Chan Before Chan

STUDIES IN EAST ASIAN BUDDHISM 28

Chan Before Chan

MEDITATION, REPENTANCE, AND VISIONARY EXPERIENCE IN CHINESE BUDDHISM

Eric M. Greene

A KURODA INSTITUTE BOOK

University of Hawai'i Press

Honolulu

Library of Congress Cataloging-in-Publication Data

Names: Greene, Eric M., author.
Title: Chan before chan : meditation, repentance, and visionary experience
in Chinese Buddhism / Eric M. Greene.
Other titles: Studies in East Asian Buddhism ; no. 28.
Description: Honolulu : University of Hawai'i Press, 2021. | Series:
Studies in East Asian Buddhism; 28 | "A Kuroda Institute book." |
Includes bibliographical references and index.
Identifiers: LCCN 2020026503 | ISBN 9780824884437 (hardcover) | ISBN
9780824886875 (adobe pdf) | ISBN 9780824886882 (epub) | ISBN
9780824886899 (kindle edition)
Subjects: LCSH: Meditation—Zen Buddhism. | Zen Buddhism—China.
Classification: LCC BQ9288 .G74 2021 | DDC 294.3/44350951—dc23
LC record available at https://lccn.loc.gov/2020026503

The Kuroda Institute for the Study of Buddhism is a nonprofit,
educational corporation founded in 1976. One of its primary objectives
is to promote scholarship on the historical, philosophical, and cultural
ramifications of Buddhism. In association with the University of Hawai'i Press,
the Institute also publishes Classics in East Asian Buddhism, a series devoted
to the translation of significant texts in the East Asian Buddhist tradition.

University of Hawai'i Press books are printed on acid-free
paper and meet the guidelines for permanence and
durability of the Council on Library Resources.

For Lauren

Contents

Acknowledgments

THE BUDDHA, I have heard, urged us to consider that we are not individuals, as we think we are, but the temporary coming together of other causes and conditions. For modern academic authors, for better or worse, a contrary ideology reigns. Though our work is arguably no more than a particular summation of those who have influenced us, we still must sign our names as if it were ours alone. Even our careful practices of citation are, perhaps, but an expression of the anxiety of influence: by purporting to have meticulously clarified the limits of others' thoughts, we give greater relief to what we hope to persuade our readers, and ourselves, are ours and ours alone. Fortunately, by convention we are permitted to drop these pretenses here, in the liminal space of the acknowledgments, and confess the deeper truth that, whatever it says on the cover, without the help of our colleagues and teachers—to say nothing of our friends and families—none of it would have happened at all.

First and foremost, this book would not exist without the unstinting instruction, advice, conversation, and support of Robert Sharf. I studied with many others at Berkeley who have in ways great and small contributed to the final shape of this book and, more broadly, to my own sense of what scholarship should be, including Robert Ashmore, Alexander von Rospatt, Jacob Dalton, Mark Csikszentmihalyi, T. Griffith Foulk, Patricia Berger, Sally Sutherland Goldman, Michael Nylan, Duncan Williams, David Johnson, William Hanks, Jens-Uwe Hartmann, Giulio Agostini, and Bruce Williams.

The research for this book began in earnest while I was in Kyoto, in 2009 and 2010, where I had the great fortune to work with Professor Funayama Tōru 船山徹 at the Institute for Research in the Humanities. I am indebted to him for facilitating my stay in Japan and, more significantly, for the instruction he provided me, and has continued to provide over the years, in all things pertaining to medieval Chinese Buddhism. Other teachers in Japan whose help was essential include Mugitani Kunio 麦谷邦夫, Kinugawa Kenji 衣川賢次, Kogachi Ryūichi 古勝隆一, Iyanaga Nobumi 彌永信美, and Ochiai Toshinori 落合俊典. In Japan, I also finally met Yamabe Nobuyoshi 山部能宜, whose research first inspired my interest in the fifth-century Chinese

Buddhist meditation manuals and who has been very generous with his knowledge whenever I have asked.

At the great risk of leaving someone out, I also want to thank the many others whose help has been essential to this book. I owe an intellectually stimulating three years to my former colleagues in the department of religion and theology at the University of Bristol: Rita Langer, Gavin D'Costa, Jon Balserak, John Lyons, Jonathan Campbell, Carolyn Muessig, David Leech, George Ferozoco, and Rupert Gethin. A stroke of good luck brought me together with Lothar Ledderose, Claudia Wenzel, and Tsai Suey-ling 蔡穗玲 of Heidelberg, and this meeting has greatly enriched Chapter 5. Miyaji Akira 宮治昭 generously provided copies of his photos and line drawings of Toyok caves 42 and 20, and April Hughes kindly let me use her photographs of the Wofoyuan. Steve Bokenkamp, Webb Keane, Max Brandstat, Robert Ford Campany, Alan (Yi) Ding, and Lucas Bender offered me their learned comments on drafts of chapters (or in some cases the entirety) of this book and it is much better because of their help. I also want to thank the anonymous reviewers for the Kuroda series whose suggestions, comments, and criticisms have greatly improved this book. The enthusiasm, support, and assistance of Robert Buswell, general editor of the Kuroda series, Stephanie Chun of the University of Hawai'i Press, and Stuart Kiang, my patient but firm copy editor, have also been instrumental in making this book a reality and they have my sincere thanks. Since 2015, the Department of Religious Studies at Yale has been a supportive environment as I have brought this book to completion. I owe a great debt to all my colleagues who have helped me in matters both large and small, institutional and intellectual, most particularly Phyllis Granoff, Koichi Shinohara, Valerie Hansen, Kathryn Lofton, Andrew Quintman, and Hwansoo Kim. In no special order I also want to thank, for their suggestions, answers to specific questions, and other help, Neil Schmid, Wendi Adamek, Jonathan Silk, Kate Crosby, David Brick, Mark Blum, Jinhua Chen, Juhn Ahn, Michael Radich, Stefan Baums, Natasha Heller, Cuilan Liu, Robert Kritzer, Antonello Palumbo, Nate Lovdahl, David Carpenter, Daniel Stuart, Bryan Lowe, Paul Groner, Peirce Salguero, Amanda Goodman, Paul Harrison, John Kieschnick, Jan Nattier, Hao Chunwen 郝春文, Stephen (Buzzy) Teiser, James Robson, James Benn, Teng Weijen 鄧偉仁, Keng Ching 耿晴, and, finally, my friend and teacher Stefano Zacchetti, whose untimely passing came just as this book was going to press.

Funding from the Tianzhu Global Network for the Study of Buddhist Cultures allowed me to spend an enjoyable week in Berkeley in February of 2018, where I was able to get valuable feedback on the material that has gone into Chapter 5. Funding was also provided, at various stages, by the Group in Buddhist Studies (Berkeley), the Center for East Asian Studies (Berkeley), the Fulbright-Hays program, the International College of Postgraduate Buddhist Studies (Tokyo), and, most recently, the Morse Fellowship and Frederick W. Hilles Publication Fund at Yale University. I want to thank these organizations for their generous support.

Conventions and Abbreviations

ALL TRANSLATIONS ARE my own unless otherwise noted. The original text has been provided in the notes whenever possible. Emendations to Chinese texts are noted as X[>Y], meaning X has been emended to Y.

My translations of T.613 and T.620, cited as *Chan Essentials* and *Methods for Curing*, respectively, are published in *The Secrets of Buddhist Meditation: Visionary Meditation Texts from Early Medieval China* (Greene 2021, cited in the notes as *Secrets of Buddhist Meditation*), which interested readers should consult for text-critical notes, pertaining to passages from those texts, that are largely omitted here.

"Song dynasty" refers to the Liu Song 劉宋 dynasty (420–479) unless otherwise noted. All dates are CE unless otherwise noted.

Chinese words are transcribed in Pinyin. I silently convert to Pinyin any citations using other systems except in book and article titles and names of published authors. The character 祕 is always transcribed in its informal modern pronunciation *mi*, not its formal pronunciation *bi*. In bibliographic contexts, and in all cases when transcribing the titles of Chinese texts, I use the Library of Congress guidelines which call for a space between *each* character (*lao shi* 老師) except for toponyms (Beijing 北京) and proper names (Zhiyi 智顗); to these conventions I add the further rule of joining the syllables of Chinese transcriptions of Indic words (*pusa* 菩薩). In nonbibliographic contexts, I follow the Pinyin standard of joining syllables to make "words" when appropriate (*zuochan* 坐禪, *chanhui* 懺悔, and so forth).

Since the perspective of this book is largely that of Chinese Buddhism, I use the terms "Indian Buddhism" and "India" in a relatively loose fashion—suffice it to say that any comments about those entities do not necessarily apply to everything that can or could be subsumed under those categories. I occasionally speak of "Central Asian" Buddhism in reference to people, texts, or places that are more localizable to that region. Because its precise variant in any given case is usually uncertain, I use the word "Indic" to denote the original language from which Chinese Buddhist texts were translated. To retain consistency, I give the Sanskrit form of Indic vocabulary, even when discussing sources written in Pāli, unless I am directly citing those texts.

The names of modern Chinese, Japanese, and Korean authors are given surname first except when an author's publications, as listed in the bibliography, follow the Western format exclusively.

Abbreviations

BQNZ   *Biqiuni zhuan* 比丘尼傳

CDFM   *Shi chan boluomi ci di fa men* 釋禪波羅蜜次第法門

CMY   *Chan mi yao fa jing* 禪祕要法經

CSZJJ   *Chu san zang ji ji* 出三藏記集

DMDL   *Damoduoluo chan jing* 達摩多羅禪經

DZDL   *Da zhi du lun* 大智度論

GFSMH *Guan fo sanmei hai jing* 觀佛三昧海經

GHMJ   *Guang hong ming ji* 廣弘明集

GSZ   *Gao seng zhuan* 高僧傳

HMJ   *Hong ming ji* 弘明集

HY   Dao zang 道藏. Passages are cited by page number (of each text) and column (a / b) using the text numbering system given in *Dao zang zi mu yin de* 道藏子目引得.

P.   Pāli

Skt.   Sanskrit

T   *Taishō shinshū daizōkyō* 大正新修大藏經. Passages are cited by text number, followed by volume, page, register (a, b, or c), and line number(s).

WMCJ   *Wu men chan jing yao yong fa* 五門禪經要用法

XGSZ   *Xu gao seng zhuan* 續高僧傳

Z   *Shinsan Dai Nihon zoku zōkyō* 新纂大日本續藏經. Passages are cited by text number, followed by volume, page, register (a, b, or c), and line number(s).

ZCB   *Zhi chan bing mi yao fa* 治禪病祕要法

ZCSM   *Zuo chan sanmei jing* 坐禪三昧經

Chan Before Chan

Introduction

YOU HAVE SEEN IT BEFORE: the seated figure, body upright, legs crossed, hands clasped in the lap, eyes serenely lowered or perhaps closed, as they are in the image on this book's cover. Even those who know nothing about Buddhism know that here, in the pose immortalized in countless paintings and statues, sits the Buddha, or Buddhist adept, in meditation.

But what is Buddhist meditation? What is going on—and what should be going on—behind those closed or lowered eyelids? And in what ways and to what ends have the answers mattered for Buddhists themselves? This book is an attempt to answer these questions in the particular setting of medieval China between roughly the years 400, when Buddhist meditation became established as a regular feature of Chinese Buddhist life, and 750, the end of the first generation of the Chan School (*chanzong* 禪宗), the so-called Meditation School that would later spread throughout East Asia and, under its Japanese name, Zen, would become well known in all parts of the modern world.

The prominence of the Chan School both in modern scholarship on Buddhism and among Western Buddhists has often led to a foreshortened perspective, with Chinese Buddhist meditation imagined to be identical with what has for centuries been the distinctly Chan or Zen approach to it. This book seeks to deepen that perspective and expand our sense of what meditation was and is in China and throughout East Asia. Building on the work of those who have long called for a wider excavation of the ritual and contemplative worlds of Chinese Buddhism, it sheds light on what was, throughout the formative, early medieval period of Chinese Buddhist

1

history,[1] a pervasive and thoroughly nonsectarian set of ideas, methods, and ideologies concerning meditation, its practice, the experiences to which it leads, and the way those experiences can become meaningful for individuals and the communities to which they belong. While my focus is on China, the materials I take up in this book also have a place in the wider history of Buddhism. Indeed, the early medieval record in China, though characterized by its own trajectories and contexts, preserves valuable evidence of broader, pan-Asian cultures of meditation for which our other sources are limited but which flourished during the long "middle" period of Indian Buddhism, between the time of the early scriptures and the later rise of Tantra.

Even the very earliest Chinese Buddhists recognized that meditation is normatively central to Buddhism. The first written Chinese Buddhist texts—the translations of Indian scriptures made during the late Eastern Han dynasty (25–220)—already speak of *chan*, a transcription of the Indic word *dhyāna*, and discuss and analyze it in detail. The purely phonetic rendering *chan* was used during this embryonic period of Chinese Buddhism by all translators, even those who otherwise adopted a rigorous policy of finding semantic Chinese equivalents for Indic technical terms.[2] Buddhist meditation, introduced as *chan*, was in this way marked as something foreign to the Chinese religious imaginaire and endowed with an exoticism comparable to that of "Zen" in modern English. Even in later eras, when almost no Buddhist vocabulary escaped borrowing and appropriation by other Chinese religious and philosophical movements, the word *chan* always retained a specifically Buddhist connotation.[3] Ironically, then, Buddhist meditation was arguably

---

1. The term "early medieval" is typically used by Western historians of China to refer to the period between 220 (the fall of the Han dynasty) and 589 (the reunification of China by the Sui). I use it here in a slightly different way and only as a convenient label for the eras I cover, not to make any larger claims about periodization—though 755, the start of the An Lushan rebellion and approximate end of the period I cover, is an important date for such questions. China, for much of this period, was not necessarily a single culture bounded geographically, politically, or ethnically (Chittick 2020, 3–35). Nevertheless, I will speak heuristically of China and more specifically of Chinese Buddhism. By the latter I mean to point to a Buddhist culture that analytically can be thought of as united by written, literary Chinese as its lingua franca and a canon of texts in that language—a canon not everywhere identical and still in active formation during the time period that concerns us. There were great variations in the extent to which any individual who engaged in activities we might wish to call Buddhist participated in "Chinese Buddhism" thus defined. But to speak of Chinese Buddhism in this sense—as akin to what Steven Collins (1998) called the "Pāli imaginaire" in the case of Southeast Asian Buddhism—is not, I would insist, a negation of the existence of divergent understandings, practices, and values. It is simply a conscious directing of our attention to a particular shared space, one that itself had a historical trajectory and was not static, consisting of ideas, texts, practices, ideologies, and patterns of material culture, among other things.

2. Notable in this regard is An Shigao, the first known translator of Buddhist texts into Chinese, who generally used transcriptions only for proper names (Nattier 2008, 44).

3. This borrowing of originally Buddhist vocabulary extended even to the word "Buddha"

more "Buddhist" in China than it ever was in India, where its cross-legged posture and most of its technical vocabulary were shared by other religious traditions as well.[4]

A distinctly Chinese vocabulary did eventually develop to describe the various facets of Buddhist meditation. But throughout the early medieval period and arguably well beyond, *chan* remained the most common way of referring to it in its entirety. It is this concept, therefore, that forms the contours of my study, and in this book by *meditation* I generally mean *chan*. In other words, the focus of this book is not "meditation" as a second-order category, instances of which I will seek wherever I can find them, but *chan* as a Chinese social fact—that is, as both a real practice carried out by Chinese Buddhists on the ground as well as a domain of value that articulated with other aspects of culture and society. It was in the fifth century, as Chapter 1 explains, when *chan* first came to have this kind of existence.

The specifically Buddhist implications of *chan* in early medieval China stand in contrast to the fluid meaning of the contemporary English term "meditation," which points on the one hand to a generic form of mental training believed to be universally accessible—an "attention-based technique for inner transformation," as one scholar puts it (Eifring 2016, 1)—and a recondite pearl of Buddhist or at least "Asian" wisdom on the other.[5] This ambiguity speaks to the long history of "meditation" as a term of Western anthropological description. The first to use it in this manner were Jesuit missionaries in Japan in the sixteenth century (App 2012, 24), the very point of origin of modern Western knowledge of Buddhism, who chose the Latin word *meditatio*, a concept with its own rich histories in medieval Christian thought and practice (Karnes 2011), to describe what they thought the Zen monks they observed were doing while sitting cross-legged. With this as the starting point, through a process whose full history has yet to be traced, "meditation" in both English and other modern European languages has become the common description of an increasing number of Asian yogic or contemplative disciplines. Among other things, this has helped make plausible a central conceit of a now booming subdivision of the modern wellness industry: that in such practices we have something both ancient and pure as well as modern and real, something verified by generations of Buddhist

---

(*fo* 佛), used by Manichaean and Christian missionaries in the Tang dynasty to translate "God" (Bryder 1985, 83; Tang 2004, 132). In late imperial China, the word *chan* was sometimes a generic designation for Buddhism, as opposed to Daoism (Goossaert 2004, 708).

4. Scholars debate the extent of the debt that Buddhist *dhyāna* owes to non-Buddhist practices (W. King 1980; Bronkhorst 1986). What is undeniable is that the words denoting Buddhist meditation and its various aspects, words such as *dhyāna, samādhi, yoga,* and *bhāvanā,* were shared by many Indian religious traditions.

5. No less an authority than Wikipedia, in two back-to-back sentences, says that "meditation" has long been practiced in many religious traditions, but also that its origins lie in India specifically (https://en.wikipedia.org/wiki/Meditation, accessed April 2018).

virtuosos but also by contemporary science.[6] Meditation, in this way, partakes of a dual authority that has proven attractive. Popular books on meditation (now often "mindfulness") increase in number each day. Dorms at American universities offer their stressed-out undergraduates spaces for "meditating" complete with sandboxes modeled on the dry rock-gardens that popular culture links to Zen.[7] Hundreds of scientific studies now claim to show that meditation "works," in cognitively identifiable ways (Lutz, Dunne, and Davidson 2007), and an emerging field of Contemplative Studies, backed by well-funded research centers and a dedicated group at the American Academy of Religion, seeks to combine these insights with the work of scholars of religion, philosophy, and other humanistic fields.[8]

Although this book does not address these contemporary developments directly, I mention them here because in trying to reimagine what Buddhist meditation was and often still is, it does aim to challenge the usually ahistorical and modernist perspectives on it that are presently being put to these various uses. Though I have conceived this study as offering such a challenge, at the same time I want to distinguish its methods and aims from the many influential critiques of modernist depictions of Buddhist meditation that have taken the form of an *unmasking*. Such arguments draw from different archives but frequently partake of a common pattern. They usually begin by pointing out that the dictum that meditation is the "very core of the Buddhist approach to life" (Conze 1975, 11), as even professional historians were once wont to say, has a suspicious genealogy, one that passes through the crucible of colonialism, Orientalist scholarship, and the "strategic Occidentalism" of modern Asian reformers.[9] They then note that this idea did not derive from actual observation of what living Buddhist traditions in Asia hold or have held to be most important in practice, but emerged only by extracting from a selective reading of the early canonical scriptures a notional "pure" or "original" Buddhism that emphasizes meditation above all else. And the conclusion, upon tracing this genealogy, is that by focusing on meditation as the heart and soul of Buddhism we—modern scholars and modernist Buddhists alike—wrongly exclude from the history of their own religion the practices and beliefs of most Buddhists throughout history.

---

6. The literature is vast; see Wallace 2009 and Flanagan 2011 for recent examples of how the case is made.

7. Lorenzo Arvanitis and Julianna Lai, " 'Good Life Center' Opens in Silliman," *Yale Daily News*, September 20, 2018, https://yaledailynews.com/blog/2018/09/20/good-life-center -opens-in-silliman.

8. Wilson 2014 and McMahan and Braun 2017 provide useful introductions to these trends and the critiques of them. For more trenchant critiques, see Lopez 2008, 197–210, Sharf 2015, Faure 2017, and Kellner 2019, among others.

9. On "strategic Occidentalism," see Ketelaar 1991. The modern Asian Buddhist movements that emphasize meditation above all else, and promote it as accessible and necessary for the laity as well as the clergy, stem at least in part from these colonial-era revisions. On these movements, see Gombrich and Obeyesekere 1988, Cook 2010, Cassaniti 2015 and 2018, Jordt 2007, Braun 2013, and Stuart 2017b.

Such critiques follow a rhetorical mode in which the primary intellectual task is to "interrogate" and thereby dissolve a problematic normative paradigm rather than replace it with a new one (Felski 2015). Accordingly, these arguments often imply not just that we in the modern West have misapprehended particular aspects of Buddhism, but that we have wrongly grasped its very content. Meditation often serves in these unmaskings as emblematic of the issues at stake. If, as Donald Lopez suggests, scholars must critique the Orientalist view that "the essential practice of Buddhism is meditation, with the rituals of consecration, purification, and exorcism so common throughout Asia largely dismissed as late accretions of popular superstition" (2005, 2), then the path to better understanding of Buddhism appears to require *de-privileging* meditation, relative to its misbegotten and dubiously acquired pride of place in popular consciousness, in favor of different topics. Historically and ethically responsible scholarship therefore turns from "liberation" to "lentils," as Vasudha Narayanan (2000) puts it in her analogous reassessment of Hinduism. It turns away from those things that fascinated Orientalist scholars and toward what they dismissed as popular superstition but which a gaze free of colonialist biases would restore to their rightful place of importance.

Over the past thirty years, this approach has opened up entirely new fields of study, producing a voluminous bibliography on long-ignored topics instrumental to the history of Buddhism such as relic worship, the cult of images, the spirit world, and so forth. But by the same token, when it has come to Buddhist meditation (and many other aspects of "elite" Buddhist culture as well), the critical scholar now often speaks in primarily negative terms. Most Buddhists in Asia, we are reminded, did not and do not meditate and do not think they should. Indeed, to hold that the practice of meditation has or had a particular importance for Buddhists is seen as an outmoded view akin to the patently Orientalist fantasies that Buddhism is atheistic, that it knows no dogma, that it has no concern with the afterlife, or that it is fundamentally individualistic. Furthermore, this outmoded view of Buddhist meditation is not just wrong; it is *inverted*. Firsthand meditative experience, which Buddhism holds in particular esteem according to many modernist Buddhists or Buddhist sympathizers, in fact held *no* authority, nor played any role at all, among traditional Buddhists in Asia, for whom exalted states of meditation were "not considered the goal of practice, were not deemed doctrinally authoritative, and did not serve as the reference point for . . . understandings of the path."[10]

These critiques of modernist misprisions pack their punch from the margins, when they serve, as they did when first articulated, to disabuse

---

10. Sharf 1998, 99. See also Sharf 1995. In more recent work (2014b), Sharf argues that personal meditative experience *was* sometimes held up as a source of authority, but only in contexts decidedly atypical of premodern Buddhism—specifically, when meditation was being taught to laypeople.

readers of their naïve ideas. They eschew a positive reformulation of Buddhist meditation in favor of exposing the genealogy of modern misunderstandings. And no doubt, this kind of critique is all that is warranted in some cases. To ask for a better account of Buddhist *atheism*, for example, would be to miss the point that this object is itself a kind of fantasy. But the same cannot be said for Buddhist meditation. This, at least, is the perspective I adopt in this book, which assumes its readers are already skeptical of the popular modern construal of Buddhist meditation as an accurate telling of what Buddhists throughout history have thought this activity was, how they carried it out, and to what ends they did so. In other words, this book is written for those who already know or suspect what Buddhist meditation is *not,* but who also want to ask: well then, what is it? Its aim is to widen our understanding not by showing that modernist representations of Buddhism are utterly wrong—that meditation, psychology, or personal experience are, in fact, less important in Buddhism than gods, relics, or funerary rites—but rather by showing that "Buddhist meditation" has a history. It is, in short, an attempt to better understand the past and present of Buddhism by going through, not around, a part of it that, for reasons due partially but not entirely to our own parochial interests, has become central to many modern understandings of this religion.

Historiography

In thinking about what Buddhist meditation was in early medieval China, I make a series of arguments in this book ranging from the specific to the more general. These arguments pertain to particular problems in the historiography of Chinese Buddhism; to the nature and historical value of the category of Buddhist literature often called "meditation manuals" or "meditation texts"; to the relationship between elite Buddhist practices such as meditation and the broader religious and cultic worlds in which they took place; and finally to how if at all we should approach the thorny topic of religious or mystical "experience"—a rubric under which Buddhist meditation has often been studied and for which its literature is often held to offer special insight as a repository of time-tested techniques for generating it.

The book's title *Chan Before Chan* points to the first of these questions and the specific gap in historical knowledge it redresses: the nature of Buddhist meditation in China *before* the rise, around the year 700 in the mid-Tang dynasty, of the so-called Chan School. The prehistory of Chan is not, to be sure, a new topic. Recent scholars have often taken up questions such as Chan's debt to earlier doctrinal developments and the antecedents in Chinese Buddhism to the ideology of lineage in which the Chan School became particularly invested.[11] Yet because Chan (big-C) eventually managed to appropriate the previously generic concept of *chan* (small-c), adopting it

---

11. See, for example, Buswell 1989, Faure 1986b, Adamek 2007, and Young 2015.

as its own name while interpreting its purport in novel ways and even dis-associating it at times from any concrete practices whatsoever, a presectarian history of *chan* as *meditation* has remained elusive. Western scholars have rarely looked farther back than the Tiantai patriarch Zhiyi 智顗 (538–597), the Thomas Aquinas of medieval Chinese Buddhist contemplative theory, who is often seen, by historians of the Chan School, as representative of the traditional or "Indian" approach to meditation that Chan aimed to super-sede (Bielefeldt 1988, 78–106). Conversely, scholars of Tiantai, especially sectarian Japanese scholars, have usually seen Zhiyi as the truly innovative figure, treating the Chan School's take on meditation as a reactionary "Lesser Vehicle" or Hīnayāna approach. In either case, it is agreed that only in the Sui-Tang era (581–907), traditionally seen as the golden age of Chinese Buddhism, did Chinese approaches to Buddhist meditation, with either Zhiyi or the early patriarchs of the Chan School in the forefront, come into their own in a cultural (as authentically "Chinese") and theological (as properly "Mahāyāna") efflorescence that has supposedly remained the norm in East Asia down to the present.[12] This study began as an attempt to revise this tale by providing a nonteleological, nonsectarian history of Buddhist meditation in early medieval China, one in which the famous early Tiantai and Chan School writings would certainly appear but without being reified as the cul-mination of everything that preceded them or the essential font of all that followed.

What attracted me as a point of departure for such a history was the sur-prisingly large and varied corpus of meditation manuals traditionally called "*chan* scriptures" (*chanjing* 禪經) that date from the fifth century and are largely preserved in the Chinese Buddhist canon. While premodern catalogs classify these texts as translations of Indian treatises devoted to meditation, at least some seemed to be Chinese compositions, and those in particular, I thought, might show us how Chinese Buddhists had taken up the practice and theory of Indian Buddhist meditation in the era before Chan or Tiantai. Modern scholarship had certainly been aware of these manuals.[13] But because these texts do not engage with the Mahāyāna philosophical idiom of emptiness and nonduality that would become so prominent in both Chan and Tiantai literature, they had usually been passed over quickly and seen as little more than relics of the Indian or Hīnayāna approaches to medita-tion that Chinese Buddhists had been exposed to, through the translations of Indian texts, but that ultimately failed to satisfy them.

The problem with this reading, I soon realized, is that it does not square with the historical record, which instead shows that for several centuries Chinese Buddhists viewed the fifth-century *chan* scriptures—particularly

---

12. For further consideration of these issues, see *Secrets of Buddhist Meditation*, chap. 1.

13. Two monumental pieces of earlier Western scholarship that brought these sources to my attention are Demiéville 1954 and Yamabe 1999b. Neither takes the fifth-century *chan* scriptures as their primary focus, however.

those now suspected of being Chinese compositions—as authoritative expositions of the path and practice of meditation. At the same time, it also became apparent upon examining them firsthand that these texts were quite different from the traditional Indian Buddhist meditation literature that I had been acquainted with.[14] The following passage, from one of the fifth-century *chan* scriptures authored in China, is typical of the genre:

> Again he must be instructed to fix his thoughts and contemplate [the bodies] of others. Contemplating external objects, because he has directed his imagination outward he suddenly sees a tree on which rare sweet fruit is growing. There are four fruits, shining with four kinds of light, and this fruit tree, like a tree of beryl, spreads over everything.
>
> Seeing this tree, he sees sentient beings of various kinds come before him begging for food, oppressed by the fires of hunger.... He looks upon these beings who beg from him as he would his own parents undergoing great torment, thinking: "How can I save them?" With this thought, he contemplates his own body, and as before it turns into pus and blood. Going further, he turns it into chunks of meat, which he gives to the hungry beings. These hungry ghosts rush forward madly to eat it.[15]

Rather than describing concrete methods for calming the mind and gaining knowledge of abstruse Buddhist truths, many of the fifth-century *chan* scriptures devote their attention to an unrelenting slideshow of elaborate and often enigmatic visions which meditators, it is claimed, will or should experience. Though their methods often seem vaguely comparable to the visualization practices developed later in Tantric Buddhism, these texts are several centuries younger than known examples of Tantric literature and furthermore contain few if any characteristically Tantric doctrines. The early history of Buddhist meditation in China, and perhaps elsewhere, was evidently more complex than I had been led to believe.

Meditation, Meditation Literature, and Meditative Experience

And yet for what kind of historical analysis might sources such as the *chan* scriptures serve? What questions related to the practice of Buddhist meditation in medieval China can their elaborate descriptions of visions and other meditative encounters help us answer? Because these texts seem at times to speak of nothing else, we must confront here the hoary topic of religious *experience*, once a field-defining object of inquiry for scholars of religion but a category that in recent decades has come to be regarded by many critics as

---

14. One fragmentary Indic source, the so-called *Yogalehrbuch*, does closely resemble these texts, as has been shown in detail by Yamabe (1999b). I discuss some of these parallels in Chap. 2.

15. *Chan Essentials* 3.26.8 (*CMY*, T.613:15.260c19–27).

problematic. The reasons for this fall from grace have been at once ontological, because experiences, it is argued, are caused by, and are not the unmediated causes of, religion's social, cultural, and linguistic contexts; epistemological, because it is deemed that what matters are not experiences per se but the public language games in which talk of inner states figures; and critico-historical, because emphasizing a distinctive kind of "experience" as what religion is truly about is, supposedly, a suspiciously Protestant perspective that unjustly relegates rituals, institutions, and material objects to the status of secondary vulgarizations.

The proposition that experience might be a slippery or even a best-forgotten beast poses a particular problem for any history of Buddhist meditation for which formal meditation texts are key sources, because this literature takes as a central concern something we can only call the *experiences* of Buddhist meditators. However we might ultimately choose to read them, these documents do devote much of their attention to something akin to the "feelings, acts, and experiences of individual men in their solitude," as William James famously defined religion in his *Varieties of Religious Experience*. Whatever problems we might now see in taking such categories for granted, it is not entirely without reason that Buddhist meditation literature has often served as fertile source material for claims about the nature of mysticism or the primacy of experience for religion in general.[16]

But if James' definition of religion is unacceptably limited, and if the study of Buddhism requires more than merely curating emic claims to, or prescriptions for, extraordinary experiences—and these points I take for granted—what if anything can traditional Buddhist meditation literature usefully tell us? A way out of this conundrum opened when I realized that the fifth-century Chinese meditation manuals I was reading did more than merely prescribe meditative techniques or describe the experiences of ideal meditators. Sometimes overtly and sometimes implicitly, these texts also contain other information whose presence permits a more nuanced assessment of the uses to which these documents were put and their evidential value for the history of Buddhism in China. Consider the following passages from a short and at times pointedly enigmatic manual called the *Five Gates* (*Wu men chan jing yao yong fa*):

> The master must instruct him further, saying: "From now on put aside the previous two contemplations. Concentrate your mind on your navel." After receiving the master's instructions, [the meditator] single-mindedly contemplates his navel. After contemplating his navel for a short time, he feels something moving there....He sees something in his navel like a heron's egg, white in color.
>
> He goes and tells the master. The master says: "Look further at this place."

---

16. Classic studies that uphold Buddhist meditation as a representative example of a pan-religious category of "mysticism" or "religious experience" include Heiler 1922, Smart 1958, Eliade 1969, and W. King 1988.

He does as the master instructs. Having contemplated it, [he sees] a lotus flower, with a beryl stem and a golden dais.[17] On the dais is a buddha, sitting cross-legged....

The meditator then tells the master what he has seen. The master says: "Good! You have applied your mind well to contemplation. This is the sign of the attainment of concentration [by way of contemplation of] the body."

The master instructs him: "Further contemplate within the navel." [The meditator] then contemplates as instructed. He sees on the crown of the buddha's head a five-colored light. Seeing this, he tells the master.... [The master] further has him contemplate the buddhas within the five lights. In each, he sees that from the buddha's navel five lions emerge and eat the flowers from which [that buddha had] emerged and then reenter the navel of the buddha....This is called "the sign of the lion's awe-inspiring presence *samādhi*."[18]

Like many formal Buddhist meditation texts, the *Five Gates* describes an ordered sequence of meditation methods and the experiences that should result from them, and then classifies the results in accordance with named stages of attainment. But it also provides something more unusual: a model of how these three things might coexist in a social world. That is, while it presents many details concerning the personal experiences of successful meditators, it does not frame these experiences merely as psychological states that the meditator obtains and then enjoys. Rather, it describes these experiences as concrete events that the meditator must report to someone else, whose responsibility is then to evaluate them and declare their significance—for instance, that the meditator should now pursue a different technique, or that the reported vision is the sign of a nameable, normatively valued attainment.

In emphasizing these things, the *Five Gates* invites questions about Buddhist meditation and meditative experience, and about what historical analysis of these things meditation texts might support, that are somewhat different than those usually posed. Before formulating the positive version of what those questions are, let me first identify what the evidence of the *Five Gates* suggests we needn't worry about too much: namely, how to *explain*—to account for causally—the experiences of medieval Chinese Buddhist meditators, whether in reference to their mental or physiological practices, the prescriptions of the normative texts they accepted, or the cultural or religious contexts in which they lived.

That seeking explanations of this kind is the proper task of a scholar investigating religious or other unusual experiences is an idea closely entwined with the origins of the academic study of religion in the nineteenth

---

17. "Dais" (*tai* 臺) here refers to the prominent carpellary receptacle of a lotus flower.

18. 師復更教言。汝從今捨前二觀，係心在齊。即受師教，一心觀齊。觀齊不久，覺齊有動相...見齊有物，猶如鴈卵，其色鮮白。即往白師。師言。汝更視在[>此]處。如師所見。觀已，有蓮花，琉璃為莖，黃金為臺。臺上有佛，結跏趺坐...即以所見白師。師言。大善。汝好用心觀。此身成定相也。師教言。更觀齊中。即如教觀。見頂有五色光焰。見已白師...更今觀五光中佛。一見佛齊中有五師子出。師子出已，食所出諸花已，還入五光中佛齊中...此名師子奮迅三昧定相也。(*WMCJ*, T.619:15.326a14–b6)

century (Taves 1999). As Wayne Proudfoot (1985) formulates the argument in his justly influential book *Religious Experience,* to avoid the charge of "reductionism" the critical scholar must indeed first *describe* religious experiences accurately in terms recognizable to those who claim them, but then must also *explain* them in terms acceptable to everyone else—in other words, we must provide an account of why a given experience occurred rather than some other, why someone saw the Virgin Mary, not the Buddha, or experienced nirvana, not the boundless love of God. This kind of explanation, Proudfoot suggests, requires situating religious experiences in their historical, cultural, disciplinary, or theological contexts. Although this call to locate even putatively unmediated experiences as the products rather than the causes of their social and cultural settings has often been criticized by those who would instead ground them in a *sui generis* domain, over the past decades it has been embraced by many scholars of religion (S. Katz 1978; 1983), historians (Scott 1991), and anthropologists (Desjarlais 1997).[19] As Russell McCutcheon puts it: "What some might understand as the supposed immediacy of experience . . . may actually be but an internalized residue of an earlier social world (its calculus), invented by others and that, through the actions of others, has been imprinted on us—or better put, *within* us" (2012, 8).

That experience is not what does the explaining but what must itself be explained dovetails with long-running themes in humanistic scholarship that treat even our putative interiority as the trace or testament of an external discourse or power. Yet, interestingly, that religious experiences are above all in need of causal explanation is a conviction also held by scholars who work in or on the borders of the so-called cognitive science of religion. Studying modern American Evangelicals who claim to hear God, Tanya Luhrmann (2012) asks: "But are they crazy?" She answers no by arguing that their technologies of prayer, with practice, do in fact induce a biologically grounded state she calls "absorption," in which vivid experiences of internal auditory perception more easily occur. Those who pray "actually have different sensory evidence with which to interpret the claims they make about reality."[20] For analysts who see such experiences emerging from objective forms of cognitive training, no less than for those who see them as the residue of prior social or linguistic worlds, religious experiences must, it seems, be *explained.* And this explaining is compelling, it is implied, precisely to the extent that it serves as an alternative to the claims of the insiders, for whom the same events are

---

19. This is not to say that these positions have been universally accepted (recent pushbacks by scholars of religion include Blum 2014; Fong 2014; Shushan 2014; and Orsi 2016). A lively discussion also continues among philosophers, whose long running debates about consciousness, experience, "qualia," and related topics have influenced scholars of religion studying these topics (see Strawson 2017).

20. Luhrmann and Morgain 2012, 386. Elsewhere, Luhrmann and her collaborators take into account both biological and "cultural" causes of religious experiences, which they argue often operate together in patterned ways (Cassaniti and Luhrmann 2014).

proffered as evidence for the existence of the contested things held to be their cause: God, the soul, pure consciousness, enlightenment, and so forth.

For historians of Buddhist meditation, the methodology of explaining experience has meant reading the literature of meditation as prescriptive. That is to say, rather than taking meditation texts or other literary accounts of meditation practice as unproblematically recording the experiences or activities of past mystics (as if Buddhism had simply emerged from the un- mediated experiences of its founders), these documents are understood as themselves constituting the tools through which the Buddhist tradition in- culcates the forms of experience and knowledge it values.[21]

Yet for the *chan* scriptures of early medieval China, this way of reading the import of formal Buddhist meditation manuals often seems less than complete. To take the *Five Gates* passage cited above merely as prescriptive of the given meditative experiences, in either intention or application, pro- duces a rather thin reading. This document provides only the most cursory discussion of anything we could call a meditation "technique." Nor does it show any trace of the minute analyses of the cognitive qualities of particular meditative states that often fill the pages of traditional Buddhist meditation literature—analyses that are indeed profitably read as prescriptive tools in- tended to help the meditator internalize and (re)create these selfsame, nor- mative experiences. The meditative experiences the *Five Gates* describes, such as the enigmatic vision of a "heron's egg" within the meditator's navel, frequently do not in any obvious way instantiate Buddhist norms or ways of being in the world. More to the point, even the ideal meditator, as depicted in this text, will not think that they do. Indeed, the meditator does not know the import, if any, of the visions that will, apparently, come. This import must be worked out by someone else, and it is in the service of this working out that the details of the meditator's personal experiences are to be solicited, reported, and then evaluated. The *Five Gates* clearly is still a prescriptive rather than a descriptive text. But its prescriptions have less to do with spe- cific cognitive practices or meditative experiences than with a process for rendering judgment on those experiences.

What the *Five Gates* provides us is a preliminary sketch of something we might call the social life of meditative experience. It gives a portrait of how *those things which others deem the meditator alone necessarily and reliably privy to* were thought to be properly handled. As we will see in the course of this study, comparable ideas about the experiences to which Buddhist medita- tion leads were widely accepted and put into practice in early medieval China, and charting the emergence and historical evolution of these ideas, and the forms of interaction they made possible, is this book's primary task. For now, let us note simply that the social life of Buddhist meditative experience, as

---

21. Gimello 1978; Buswell and Gimello 1992, 11; Samuel 2014, 570; McMahan 2017. For some alternative perspectives, see Kapstein 2004 and Dreyfus 2011.

imagined in the *Five Gates,* is neither entirely private nor completely public.[22] We see in it neither the attitude of the modernist Buddhist, for whom personal meditative experience is apodictic at least in theory, nor the converse position that vests all certainty and authority in externally observable public criteria. Meditators, the *Five Gates* implies, have *experiences*—visions to which they and they alone have access. And the content of these experiences is indeed the proof of their attainment. But in contrast to the way that claims to firsthand experience are wielded in some religious contexts, in the *Five Gates* this content is not perception-like evidence of a contested object. It is rather a *sign* that conveys information about the one to whom it appears only when read correctly. Here, accordingly, the problematic of Buddhist meditative experience is one not of perception but of divination; not of representation, judged to be reliable only when it is mirrorlike, but of semiotics (more on this in a moment), in which one thing can produce knowledge of another in a wider variety of ways.[23]

In short, the *Five Gates* suggests that uncovering the specific techniques, the underlying psychological or biological processes, or the social or cultural factors that *caused* Buddhist meditative experiences in early medieval China would still not answer the most important questions. What proves most interesting, and what the *Five Gates* and similar meditation texts can help us understand, is not the causes of meditative experiences but the sociality of their effects. "How experiences become real to subjects" (Taves 2009, 159) is therefore not the right question here. In early medieval China, meditative experiences were assumed to be real, that is, to be sites where messages are transmitted. The question was whether one could read those messages accurately and what any given one meant, suggesting that our questions too should concern how this worked and why it took the forms it did.

Semiotic Ideology

Writing in implicit criticism of those who would explain unusual religious experiences in terms of their cognitive mechanisms, Webb Keane observes that such explanations, no matter how sophisticated, offer less than their proponents think:

---

22. For an analysis of the role of "experience" in later Tibetan Buddhist contemplative literature that reaches similar conclusions, see Gyatso 1999 and 2002.

23. Arguments about the inferential validity of "yogic perception" (*yogipratyakṣa*) are an important topic in some late Indian Buddhist traditions (Taber 2009). Significantly, however, these arguments tend to appear in the context of debate, actual or implied, with non-Buddhists, when it was necessary to offer an evidential ground for otherwise difficult to establish truths preached by the Buddha, truths that were not, in other contexts, ordinarily called into question. As Vincent Eltschinger has noted (2012), prior to around the year 500 Indian Buddhists seem to have only rarely engaged in this kind of polemic debate with outsiders.

Suppose one day I am strolling home from the office and I encounter the Virgin Mary, or at night I dream I have been granted powers by a jaguar spirit, or suddenly start to speak fluently in a voice and language that are not my own. Certainly people have such experiences, and we may even grant that each involves identifiable cognitive processes. But what makes these respectively a vision, a prophetic experience, and a case of spirit possession rather than, say, fantasies, dreams, psychotic episodes, the effects of drugs, or a sudden head injury? They are instances of categories recognizable to other people. This is not an automatic business: even in places where shamanism or spirit possession are well accepted, in any given instances local communities have to decide whether they now have a case of possession or, say, madness, fraud, or error. (2008, 114)

The crux of Keane's point lies at the interface between the word "recognizable" and the observation that such recognition is not *automatic*. The point here is not the familiar one that "experiences" are generated by local rather than universal possibilities and are thus the "residue of an earlier social world," as McCutcheon put it. It's that *how* they are generated is not the most important thing, because whatever their causes or antecedent histories, they become relevant only when taken up as instances of a known kind of thing, even as this "taking"—the decision, on the part of individuals or groups, that *this* is an instance of *that*—is not simply given, in the way that cultural meanings or language games are often presumed to be. Rather, such taking is the result of real social work, of judgments that are based on tangible, discursive, or material forms, that have historical trajectories, that are possibly contested, are carried out in time under various conditions and to various ends, and which for all these reasons are of uncertain outcome in any given case.

To ask questions about how such matters play out is to investigate what Keane calls *semiotic ideology,* which he defines as "people's underlying assumptions about what signs are, what functions they do or do not serve, and what consequences they might or might not produce."[24] The terms "semiotics" and "ideology" as Keane uses them deserve a word of explanation. First, the "semiotics" he has in mind lies in the tradition of Charles Sanders Peirce, whose definition of a sign as "something which stands to somebody for something in some respect" (1931–1966, 2:228) makes room for semiotics to be not just the study of abstract, static sign systems (as for Saussure and the traditions of cultural analysis he inspired) but an investigation of *communication* as an ongoing social event—one that is undertaken by real people in particular contexts and for particular ends, and is constrained by the real world and

---

24. Keane 2018, 65. With "semiotic ideology" Keane extends the notion of "language ideology" or "linguistic ideology" (in the sense of a given community's own understanding of how its language works and should work) so as to include nonlinguistic signifying media such as material objects. See also Keane 2003; 2005; and 2007; Silverstein 1979; and Schieffelin, Woolard, and Kroskrity 1998.

the properties of tangible media of representation.[25] "Ideology," meanwhile, here refers not to a false consciousness about this communication that we purport to see through (so as to conclude, for example, that what the natives think are true signs are in fact interested cultural conventions), but to people's own, self-reflexive understandings about their communicative practices. Semiotic ideology, then, points to the forms, practices, and spaces in which the people who use signs think and argue with each other about how those signs work or are supposed to work.

This concept provides a robust framework for asking questions about the literature, practice, and experience of Buddhist meditation in medieval China. But talk of "signs" and "semiotics," especially in conjunction with the topic of "experience," may already be making some readers wary. Is not the notion that religion traffics primarily in signs the chief characteristic of a parochial, Protestant reading of it? And one worth moving beyond, not least because, by taking them only as symbols of something ethereal, it devalues the particularity of the objects, presences, and bodies that most if not all religions seem in fact to be about when we examine them in action?[26] This kind of criticism makes an important point, but its true target is the specifically Saussurean model in which studying cultural objects as "signs" has tended to mean focusing on a purely abstract system of ideas linked only arbitrarily to things in the world. Semiotics in this sense indeed risks minimizing the concrete, embodied world to which most religions happily devote their attention in both practice and theory in favor of the putatively formless and transcendent objects of religious symbols.

Yet, to ignore semiotics in the broader, Peircian sense of a semiotic ideology risks producing an equally distorted picture in which cultural forms, for those who use and interact with them, are uncontested and uncontestable, and where, consequently, there can be no change or history. Critics of a naïve Saussurean model of cultural signification sometimes seem to end up heading in this direction in their efforts to direct the attention of scholars of religion back to the material world. Lin Wei-cheng, for example, notes that in premodern China auspicious omens such as the appearance of an unusual fungus or animal did "not so much refer as respond (*ying*) to the ruler's virtue" and concludes from this that "signs" are therefore "not always passive and static" but also "vital and invocatory, bringing about immediacy rather than exegesis" (Lin 2015, 203).

Part of Lin's point is well taken: in Peircian terms, omens in premodern China were indeed approached not just as *symbols*, in the sense of signs whose referent is known by way of convention, but also as *indexes*, signs taken to have

---

25. Singer 1984, 62. Anthropologists inspired by Peirce often call their approach "semiotic anthropology" and distinguish it from the "symbolic anthropology" of someone like Geertz, seen as drawing from a more Saussurean model; see Parmentier 1994 and 2016, and Mertz 2007.

26. For two recent studies making this point, see Orsi 2016 and Morgan 2018.

a causal connection to their objects (in this case, the ruler's virtue). But to conclude from this that Chinese omens "brought about immediacy rather than exegesis" is to miss something important. For even if auspicious omens really do exist, for anything to operate as an omen it must, additionally, be *taken* as such by someone. In fact, we can be certain that Chinese omens did not bring about "immediacy" because, as Lin himself notes, records of them were collected, compiled, publicized, and commented on—a necessary enterprise precisely because whether any given thing or event was an omen needed working out. And to ignore the activities and ideologies that effectuated and informed this working out would be to abdicate much of what needs discussion: why these kinds of things in particular were held to index the ruler's virtue; what material and social conditions allowed for the circulation of tools (such as omenological treatises) making it possible or plausible to take new events as omens; and how the handling of such events changed over time.[27] It would leave us, finally, with no way to discuss, even in the abstract, the debate, doubt, or anxiety that, given the stakes, the taking of any particular event as an auspicious omen surely occasioned, whether or not ancient Chinese historians recorded that debate for posterity.

This book therefore approaches the practice of Buddhist meditation in medieval China as a matter of sign reading. Not, however, as its method—not, that is, in an effort to read the events, practices, and experiences of an unfamiliar time and place as symbols or texts that might be decoded and used to reconstruct the abstract system or culture they represent—but as its object of study. By attending to the domains where social actors struggle to work out the meanings of real things—unusual fungi, winks, or, in the case at hand, the experiences of Buddhist meditators—it aims to uncover their assumptions (and track their debates concerning those assumptions) about what can be a sign at all, the manner in which any given kind of sign should be taken as such, the objects to which signs can refer, and the consequences that given instances of sign reading can plausibly entail.[28] A central argument of this book is that Buddhist meditation manuals, because rather than in spite of their normative or prescriptive status, can inform us about these assumptions and therefore can help us reconstruct the semiotic ideology of Buddhist meditative experience in early medieval China. Indeed, they can be seen as having served as tools themselves for guiding the application of that ideology. More broadly, the claim put forward in this book is that thinking about these sources in this way gives us a means of studying the history of Buddhist meditation without, on the one hand, unduly privileging it as a site of personal experience or,

---

27. Chinese Buddhists, for example, eventually had some success arguing that earthquakes are auspicious, not inauspicious (Sun 2014, 242–284).

28. We should also distinguish these questions from an analysis of what we might call the "semiotics of the sacred," that is, emic theories concerning how transcendent realities can or cannot be represented, a topic about which Buddhists certainly had much to say (Rambelli 2013).

conversely, reducing it to a scriptural ideal professed in theory but having minimal impact on real lives. Seen from this perspective, Buddhist meditation manuals become sources for something beyond their own literary history. They inform us about a world beyond the activity of meditation itself and point us to other sources, topics, and activities in service of a history that encompasses private experiences, cultural norms, social statuses, and the people, not least, who in specific instances did the work of tying these things together.

Chapter Summary

Chan Before Chan presents the early history of Buddhist meditation in China as a history of the semiotic ideology of meditative experience and meditative attainment, stretching from the first era in which there was such an ideology, beginning around the turn of the fifth century, to the first sustained challenge to it, presented by the early Chan School of the mid-Tang dynasty, some three hundred years later. I have not analyzed everything that Chinese Buddhists wrote, thought, or did concerning meditation over the course of the three centuries this book covers. Collectively, its chapters are intended to be representative rather than comprehensive, and I have privileged the sources—especially the fifth-century *chan* scriptures—that I think offer special insight into the questions I raise. Nevertheless, despite necessarily leaving many variations undiscussed, the view presented in this book until the last chapter is of a *longue durée,* a period of history characterized by a stable and broadly shared approach to the semiotics of Buddhist meditation, meditative attainment, and meditative experience that went largely unchallenged for several centuries.

Chapter 1 argues that it was not until the early fifth century that Buddhist meditation came to have a social and cultural life in China. Long before this, Buddhists and others in China had known that the Buddha taught something called *chan*, a practice carried out in the distinctive seated posture of the Buddhist yogi and reputedly a source of power and salvation. But Chinese interest in this pursuit remained largely theoretical for a long time. By tracing the changing assumptions and expectations revealed in hagiographical and similar literary accounts, we can infer that not until the early fifth century did Buddhist meditation become something that a wide variety of Chinese monks and nuns might plausibly be expected to learn or perform. It was only in this era that meditative attainment became what we may call a "real ideal," a social category in terms of which living people in China were classified and understood and on the basis of which they gained fame and authority. What emerged for the first time in the early fifth century was a discernible social "field" of meditation consisting of (1) concrete practices that were relatively accessible to monastic and occasionally even lay Chinese Buddhists; (2) socially relevant positions and formal titles pertaining to these practices, held by living individuals in positions of institutional power and authority, notably the new rank and title of the "*chan* master" (*chanshi* 禪師); and (3) broad ideologies, and specific concrete actions, concerning the possibilities and mechanics of assigning, claiming, and occupying such positions.[29]

A social field comprising meditation practices, meditation masters, and ideologies concerning the relationship between the two provides the context for the many Buddhist meditation texts—the so-called *chan* scriptures—that appeared in China at this time. Chapter 2 turns to the content of these texts and to the well-known Indian *chan* masters they were associated with. How do these texts propose that meditative attainment should be recognized? What tools do they provide to effectuate such recognition? These sources, augmented by other contemporaneous examples from different genres and media, provide various instantiations of what became, over the course of the fifth and sixth centuries, a widely shared understanding—namely, that significant meditative attainment is signaled by concrete (but partially enigmatic) visions, of which the paradigmatic examples were those described in the *chan* scriptures themselves. These confirmatory visions, as I call them, were accepted as events whose occurrence and content would only be known to the one to whom they had occurred (they were *experiences* in this sense), but their meaning—what if anything they indicated about the meditator's attainment—was not self-evident; only a teacher skilled in reading these signs could discern it. Mastery of this interpretive task was characteristic of the *chan* master, who was in this respect analogous to what Steven van Zoeren (1991) has called the "moral-hermeneutical adept" of early Chinese literature: the saintly figure, such as Confucius, whose status as such is revealed by the ability to identify and understand the signs that attest to the virtue (or lack of virtue) in others.

In Keane's definition, a semiotic ideology encompasses assumptions about "what signs are, what functions they do or do not serve, and what consequences they might or might not produce." Chapters 3 and 4 turn to the second and third of these aspects: the functions that confirmatory visions served and the consequences they could produce. In asking what exactly meditative attainment was thought to be, Chapter 3 reconstructs the religious context in which the practice of meditation was carried out and the ends to which Chinese Buddhists put it. Sources drawn from the fifth, sixth, and seventh centuries affirm that the confirmatory visions experienced in meditation were not seen as goods in and of themselves but as indicators of the presence or absence of the same kind of purity that one might otherwise hope to obtain through rituals of repentance (*chanhui* 懺悔) undertaken to eliminate bad karma. This understanding was grounded in ancient Buddhist ideas about the dependence of meditation on purity with respect to the monastic disciplinary restraints. But rather than purity being a mere precondition for meditation practice, visionary meditative experiences were under-

---

29. This characterization of a social field, in the tradition of Bourdieu, I adapt from Hanks 2010, 91–93.

stood to be revelatory, to those who could read them, of otherwise hidden information about past sins. The point to emphasize here is that meditative attainment was not considered, even ideally, an abstract or ethereal thing. It was not merely an inner mental transformation. Nor did it only point "upward," or away from the mundane or material world toward a formless liberation or nirvana. In addition, perhaps primarily, it also mediated one's relationship to a wider world of concrete Buddhist rituals and practices. And that it did so was not just the way things worked out in practice, in contrast to a supposed doctrinal ideal: even elite scriptural sources depict ideal meditative experiences as confirmatory visions and hence as similar to the miraculous happenings in dreams and deathbed visions that were generally thought to be accessible to anyone. All these events were understood to be generated in similar ways, carried a similar range of possible meanings, and similarly implicated decisions about one's engagement with the rituals of repentance and karmic purification that were among the most common forms of Buddhist religious practice in medieval China.

Chapter 4 addresses these rituals of repentance broadly, including a look back to their pre- and non-Buddhist histories in China. But in discussing the specific forms of repentance that appear in meditation manuals and other genres of medieval Chinese Buddhist literature, repentance proves to be more than just one form of ritual among others; conceptually, it was closer to the overall frame within which religious activity took place. This again was not just a matter of practice in contrast to theory. It was never the case that meditation constituted the normative Buddhist goal promoted by canonical scripture and pursued by a few rare virtuosos while most Buddhists on the ground were preoccupied with repentance and the purification of sin. Even high scholastic doctrine conceived of meditation as a *form* of repentance, that is, as something useful for the same ends as (and inherently of a piece with) the rituals of prayer and pleas for mercy that were ubiquitous throughout medieval Chinese Buddhism and medieval Chinese religion as a whole. Here the semiotic ideology of meditative experience, by pointing to the *consequences* of sign reading, leads us well outside the practice of meditation itself into a wider domain of religious activity in which medieval Chinese practitioners of all classes, aspirations, and abilities participated.

Finally, Chapter 5 shifts our perspective from a shared space to the tumultuous ideological change that occurred when the Chan School of the Tang dynasty brought a novel approach to Buddhist meditation into the picture. By setting their writings on this subject against the understanding of meditation that I reconstruct in the earlier chapters, it becomes apparent that the early Chan School proposed neither new methods of meditation nor, conversely, merely a new rhetoric of meditation that had little impact on the ground. It introduced, rather, a new semiotic ideology of meditative experience, a new set of claims about what should count as the evidence of meditative attainment. These arguments were finely aimed. They rejected, above all, the previously uncontroversial understanding that concrete meditative visions were the kind of thing that could potentially confirm true attainment. That the early Chan School offered this kind of higher-order criticism accounts for some of the apparent radicalness of its message and for the way its proponents eventually felt the need to seek out new norms, involving the wholly new literary forms for which Chan is justly famed, in order to establish the authority of "chan" attainment, which they argued could not truly be confirmed in the manner it once routinely had been.

The book concludes with a short epilogue bringing to a close the various threads running through it. Drawing on a unique manuscript that provides a rare, documentary record of how meditative visions were evaluated at Dunhuang in the early 900s, it gestures toward another history that this book does not tell but whose existence it is important to signal: that of later eras when *chan* before Chan often continued on as *chan* after Chan, letting us see that while the Chan School introduced to Chinese and East Asian Buddhism a new model of meditative experience and attainment, it did not entirely displace the old one.

1

Meditation Practice, Meditation Masters, and Meditation Texts

ON PAPER, the history of Buddhist meditation in China stretches back to the very beginning, with detailed writings on meditation figuring prominently among the earliest Buddhist texts in Chinese—those translated in the late Han dynasty by An Shigao 安世高 (fl. 148–168).[1] An Shigao, or more precisely the translation team(s) associated with this name, coined much of the vocabulary that would define this subject throughout its subsequent history in East Asia, including, centrally, the word *chan* 禪, the transcription of a middle-Indic form of the term *dhyāna* that has served as the basic Chinese expression for Buddhist meditation ever since.[2]

Those telling the history of Buddhist meditation in China have long done so in a manner befitting these seemingly ancient origins. Huijiao 慧皎 (497–554), at the conclusion of his collection of biographies of famous "practitioners of meditation" (習禪), gives the following account of its development up until around the beginning of the fifth century:

> Ever since Buddhism came from India to China, the path of *chan* has also been transmitted. In the beginning, [foreign missionaries such as] An Shigao and Dharmarakṣa translated *chan* scriptures. [Chinese monks] such as Sengguang and Tanyou cultivated their minds based on these teachings, ultimately attaining supreme achievement. As a result, inwardly they were joyous and happy, while outwardly they were able to subdue demonic apparitions. Amid multistoried cliffs they drove away devilish ghouls, and on solitary crags they caught glimpses of divine monks [who appeared miraculously in response to their practice].[3]

---

1. For a survey of An Shigao's authentic corpus of translations, see Zacchetti 2010.

2. An Shigao's translations also provide the first examples of the expression *zuochan* 坐禪, "to sit in meditation." It is possible, of course, that An Shigao and his team did not invent these words but borrowed them from other sources that no longer survive.

3. 自遺教東移禪道亦授。先是世高法護譯出禪經。僧先[>光]曇猷等並依教修心，終成勝業。故能內踰喜樂，外折妖祥。擯鬼魅於重巖，覩神僧於絕石。(*GSZ*, T.2059:50.400b25–28). In citations and translations from the *Gao seng zhuan* (*GSZ*), I have profited from the modern Japanese translation by Yoshikawa and Funayama 2009–2010.

For Huijiao, the path of *chan* had been "transmitted" (授) since the advent of Buddhism in China, beginning with An Shigao's translation into Chinese of what Huijiao calls the "*chan* scriptures" (*chanjing* 禪經). The teachings contained in these authoritative Indian texts were then instantiated, Huijiao goes on to say, by the likes of Sengguang and Tanyou, Chinese hermit-monks who realized the fruits of meditative practice in their subduing of demons and experience of miraculous visions.

Huijiao here weaves together two things that we, in the service of our own historical projects, should not unthinkingly conflate: the history in China of a particular tradition of literature (authoritative Buddhist texts about meditation) and the history of a particular kind of person (Buddhists famous for their meditation practice and meditative attainments). We should notice both that Huijiao wanted to make this connection, but also that he had to stretch his sources to do so. The Chinese monks Sengguang and Tanyou lived, according to Huijiao's own biographies of them, nearly two hundred years after An Shigao's time and close to a century after Dharmarakṣa's.[4] Neither's biography mentions the meditation texts of either An Shigao or Dharmarakṣa, or any other examples of early Chinese Buddhist meditation literature. Nor, indeed, do the biographies that Huijiao collected of any of the other "meditation practitioners" who lived or were active before roughly the year 400. As for An Shigao and Dharmarakṣa, the Indian meditation texts they translated were indeed studied by several generations of Chinese Buddhists, as prefaces and commentaries to them attest.[5] Yet neither figure is anywhere said to have been a teacher of the practice of meditation or even to have engaged in this activity himself, much less to have reached any noteworthy meditative attainment.[6] Apart from his assumption that good Buddhist meditation conforms to the prescriptions of authoritative texts, Huijiao, it seems, had little evidence to show that the earliest Chinese meditation texts held any particular significance for the earliest *people* in China known or remembered as actual practitioners of meditation.

Modern scholars who discuss the early history of Buddhist meditation

---

4. *GSZ*, T.50:2059.395c6–25 and 395c27–396b17, respectively.

5. Commentaries to An Shigao's *Anban shou yi jing* 安般守意經, his most famous meditation text, were written by Kang Senghui 康僧會 (d. 280), Dao'an 道安 (312–385), and Xie Fu 謝敷 (fl. fourth century). Each of these authors also wrote prefaces to the text (Link 1976). Zhi Dun 支遁 (314–366) is also said to have authored a commentary to it (*GSZ*, T.2059:50.348c22–23). The popularity of Dharmarakṣa's meditation text—the *Xiu xing dao di jing* 修行道地經, translated in 284 (Boucher 2006, 24)—is less clear, though there is a record of a commentary written to it in the fifth century (*GSZ*, T.2059:50.372b4–5).

6. An Shigao has been described by some modern scholars as an accomplished *practitioner* of meditation (Tsukamoto 1968, 304; Yamabe 1997, 824; Kanno 2010, 159). His earliest biographies say only that he "recited and preserved the *chan* scriptures" (諷持禪經), and this is presented as a subspecialization within his mastery of the Abhidharma (*GSZ*, T.2059:50.323b3; *CSZJJ*, T.2145:55.95a17–18). Details of An Shigao's life are also discussed in early prefaces (Forte 1995, 66–82), and here too meditation is mentioned only as the topic of the literature he translated (*CSZJJ*, T.2145:55.44c19–22).

in China have unwittingly, perhaps, tended to follow in the footsteps of Huijiao's comments. Owing to strong interest, particularly in Japan, in the
origins of the schools of Chinese Buddhism that formed in later periods,
histories of meditation practice have most frequently been told as *pre*-
histories, notably as origin stories of the Chan School, which arose in the
late seventh century as an elite lineage tracing its inception to the legendary,
sixth-century patriarch Bodhidharma.[7] In nonsectarian sources Bodhidharma and his immediate successors were called "practitioners of meditation" or "meditation masters" (*chanshi* 禪師), and later partisans of the Bodhidharma lineage did indeed propose novel approaches to meditation.[8] As the
Bodhidharma lineage grew in prominence, "meditation" (*chan*) often served
as its proper name, producing what became known in China as the Chan
School.

When modern scholars first tried to give an objective history of the
origins of the Chan School, they naturally (but not necessarily rightly)
turned to sources such as Huijiao's *Biographies of Eminent Monks,* which describes, as we have seen, a tradition of *chan* practitioners dating to the earliest days of Chinese Buddhism. For the many influential scholars of Chan in
Japan, however, more was needed lest the Chan School, and hence the Japanese Zen sect with which many of these scholars were associated, be nothing
more than the continuation of a common, widely practiced facet of early
Chinese Buddhism (Foulk 1987, 227). Nukariya Kaiten, in his influential
history of Zen (1925), thus divided pre-Bodhidharma forms of *chan* into two
categories (1:183–210). First were the teachings contained in the early meditation texts translated by An Shigao and others. These teachings, Nukariya
suggested, were what Huijiao's "meditation practitioners" had followed, consisting of traditional Indian methods such as the contemplation of impurity
(*aśubha-bhāvanā*) and the four trances (*dhyāna*), which led to the attainment
of magical powers (*abhijñā*) and the four levels of sainthood. Nukariya classified these practices as "Hīnayāna" meditation. He contrasted them with
the "Mahāyāna" meditation teachings of radical emptiness that would
become prominent in later Chan and which he traced to a different stream
of early Chinese Buddhist literature, one associated with the translator
Lokakṣema (fl. 178–189). The Chan of Bodhidharma, Nukaryia concluded,
could be understood historically as the fusion of these two branches, both
with ancient roots in China and in Buddhism, producing what he called
"pure zen" (*junzen* 純禪).

Over the years other scholars have offered many close variations on this
telling of the history of Chinese Buddhist meditation, sometimes in service

---

7. The "schools" (*zong* 宗) of Chinese Buddhism were in general scholastic or spiritual
lineages, not separate institutions as they often became in Japan (Foulk 1992).

8. Scholars debate the extent to which the early Chan School emerged from a sustained
engagement with meditation practice, as opposed to it being primarily a novel understanding
of lineage (Foulk 2007; Sharf 2014b, 937–938). I will take up this question in more detail in
Chap. 5.

of explaining, or at least including, other later schools of Chinese Buddhism as well.[9] But all of these accounts share two characteristic moves: first, the *chan* of the early *chan* scriptures is deemed an incomplete or inferior "Hīnayāna" variety in relation to the "Mahāyāna" approaches to meditation that flourished later;[10] and second, no attempt is made to question the relationship between texts and people, to differentiate between Buddhist meditation as something written about in sacred religious scriptures and Buddhist meditation as a practice carried out by living people and as a socially defined attribute of such people.

This latter distinction would have less consequence if Buddhist meditation were an activity akin to, say, tennis. In such a domain, textual and social or cultural history could be more readily assumed to have some mutual connection. From a book about tennis written in the 1920s we would necessarily be able to learn things bearing at least some relevance to at least some people living in that era, even if none of their names or life stories were known and no tennis courts or other physical evidence of playing tennis had survived. Even if, as skeptical historians, we refrained from assuming that the recommendations of this book for using tennis to meet new business partners had ever been put into practice, we could still infer something of the social circles where tennis was sometimes played and could conclude that tennis was imagined as something that a businessman—whose existence at the time, as a kind of person, is not in doubt—might so use. In other words, the written source could here be safely treated as reflecting, if only through a glass darkly, ideas that real people employed to characterize an activity that they, or those they knew or had heard of, sometimes engaged in.

But Buddhist meditation is not like tennis, for several reasons. First, although "Buddhist meditation" in English calls to mind a concrete activity, the Indian word *dhyāna* and the Chinese word *chan* that transcribed it encompass not only the practice of meditation but also its normative fruits, including the attainment of particular states of mind with precisely defined

---

9. See, for example, Itō 1931, 8–18; Hu 1937; Sakaino 1935, 858–862; Tang Y. 2001, 1:115–117; Mizuno 1957; Kamata 1982, 1:162; Ren 1985, 1:371–380; Jan 1990, 1–13; Du and Wei 1993, 6–15; Xuan 2001, 235–271; and Xu W. 2004, 13–29. Sasaki [1936] 1978, 41–57, is notable as a response to Nukariya that emphasizes Zhiyi, not Bodhidharma, as the first proponent of truly Mahāyāna meditation. Other scholars refrain from tracing Chan's prehistory back to the Han dynasty but still describe the pre-Bodhidharma scene in similar terms (Yanagida 1970). Western scholars who have covered this ground have also tended to see it as a prelude to later Chan and / or Tiantai and have similarly emphasized the supposedly Hīnayāna character of earlier forms of Chinese Buddhist meditation and their gradual supplanting by the Mahāyāna approaches of Chan and Tiantai; see Dumoulin 1994, 1:63–83; Donner 1977; W. Lai 1983, 65–71; and Sørensen 2012, 58.

10. Alternatively, it is faulted for being purely Indian and not yet suited to the Chinese temperament—and therefore, in the long run, not particularly relevant for the history of Chinese Buddhism. The reading that identifies the Chan School in particular as the most "Chinese" form of Chinese Buddhism was pioneered by Hu Shih 胡適 (1891–1962); see Gong 2006, 42–50.

attributes, magical powers, or rebirth in a specific set of heavenly realms.[11] In Buddhist literature, *dhyāna* is furthermore the activity through which the Buddha reached awakening and also the state in which he died. The Buddhist tradition was always concerned with scholastic analysis of the path followed by the Buddha, and texts on Buddhist meditation were an inextricable part of that activity. In short, Buddhists have always had innumerable purely doctrinal reasons to be interested in the literature of meditation, and calling such documents meditation "manuals," as we sometimes do for convenience, risks predetermining how any given example was in fact used or intended to be used. That Buddhist meditation texts had the potential to function as doctrinal compendia introduces a second issue: namely, that the transmission of Buddhist teachings in the form of sacred written texts was always seen as a meritorious activity in and of itself. Therefore, the preservation of given Buddhist scriptures, and in China their very creation as translations from Indic languages, always had the potential to be motivated by concerns that had little to do with the discursive content of the texts in question.[12]

Together these two issues raise the question of relevance. If even the most concrete scriptural directive for the practice of meditation is a document whose connection *as such* to the daily lives of those who transmitted, studied, or wrote it cannot be assumed, before we can use the textual record to reconstruct the medieval Chinese approach to Buddhist meditation we must first ask which parts of that record were relevant, and how they were relevant, to which groups of Chinese Buddhists. We must, in other words, bring the history of Chinese Buddhist meditation literature into some kind of connection with the history of Buddhist meditation itself, both as a real and as an actively imagined part of the Chinese Buddhist world.

Meditation in China before 400

As an alternative to Huijiao's tidy history, in which meditation texts and meditation practitioners form a necessary and coherent whole, let us consider a somewhat earlier document: a preface written by the Chinese monk Sengrui 僧叡 (352–421/439) to a meditation text translated by the Central Asian monk Kumārajīva, arguably the most influential translator in the history of Chinese Buddhism, shortly after he arrived in the city of Chang'an early in 402.[13] To introduce the text and explain to readers its putative significance within the history of Buddhism in China, Sengrui writes:

---

11. For these reasons, ideas about Buddhist meditation were intimately linked to theories about Buddhist cosmology (Gethin 1997).

12. On such "non-hermeneutic" uses of Buddhist scriptures, see Campany 1991 and Lowe 2017. On translation as a merit-making activity, see Hureau 2006.

13. The *Meditation Scripture* (*Zuo chan sanmei jing* 坐禪三昧經), discussed in Chap. 2. On the question of the date of Sengrui's death, see Felbur 2018, 334–335.

The method of *chan* is the first gateway toward the Way, the salvific route leading to nirvana. Formerly here in China translations were made of [meditation texts such as] the *Scripture on the Stages of Cultivation* [by Dharmarakṣa], and the larger and smaller versions of the *Scripture of the Twelve Gates* and the larger and smaller versions of the *Scripture on Breath Meditation* [by An Shigao].[14] Those texts do indeed pertain to this matter. But they are not sufficiently detailed, and furthermore no one has transmitted [or: "received"] their methods. Regulations for those wishing to learn [*chan*] have thus been wanting.

The master Kumārajīva, travelling from Guzang, arrived in Chang'an on the twentieth day of the twelfth month of the year Xinchou [February 9, 402], and on the twenty-sixth day of that month I received from him the methods for *chan*. Only by being blessed with this edifying instruction did I know that in learning [*chan*] there is a prescribed standard, and that its methods have a prescribed arrangement. This is indeed the meaning of what is said in the *Śūraṅgama-sūtra*, that even if one studies the Way in the mountains, without a master one will never succeed. Inquiring further, I was fortunate enough to receive [from Kumārajīva] these three fascicles of compiled excerpts from the *chan* manuals of various [Indian Buddhist] masters.[15]

Kumārajīva was famous as an interpreter of Mahāyāna doctrine, and his later translations include versions of key treatises and scriptures such as the *Lotus Sutra,* the *Diamond Sutra,* and the *Vimalakīrti Sutra* that remain to this day among the most widely used and studied Chinese Buddhist scriptures. It is also the case that, unlike the *chan* texts previously available in China, Kumārajīva's contains a section with instructions for "bodhisattva" meditation practice.[16] Some scholars have concluded from this that Kumārajīva, who is not elsewhere known for expertise in meditation, must have translated this text because his Chinese students were dissatisfied with the "Hīnayāna" meditation methods they previously had access to and were eager to learn specifically Mahāyāna ones.[17]

---

14. The *Scripture of the Twelve Gates* (*Shi er men jing* 十二門經), one of An Shigao's meditation texts, was long thought to be lost, but a copy was rediscovered recently in Japan (Zacchetti 2003 and 2008).

15. 禪法者，向道之初門，泥洹之津徑也。此土，先出修行、大小十二門、大小安般。雖是其事，既不根悉，又無受法，學者之戒蓋闕如也。究摩羅法師，以辛丑之年十二月二十日自姑臧至常安。予即以其月二十六日從受禪法。既蒙啟授，乃知學有成准，法有成條。首楞嚴經云，人在山中學道，無師道終不成，是其事也。尋蒙抄撰眾家禪要，得此三卷。(*CSZJJ*, T.2145: 55.65a20–27). For a richly annotated English translation of this entire preface, see Felbur 2018, 253–261.

16. *ZCSM*, T.614:15.281a22–286a11. In the received, two-scroll recension, the bodhisattva section begins, without a separate title, in the middle of the second scroll. In the three-scroll manuscripts from Nanatsudera 七寺 and Kongōji 金剛寺, which I have examined, the bodhisattva section is set apart, as the entirety of the third scroll. The three-scroll format seems to be the original one, as the earliest catalogs indicate (*CSZJJ*, T.2145:55.11a14), and its arrangement conforms with Sengrui's comments that the bodhisattva section was compiled and added at a later date (*CSZJJ*, T.2145:55.65b5–6).

17. Donner 1977, 58; Ōchō and Suwa 1982, 216; Kamata 1982, 2:267. On Kumārajīva's

Yet Sengrui, in his preface, says nothing about any such concerns.[18] He says only that the previously available *chan* texts of An Shigao and Dharma-rakṣa, the same translators mentioned by Huijiao above, were "not sufficiently detailed" and also that "no one has transmitted their methods." It would seem that the most exciting thing about Kumārajīva's meditation text for Sengrui was not its radically new doctrines or methods but that it came with the instructions of a living teacher. Sengrui's remarks, of course, occur within a preface, where praise of text and translator is expected by convention, so we must take with a grain of salt any comments here that extol Kumārajīva in particular. Yet it is worth noticing that Sengrui's former teacher Dao'an 道安 (312–385) had expressed similar concerns about the absence of living representatives of Buddhist meditative attainment a generation or two earlier:

> Here in China, the practice of *chan* contemplation has been neglected, so while there are many students [of Buddhism] none have extinguished their defilements. Why is this so? Because it is through *chan* meditation that one guards the mystery, refines the subtle, and enters tranquility, such that one may attain whatever destiny one desires just as readily as one can discern an object held in the palm of one's hand. With this essential method being abandoned, it is no wonder that it has been difficult for those hoping for realization.[19]

Dao'an indicates here, in his own preface to one of An Shigao's meditation texts, that despite the long standing presence of authoritative texts on the subject of *chan*, few Chinese Buddhists had undertaken its practice and none had yet mastered it.

Although neither of these two prefaces can be considered documentary evidence of how or by whom Buddhist meditation was or was not practiced in late fourth-century China, we should still take note of how both authors frame the problem. Neither claims that the meditation texts available to them were wanting in content, and certainly neither one claims that the texts were "Hīnayāna" in character. What both authors express their concern with is the relationship between texts and people. Where Huijiao would celebrate a coherent tradition transmitted since the earliest days of Buddhism in China, Dao'an and Sengrui saw a fragmented terrain. Despite the availability of authoritative texts about meditation, for Dao'an, and for Sengrui prior to Kumārajīva's arrival, there was a conspicuous absence of people standing in an authoritative relationship to such texts, either as teachers of their methods

---

life and times, see Ōchō and Suwa 1982; Lu 2004; and Felbur 2019. The *Gao seng zhuan* does report that Kumārajīva's mother, who was a Buddhist nun, was skilled in meditation (*GSZ*, T.2059:50.330b2).

18. Moreover the "bodhisattva" methods that Kumārajīva's text does present are, in fact, very similar to those it provides for the non-bodhisattva practitioner (Yamabe 2009).

19. 斯晉土，禪觀弛廢。學徒雖興，蔑有盡漏。何者，禪思守玄，練微入寂，在取何道，猶覘于掌。墮替斯要，而悕見證，不亦難乎。(*CSZJJ*, T.2145:55.45a2–4)

or as those who claimed, or were thought by others, to have mastered or attained what these texts describe.

The Meditation Master as a Social Category

The contrast between Sengrui's and Dao'an's accounts of meditation in early Chinese Buddhism and that of Huijiao, writing roughly 150 years later, points to a decisive change in how *chan* was understood, one for which Kumārajīva's translation of meditation texts for Sengrui in the year 402 serves as a convenient marker. This change was not limited to the production of new writings' about meditation, though it was also that, and the new meditation texts that appeared during the fifth century in particular will occupy us at length later in this book. More than that, it was a change in which *chan* went from being a mythic practice linked to saints from far away or long ago, and only read about in books or known through legend, to something with a real existence in China, something that Chinese Buddhists could hope to accomplish, and under whose guise living people and their activities were named, classified, and valued.

The main sources purporting to reveal information about the practice of meditation among Chinese Buddhists of the second through sixth centuries are hagiographical collections such as the *Biographies of Eminent Monks* and the *Lives of the Nuns*.[20] Although these collections do contain ample measures of historically accurate information, when it comes to their depictions of normatively significant practices such as meditation, we must, of course, approach them not as records of the lives of specific individuals but as exemplifications of ideals (Kieschnick 1997). Yet because such biographies show us the nature of Buddhist excellence as it was in fact commemoratively attributed, in many cases to real historical persons, these stories are nonetheless revealing. Precisely because they are idealizing, they are sources for the real history of ideals. From this perspective, there is "no profound gap... between hagiographic or historical narrative on the one hand, and the religious and social life setting in which those narratives were formed on the other" because "stories are already part and parcel of religious life as it is lived" (Campany 2009, 13). The idealizing nature of hagiographic depictions of Buddhist meditation, far from a barrier to our perception of what "really" happened, actively contributes to our understanding of how Bud-

---

20. Many scholars have studied the biographical records of early (pre-Tang) Chinese monks remembered for their practice of *chan*, though this scholarship has almost always focused on monastic hagiography at the expense of other pertinent sources such as miracle tales, and has almost entirely ignored nuns' hagiographies (exceptionally, see Zhou 2014). See, among others, Matsumoto 1911, 222–306; Sakaino 1935, 906–939; Mizuno 1957; Ōtani 1970, 1972; Murakami 1961; Furuta 1980; Sakamoto 1981; 1982; Mutō 2004; 2009; and J. Chen 2014a; 2014b.

dhist meditation was thought about and the role it was imagined to have in Chinese society and in the lives of Chinese Buddhists.

It may also be possible, in some cases, for these sources to support observations about the way perceptions of Buddhist meditation, together with the ideals and expectations concerning it, changed over time and what those changes may reflect of events that occurred outside the world of the texts themselves. Here we must proceed with caution. The major surviving collections of early Chinese Buddhist monastic hagiography were compiled in south China during the Liang dynasty (502–557), a period of lively interest in systematic bibliographical projects.[21] The chronology of the composition of the biographies in these collections does not, therefore, necessarily match the chronologies of the relevant figures themselves.

Still, while there may be examples where the biography of a second-century monk reached its final form later than the biography of a fifth-century monk, such cases surely form a minority. We know that the early sixth-century hagiographic collections made liberal use of earlier collections and also drew from funerary epitaphs and other ancient sources (Shinohara 1988). *On average* we can infer something about the relative chronology of composition from the chronology of the figures themselves. The specific patterns I discuss below, in particular the evident lack of importance given to meditation in the stories of pre-400 monks and nuns, lend plausibility to this approach inasmuch as they make the early Chinese monastic establishment look less than optimal in light of later ideals. By the "criterion of embarrassment," we may conclude that these records do really show us the ideals about meditation characteristic of that earlier era, ideals that had evidently changed in certain ways by the early sixth century.

Pre-400: The Chinese Recluse

Let us begin with a simple question: who was thought to practice meditation in early Chinese Buddhism? Remarkably, to the extent that they were remembered and extolled in hagiography *foreign* Buddhists, from India or the "western regions" of Central Asia, were not known for any particular connection to meditation prior to the early fifth century. Not only do the hagiographies never describe such monks as masters or teachers of meditation, but even the mere practice of meditation goes unmentioned in the accounts of their lives. Before the fifth century, foreign Buddhists in China were remembered and celebrated for having excelled in only two ways: as translators of Indian texts who gained fame for some combination of prowess in memorization, skill in translation, and mastery of Buddhist scriptural sources, or

---

21. On the character of Liang-dynasty Buddhism, see Funayama 2015. One important set of surviving biographies, those in the *Chu san zang ji ji*, were completed by the end of the immediately preceding Qi 齊 dynasty; they refer to Chinese as "the language of Qi" and the year 503 is the latest date they mention (Palumbo 2003, 197n87).

as exotic miracle workers who could predict the future, cure diseases, and wield supernatural powers (Zürcher 1999).[22]

Even early translators whose oeuvre included specialized meditation texts, such as An Shigao or Dharmarakṣa, were not themselves remembered as practitioners of meditation. The case of An Shigao is particularly interesting in this respect, because for him we have, in addition to his monastic biographies, an early miracle tale preserved in the fifth-century *Records of the Hidden and Visible Worlds* (*You ming lu* 幽明錄), a source that predates surviving monastic hagiographical accounts by almost a century and also reflects the preoccupations of a slightly different literary genre.[23] This tale says nothing of An Shigao's activities as a translator, the emphasis in his monastic biography, and depicts him solely as a wonder worker capable of quelling spirits and other stupendous feats (*Gu xiao shuo gou chen*, 430–431). To judge from the surviving evidence, then, the two roles of translator and exotic holy man defined the range of possibilities for the foreign monk in China through the first several hundred years of Chinese Buddhism.

It is true that in later Buddhist hagiographies a connection is often made between thaumaturgy and *chan* practice. Hujiao's concluding comments to his biographies of the "*chan* practitioners" explicitly posit supernatural power as a key marker of meditative attainment.[24] Yet the converse is not true: those whom Huijiao classifies as miracle workers are only rarely linked to meditation practice, and never so in the case of specifically foreign miracle workers.[25] To take one example, the *Biographies of Eminent Monks* describes the training and skills of Fotucheng 佛圖澄 (d. 348), who served as a court monk for the military rulers of north China during the mid-fourth century and is the best documented of the early foreign miracle workers, only as follows:

> Fotucheng was a native of Central Asia. He was originally a member of the Bo clan. When he was young, he became a monk and devoted himself diligently to his studies. He could recite several hundreds of thousands of lines of scripture, and well understood their meaning.... He said that he had twice traveled to Gandhāra, where he received instruction from famous masters. Everyone in Central Asia said that he had attained the Way.[26]

---

22. Even after the fifth century, when other possibilities opened up for foreign Buddhist missionaries in China, the *Gao seng zhuan* classifies foreign monks only as translators or miracle workers. This, however, seems to have been a feature of this collection alone. The table of contents of the *Ming seng zhuan*, for example, lists ten foreign monks under the category of "foreign *chan* masters." However, none of these figures were present in China prior to Kumārajīva (*Meisōden shō*, Z.1523:77.348b22–c4).

23. On the *You ming lu*, see Campany 1996, 75–77, and Zhang 2014.

24. *GSZ*, T.2059:50.400c3–8.

25. Only three of the twenty principal biographies of "miracle workers" (*shen yi* 神異) in the *Gao seng zhuan* mention the practice of *chan*: Tan Daokai 單道開 (T.2059:50.387b16–17), Heluojie 訶羅竭 (T.2059:50.389a6–9), and Baozhi 保誌 (T.2059:50.394a15–16). All three were Chinese. (Heluojie's name suggests foreign ancestry, but he is said to have been born in China.)

26. 竺佛圖澄者。西域人也。本姓帛氏。少出家清真務學。誦經數百萬言，善解文義 ... 自云再到罽

The few places in the remainder of the biography that touch on the source of Fotucheng's powers speak only of exotic rituals and spellcraft. It would seem, then, that Fotucheng's magical abilities were not connected to Buddhist meditation practice in any clearly identifiable way by the Chinese public who recorded and remembered his exploits.

In contrast to these foreign translators and magicians, the pre-fifth-century *chan* practitioners identified in the *Biographies of Eminent Monks* were all native-born Chinese. This seeming selectivity is not an editorial quirk of this collection alone; in the fully surviving table of contents of the slightly earlier *Biographies of Famous Monks* (*Ming seng zhuan* 名僧傳),[27] those who are identified as *chan* masters are explicitly classified as foreign or Chinese, and no one in the former group arrived in China before the early fifth century.[28] The same result obtains even if we ignore the collections' potentially arbitrary categorization of the figures in question: no pre-fifth-century foreign monks of any kind are ever described, even in passing, as having practiced meditation at all.[29]

Thus, before the fifth century, it appears that *chan* was something associated exclusively with *Chinese* Buddhist monks. The way that hagiographies depict these figures' practice and mastery of meditation also differs in

---

賓，受誨名師。西域咸稱得道。(*GSZ*, T.2059:50.383b16–20). On Fotucheng (also read Fotu*deng*), see Wright 1948 and Shinohara 2018.

27. On the *Ming seng zhuan*, see Wright 1954, 408–412; Ji 2009, 198–234; Sangyop Lee 2020. I have used Kasuga's (1936) editions of the three different works of the Japanese monk Sōshō 宗性 (1202–1278) that preserve fragments of the *Ming seng zhuan*, but for convenience I give references to the *Meisōden shō* 名僧傳抄 (Z.1523), a modern compilation of these sources.

28. *Meisōden shō*, Z.1523:77.348b22–c6. For this table of contents, see also Sangyop Lee 2020, 39–83. This table of contents helps resolve some ambiguous figures from the *Gao seng zhuan* with surnames such as Bo 帛 or Zhi 支, which could refer either to foreign Buddhist monks or to their Chinese students. All the early *chan* practitioners included in the *Gao seng zhuan* who had such surnames are, in the table of contents of the *Ming seng zhuan*, classified as Chinese rather than foreign meditation masters. The *Ming seng zhuan* also includes, as foreign *chan* specialists, some monks the *Gao seng zhuan* classifies as translators. These monks too all arrived in China only after the early fifth century.

29. Mutō 2004 has compiled a helpful chart of all references to meditation practice in the *Gao seng zhuan*. The only pre-fifth-century foreign monks he lists are linked to meditation solely by their translation of meditation-themed texts (such as An Shigao). The one exception is Shilimiduoluo 尸梨密多羅 (*Śrīmitra), active during the early Eastern Jin (317–420), who is portrayed as an exotic foreigner capable of participating in the witty exchanges of the literati salons of the day, and remembered for his skill in the melodic chanting of mantras (*GSZ*, T.2059:50.327c12–328a27; Shih 1968, 42–46). Mutō includes Śrīmitra in his list based on a single line from his biography: "he frequently carried out austerities east of Boulder Hill" (常在石子岡東行頭陀). In the *Gao seng zhuan* the word "austerities" (*toutuo* 頭陀; Skt. *dhuta*), nominally referring to the twelve or thirteen canonical ascetic practices (Dantinne 1991), primarily describes monks who live in uninhabited areas and is not inherently connected to meditation. In any case, the biography mentions this only to explain why Śrīmitra was buried in this location. The *Chu san zang ji ji*, meanwhile, contains the biographies of eleven pre-Kumārajīva foreign translators (and one Chinese translator, Zhu Shixing 朱士行)—none of these mention *chan* practice at all (*CSZJJ*, T.2145:55.95a7–100a6).

revealing ways from how even the same collections depict it for monks (and then also nuns) living after this time. The *Biographies of Eminent Monks* portrays all the earliest "practitioners of *chan*" as hermit-like recluses living in remote locations and unconnected to any larger social networks, Buddhist or otherwise. (The few examples where such networks are mentioned treat them cursorily.) How these monks learned to practice *chan* is never explained. Their background is rarely described in more than a few brief sentences, and there are no accounts of discipleship under Indian or Chinese Buddhist masters. Of Bo Sengguang 帛僧光 (d. ca.376–396), for example, we only learn that "his origins are unknown. In his youth he cultivated the practice of *chan*."[30] Only slightly more informative is the biography of Zhu Faxian 竺法顯 (fl. 318–322): "He was from the north. He was resolute in his asceticism and enjoyed restraint. He did not eat meat, chanted the scriptures, and endeavored at *chan* as his major occupation. He frequently lived alone in the mountains and forests, practicing austerities beyond the reach of men."[31] Zhu Faxian later crossed into south China, where he is described, in similarly anonymous terms, only as "having spent time in famous monasteries, where he practiced his usual activity [of meditation]."[32]

The *Biographies of Eminent Monks* provides essentially equivalent biographies for a few early figures not classified as "*chan* practitioners" but still reported to have intensively engaged in *chan*.[33] Daoli 道立 (fl. late fourth century), grouped among the exegetes, was also famous for entering states of meditative trance lasting up to seven days. He "kept his spirit pure and did not interact with the society of his day.... He remained in reclusion on Mount Fuzhou, living alone on the cliffs and not accepting patronage."[34] Unlike the typical early *chan* practitioner in the *Biographies of Eminent Monks*, Daoli is depicted as the disciple of a famous Chinese monk, the well-known Dao'an. Noticeably, however, the biography does not say that he studied meditation under Dao'an, only certain Buddhist scriptures. His practice of meditation is also described as a solitary affair taking place outside the orbit of Dao'an and his community.

A final aspect of the hagiographic portrayal of the pre-fifth-century Chinese monks known for their practice of meditation is worth stressing: that these figures were not remembered as associating with or being patronized by prominent laypersons, government officials, or other persons of

---

30. 未詳何許人。少習禪業。(*GSZ*, T.2059:50.295c6)

31. 北地人。貞苦善戒節。蔬食誦經，業禪為務。常獨處山林，頭陀人外。(*GSZ*, T.2059:50.295b24–25)

32. 復歷名山修己恒業。(*GSZ*, T.2059:50.295b28)

33. Some of these same figures were included in the "*chan* master" section of the *Ming seng zhuan* (*Meisōden shō*, Z.1523:77.348c5–349a3). This includes the fourth-century Lingshao 令韶, whose biography in the *Gao seng zhuan* appears in the exegete section (*GSZ*, T.2059:50.347b19–24), as well as Faxiang 法相, listed as a Chinese *chan* master in the *Ming seng zhuan* but classified as a "scripture reciter" (*songjing* 誦經) in the *Gao seng zhuan* (*GSZ*, T.2059:50.406c8–20).

34. 性澄靖不涉當世 . . . 隱覆舟山，巖居獨處，不受供養。(*GSZ*, T.2059:50.356b17–24)

power. The closest we come to any depiction of such patronage is in the
biography of Zhu Tanyou 竺曇猷 (fl. early fourth century):

> On the mountain [where he had settled] there was a single high cliff that rose
> up through the layers of clouds. Tanyou dug out the rock to make a ladder and
> ascended the cliff where he sat in peace, using connected pieces of bamboo to
> deliver water for his daily needs. A dozen or so students of meditation came to
> him there. Wang Xizhi heard of him and came to visit. Looking up at the peak
> he bowed to its loftiness, presented his respects, and then departed.[35]

Here, Tanyou's spiritual loftiness is shown by the biographer in the *failure* of
the famous politician-cum-poet-calligrapher Wang Xizhi (303–361) to ever
meet him despite his best efforts to do so. Though Tanyou is imagined as
having a certain renown in the wider world, this does not translate into any
contact with that world. The kinds of social interactions that were imagined
as possible for the early *chan* practitioners were thus considerably different
than those routinely engaged in by the salon-frequenting, bon-mot-dispensing
monks of the "gentry Buddhism" that captivated the Chinese elite during this
same era (Zürcher 1972, 71–80).[36]

Post-400: A New Model

The portrayal of Buddhist meditators as cave-dwelling hermits who disdained
association with the famous and powerful and even with their own fellow
seekers is clearly indebted to Chinese literary conventions having to do with
"recluses" (*yin* 隱) and "transcendents" (*xian* 仙).[37] The tale of Wang Xizhi
and Zhu Tanyou, for example, would find a ready home among the medieval
Chinese poems in which the recluse's "lofty" nature is shown when he cannot
be found by a would-be visitor (Varsano 1999). Yet for all their shunning of
the world, the recluses and seekers of immortality of ancient and early medieval Chinese literature are rarely exclusively otherworldly. Instead, they
are frequently shown displaying their arts for patrons and clients. Robert
Ford Campany (2009, 151–215) sees in these interactions ground for arguing

---

35. 山有孤巖，獨立秀出千雲。猷搏石作梯升巖宴坐，接竹傳水以供常用。禪學造者十有餘人。王羲之聞而故往。仰峯高挹致敬而反。(*GSZ*, T.2059:50.396a15–18)

36. Biographies of pre-400 Chinese monks who did interact with elite society do occasionally refer to the ideal of meditation. The biography of Zhi Dun 支盾 (314–366), one of the most famous monks of the mid-fourth century, reports that "in his later years he moved to Mount Shicheng, where he founded the Xiguang temple. He sat quietly [in meditation] in his mountain abode and let his mind roam freely in the grove of *chan*" 晚移石城山。又立棲光寺。宴坐山門遊心禪苑。(*GSZ*, T.2059:50.348c21–22). Yet as a percentage of the total space devoted to Zhi Dun's monkish activities—which, in a lengthy biography, include his study of scriptures, his composition of commentaries to Buddhist and secular literature, and his interaction with secular elites—this one brief mention of meditation is vanishingly small. Meditation, in other words, is not posited here as a source of Zhi Dun's reputation and authority.

37. On the literary portrayal of Chinese recluses and transcendents, see Berkowitz 2000 and Campany 2009.

that being a "transcendent" in early medieval China was not an individual pursuit carried out alone in the mountains so much as a kind of performance requiring both actor and audience. From an historical perspective, the tales Campany investigates also show us that such interactions were considered plausible occurrences—in other words, that people really did exist then who claimed or were considered to be seekers of transcendence, and that encountering such a person was thought of as a real possibility for rulers, ministers, and other persons of power.

It is this presumption that is lacking in the biographies of the *chan* practitioners before the fifth century. And yet when we turn to figures active in the early fifth century and beyond, there is a clear shift. Although the tropes of eremitism continue, we also find a new profile: the well-connected or even politically active meditation master.[38] The biography of Xuangao 玄高 (d. 444), one of the most important Buddhist monks in north China during the first half of the fifth century, provides a model of the new career possibilities now apparently available for those with expertise in *chan*.[39] Xuangao supposedly studied *chan* with the Indian monk Buddhabhadra in Chang'an and later served Juqu Mengsun 沮渠蒙遜 (r. 401–433), ruler of the Northern Liang kingdom and a great patron of Buddhism. When the Wei armies drove the Northern Liang rulers into Central Asia in 439, Xuangao offered his services to the Wei court, eventually meeting a tragic end when he was executed for plotting a rebellion with an imperial prince (Tang Y. 2001, 2:98–100).

But in addition to his illustrious if ill-fated career as a court monk under two different dynasties, Xuanggao's biography also emphasizes his attainments in *chan* and his discipleship under, and confirmation by, a famous Indian "meditation master":

> Xuangao then heard that *chan* master Buddhabhadra was transmitting the teachings at the Shiyang monastery near Chang'an, so he went there and took him as his teacher. After a dozen or so days he had reached a profound mastery of the teachings of *chan*. Buddhabhadra said to him: "Excellent indeed, O child of the Buddha, is your profound understanding." Thereafter Buddhabhadra became deferential towards Xuangao and refused to be treated as his teacher.[40]

Xuangao was not the only meditation master of his day who reached such political heights. An appendix to his biography mentions another who "gained fame through the vocation of *chan*" (以禪業見稱) in this same era:

---

38. On the fifth- and early sixth-century Chinese monks known for their association with meditation practice, see J. Chen 2014a and 2014b.

39. *GSZ*, T.2059:50.397a3–398b11. On Xuangao see W. Lai 2003, 152–158, who provides an English translation of his biography.

40. 聞關中有浮馱跋陀禪師在石羊寺弘法，高往師之。旬日之中妙通禪法。跋陀歎曰。善哉佛子，乃能深悟如此。於是卑顏推遜，不受師禮。(*GSZ*, T.2059:50.397a19–24). Xuangao's powers and the meditative attainments of his many students are described in the later portions of his biography.

the monk Tanyao 曇曜.[41] Although the *Biographies of Eminent Monks* speaks of him only in passing, Tanyao was in fact the government-appointed monastic superintendent (*shamen tong* 沙門統) under the Wei in the 460s and essentially the most powerful Buddhist monk in north China.[42]

The *Biographies of Eminent Monks* records many other cases of monks famous for their practice of meditation who held, or who were depicted as holding, lesser, though still important institutional roles. Sengliang 僧亮, a disciple of another eminent Chinese *chan* practitioner named Sengzhou 僧周, supposedly spearheaded the reestablishment of Buddhism in Chang'an following the death of the Wei emperor Taiwu 太武 (r. 424–452), who in 446 had instituted a suppression of Buddhism. Sengliang's biography reports that he was greeted with great fanfare when he returned to Chang'an at the invitation of the prince of Yongchang 永昌, a member of the Wei imperial family then serving as governor of the region:

> Before [Sengliang] arrived in Chang'an, the prince and the local people swept and cleaned the streets and alleys, and everyone came out to greet him. The prince came personally to humbly welcome him, touching [his head] to Sengliang's feet to express his reverence.[43]

We need not take any of these accounts as historically descriptive to conclude that by the middle of the fifth century mastery of *chan* had become attributable not only to reclusive hermits but also to famous monks who associated with wealthy patrons, government officials, and even the rulers of states large and small.

Such patronage was deemed equally if not even more common in south China, under the Song 宋 (420–479) court, where by the mid-fifth century numerous foreign and native Buddhist teachers were known for their practice and mastery of *chan* (J. Chen 2014a). Many references in the *Biographies of Eminent Monks* describe the support that even the highest echelons of Song society gave to monks whose status and authority derived from their (claimed or imputed) mastery of meditation. (In a seemingly related trend, Buddhist temple names incorporating the word *chan* suddenly became quite fashionable in this same era.)[44] That our stories sometimes mention such connections only in passing confirms that the possibility of such occurrences was by then taken for granted. The biography of a certain Zhicheng 智稱 (d. 501) reports that he had studied in his youth with a certain *chan* master Yin 印, an "imperial teacher" (*dishi* 帝師) who had been invited to the southern capital

---

41. *GSZ*, T.2059:50.398b10.

42. On Tanyao's life, see Tsukamoto 1957. Tanyao was instrumental in the construction of the early Yungang caves, sponsored by the Wei rulers (Yi 2018, 53–77).

43. 未至之頃，王及民人，掃灑街巷，比室候迎。王親自枉道，接足致敬。(*GSZ*, T.2059:50.398c1–2). See Tsukamoto 1957, 368–369.

44. *Song shu*, 87.2200, reports that Xiao Huikai 蕭慧開 (d. 471) endowed four Buddhist temples on behalf of his deceased father, with each temple name containing the word *chan* 禪.

by the Song emperor Xiaowu 孝武 (r. 453–464).[45] Other references are more
detailed, such as the biography of Huilan 慧覽 (d. ca. 457–464), a colleague
of Xuangao's who eventually ended up in the south. Born in what is now
Gansu province, Huilan reportedly traveled across Central Asia to Gandhāra,
where he studied under Indian meditation masters. Upon his return to
China, he was invited by Emperor Wen 文 (r. 424–453) to reside at the
imperially supported Dinglin 定林 temple near the capital. When the next
emperor, Xiaowu, had the Zhongxing 中興 temple built, Huilan moved there,
where he was patronized by prominent laymen and came to be known as the
instructor of "all the *chan* monks in the capital region."[46] Huilan may not
have reached quite the same heights as Xuangao, but both figures, unlike
the reclusive *chan* practitioners of the fourth century and earlier, were depicted as having a clear pedigree of *chan* training, as teaching known disciples, as living in imperially sponsored temples, and as having received the
patronage of aristocrats.

Beginning from the early fifth century, then, the kinds of figures to
whom mastery of meditation was attributed changed significantly. No longer
the sole preserve of hermit-like figures who declined to interact with the
world, mastery of meditation became something that one might also expect
of powerful monks who frequented emperors.

Nuns and Meditation

This shift may be responsible for another noteworthy change: in the fifth
century the practice of *chan* also became an imaginable attribute of Buddhist
nuns. Our most important source for the medieval Chinese understanding
of the ideal Buddhist nun is the early sixth-century *Lives of the Nuns* (*Biqiuni
zhuan* 比丘尼傳), which chronicles over sixty-five Chinese nuns living between
the early fourth century, when the Chinese nuns' order was first established,
and the early sixth century.[47] Unlike the *Biographies of Eminent Monks*, the
Lives of the Nuns does not classify its subjects by monastic vocational specialization. The preface, however, specifically mentions meditation (*changuan*
禪觀) as one of four areas in which these nuns had gained renown.[48] This is
confirmed by the biographies themselves, which frequently discuss the nuns'

---

45. *GSZ*, T.2059:50.402b10–11; *GHMJ*, T.2103:50.269a2. The monk Yin might possibly
be the *chan* master Huiyin 慧印, mentioned in passing (but in a manner suggesting he was well
known) in a fragment of the *Ming xiang ji* (*Fa yuan zhu lin*, T.2122:53.1003c29–1004a4; Campany
2012, 323).

46. 京邑禪僧皆隨踵受業。(*GSZ*, T.2059:50.399a11–22). See also *Meisōden shō*,
Z.1523:77.356a7–15.

47. See Tsai 1994 for a complete translation and introduction. Fifth- and sixth-century
miracle tale collections also preserve some stories about Buddhist nuns (Georgieva 1996).

48. *BQNZ*, T.2063:50.934b20–22. The three other areas are ascetic practice (苦行), "firmly
maintaining one's intention" (立志貞固, i.e., resisting marriage), and "spreading the teachings
far and wide" (弘震曠遠).

practice and mastery of meditation, proportionally more often, even, than do hagiographies of monks from the same era.[49]

However, a clear historical change is also evident in the frequency of such descriptions. Of the thirteen nuns who died before 420 (the beginning of the Song dynasty), only one is mentioned—and only in passing—as having practiced *chan:* Kang Minggan 康明感, the founder of the first nunnery in south China.[50] In contrast, the practice of *chan* is mentioned, sometimes at length, in the biographies of twenty-five of the remaining fifty-two nuns who received full entries.[51] This evolution is readily understandable in light of the changing historical patterns discussed above for monks' biographies. For in the *Lives of the Nuns,* Chinese nuns are never depicted as wandering ascetics or hermits. They always appear as residents of temples in or near major cities, usually with the support of wealthy patrons.[52] It was only when *chan* became imaginable as something accessible to those living in such circumstances, it seems, that nuns too could become recognized for their association with and mastery of this practice.

The *Chan* Master

These changes in the depiction of those who practiced *chan* went hand in hand with a parallel and historically undoubtedly related development: the first appearance in China of Indian or Central Asian Buddhist missionaries remembered as *teachers* of meditation. Before the fifth century, there were no foreign monks answering to that description at all, or at least none that were remembered. Beginning soon after the turn of the century, however, a wave of foreign missionaries claiming to be or regarded as teachers of *chan* arrived in China, at least some of whom achieved renown without recourse to accustomed areas of expertise such as translation.

Many of these foreign teachers were known in their lifetimes under the title of "*chan* master" (*chanshi*). This title, so familiar from subsequent Chinese Buddhist history, was a new one at the time. As far as can be judged from written sources, the first person to carry it was Buddhabhadra, who arrived in Chang'an in 406, not long after Kumārajīva, as one of several prominent

---

49. On meditation in the *Biqiuni zhuan,* see Adamek 2009, 14–16, and Zhou 2014.

50. *BQNZ,* T.2063:50.935b29–c20.

51. A more precise calculation yields even starker figures. Apart from Kang Minggan, the first nun whose biography mentions meditation is Fasheng 法勝 (*BQNZ,* T.2063:50.938c28–939a16). Fasheng's life is undated, but the entries are chronological and her biography is placed between two figures who died in 442 and 448, respectively. Taking Fasheng's biography as the dividing line, of the twenty-two nuns who died earlier only one (4.5 percent) is described as having practiced *chan,* versus an astonishing twenty-five out of the forty-three (58 percent) who died later.

52. Indian Buddhist nuns too may have been primarily *urban* residents (Schopen 2014a, 3–72). Tellingly, no nun in the *Biqiuni zhuan* is said to have practiced the *dhutas* (*toutuo* 頭陀), the ascetic practices that in monk's biographies typically characterize those without a fixed residence. In later eras, however, many Chinese nuns did come to be associated with these ideals (Adamek 2009).

Indian masters assembled under the patronage of the warlord Yao Xing 姚興 (r. 399–416). Although Buddhabhadra eventually settled in south China and became a noted translator, his initial reputation was gained solely as a teacher of meditation (J. Chen 2014b). In a letter written to Liu Yimin 劉遺民 (d. 410), Sengzhao 僧肇, who studied under both Buddhabhadra and Kumārajīva, refers to Buddhabhadra as the "*chan* master" and contrasts his teaching of meditation with the pursuits of the other Indian missionaries then in Chang'an who were translating scriptures or giving exegesis.[53]

The *chanshi* title may have begun as a Chinese translation or interpretation of the Indian title *yogācāra,* meaning a practitioner of *yoga,* that is, meditation.[54] Indeed, Buddhabhadra is known to have translated texts associated with a loosely defined group whose members were sometimes called *yogācāra*s.[55] Whatever its origin, what is historically most significant is that the very idea of a "*chan* master" was seemingly unknown in China before the early fifth century, when the word is first attested.[56] Tellingly, the *Biographies of Eminent Monks* does not use this title to refer to any of the pre-fifth-century "*chan* practitioners" it memorializes, all of whom were Chinese, even as it does sometimes call them by other titles such as "Dharma master."

Whether or not Buddhabhadra was truly the first person in Chinese history to be called a *chan* master, he was the first to become famous enough as such to have his name remembered.[57] It is also clear that soon thereafter

---

53. *Zhao lun,* T.1858:45.155c14–15 (Tsukamoto 1955, 44–45); *CSZJJ,* T.2145:55.20c12–21. Other sources confirm that Buddhabhadra was called a "*chan* master" even while alive. See Sengrui's "Explications for the Confused" (*Yu yi lun* 喻疑論; *CSZJJ,* T.2145:55.41b17–18), the colophons to Buddhabhadra's translation of the *Mahāsāṅghika-vinaya* (*CSZJJ,* T.2145:55.21a9; *Mohesengqi lü,*T.1425:22.548b9) and the *Hua yan jing* 華嚴經 (*CSZJJ,* T.2145:55.61a4; *Hua yan jing,* T.278:9.788b6), as well as the travel records of Faxian (*Gao seng Faxian zhuan,* T.2085:51.866b16–17).

54. Another possibility would be the title *prāhāṇika* (one who strives, i.e., a meditator), attested in early Indian Buddhist inscriptions among other places (Schopen 1997, 31).

55. On the term *yogācāra* as used in Indian Buddhist texts, see Silk 1997 and 2000; and Stuart 2015, 225–242. On the *yogācāra*s as a loosely defined group behind the composition of the meditation texts translated into Chinese by Buddhabhadra and others, see Odani 1996. The relationship between these *yogācāra*s and the later Yogācāra philosophical school is a subject of ongoing debate among scholars.

56. The word is rare in *translated* texts of any era. The earliest example may be Zhu Fonian's 竺佛念 *Chu yao jing* 出曜經, a commentary to the *Dharmapada.* The catalog of the *Chu san zang ji ji* says this text was translated between 373 and 383 (*CSZJJ,* T.2145:55.10c5–6), but Zhu Fonian's (earlier) biography dates it later, to after Kumārajīva had arrived (ibid., 111b21–23) and hence perhaps only after Buddhabhadra had already become famous as a "*chan* master" (on Zhu Fonian's problematic corpus, see Nattier 2010). The commentary portions of the *Chu yao jing,* where we find the term *chanshi,* were also at least in part composed by Zhu Fonian himself (Hiraoka 2007), making the link between this word and any specific Indic term even less clear.

57. The *Ming seng zhuan* gives the names of two other "foreign *chan* masters" present in Chang'an at this time: Puṇyatāra 弗若多羅 and Dharmayaśas 曇摩耶舍 (*Meisōden shō,* Z.1523:77.348b22–24). Dharmayaśas later settled in the south and taught meditation (*GSZ,* T.2059:50.329b16–c27). Puṇyatāra is better known as the first reciter of the *Sarvāstivāda Vinaya* (*Shi song lü*) for Kumārajīva's translation (*GSZ,* T.2059:50.333a13–24); why he is here called a *chan* master is unclear.

many other similarly imagined foreign monks reached positions of authority and prestige in various Chinese Buddhist communities. In north China, under the Northern Liang dynasty that ruled the Gansu region during the early fifth century, the Indian monk Dharmapriya became sufficiently important for his portrait to be painted on the wall of cave 169 at Binglinsi 炳靈寺 (he seems to have been one of the sponsors of part of the cave), and a partially surviving inscription, likely from 420 or 424 (Kuramoto 2016, 525n78), refers to him explicitly as "the great *chan* master" (大禪師). Although Dharmapriya was seemingly not remembered as the translator of any Indian texts—and perhaps for that reason the *Biographies of Eminent Monks* mentions him only in passing[58]—he was clearly an important figure in his day, at least locally. By 420, it would seem, a foreign Buddhist monk could gain patronage and position primarily on his reputation as a "*chan* master."

Foreign *chan* masters were equally if not even more prevalent in south China during the Song dynasty. Many passed through the Jetavana (Qihuan 祇洹) temple near the southern capital of Jiankang (modern Nanjing), a large monastery whose first abbot, Huiyi 慧義 (372–444), had helped the founding Song emperor overthrow the preceding dynasty by obtaining favorable omens (Tsukamoto 1975, 77). Huiyi's biography records the Qihuan temple's hosting of numerous foreign monks, "some of whom translated scriptures while others gave instruction in the practice of *chan*," during the early years of the dynasty.[59] Also in the southern capital was the Douchang 鬪場 temple (also called Daochang 道場), where the *chan* master Buddhabhadra lived at the end of his life. This temple became so well known as the home of meditation teachers that it was styled, in contrast to another local temple famed for its scriptural exegesis, the "grotto of the *chan* masters" (禪師窟; *Song shu*, 97.2392).

Among the foreign meditation teachers who spent time at the Qihuan temple was the Gandhāran *chan* master Dharmamitra 曇摩密多 (d. 442). Having first made a name for himself in Sichuan, he lived briefly in the Qihuan temple before founding, also near the capital, the famous Dinglin 定林 temple.[60] Like Xuangao in the north, Dharmamitra was both a *chan* master and a court monk. He taught meditation to Chinese students—who, it is said, called him "the great *chan* master"—and also enjoyed close connection with the imperial family, especially the empress, for whom he performed rituals and initiations.[61] A number of other, less famous foreign *chan* masters also found a place for themselves in and around the southern capital

---

58. A figure called Tanwupi 曇無毗, assumed to be the Dharmapriya whose name in the inscription is written as Tanmopi 曇摩毗, is mentioned in the biography of Xuangao (*GSZ*, T.2059:50.397a28). A (different?) Tanmopi 曇摩蜱 is mentioned in scriptural catalogs as a translator active in Chang'an in the 380s (Mei 2005; Palumbo 2013, 13).

59. 或傳譯經典，或訓授禪法。(*GSZ*, T.2059:50.368c20)

60. *GSZ*, T.2059:50.342c8–343a29; *CSZJJ*, T.2145:55.105a–b16; *Meisōden shō*, Z.1523:77.355b1–11; Schuster 1984.

61. *GSZ*, T.2059:50.343a2–3.

Figure 1. Binglingsi cave 169. On the left is Dharmapriya, with a partially surviving cartouche reading "Portrait of the great *chan* master Dharmapriya from...country" (□□國大禪師曇摩毗之像). On the right is the barely visible portrait of Daorong 道融, titled "monk" (比丘). Daorong is mentioned in the inscription above the portraits as one of the sponsors of the images carved and painted nearby. *Yongjing Bingling si*, pl. 25.

at this time, such as Saṅghananda 僧伽難陀, who is mentioned briefly in the biography of the Chinese monk Tanyi 曇翼 but is unknown from other sources.[62]

Lineages and Spaces of Meditation

At the same time that foreign monks known as "masters of meditation" were becoming an increasingly visible presence in China, the experience of actually studying *chan* under such a person became an expected part of the training possessed by anyone claiming expertise in this subject. Accordingly, a period of such discipleship becomes a standard element in biographies of eminent *chan* practitioners, both monks and nuns, even in brief ones otherwise short on details. The early fifth-century monk Huitong 慧通, it is said,

> was from the region around Chang'an. As a youth, he stayed for a while at the Taihou temple in Chang'an. He did not eat meat and knew spells. He could recite the *Ekottarikāgama* scripture. He first received instruction in *chan* from *chan* master Huishao of Liangzhou, and he roamed masterfully through many different contemplations.[63]

Huitong's short biography would in most respects be at home among those of the hermit-like fourth-century *chan* practitioners discussed earlier. But Huitong's biography adds to the repertoire of ideals a new element: an accounting, however brief, of Huitong's *lineage*—a claim of his having studied meditation under a qualified teacher, a "*chan* master" who even though himself seemingly unknown from other sources is nonetheless identified by name and location.

Biographies of nuns adhere to this same convention. Huisheng 慧勝 (425–505), famed later in life for her practice of meditation, in her youth "followed the nun [Hui]xu of the Jishan temple in learning the five gates of *chan*."[64] Huixu 慧緒 (d. 499) too has a biography in the *Lives of the Nuns,* and she in turn supposedly studied meditation with the *chan* master Xuanchang 玄暢, himself a student of Xuangao.[65] Huisheng's *chan* pedigree is thus clearly traceable over two generations to a qualified master whose expertise is certified by reference to earlier *chan* masters going back through Xuangao to

---

62. *GSZ*, T.2059:50.356a7–8.

63. 釋慧通關中人。少止長安太后寺，蔬食持呪，誦習一阿含經。初從涼州禪師慧紹諮受禪業，法門觀行多所遊刃。(*GSZ*, T.2059:50.398c7–14). The *Ekottarikāgama* was first translated in Chang'an between 384 and 385 (Palumbo 2013, 9–96). Meanwhile Huitong's teacher Huishao 慧紹 of Liangzhou is recorded elsewhere as having died during the late Jin, hence before the year 420 (*Meisōden shō*, Z.1523:77.348c9). Huitong was thus presumably active during the early fifth century. Some scholars have suggested that this Huishao may be the same person as Xuanshao 玄紹, a disciple of Xuangao (Jan 1990, 18).

64. 隨集善寺緒尼學五門禪。(*BQNZ*, T.2063:50.946c6–8)

65. *BQNZ*, T.2063:50.944a9–11; *GSZ*, T.2059:50.377a3–b21.

Buddhabhadra. It is also of interest that the "*chan* masters" mentioned in the biographies of Huitong and Huixu seem to have been Chinese. It would appear that soon after the title *chanshi* began to be used in the early fifth century, the possibility arose that Chinese-born monks—and eventually, though less commonly, nuns—might themselves acquire this status.[66]

These accounts of "lineage" must be taken with many grains of salt. It would be asking too much of these sources to use them to reconstruct real historical connections between the named individuals. What we can say, however, is that the *idea* of lineage in connection with the practice of *chan* emerged in a loose way during this era, at least in south China where most of the records cited earlier were composed, as part of a broad historical change in which meditation came to be regarded as a domain of Buddhist expertise with which Chinese Buddhist monks and nuns could and did claim association.

Another sign of the growing accessibility of meditation to a wide swath of the Chinese Buddhist world in the fifth century was the advent of new kinds of communal spaces where the practice of meditation could be carried out. Together with "*chan* masters" both foreign and domestic, these spaces began to fill the physical and imaginative landscape of Chinese Buddhism during this era. Biographies, poems, official histories, and other sources begin, around the year 400, to mention Buddhist temples endowed with structures with names such as *chan* cloister (*chanyuan* 禪院), *chan* quarters (*chanfang* 禪房), *chan* ward (*chanfang* 禪坊), *chan* hall (*chantang* 禪堂), *chan* platform (*chanji* 禪基), *chan* workshop (*chansi* 禪肆), and *chan* pavilion (*chan'ge* 禪閣).[67] Before the fifth century, even the idea of accommodations such as these appears not to have existed in the common understanding of how the physical space of a typical Buddhist temple was to be apportioned.[68] None are mentioned in biographies of monks or nuns living before then, and the earliest references to such structures in Chinese translations of Indian Bud-

---

66. The *Biqiuni zhuan* preserves only a single example of a nun called a "*chan* master," Jingxiu 淨秀 (*BQNZ*, T.2063:50.945a20–25). However, this title is used in a dialog, not as an official designation. Jingxiu's "record of conduct" (行狀), written shortly after her death, does not use this title in its otherwise identical account of this incident (*GHMJ*, T.2103:52.270c16). The copious Northern Wei inscriptional record also yields no references to women *chan* masters, despite many such monks (Balkwill 2015, 258). By the Tang dynasty, however, women *chan* masters were common (*Baoshan Lingquan si*, 88–89; Adamek 2009).

67. For the term "*chan* workshop," see *XGSZ*, T.2060:50.554b18 (the biography of the meditation master Sengchou 僧稠). The unusual term "*chan* platform" is mentioned in the story of an early fifth-century nun from the *Ming xiang ji* cited in the *Fa yuan zhu lin* (T.2122:53.407b22). A different version of this story here reads "foundation for a meditation hall" (禪堂基; *Ji shen zhou san bao gan tong lu*, T.2106:52.418b12), but the concept of a "*chan* platform" (an open-air space designated for meditation?) was not unknown in the fifth century, to judge from the "Temple of the *Chan* Platform" associated with the nun Senggai 僧蓋 (*BQNZ*, T.2063:50.943a22).

68. Notably, Huiyuan's 慧遠 (d. 416) "*chan* grove" (*chanlin* 禪林) on Mount Lu seems to have been an *outdoor* garden space (*CSZJJ*, T.2145:55.109c2; *GSZ*, T.2059:50.358b6–7), suggesting the absence, as late as the turn of the fifth century, of the notion of a purpose-built meditation hall.

dhist texts also occur beginning in the early fifth century, in translations of Indian monastic codes.[69]

Possibly the earliest example of a building of this type is mentioned in the *History of the Wei* (*Wei shu* 魏書) of Wei Shou 魏收 (506–572), which states that in 398, shortly after establishing his capital in Datong, Emperor Taizu 太祖 (r. 386–409) built a major Buddhist temple consisting of a lecture hall (*jiangtang* 講堂), a *chan* hall (*chantang*), and monks' quarters (*shamen zuo* 沙門座), among other structures.[70] The present state of knowledge regarding Chinese Buddhist architecture before the Tang dynasty does not allow us to estimate how many Chinese temples had "*chan* halls" or "*chan* cloisters" in the fifth century,[71] but they were common enough to be mentioned in biographies of the eminent *chan* practitioners of this era, and eventually they came to be accepted as part of what a complete Buddhist temple should look like.

Of course, in invoking the idea of mental tranquility, names such as "*chan* pavilion" readily serve as poetic titles. Surely not every such building was used, or was even intended to be used, exclusively or primarily for communal meditation. We have records, for example, of a *chan* quarters being used, during the fifth century, as a translation workshop.[72] And it was in a *chan* pavilion at the Changsha 長沙 temple in Sichuan that the *chan* master Dharmamitra fervently prayed for the miraculous appearance of a relic of the Buddha.[73] But in other cases such words clearly point to communal meditation halls of some kind. In recounting an anecdote about a miraculous occurrence attesting to her prowess in meditation, the biography of the nun Jingxiu 淨秀 (d. 506) unambiguously describes the "*chan* quarters" of her temple as a large, communal meditation hall, or at least as being used as such on that occasion.[74] A sixth-century record of monastic architecture even describes such places as the hall or room where "monks who practice quiescence sit on corded meditation chairs."[75]

The specific use of any particular building is not the issue here. The

---

69. On "meditation halls" (*prahāṇa-śāla* is one attested Indic term) as discussed in *vinaya* texts, see Greene 2013, 272. Pre-fifth-century Chinese texts do use the terms *chanshi* 禪室 (*chan* chamber), *chanku* 禪窟 (*chan* cave), and *chankang* 禪龕 (*chan* niche). These point not to meditation halls in temples but individual cells or caves in the mountains or other remote locations (see, e.g., *GSZ*, T.2059:50.387b16–17; 396b16). On Buddhist temple architecture as depicted in early Chinese texts translated from Indian languages, see Pettit 2013, 60–75.

70. *Wei shu*, 114.3030 (Tsukamoto 1974, 151). Hurvitz (1956, 52) interprets *shamen zuo* as a living space for monks; the word is unattested elsewhere. On the other structures here, see Mcnair 2013, 20–26.

71. On the layout of pre-Tang Buddhist monasteries, see Su B. 1997.

72. *CSZJJ*, T.2145:55.13a18–19.

73. *GSZ*, T.2059:50.342c27; *CSZJJ*, T.2145:55.105a18; the latter calls it a "*chan* lodge" (*changuan* 禪舘), a term unattested elsewhere. Praying for a relic could also have been part of what *chan* practice was thought to entail.

74. *BQNZ*, T.2063:50.945a22–25; cf. *GHMJ*, T.2103:52.270c12–17, which says "Buddha hall" (*fodian* 佛殿).

75. 靜行之僧繩坐其內。(*Luoyang qielan ji*, T.2092:51.1004a27). A corded meditation chair is depicted in the cover image.

point is simply that because it was now assumed that many famous Chinese monasteries had spaces for the practice of *chan*, we know that meditation was no longer seen as something for which instruction would be nearly impossible to obtain, as Sengrui had described it in the spring of 402; it was now an activity for which qualified teaching personnel and facilities were relatively widely available. It was not impossible, then, to imagine a *chan* master with five hundred disciples, as the monk Huiquan 慧全, living in the Song dynasty, is portrayed in an anecdote in the *Records of Signs from the Unseen Realm* (*Ming xiang ji* 冥祥記), a late fifth-century collection of Buddhist miracle stories (Campany 2012, 225–226). The study of *chan* is here something *accessible*, to even comparatively ordinary monks and nuns, in a way that stands in clear contrast to its representations, in earlier times, as something carried out exclusively by solitary hermits or the chosen few on remote, mist-enshrouded peaks.

By the middle of the fifth century, it was not even out of the question to think that a layman might learn meditation under a *chan* master. The *Records of Signs from the Unseen Realm* also tells the story of Cheng Dedu 程德度, a minor military official of the early Song dynasty who meets the *chan* master Daogong 道恭 and undertakes to study *chan* with him, reaching a deep understanding that is later confirmed by auspicious fragrances emanating from his household ritual hall.[76] The *Records in Proclamation of Manifestations* (*Xuan yan ji* 宣驗記), a slightly earlier collection of miracle stories, also contains a story of a layman who practices *chan* and reaches an advanced attainment—in this case, an auspicious vision.[77] Northern epigraphical sources too, in a slightly later era, mention Buddhist laymen remembered for their practice of *chan*,[78] and we even have one record of a set of written meditation instructions, no longer extant, that circulated in south China in the second half of the fifth century and was specifically intended for use by laypeople.[79] Nor was it only *men* who were deemed capable of *chan* practice and attainment as householders. According to the biography of the nun Huixu, a thrice removed descendant of the *chan* master Buddhabhadra, her patron, the imperial prince Xiao Ni 蕭嶷 (444–492), *together with his wife*

---

76. *Fa yuan zhu lin*, T.2122:53.492b9–17; Campany 2012, 218–219. Daogong had a biography in the *Ming seng zhuan*, but it does not survive (*Meisōden shō*, Z.1523:77.348c13).

77. Cited at *Bian zheng lun*, T.2110:52.539c13–15. I discuss this story in Chap. 2. On the *Xuan yan ji*, compiled by Liu Yiqing 劉義慶 (403–444), see Gjertson 1981, 292–293; and Campany 1996, 77.

78. The funerary epitaph of the Buddhist layman Daoming 道明 (d. 552) says he not only made pious donations to the Buddhist church but also "cultivated *chan* and practiced trance, producing a mind of concentration" (修禪習定，專心內起; *Han wei nan bei chao mu zhi hui bian*, 388). Buddhist laymen said to have practiced *chan* were, to be sure, the exception not the rule.

79. This text, the "Procedures for practicing *chan*: Methods for cultivating trance as a layperson" (*Xiu chan ding yi zai jia xi ding fa* 修禪定義在家習定法) is listed at *CSZJJ*, T.2145:55.84b5 (cf. *Da tang nei dian lu*, T.2149:55.328c12), reproducing the table of contents of the *Fa lun* 法論, compiled by Lu Zheng 陸澄 (425–494; *Nan qi shu*, 9.681–685) between 465 and 469; on this dating, see Pelliot 1920, 266n1.

"received [from Huixu] the methods of *chan*" (從受禪法).[80] While in reality these two historical personages may not have learned meditation from the nun Huixu, this story still suggests that by the early sixth century, when Huixu's biography was composed, it was not outlandish to think that they might have done so. Even imperial princes and their wives could now imagine themselves studying meditation with a famous nun remembered as a lineal descendant of one of the original Indian *chan* masters who had arrived in south China in the early fifth century.

The *Chan* Scriptures

Although some foreign *chan* masters achieved renown in fifth-century China without being prolific translators, and some native Chinese *chan* masters acquired prestige without excelling in doctrinal or scriptural exegesis, the practice and mastery of meditation were nonetheless inextricably associated with texts. Already in the writings of Sengrui and Dao'an discussed earlier, we saw that Chinese Buddhists, when surveying their translations of Indian scriptures, identified a certain subset as particularly connected to the domain of *chan*. So too, when Sengrui reported that he had received the "methods for *chan*" from Kumārajīva, it seems clear that he meant, at least in part, the newly translated text for which he was writing a preface. This would be only the first of many new texts purporting to contain essential information about *chan* that appeared in China during the fifth century, many of them translated from Indian languages, but others seemingly composed in China either partially or entirely.

These texts were collectively called the "*chan* scriptures" (*chan jing* 禪經), a term that has been widely adopted by modern scholars writing in Japanese and Chinese and frequently translated into English as "meditation manual." The word "*chan* scripture," however, is not a purely generic description but was an indigenous Chinese Buddhist classification, a bibliographic counterpart to the title *chanshi* or "*chan* master," which, as we have seen, was during this same era becoming an accepted way to categorize the particular form of expertise attributed to certain living Buddhist teachers.

In the sense of a subset of the Buddhist scriptural corpus, the term "*chan* scriptures" is first attested in the writings of Dao'an in the mid-fourth century. In his preface to the *Scripture on the Twelve Gates* (*Shi er men jing* 十二門經), whose translation was attributed to An Shigao, Dao'an calls this text "the most detailed of all the *chan* scriptures."[81] It is unclear what other texts Dao'an counted among these "*chan* scriptures," and he does not use this word again

---

80. *BQNZ*, T.2063:50.944a12–13.

81. 比諸禪經最為精悉。(*CSZJJ*, T.2145:55.46b7–8). The *Gao seng zhuan* cites a source that claims that An Shigao himself, in the late *third* [sic] century, wrote a letter predicting who in the future would "transmit [my] *chan* scriptures" (傳禪經者; *GSZ*, T.2059:50.324a17). Huijiao argues against the authenticity of this letter, and in any case the source Huijiao cites may not itself be any earlier than Dao'an's preface.

in his surviving writings. Significantly, the term *chan* scripture does *not* appear to correspond to any known Indian bibliographic category.[82] Although it appears several times in Kumārajīva's massive *Great Treatise on the Perfection of Wisdom* (*Da zhi du lun*), it seems to be a proper noun in most of these instances.[83] Chinese authors, in contrast, tended to follow Dao'an in thinking of the *chan* scriptures as a genre. In his preface to the meditation text translated by Buddhabhadra that survives under the title *Chan Scripture of Dharmatrāta* (*Damoduoluo chan jing* 達摩多羅禪經), Huiyuan, with whom Buddhabhadra had been staying while making the translation, offers the explanation that the *chan* scriptures were a body of texts compiled by a select group of Indian masters several generations after the Buddha died. The first generations of these masters "possessed merit that transcended words and was beyond what was described in the scriptures," and as Buddhism began to decline in the era following the Buddha's death, those who had inherited the transmission of these teachings "began to fear that the great Dharma might decay. Sorrowing profoundly over this, they each transmitted and promoted '*chan* scriptures' to ensure the flourishing of the supreme endeavor [of Buddhism]."[84]

Huiyuan's preface contains one of the earliest versions of the list of Indian patriarchs that would eventually become the mind-to-mind transmission lineage of the Chan School in the late seventh and early eighth centuries. For this reason, this document has been intensively studied by scholars tracing the formation of the ideology of the Chan lineage.[85] However, while the later Chan lineage would present itself as a special transmission lying *outside* written texts, Huiyuan's preface itself champions a very different understanding: that the special transmission in question, though embodied in the persons of *chan* masters such as Buddhabhadra, is also indissolubly linked

---

82. Deleanu 2006, 1:157. Interestingly, the term *chanjing* appears in the *Shi er men jing* itself (Ochiai 2004, 198, line 411). Here, however, *jing* 經 probably translates not *sūtra* but *dharma*, as it often did in the Han dynasty (Vetter and Zacchetti 2004). But Dao'an may have used the word in his preface having read it in the text and interpreted it as a class of canonical literature. Some (but not the earliest) catalogs actually title the text *Shi er men chan jing* (*Zhong jing mu lu*, T.2146:55.137c25), a title used at the end (but not the beginning) of the surviving manuscript. But here the operative word is surely *shi er men chan*, the "twelve gates of *chan*," a concept discussed within the text. In the *Yogalehrbuch*, we find the term *yoga-śāstra* (Schlingloff 1964, 86), a plausible Indic equivalent for *chanjing* but not a term regularly used in Buddhist writings (the same holds true of the similar term *yoga-sūtra*).

83. *DZDL*, T.1509:25.185c1–27; 228a2–3; 239b8; 264c25–265a5; 705b7. Kumārajīva's principal meditation text, for which Sengrui wrote his preface, was originally titled *Chan jing* 禪經 (*CSZJJ*, T.2145:55.11a14–15), and the intention may have been to refer to this text. However, the passages the *Da zhi du lun* cites under this title are not found in the extant *Zuo chan sanmei jing* (nor in T.616, another *chan*-related text that Kumārajīva translated).

84. 功在言外經所不辨 . . . 咸懼大法將頹。理深其慨，遂各述讚禪經以隆盛業。(*CSZJJ*, T.2145:55.65c11–19). "Transmit" (*shu* 述) invokes the precedent of Confucius' having transmitted rather than "created" (作) the Chinese classics.

85. Yanagida 1967, 38–39; McRae 1986, 80–92; and Adamek 2007, 33–40. See also Young 2015, 57–59.

to a special set of texts—the *chan* scriptures compiled for the benefit of those living in the later ages of the declining Dharma. Indeed, the surviving exemplars of the texts whose Indian origin is relatively certain do seem stylistically similar to Indian Buddhist commentarial literature, conforming to the understanding that the *chan* scriptures were not discourses of the Buddha but compilations put together by later masters.[86]

The Three Trainings as a Bibliographic Scheme

The notion of a corpus of authoritative Indian Buddhist texts devoted specifically to meditation captured the imagination of Chinese Buddhists throughout the fifth and sixth centuries. Most often called the "*chan* scriptures," this collection occasionally went by other names such as the "*chan* canon" (*chandian* 禪典).[87] This conception of the *chan* scriptures as a coherent subset of Buddhist canonical literature was facilitated by a tendency, observable beginning in the fifth century, to conflate the traditional "three baskets" (*tripiṭaka*) of the Buddhist canon with the so-called three trainings of discipline (*śīla*), meditation (*samādhi* or *dhyāna*), and wisdom (*prajñā*), a common classification of the totality of Buddhist practice. Chinese catalogs of Buddhist literature, when they attempted to organize the entire canon, generally followed the traditional scheme of *sūtra* (discourses of the Buddha), *vinaya* (monastic rules), and *abhidharma* (canonical doctrinal exegesis)—the three baskets—to which they added various refinements, separating the contents of each basket into texts of "Mahāyāna" and "Hīnayāna" orientation and the like.[88] But in the fifth and sixth centuries, some catalogs also followed a completely different system. The *Catalog in Seven Sections* (*Qi lu* 七錄), compiled for the emperor by Ruan Xiaoxu 阮孝緒 (479–536) in 523, grouped Buddhist texts under five divisions: precepts and regulations (戒律), *chan* meditation (禪定), wisdom (智慧), works of dubious authenticity (疑似), and essays and records [by Chinese authors] (論記).[89] Ruan's scheme, which augmented the tripartite classification of precepts, meditation, and wisdom with two additional categories, followed the precedent of recent imperially sponsored catalogs in which the *chan* scriptures had been highlighted as a major division of

---

86. The only two examples written as actual sutras—the *Chan Essentials* (T.613) and *Methods for Curing* (T.620), which I discuss in in Chap. 2—are precisely the ones that seem to have been composed in China. Even these texts were often classified in catalogs as "compilations of [past] saints and sages" (賢聖撰), meaning compilations made after the Buddha's death (*Zhong jing mu lu*, T.2146:55.144b25). Beginning with the *Kaiyuan shi jiao lu* 開元釋教錄 in 730, they were reclassified as sutras.

87. *CSZJJ*, T.2145:55.66b4; *Zhao lun*, T.1858:45.160c25 (here it may be a proper name for the *Zuo chan sanmei jing*; see Felbur 2017, 135n181). This term was rare after the fifth century.

88. For an overview of the early Chinese catalogs of Buddhist texts and their organizational schemes, see Hayashiya 1941, 43–110; Drège 1991, 177–186; and Storch 2014, 192–208. Concerning the formation in China of the notion of the "canon" as a complete collection of all the Buddhist scriptures, see Zacchetti 2016.

89. *GHMJ*, T.2103:52.111a14–19. On the Buddhist section of the *Qi lu*, see Li and He 2003, 62–63.

Buddhist canonical literature. These instances included the 518 catalog of Baochang 寶唱,[90] whose first three divisions were sutras (*jing* 經),[91] *chan* scriptures, and precepts, and a fifth-century collection of Chinese Buddhist writings compiled for the Song emperor Ming 明 (r. 465–472) by Lu Cheng 陸澄 (420–494), which included, among other categories, a "basket of discipline" (律藏), a "basket of meditation" (定藏), and a "basket of wisdom" (慧藏).[92]

Using the three trainings as a bibliographic scheme may have been inspired by theories found in Indian texts translated into Chinese during the late fourth and early fifth centuries. The earliest of the three Chinese translations of the massive compendium of commentary and lore known as the *Vibhāṣā*, carried out in the year 383, interprets the three baskets in connection with the three trainings: the *vinaya* discusses precepts, the sutras meditation, and the Abhidharma wisdom.[93] This same typology, also found in an Indian *vinaya* commentary translated into Chinese in the early fifth century, was evidently an accepted interpretive model in Indian Buddhist scholastic literature, and it was subsequently taken up in commentaries and treatises by Chinese Buddhist writers.[94] The pairing here of *vinaya* with discipline makes obvious sense, and a link between the Abhidharma—devoted to systematic analysis of Buddhist doctrine—and wisdom is also not hard to fathom. But given the diversity of topics they cover, to posit a generic connection between the sutras and meditation seems much less straightforward.

Whether out of dissatisfaction with this Indian model, or for some other reason, Chinese authors in the early fifth century began to connect wisdom not to the Abhidharma but to sutras (*jing* 經) or sutras and treatises (*jing lun* 經論), freeing meditation to be associated with what was imagined to be its own collection of texts.[95] Huiyuan, in his preface to Buddhabhadra's meditation manual, makes a first outline of this move:

90. The table of contents is preserved at *Li dai san bao ji*, T.2034:49.126b5–c9 (Hayashiya 1941, 68–72; Storch 2014, 53–55). Its authenticity has been called into question by Tan (1991, 185).

91. Though Baochang's catalog does not explicitly equate sutras with "wisdom," in Ruan Xiaoxu's catalog this must have been the understanding, as the wisdom category had 2,077 texts, far more than the others (*GHMJ*, T.2103:52.111a16). The bulk of the available Buddhist texts, which were sutras, must have been placed here.

92. *CSZJJ*, T.2145:55.84a2–b23.

93. *Piposha lun*, T.1547:28.416b24–c9. The word "higher consciousness" (增上意) here translates *adhicitta-śikṣāpada*, which means meditation (Ōchō 1958–1979, 1:151). Several different versions of "the" *Vibhāṣā* were translated into Chinese (Willemen, Dessein, and Cox 1998, 229–239).

94. *Sapoduo pini piposha* (*Sarvāstivāda-vinaya-vibhāṣā*), T.1440:23.514b2–4. On this text see Hirakawa 1960, 259–260; Funayama (1998, 280–282) argues it is a commentary delivered by an Indian *vinaya* master living in China. For examples of this typology from later Chinese writings, see Gimello 1976, 376. For examples from Pāli commentaries, see Heim 2018, 50n52.

95. Another possible Indian inspiration for these ideas might have been the scheme seen in the *Sapoduo pini piposha* (T.1440:23.503c27–504a1), in which the four Āgamas were

> I have frequently lamented that, ever since the advent of Buddhism in China, [texts on the] "*chan* numbers"[96] have been especially rare. With the three trainings still incomplete, the noble way has been in danger of decline. But now that Kumārajīva has transmitted the works of Aśvaghoṣa, this training has finally been established [here in China].[97]

By citing Kumārajīva's recently translated meditation text as having laid the foundation for "training" (*ye* 業) in *chan,* Huiyuan places Kumārajīva's contribution firmly within the "three trainings" of precepts, meditation, and wisdom. Yet what Huiyuan considers necessary for the completion of the three trainings are specific kinds of *texts,* and his biography makes clear what these were thought to be:

> When the scriptures first came to south China, many were missing. Little was heard of methods for *chan,* and the basket of the discipline was fragmentary. Grieving that the Way was incomplete, Huiyuan sent his disciples Fajing, Faling, and others to seek scriptures in distant lands. They traversed mountains and deserts, returning only after long years. All obtained Indian texts, which were eventually translated.[98]

In this passage "scriptures," "methods for *chan,*" and "basket of the discipline" seem to refer to three categories of texts, an interpretation confirmed in the ensuing lines which note that after Buddhabhdra had translated his *chan* text: "methods for *chan,* scriptures, and precepts were thereby all translated at Mount Lu, totaling nearly a hundred fascicles."[99] While there is no indication that this collection of translations was thought to be a complete Buddhist canon, it is nonetheless implied that meditation texts, "scriptures," and precepts (i.e., *vinaya* texts) together comprise the three essential divisions of canonical Buddhist literature.

The Three Trainings as a Model of Buddhist Excellence

Chinese authors of the fifth century thus imagined the Buddhist textual corpus as divisible into categories corresponding to the three domains of mastery expected of accomplished Buddhist practitioners. Yet because

---

divided according to content and purpose, with the *Saṃyuktāgama* being for those who study meditation.

96. The term "*chan* numbers" (*chanshu* 禪數) is used by Dao'an, among other places, in reference to the translations of An Shigao (*CSZJJ,* T.2145:55.46a12).

97. 每慨大教東流，禪數尤寡，三業無統，斯道殆廢。頃鳩摩耆婆宣馬鳴所述，乃有此業。(*CSZJJ,* T.2145:55.65c28–66a1)

98. 初經流江東，多有未備。禪法無聞，律藏殘闕。遠慨其道缺，乃令弟子法淨、法領等，遠尋眾經。踰越沙雪，曠歲方反，皆獲梵本，得以傳譯。(*GSZ,* T.2059:50.359b15–18; *CSZJJ,* T.2145:55.110a14–17 is nearly identical). I have benefited here from Zürcher's translation of this passage (1972, 246).

99. 所以禪法、經、戒，皆出廬山，幾且百卷。(*CSZJJ,* T.2145:55.110a20–21)

Chinese expressions such as "methods for *chan*" point equally to the practice of meditation and to authoritative texts about it, when individuals are described as having attained proficiency in these areas it is often difficult to distinguish mastery of texts from mastery of their contents. The biography of the monk Xuanchang 玄暢 (416–484), for example, describes him as "deeply versed in the essentials of *chan*."[100] But reading this we are left to wonder if this means that he himself had advanced meditative attainment, or if he was merely well versed in the content of meditation *texts,* some of which were titled "essentials of *chan*."[101] What this conflation shows us is that the notion that precepts, meditation, and wisdom comprised the totality of Buddhist study was much more than a purely abstract bibliographic classification. It was a typology actively used to imagine and commemorate the forms of mastery attained by members of the Buddhist community.

Countless hagiographies describe the achievements of fifth-century and early sixth-century nuns and monks in these terms. The monk Fa'an 法安, for example, "properly maintained the precepts, could expound on the scriptures, and furthermore trained in *chan*."[102] Conversely, when the nun Huisu 慧宿 was disparaged by her peers, it was on account of "never having set her mind on the scriptures or monastic rules of Buddhism, and not having trained in the practice of meditation."[103] In some cases, the attainments associated with "wisdom" were limited to the memorization and chanting of scriptures. The nun Jingcheng 靜稱 "was diligent and austere with regard to training in the precepts, could chant four hundred fifty thousand words of scripture, and in the wooded hills by her temple where it was free of distraction let her mind roam in the silence of *chan*."[104] So too the Gandhāran *chan* master Dharmamitra was known in his youth for "reciting the basket of scriptures, firmly upholding the regulations, and being especially fond of *chan*."[105] Guṇavarman (求那跋摩), yet another foreign master active in south China during the early Song dynasty, is described in almost identical terms: "He could recite tens of millions of words of scripture; he had deeply mastered the corpus of the monastic regulations; and he was marvelously proficient in the essentials of *chan*."[106] In other cases, the attainment of "wisdom" is more clearly the *understanding* of Buddhist doctrine. The nun Yeshou 業首 "was upright and austere in her deportment, so purely did she practice the precepts; she had a deep understanding of the Mahāyāna and proved adept in wielding its wondrous doctrine; and being especially fond of *chan* and chanting she carried them out continuously without ever slacking."[107] (Here, *chan*

---

100. 深入禪要。(*GSZ*, T.2059:50.377a15–16)

101. See, e.g., *GSZ*, T.2059:337a13–14; *CSZJJ*, T.2145:55.65a29–b2.

102. 善持戒行，講說眾經，兼習禪業。(*GSZ*, T.2059:50.362b29)

103. 佛法經律曾未厝心。欲學禪定又無師範。(*BQNZ*, T.2063:50.940a25–26)

104. 戒業精苦。誦經四十五萬言。寺傍山林無諸囂雜。遊心禪默。(*BQNZ*, T.2063:50.940a5–7)

105. 諷誦經藏，堅持律部，偏好禪那。(*Meisōden shō*, Z.1523:77.355b2)

106. 誦經百餘萬言，深達律品，妙入禪要。(*GSZ*, T.2059:50.340a27–29)

107. 風儀峻整戒行清白。深解大乘善搆妙理。彌好禪誦造次無怠。(*BQNZ*, T.2063:50.940b6–7). I have adapted this translation from Tsai 1994, 57–58.

is joined with chanting, as if the third area of expertise were ritual practice broadly considered.) In many cases, mastery of the precepts is expressed as achievement in asceticism. The nun Faquan 法全 (412–494) "could expound at length on the abstruse texts of the Mahāyāna, was a guide on the secret pathways of *samādhi*, and maintaining a vegetarian diet limited her clothing to what was just enough to cover her body."[108] For others, monastic discipline is mainly a matter of familiarity with *vinaya* texts, as it was for the monk Daoshao 道韶 (fl. fifth century), who "read and recited Mahāyāna [scriptures], carefully examined [the texts] of the precepts and regulations, and comprehensively studied all forms of *chan*."[109]

Let us note, finally, that while the previous examples are drawn from literary compilations made in south China, which are our most comprehensive sources, similar tropes appear in northern sources, which are primarily epigraphical during this era. The funerary epitaph of the nun Sengzhi 僧芝 (d. 516), for example, states that "when she left home at seventeen, she practiced the precepts spotlessly, and by the age of twenty she possessed a virtue most profound; in her practice of *chan* she attained the six powers, and in her calm recitation of scriptures she was able, after but one hearing, to recite more than twenty scrolls of the *Nirvana, Lotus,* and *Śrīmālādevī Sutras*."[110]

Dharma Masters, *Vinaya* Masters, and *Chan* Masters

The notion that mastery of scripture, the monastic rules, and *chan* are the three principal areas of clerical achievement found concrete expression in the three titles that were most widely applied to eminent Buddhist monks and nuns in medieval China: Dharma master (*fashi* 法師), *vinaya* master (*lüshi* 律師), and *chan* master (*chanshi* 禪師). We do not know precisely how these titles were chosen or assigned, either informally by local communities or by clerical or secular authorities. However it occurred, the mere existence of this tripartite classification, firmly in place by the middle of the fifth century,[111] is significant as a distinctly Chinese division of the domains of Buddhist mastery that provided the categories through which disciples and descendants honored and remembered their teachers, both living and dead.

This system of titles was indebted to Indian Buddhist classifications of monastic specialization, but it was not a mere copy of them. We can even watch, in some cases, as Indian Buddhists classified under slightly different

---

108. 大乘奧典皆能宣講。三昧祕門並為師匠。食但蔬菜衣止蔽形。(*BQNZ*, T.2063:50.943b11–13)
109. 讀誦大乘，披覽戒律，備學諸禪。(*Meisōden shō*, Z.1523:77.355b23–24)
110. 十七出家戒行清純，暨於廿，德義淵富。安禪屆於六通，靜讀幾於一聞誦湟槃、法華、勝鬘廿餘卷。(Zhao and Zhao 2006, no. 20, cited in Balkwill 2015, 333).
111. The first "*vinaya* master" in China was Vimalakṣa (卑摩羅叉), who helped with the translation of the *Sarvāstivāda Vinaya* in the early 400s (*GSZ*, T.2059:50.333c14; Funayama 2004, 100–102). Like *chanshi*, the title of *vinaya* master was used to name living Buddhist teachers in China *before* it is attested in Chinese translations of Buddhist texts (the first example seems to be *Da bannihuan jing*, T.376:12.881c23, translated by Faxian in 418).

rubrics were re-imagined in China under this more appealing framework. Sengzhao's letter to Liu Yimin, written before 410, describes the Indian Buddhist masters then active in Chang'an as follows:

> [In addition to the Dharma master Kumārajīva] one Mahāyāna *chan* master, one Dharma master versed in the three baskets, and two Dharma masters of the Vaibhāṣika [school] have been invited. Kumārajīva has been translating the new scriptures at the Dashi temple. . . . In the Waguan temple the *chan* master [Buddhabhadra] gives instruction in the path of *chan* . . . while in the Zhong temple the Dharma master versed in the three baskets has been translating the basket of the *vinaya*. . . . [Finally,] at the Shiyang temple the Vaibhāṣika Dharma masters are translating [an Abhidharma text, the] *Śāriputrābhidharma*.[112]

Sengzhao contrasts the Dharma masters, who recite, translate, or expound on Buddhist texts, with the one *chan* master, who teaches meditation practice. Originating in Indian Buddhist literature,[113] this twofold division between meditators and textualists undergoes subdivision when Sengzhao separates the latter according to their expertise in the three baskets of the canon: sutras, *vinaya,* and *abhidharma.* The resulting fourfold classification corresponds to one also found in contemporaneous Chinese translations of Indian texts to which Sengzhao would have had access.[114] Thus, Sengzhao here depicts the flourishing of Buddhism in Chang'an by noting the presence of a complete set of foreign masters, corresponding to an accepted Indian classification of the four key areas in which a Buddhist cleric could obtain renown.

Writing at least a decade later, after many of the protagonists had either died or moved on, Sengzhao's colleague Sengrui, however, remembered the same persons and events in slightly different terms:

> [At that time] Buddhist masters and [new] scriptures were all assembled. Dharma master Kumārajīva came from Kucha, masters of the canon versed in the *vinaya* came from Gandhāra, and the *chan* master [Buddhabhadra] and his

---

112. 請大乘禪師一人、三藏法師一人、毘婆沙法師二人。什法師於大石寺出新至諸經 . . . 禪師於瓦官寺教習禪道 . . . 三藏法師於中寺出律藏 . . . 毘婆沙法師於石羊寺出舍利弗阿毘曇。(*Zhao lun,* T.1858:45.155c12–18; Tsukamoto 1955, 43–44). On the identification of the figures listed, see Felbur 2017, 92, from whom I have benefited.

113. The "two vocations" of meditation and recitation are spoken of frequently in the *Mūlasarvāstivāda-vinaya (Gen ben shuo yi qie you bu pi'naiye za shi,* T.1451:24.267c4–5). Pāli sources make a similar division (Gombrich 1988, 152–153). These divisions do not imply mutually exclusive paths (Cousins 2009, 41–44).

114. The *Sarvāstivāda Vinaya,* whose ongoing translation Sengzhao mentions in his letter, says that a dying monk should be lauded based on his principal vocation: either meditation or study of the sutras, *vinaya,* or *abhidharma (Shi song lü,* T.1435:23.205c20–27). The *Sapoduo pini piposha* similarly says that it is a transgression to claim, if it is not true, that one is (1) a reciter of the four Āgamas, (2) an *abhidharma* master, (3) a *vinaya* master, or (4) a forest-dwelling meditator (T.1440:23.519a14–18).

disciples also gathered. For over a dozen years the Chang'an area was a flurry of activity. Truly it was the second flourishing of the great teaching![115]

Here Sengrui reduces Sengzhao's fourfold classification to a simpler scheme of Dharma master, *vinaya* masters, and *chan* master—experts in wisdom, discipline, and meditation, respectively. This tripartite framework soon became the most common Chinese way of conceptualizing the ideal contours of Buddhist practice, and texts of all genres consistently used it to embrace and define the possible forms of excellence for monks and nuns.[116] Even in much later periods, the influence of this model can be detected in new and different guises. In the mid-ninth century, for example, the emperor replaced the older government exam for aspiring Buddhist clerics with a new one in which candidates would be tested in their mastery of one of the three categories of precepts, meditation, or wisdom.[117] And we may infer that it was this idea that Buddhist masters are experts in doctrine, precepts, or *chan* that informed the titles claimed by the three lineages that dominated the abbacies of public monasteries during the Northern and Southern Song dynasties (960–1279): the "teachings" (*jiao* 教) lineages of Tiantai and Huayan, the *vinaya* tradition of the Nanshan 南山 lineage, and of course the Bodhidharma lineage of Chan, which had by then long since rhetorically separated itself from the tradition of *chan* masters that began in the fifth century while remaining associated with it in name.[118]

In sum, during the fifth century Chinese Buddhists came to think of the "*chan* scriptures" as a discrete body of textual knowledge. The formation of this category, I have argued, is more than just an index of the increasing volume of canonical Buddhist scriptures to which Chinese Buddhists of this era had

---

115. 持法之宗亦並與經俱集。究摩羅法師至自龜茲，持律三藏集自罽賓，禪師徒眾尋亦並集。關中洋洋十數年中，當是大法後興之盛也。(*CSZJJ*, T.2145:55.41b16–19). For a complete English translation of this essay, see Felbur 2018, 287–338, who dates it to sometime between 417 and 418. Others, following a different reconstruction of Sengrui's life, place the essay in the 430s (Wright 1957, 286–288).

116. To take just four examples, drawn from diverse genres between the fifth and seventh centuries, consider: (1) a lay-oriented apocryphal scripture from the late fifth century (*Xiang fa jue yi jing*, T.2870:85.1337a27–28), (2) the *Dui gen qi xing fa* 對根起行法, a sixth-century doctrinal treatise associated with the Three Levels (*San jie jiao* 三階教) movement (Nishimoto 1998, 480–481), (3) a seventh-century meditation manual authored in China by an Indian master (*Xiu chan yao jue*, Z.1222:63.17b5–7), and (4) a seventh-century record of a vision of the ideal Buddhist temple filled with saints (*Lü xiang gan tong zhuan*, T.1898:45.878a8–12; see also *Fa yuan zhu lin*, T.2122:53.598a24–29). Funerary Buddhist epigraphy of the sixth, seventh, and eighth centuries also primarily uses these three titles to describe deceased monks (Yagi 1986). Even during the second half of the Tang dynasty, literati writings tend to classify individual monks and nuns as Dharma master, *vinaya* master, or *chan* master rather than as members of any of the so-called schools (宗) of Chinese Buddhism (Ge 2001, 2:43).

117. *Fo zu tong ji*, T.2035:49.388b13–15.

118. On the classification of public monasteries in this era, see Foulk 1993, 166; and Schlütter 2005, 152–157.

access. It reflects the development of a distinctly Chinese way of conceptualizing the possible domains of Buddhist mastery, one that went hand in hand
with the emergence of new categories of persons, such as the "*chan* master."
Rather than drawing a line between textual study on the one hand and meditation practice on the other, the model was that a given area of expertise
should have its own set of canonical writings. The acceptance of meditation
as a legitimate domain in which clerics and even some exceptional laypeople
could gain renown, as occurred during this era, meant that it required a corresponding collection of authoritative texts: the *chan* scriptures. Yet while
individual Indian texts devoted to meditation did exist, there was not necessarily a pre-existing Indian Buddhist bibliographic category making for a
chan counterpart to the sutras and the *vinaya*. It may be for this reason that
many of the so-called *chan* scriptures translated into Chinese from Indian
languages were in fact compilations based on multiple sources. Sengrui's
preface describes Kumārajīva's major meditation treatise, for example, not
as the translation of a single text but as composed out of "excerpts from the
chan manuals of various [Indian Buddhist] masters." Though Sengrui here
uses the word "*chan* manual" (*chanyao*) as if it pointed to a specific genre of
texts, in the one case where we can verify Kumārajīva's sources, they prove to
have come from a famous poem, not a stand-alone meditation treatise.[119]
There thus indeed seems to have been a gap between the Chinese desire for
a canonical collection of *chan* texts and the way that the Indian Buddhist tradition had typically organized information about this subject. This gap contributed to an ongoing feeling among Chinese Buddhists that a complete
collection of the *chan* scriptures was still lacking. Such a disparity would certainly have been evident in the early sixth century, when Baochang's catalog
of Buddhist texts recorded only thirty-eight fascicles of *chan* scriptures while
the other divisions of the canon each had several hundred. It could well be
that this is why, around this same time, the Liang emperor Wu (r. 502–550)
sent a mission of monks abroad specifically charged with searching for more
of these mysterious and ever insufficient "*chan* scriptures."[120]

The Formation of a Social Field of Meditation in the Fifth Century

To the extent that hagiography reflects ideals and expectations about what
is possible, there is a real difference between the fourth and fifth centuries
regarding the significance of Buddhist meditation practice and the role of
meditation masters in China. Prior to the early fifth century, *chan* was associated almost exclusively with mysterious Chinese recluses with hazy life

---

119. These are the passages that Sengrui attributes to the Indian author Aśvaghoṣa,
which correspond to sections of his poem the *Saundarananda*. These are the only passages
from any fifth-century Chinese *chan* text for which exact Indic parallels have been found. See
Matsunami 1967, 128–144; Shi H. 2001; and Kanno R. 2002.
    120. *HMJ*, T.2145:55.93b10.

stories. These monks—and in these stories it is only monks, never nuns or laypersons—were not the kind who interacted with patrons or political figures. It was assumed, in other words, that ordinary people, even emperors and others with means, could not reasonably be expected to encounter such figures in the course of their daily lives.

But beginning in the biographies of the Buddhist monks and nuns who died (and hence whose life stories were likely first recorded) after the turn of the fifth century, a dramatic change occurs. Though reclusive *chan* practitioners living in caves and declining to interact with the world did not lose their place in social memory or imagination, Buddhist meditation practice and its mastery now figured in the biographies of men and women who were integrated into the larger Buddhist community, some of them of sufficient status to interact with the members of the imperial courts. Stories began to appear at this time about Chinese monks and nuns, and even prominent laypeople, actually learning *chan* from foreign *chan* masters and eventually their Chinese counterparts, and in some cases something akin to lineages of successive master-disciple relationships were remembered, emphasized, and even promoted. That the early fifth century was an epochal moment in the history of the "lineages" related to meditation has long been noted by modern scholars (Matsumoto 1911, 258–306). Most, however, have argued that this is significant as the first "full-fledged" (*honkakuteki;* Mizuno 1957, 30) or "systematic transmission" (Xu W. 2004, 31) of Indian meditation lineages to China. This framing tends to posit the later development of the Chan School as the teleological culmination of this process, and also treats hagiography as a more reliable source of social history than it is.

We can, however, safely take the newly evident thematization of meditation lineages in hagiography, together with the many other changing assumptions about who practiced *chan* and how they did so, as evidence of a historical shift between a Chinese Buddhism in which the practice of meditation had essentially no official place, in personal or institutional memory, and one in which it had become a recognized subdiscipline of Buddhism with certified teachers, dedicated spaces, and authoritative practices. That the study of meditation under a qualified master became an increasingly common trope in Buddhist hagiography and miracle tales can only have resulted when such training, whatever it consisted of on the ground, had become both possible and expected in a way that it had not been before. And more, that it was felt worthwhile to invest claims to mastery of meditation with an ideology of lineage—even if only loosely, in relation to where, when, and from whom a given *chan* master had learned to practice meditation— means that the stakes in making such claims had changed. Claims to mastery of meditation *mattered* in the fifth century in a new way; indeed, there is little evidence that anyone made such claims at all in earlier times. And that not just mysterious hermits but also powerful monks who frequented the court could be "*chan* masters" shows that advanced meditative attainment was no longer merely a theoretical part of Chinese Buddhism, something imagined only in reference to distant figures from legend or scripture. In the fifth century, the practice and mastery of meditation became something in terms of which the Chinese Buddhist community actively defined the activities and status of some of its prominent members living and deceased.

That in the early fifth century training in *chan* first became a real possibility for Chinese Buddhists and mastery of *chan* became a realizable goal has important consequences for how we understand the nature and significance of the surviving texts from this period that discuss this topic. Unlike the examples from earlier times, the *chan* scriptures of the fifth century were translated, composed, and circulated at a time when some Chinese Buddhists were either attempting to put such ideas into practice or were believed to have done so. Though the exact relationship between the surviving texts and specific individuals is usually unclear, most fifth-century *chan* texts were at least associated with monks known as *chan* masters, and this correlation stands in marked contrast with the lack of connection in earlier times between the activity of translating or promoting *chan* texts and personal mastery of meditation practice. Thus while a reader of the fourth century may have encountered texts describing *chan* and marveled at the attainments of obscure hermits or Buddhist saints in the magical land of India, *chan* texts would have been read in the fifth century as descriptions of the practices and experiences of at least some people presently living in China. And some Buddhist clergy and perhaps laypersons as well would have read them as descriptions of things they themselves were actively hoping to achieve.

In approaching any of these texts, we must of course fully acknowledge their prescriptive nature as expressions of religious ideals. Nevertheless, as we have seen, it is also true that these texts came into being in an environment in which practice, mastery, and claims to mastery of meditation were in fact becoming increasingly important. Living Chinese Buddhists of power and prestige claimed to be, or were held to be, "*chan* masters." The Chinese Buddhist meditation literature of the fifth century thus has the potential to show us not just abstract ideals, but the ideals actually used to characterize, imagine, and understand living Chinese Buddhists and the practices they carried out. My approach to this literature will therefore follow the path charted by scholars of religious biography who take the idealizing nature of that genre not as a limitation to be overcome, but as reflective of the humanistic perspective that what happens "on the ground" is not more important, and is even potentially *less* important, than the categories, narratives, and practices through which the infinitely variable particularities of individual experience, in the broadest sense of the term, are made intersubjectively available and then taken up as such, to real ends, within given communities. That it is productive to take such an approach not just with hagiography but also with technical meditation manuals will be a key argument of the remaining chapters of this book. It is to those sources that we next turn.

2

Confirmatory Visions and the Semiotics of Meditative Experience

Welcome to the world of models, states, stages, and visions of goals to attain. The curse and blessing of knowing all of this terminology and theory is that there is a natural tendency to begin to try to apply it to our own experiences (and those of others) and wonder what was what.... Not only have I just provided enough information for a few of you to become Master Posers on the spiritual path, I have just given some of you enough information to start obsessing way too much about "where you are" on the path. However, this is a trivial danger, and why senior dharma teachers do not ever seem to put the important details about sorting out what is what into their books is completely beyond me.

Daniel M. Ingram, self-proclaimed arhat (2008)

IN THE EARLY FIFTH CENTURY, Buddhist meditation—*chan* in its presectarian sense—became in China a newly important locus of practice, identity, and textual production. During this period, as those honored in life and in death as "masters of meditation" (*chanshi*) became increasingly consequential actors in the clergy and the wider world, and as spaces dedicated to the practice of meditation proliferated, there also appeared a new body of literature classified as a canonical repository of information about this subject. These texts—the so-called *chan* scriptures (*chanjing*)—appeared and circulated in China at a time when meditative attainment was becoming a social good of real worth. They can, for this reason, be treated as something more than a collection of abstract, doctrinal compendia. They can be read as sources disclosing the ideals that reflected, and also actively shaped, the behavior, expectations, and experiences of the increasing numbers of Chinese Buddhists who claimed mastery of this discipline or attributed it to others. For insight, then, into how this potentially esoteric domain of religious practice and attainment was understood during the era when it first came to occupy a real place in the social and cultural life of China, we must turn to the *chan* scriptures.

Evidence of Meditative Attainment

In order to use them productively as sources for the Chinese understanding of Buddhist meditation in this era, we must first ascertain what within these texts was most important for their authors and their audiences—determining the questions asked will help us recognize the answers they provided. To plot this terrain, it is worth returning for a moment to the fifth- and sixth-century biographies of monks and nuns examined in the previous chapter. What do these biographies suggest that Chinese readers most wanted to know about meditation and those who practiced it? As hagiographies, those tales have their own limitations, of course. But while they cannot reliably inform us about what concrete meditation practices any specific fifth- or sixth-century Chinese Buddhists actually engaged in, they do reveal information of a different order: namely, what kinds of things were thought to be the *evidence* of meditative attainment. Indeed, as arguments that the figures in question should be remembered as accomplished meditators, the tales themselves are instances of the mustering of such evidence. The authors and compilers of the fifth-century *chan* scriptures, as we will see, were also concerned to answer questions about the evidence of meditative attainment, and they did so in similar ways.

Meditative Visions

The section of the *Biographies of Eminent Monks* devoted to "meditation practitioners" opens with an account of Sengxian 僧顯 (fl. 318–321), a holy monk whose life of seclusion was unencumbered by fame, patronage, or contact with society. But to these external indicators of sanctity is added the following:

> Later, when [Sengxian] had become seriously ill, he directed his meditative imagination toward the Western [Pure] Land with utmost urgency. He then saw the Buddha Amitāyus descend in his true form, his light irradiating his body such that all his pain was dispelled. That evening he got up [from meditation], bathed, and told the other residents [of the temple] and his sick nurses what he had seen.... When dawn came, he died while sitting peacefully, at which point a mysterious fragrance filled the room.[1]

Although auspicious pre-death visions of this sort are common in medieval Chinese Buddhist hagiography (Shinohara 2007b, 54–60), here it is implied that Sengxian's vision had some particular connection to his accomplishments as a meditator: generated by his fervent "meditative imagination" (*xiang*想)—a key term of art in the *chan* scriptures as well—his vision is both the result of his meditative power and its confirmation. And the vision serves

---

1. 後遇疾綿篤，乃屬想西方心甚苦至。見無量壽佛降以真容，光照其身，所苦都愈。是夕便起澡浴，為同住及侍疾者說己所見...至明清晨平坐而化。室內有殊香。(*GSZ*, T.2059:50.395b28–c1)

as this confirmation not only implicitly, for readers of the tale, but explicitly in the story itself when Sengxian recounts it to his colleagues just before his death.

Medieval hagiographies frequently argued that the highest meditative achievements, whatever their external signs, would also be distinguished by visions. The famed *chan* practitioner Daofa 道法 (d. 474) was remembered for his practice of austerities, such as exposing his body to the predation of insects.[2] Yet his biography adds something more: that Daofa, after many years of meditation, entered a state of profound trance wherein "he saw [the buddha] Maitreya emit a light from his navel revealing the karmic retributions of those in the lower realms of existence."[3] Concrete visions serve as the evidence for specific meditative attainments in the biography of Puheng 普恒 (401–479), who supposedly "claimed to be able to enter the fire-radiance *samādhi*, wherein light streamed from his forehead down to the adamantine nadir [at the bottom of the universe], within which he saw numerous images."[4] Puheng's vision—narrated as something he told others he had experienced—is here linked to a named state of trance known from canonical sources.

In other stories meditative visions are initial signs of potential. The nun Tanhui 曇暉 (422–504) entered a nunnery at the age of thirteen and showed great promise:

> The very first time she received instruction, at the end of a session of seated meditation, she entered trance. She saw two lights in the east, one white and like the sun, the other blue and like the moon. While immersed in trance she thought: "The white one must [indicate] the bodhisattva path, the blue one the teachings of the voice-hearers. If this is truly so, may the blue light shrink and the white one grow brighter." Immediately, in accord with this thought, the blue light disappeared and the white one became brighter. Later, arising from trance, she told [her experiences] to the nun Fayu. Fayu was skilled in the ways of contemplation, and hearing of them she commended [Tanhui] heartily.[5]

Tanhui's trance-induced vision is here a sign of her future destiny as an accomplished meditator, as her biography later recounts.[6] Unlike the buddhas

---

2. *GSZ*, T.2059:50.399b5–14.

3. 見彌勒放齊中光，照三途果報。 (*GSZ*, 399b11–12; see also *Meisōden shō*, Z.1523:77.385a6–7). A vision of the karmic retributions of others recalls the Buddha's attainment of the first two *vidyā*s during the night of his awakening.

4. 自說入火光三昧，光從眉直下至金剛際。於光中見諸色像。 (*GSZ*, T.2059:50.399b20–22). On the fire-radiance *samādhi* (Skt. *tejodhātu-samādhi*), see Dantinne 1983, 272–274 and Anālayo 2015.

5. 裁得稟受，即於座末便得入定。見東方有二光明，其一如日而白，其一如月而青。即於定中立念云：白者必是菩薩道，青者聲聞法。若審然者，當今青者銷，而白光熾。即應此念，青光遂滅。白光熾滿。及至起定，為育尼說。育尼善觀道，聞而歡喜讚善。 (*BQNZ*, T.2063:50.946a5–11)

6. Presumably Tanhui's potential comes from her good karma. For another story linking visionary propensity to past karma, see the biography of Sengjing 僧景 (d. 497) at *GHMJ*, T.2103:52.270a14–15.

seen by Sengxian or Daofa, the content of Tanhui's vision is rather obscure. While the story eventually explains its meaning, that such an interpretation is provided at all shows that the visionary signs of meditative attainment were thought to be potentially enigmatic, a point to which we will return below.

Yet another scenario is depicted in the *Records in Proclamation of Manifestations* (*Xuan yan ji*), a mid-fifth-century collection of miracle tales, which recounts that the famous Buddhist layman Liu Yimin 劉遺民 (354–410)

> frequently suffered from illness. . . . He concentrated his thoughts through the discipline of *chan* and after half a year he saw the "sign between the eyebrows" [the white tuft of hair between the Buddha's eyebrows]. . . . Then he further saw the whole body [of the Buddha] as if in a painting. He then saw a monk presenting him with a shining pearl, and as a result his illness was cured.[7]

Though the fruit of *chan* here ascribed to Liu Yimin is the healing of his sickness rather than a formal soteriological achievement, this story still shows that meditative visions indicative of attainment were not thought to be the exclusive preserve of monks or nuns.

Visionary Experience and Meditation Literature

Like the hagiographies of visionaries, mystics, and ascetics in many religious traditions, biographies of early medieval Chinese Buddhist meditators often stress the purely external signs of their sanctity: Sengxian's death was accompanied by a mysterious fragrance, Daofa withstood the torment of insects, Liu Yimin was cured of illness, and Tanhui (later in her biography) gained, through meditation, knowledge of Buddhist doctrines that allowed her to defeat learned scholars in debate.[8] Yet these stories also claim that mastery of meditation involves something more—that it entails visionary experiences involving buddhas, flaming lights, glowing suns, or mysterious pearl-wielding monks whose appearance is the confirmation of specific attainments.

In calling these encounters visionary "experiences," it is certainly not my intention to call up any specter of the *sui generis* "religious experience" once held, problematically, to be the true origin of events such as these (Proudfoot 1985). Nor do I wish to imply that medieval Chinese Buddhists sought to ground their authority, or the authority of others, in quasi-Cartesian claims to indubitably known personal or private experience. But even if we concede, with Wittgenstein, that it does not ultimately matter whether there are beetles in anyone's box—that the ontology of private experiences is not relevant to

---

7. 體常多病...精思禪業。半年之中，見眉間相...又見全身。謂是圖畫。見一道人奉明珠，因遂病差。(*Gu xiao shuo gou chen*, 558; *Bian zheng lun*, T.2110:52.539c14–15). Liu Yimin (the style name of Liu Chengzhi 劉程之), a prominent aristocrat who frequented Huiyuan on Mount Lu, is remembered as a consummate lay practitioner of *chan* (*GHMJ*, T.2103:52.304b8–10).

8. *BQNZ*, T.50:2063.946a17–19. On the importance of external signs for the authentication of medieval Christian visionaries and saints, see Caciola 2003 and Frank 2000.

our analysis of the language games in which claims to those experiences figure (Day 2010, 294)—there is still a difference between (and hence a reason one might choose to play) games involving boxes into whose hidden depths someone can point and then speak, and those featuring only platters on which goods are displayed for others to see. From this perspective, it will be useful to say that medieval Chinese hagiographies do indeed emphasize the *experiences* of Buddhist meditators, in a way they might not have, in that they uphold as the proper evidence of attainment happenings whose details are depicted as communicatively (but not necessarily *ontologically*) private, that is to say, the kind of thing that can be made known to others only through a first-person report.[9]

Hagiographies of eminent monks and nuns tell us neither how often anyone in medieval China actually laid claim to meditative visionary experiences nor whether any specific regime of meditative training could or did reliably produce such experiences. But these tales do effectively reveal facets of what we might call the ideology of Buddhist meditative experience—what modalities of such experiences were valued and to what extent, what authority was derivable from or attributable to them, and whether and how such claims were thought to be properly presented and adjudicated.

That there indeed was such an ideology is the first thing to note. The stories cited above all posit communicatively private experiences as key pieces of evidence demonstrating meditative attainment. (Buddhist monastic law, we should note, has no blanket prohibition on true claims to meditative attainment, and even false claims are not transgressions if they are made in good faith rather than to intentionally deceive.)[10] And, second, we should note the nature of the experiences the stories claim are relevant: visions whose import lies in their *content,* in what thing or things the meditator saw. In contrast, little mention is made, if any, concerning the mental processes leading to the visions, the psychological states resulting from them, or the kind of understanding or cognition they depended on or produced.

This lack of attention to the psychic mechanisms that enable meditation (or are created by it) might tempt us to see in these stories a "popular" or noncanonical understanding of meditation and its fruits, one that differs in kind from what is found in traditional Buddhist meditation manuals that dwell on the qualities of mind characterizing the successive stages of the meditative path. We might, for example, contrast the concrete visions attesting to Puheng's attainment of the "fire-radiance *samādhi*" with the standard methods for meditation on the fire element from early Buddhist literature,

---

9. However, this communicative privacy was relative, and meditative visions were sometimes thought to be visible to others. See, for example, *Chan Essentials* 3.27.3 (*CMY,* T.613:15.262a15) and 3.29.1 (*CMY,* T.613:15.262b16); *XGSZ,* T.2060:50.555c4–9; 600c15–19; 651a16–18.

10. All known versions of the fourth *pārājika,* the prohibition on false claims of attainment, include an exception in the case of claims made from "pride" (Hirakawa 1993–1994, 1:298–323). True claims are prohibited when made to laypeople, but this is only a minor transgression (Prebish 1975, 74–75).

according to which one must first enumerate all instances of bodily fire as whatever is "fire, fiery, and clung-to, that by which one is warmed, ages, and is consumed, and that by which what is eaten is...completely digested," and then, of each of these elements, understand: "This is not mine, this I am not, this is not myself."[11] Such instructions—elaborated and expanded in post-canonical Indian sources—emphasize, and provide the conceptual and linguistic tools for, a discursive, analytic classification of the various instances of bodily fire and the "seeing" of them in conformity with the core Buddhist doctrine of "non-self" (anātman).[12] Meditative attainment, here, seems to be primarily an inner, self-known psychological achievement.

Although the differences between early Indian Buddhist meditation literature and the miraculous stories of fifth-century Chinese meditators are real, it would be wrong to conclude that they reflect an understanding of Buddhist meditation different from the "canonical" one, if by canonical we mean that which even scholastically oriented Chinese Buddhists of the time would have seen as such. For in fifth-century China the most relevant canonical texts discussing meditation were the *chan* scriptures, the most prominent examples of which similarly emphasize concrete visions.[13] According to one of these texts, someone carrying out the meditation on the "fire element" (火大):

> first contemplates the interior of his body. At the tip of his flowering heart-tree, among the leaves, there is a faint fire, like the gleam of gold. It emerges from the tip of his heart and fills his body. It then exits through his pores, gradually expanding until it fills his meditation cot...then fills his room...the building...a city...ten acres....The fire becomes white, brighter than a pearl and whiter than even crystal or a snow-covered mountain. Infused with red light, it forms a multitude of patterns, gradually expanding until it fills...the entire universe from the summit of the triple world down to the adamantine nadir. It then returns and reenters through the crown of his head.[14]

Just as in the stories of early medieval meditators, psychological analysis and abstract doctrine are passed over quickly here in favor of visually rich descriptions of the concrete objects and scenes that successful practitioners

---

11. *Dhātuvibhaṅga-sutta* (*Majjhima-nikāya*, 3.241); translation after Ñāṇamoli and Bodhi 1995, 1090, with slight modifications.

12. For some similar post-canonical examples, see *Śrāvakabhūmi*, 2:74–76 and Stuart 2015, 1:330–333.

13. Nor is correct to say, as Zürcher believed (1972, 222), that emphasis on concrete visions was in this time and place a matter of lay-friendly "Mahāyāna" approaches to meditation, in contrast to more austere and traditional "Hīnayāna" ones. Indeed, the very text Zürcher cites as an example of the latter, the *Damoduoluo chan jing*, has much to say about concrete visions, as we will see below.

14. *Chan Essentials*, 4.31.17 (*CMY*, T.15:613.266a18–b2). Broadly comparable, visually oriented presentations of the classic meditation on the fire element can be found in the fragmentary Indic meditation text from Central Asia that Schlingloff called *Yogalehrbuch* (Schlingloff 1964, 85–95; Bretfeld 2003, 172–175).

will, or should, encounter. There is no direct evidence that the authors of the hagiographies and miracle tales cited earlier were directly familiar with this *chan* scripture or similar texts, but it seems evident that the two bodies of literature shared certain basic assumptions pertaining to the nature of ideal meditative attainment.[15]

Semiotic Ideology

Chinese Buddhists of this era, when they thought and wrote about meditation either in the context of hagiography or within technical meditation manuals, did not limit their accounts to descriptions (or prescriptions) of methods for producing inner transformations they assumed to be self-evidently beneficial. They were equally concerned with the second-order question of what forms of meditative experience—the relatively private events whose entry into the social world required the personal report of the meditator—can or should count as evidence of meditative attainment and the authority that went with it. For us to inquire about the ways they asked and answered these questions is to take meditative experiences neither as inscrutable inner happenings nor as sites of privileged knowledge and authority, but rather as *semiotic forms*—instances of categories recognizable to others that are embodied in a material or linguistic form and hence capable of participating in social life in a meaningful way (Keane 2008, 114). And by inquiring into how Chinese Buddhists themselves theorized their own actual or possible interaction with these forms, we are investigating not simply the ideology of Buddhist meditative experience but its *semiotic ideology*—the culturally and historically situated assumptions and practices concerning what kinds of things can be signs, in what capacity, what their possible objects of signification are, and how those signs operate or should operate in the world (Keane 2007; 2018).

In the remainder of this chapter I will argue that in the fifth-century *chan* scriptures, particularly those composed in China, we can discern a relatively novel semiotic ideology of meditative experience—an understanding of what kinds of meditative experience might be meaningful, and to what ends—that in these sources reaches a kind of apogee for which we have few if any comparable examples in contemporaneous or earlier Buddhist literature. The understanding of meditative experience that emerges from these texts frames the discussion, in the ensuing chapters, of the meanings that visionary experiences in particular were deemed capable of communicating during the fifth, sixth, and seventh centuries. From this perspective, the new approach to meditation advocated by the Chan School in the eighth

---

15. Puheng's attainment of the "fire-radiance *samādhi*" does in fact read almost like a summary of the passage on the fire-element meditation from the *Chan Essentials* cited above. Particularly notable is the story's invocation of the "adamantine nadir" (金剛際), a cosmological term denoting the lowest level of the material universe. Similar imagery also appears in *GFSMH*, T.643:15.654a7–12, describing the moment of the Buddha's awakening.

century, examined in the final chapter, reveals itself as a fundamental rejection of the semiotic ideology of Buddhist meditative experience that had been widely if not universally shared in China since its full articulation in the fifth-century *chan* scriptures.

By focusing on the distinctly semiotic aspects of the literature of meditation, we can tie together the three domains in which Buddhist meditation had a social and historical reality in medieval China: meditation texts as repositories of canonical ideals, meditation itself as a part of living Buddhist practice, and meditation masters and practitioners as recognized bearers of an authority grounded in such practices and texts. It is possible to do so because the problem of how these things should be connected was a matter of concern for Chinese Buddhists themselves. The question of how claims to (or reports of) private meditative experiences could or could not be taken as signs that a given individual had achieved a significant, canonically sanctioned attainment posed a problem for which a newly emerging genre of canonical texts, the *chan* scriptures, provided the necessary interpretive tools. And given the right set of assumptions, it became a question that could be answered in a way that allowed the ascension of individuals to canonically sanctioned statuses to be eminently public while at the same time nontrivially dependent on the private meditative visions to which only the practitioners themselves had access.

Confirmatory Visions and Kumārajīva's *Meditation Scripture*

Of the *chan* scriptures that appeared in fifth-century China, four can provide a suitably broad template of the genre:

1. *Meditation Scripture,* translated by Kumārajīva[16]
2. *Chan Scripture of Dharmatrāta,* translated by Buddhabhadra[17]
3. *Five Gates,* translation attributed to Dharmamitra[18]
4. *Chan Essentials,* likely composed or compiled in China[19]

These four texts appeared in China during a roughly fifty-year period beginning around the turn of the fifth century, seemingly in the order listed above. The modes of their production were diverse, spanning the gamut of possibilities: no. 1 is a text with some surviving parallels in Indic-language sources;

---

16. *Zuo chan sanmei jing* 坐禪三昧經 (T.614; *ZCSM*); English trans. in Yamabe and Sueki 2009.

17. *Damoduoluo chan jing* 達摩多羅禪經 (T.618; *DMDL*). For the sake of simplicity I use the received title of this text even though its association with "Dharmatrāta" is probably the result of a later bibliographic confusion (Sakaino 1935, 910–912; L. Lin 1949, 341–346).

18. *Wu men chan jing yao yong fa* 五門禪經要用法 (T.619; *WMCJ*). I read the title to mean "essential methods [drawn from] the *chan* scriptures [that are based on] the five gates [of meditation]."

19. *Chan mi yao fa jing* 禪祕要法經 (T.613; *CMY*), or *Scripture on the Secret Essential Methods of Chan* (*Chan Essentials*). On its textual history, see *Secrets of Buddhist Meditation,* chap. 4.

no. 2 is of likely Indian origin but has no known Indian counterparts; the status of no. 3 is unclear; and no. 4 is almost certainly an apocryphal, Chinese-authored sutra.

Kumārajīva's *Meditation Scripture*

This text was the inaugural production of the famed translator Kumārajīva, and it has attracted considerable attention from modern scholars interested in the development, in India and Central Asia, of what some identify as "Mahāyāna" approaches to meditation.[20] As a compilation of the writings of a number of Indian masters, the *Meditation Scripture* can be taken broadly as an example of the kind of meditation literature that circulated during the second half of the fourth century in Gandhāra and Central Asia, the regions where Kumārajīva lived and studied.[21] Stylistically, the *Meditation Scripture* is a technical treatise describing the complete path of meditation, beginning with calming the mind and culminating in the attainment of arhatship, in accordance with a doctrinal framework more or less consistent with the Sarvāstivāda system.[22] The text devotes most of its attention to the practical details related to five introductory meditation practices, each of which can lead to the four traditional stages of trance (*dhyāna*) and from there to the higher stages of the path.[23] The five methods are (1) the contemplation of impurity (*bujing guan* 不淨觀), suitable for those afflicted by lust; (2) the cultivation of love (*cixin* 慈心), for those afflicted by hatred; (3) the contemplation of conditionality (*yinyuan* 因緣), for those afflicted by ignorance; (4) meditation on the breath (*nianxi* 念息), for those afflicted by "speculative thinking"; and (5) bringing to mind the Buddha (*nianfo* 念佛), for those whose mental defilements are equally distributed.[24] This set of five

---

20. A second meditation text translated by Kumārajīva survives as the *Chan fa yao jie* 禪法要解, or *Concise Explanations of the Methods of Meditation* (T.616). The so-called *Chan yao jing* 禪要經 (T.609) is a partial, alternate version of the first section of T.616 (Greene 2006, 170–184). On the question of the "Mahāyāna" methods in the *Meditation Scripture*, see Sakaino 1935, 879; Demiéville 1954, 356; Myōjin 1993a, 247; Tōdō 1960a; 1960b; and Abe 2006. I discuss the relative importance of Mahāyāna elements in the early history of Chinese Buddhist meditation in Chap. 1; see also Yamabe 2009, 50–59.

21. On the *Meditation Scripture* as a composite text, see Ikeda 1937. Distinct Indian sources were often compiled in China into a single "scripture" (Funayama 2006). The composition of the *Meditation Scripture* probably reflects at least some decisions made by Kumārajīva in response to the interests of his Chinese students (Zacchetti 2008, 442).

22. For a summary of the Sarvāstivāda-Vaibhāṣika path to liberation, see Guenther 1957, 215–232; Frauwallner 1995, 149–184; and Dhammajoti 2009a, 440–464. The *Meditation Scripture* follows a roughly similar system, especially for the attainments beyond the four *dhyānas* (*ZCSM*, T.614:15.279b–280c). Attainments specific to the bodhisattva path are also mentioned in the second part of the text.

23. *ZCSM*, T.614:15.271a1–277b9.

24. *ZCSM*, T.614:15.271c4–5. A later passage says *nianfo* is also suitable for "those who have committed grave sins who wish to beseech the Buddha [for pardon]" (及重罪人求索佛; *ZCSM*, T.614:15.276a7). "Speculative thinking" (*sijue* 思覺) probably renders *vitarka* (Deleanu 2012, 14). On breath meditation in the *Meditation Scripture*, see Shi H. 2001.

basic practices would become known in China as the "five gates of *chan*" (*wumen chan* 五門禪; Fujihira 1986).

Although the *Meditation Scripture*'s account of these methods gives many details concerning how one can use them to reach *dhyāna* and the higher stages of the path, what is most pertinent given our present concerns are the two occasions when it directly addresses *how it can be known* that a meditator has secured a significant meditative accomplishment. In both cases, the accomplishment in question is the first *dhyāna*. These passages connect to (and contrast with) earlier as well as contemporaneous Indian Buddhist sources in interesting ways, and similarly to the subsequent *chan* scriptures that began to appear in China slightly later. In the second of the two passages, which comes after the five basic techniques of meditation have been presented in full, the question is asked: "By what signs can it be known that one who cultivates *chan* has obtained 'oneness of mind' [i.e., the first *dhyāna*]?"[25] That person, we are told, will have a sleek complexion, lack any jealousy or stinginess, maintain the precepts purely, and be easy to converse with, humble and yielding, not argumentative, restrained in eating and drinking, and adept at chanting the scriptures.[26] Here the *Meditation Scripture* declares that meditative attainment will produce, and therefore will be discernable by, certain distinctive modes of external behavior—behavior, we should note, that generally aligns with the way early Chinese hagiographies describe the manner and lifestyle of monks and nuns remembered as skilled practitioners of meditation.

Yet this understanding of the semiotics of meditative attainment, in which a nominally internal state ("oneness of mind") is held to be communicated by external markers fully open to public view (a sleek complexion), is not the only one the *Meditation Scripture* proposes. Earlier, in the concluding instructions for the contemplation of impurity (in which a meditator must imagine his own body as a skeleton), the signs that confirm the attainment of *dhyāna* are described rather differently:

> If the mind remains fixed for a long time, it begins to accord with the factors of *dhyāna*. When one obtains *dhyāna*, there are three signs. [First,] the body will feel blissful, relaxed, and at ease. [Second,] the white bones [the meditator has been contemplating] will radiate light, as if they are made of white *ke*-jade.[27] [Third,] the mind becomes calm and still.[28]

---

25. 修行禪人，得一心相，云何可知。(*ZCSM*, T.614:15.277c13). Note the similar passage at *Chan fa yao jie*, T.616:15.287b4–11. "Oneness of mind" presumably denotes "one-pointedness of mind" (*cittaikāgrattā*), the last of the five *dhyāna*-factors that characterize the first *dhyāna*. The other factors are discussed in the next paragraph.

26. *ZCSM*, T.614:15.277c13–24.

27. *Ke* can also mean a kind of shell.

28. 若心久住，是應禪法。若得禪定，即有三相。身體和悅，柔軟輕便，白骨流光，猶如白珂，心得靜住。(*ZCSM*, T.614:15.272a20–23). The proper parsing of the three different signs is confirmed

Here the initial attainment of *dhyāna* is indicated by signs distributed across three distinct zones: (1) the body, which feels blissful, (2) the mental *object* (the "white bones," or skeleton in this case), which emits light, and (3) the mind itself, which becomes calm and still. Note that while specific states of body and mind (nos. 1 and 3) are included among these signs, the question that was asked and then answered concerns neither the ontology of *dhyāna* as a distinct configuration of those states nor the practical methods for generating such states, methods that were given earlier in the instructions for the contemplation of impurity proper. The issue, rather, is what evidence reveals if *dhyāna* has indeed been reached, and the evidence is here said to reside not in externally observable aspects of the meditator's behavior or person but in specific facets of his internal experience.

Canonical Models

That the *Meditation Scripture* asks this question at all affords a useful contrast with how the attainment of *dhyāna* is discussed in classical Buddhist literature.[29] As this matter is presented in the so-called sāmañña-phala scheme (after the title of the first text in the Pāli canon where this formulaic account of the Buddhist path appears), a meditator reaches the first *dhyāna* after he has perfected "virtue" (*śīla*), sat down with "mindfulness" (*smṛti*) established, and abandoned the so-called five hindrances of desire, ill will, sloth, remorse, and doubt.[30] The moment of attaining the first of the four levels of *dhyāna* is then described as follows:

> When he knows that these five hindrances have left him, gladness arises in him, from gladness comes delight, from the delight in his mind his body becomes tranquil, with a tranquil body he feels joy, and with joy his mind is concentrated. Being thus detached from sense-desires and detached from unwholesome states, he enters and remains in the first *dhyāna*, which is characterized by applied and sustained thought and filled with the delight and joy born of detachment. With this delight and joy born of detachment he so suffuses, drenches, fills and irradiates his body that there is no spot in his entire body untouched by it.[31]

Although often read as a set of instructions for reaching the first *dhyāna*, this passage and its many close parallels are not really practical in orientation, as Rupert Gethin notes (2004, 202)—armed with this passage alone, what

---

by the more detailed explanation in the ensuing lines. See, similarly, *Chan fa yao jie*, T.616:15.292b5–c4.

29. On *dhyāna* (P. *jhāna*) as analyzed in Pāli canonical texts and commentaries, see Cousins 1973 and Harvey 2018.

30. For consistency, except when discussing specifically Pāli technical terms I will continue to give Indic words in their Sanskrit form. On the many places this formula appears, see Gethin 2004, 202n5, and Bucknell 1984. For a study and translation of one version in light of its parallels, see Anālayo 2016.

31. *Dīgha-nikāya*, 1:73; translation by Walshe 1995, 102, with minor modifications.

exactly would one do?—but instead are a description of the attainment of *dhyāna* reached by methods unstated.[32] But what kind of description? Are expressions such as "characterized by applied and sustained thought," "filled with delight and joy," or even "his mind concentrated" intended to convey the subjective experience of entering the first *dhyāna*? (And, by extension, to describe the kind of evidence one might rely on, or inquire about if evaluating someone else, to know that this has happened?) Or do they perhaps describe only the normative ontology of *dhyāna*, claiming to tell us what *dhyāna* truly is, from an Abhidharmic point of view, without implying that such an account will align with its phenomenology?

Rather than answer this question in the case of the "sāmañña-phala" scheme, I wish simply to note that its lack of clear guidance on this point contrasts with the *Meditation Scripture,* which explicitly speaks of the *signs* indicating the attainment of *dhyāna*. To be sure, the semiotics of meditative attainment proposed by the latter does not ignore the canonical *dhyāna* formula entirely. The two signs of bodily bliss and mental concentration are clearly drawn from the list of the five qualities which the formula presents as the defining marks of the first *dhyāna*—applied and sustained thought, bodily bliss, mental joy, and one-pointedness of mind. Still, it is notable that the *Meditation Scripture* explicitly declares that these two qualities are signs, suggesting that it was not considered obvious that the factors that define the state of *dhyāna* also describe the experience that communicates its presence.[33] And for this purpose, let us note further, not all the *dhyāna* factors were deemed relevant. "Applied and sustained thought," for example, although duly mentioned earlier in the *Meditation Scripture* as an attribute of the first *dhyāna*, is not then said to be a sign of it in this sense. Moreover, the *Meditation Scripture* also proposes as a sign, beyond the two drawn from the canonical *dhyāna* formula, something else entirely: a distinctive change in the visual appearance of the *object* of the meditator's concentrated mind, the "white bones" of the contemplation of impurity, which will begin to radiate light.

Confirmatory Visions in the *Visuddhimagga*
The *Meditation Scripture*'s foregrounding of the problem of how the attainment of *dhyāna* can be known (as opposed to how it can be reached or what

---

32. Gethin argues that it is not here but rather the *smṛtyupasthāna* literature where we find the main *techniques* of meditation in the early scriptures, techniques that, he argues, promise to instill the same qualities of body and mind that formally characterize the *dhyāna*s. Gethin's argument is an implicit criticism of those who argue that the *dhyāna* formula provides an approach to meditation incompatible with, and hence historically distinct from, the one in the *smṛtyupasthāna* texts (see, e.g., Griffiths 1983).

33. The word "sign" (*xiang* 相) as used in the *Meditation Scripture* does not neatly fall on one side of the ontology / epistemology divide, and the same is true of the many potential Indic terms it might have originally translated (*nimitta, lakṣaṇa,* etc.) The point, however, is that the *Meditation Scripture* uses the word in the context of a question about identifying when a person has attained the state of *dhyāna*, making the stakes, in this instance, clear.

it is), and the idea that distinctive visionary experiences are among the necessary or probable signs, are both relatively novel when compared with early canonical models such as the "sāmañña-phala" scheme. But by the fourth century of the common era, they are moves that had become reasonably widespread in Buddhist meditation literature. An essentially identical understanding, albeit making use of quite different technical terminology, figures prominently in the well-known account of initial meditative attainment in the *Visuddhimagga* (*Path of Purification*), the famous Pāli compendium compiled, in Sri Lanka, in roughly the same era when the *Meditation Scripture* was translated into Chinese.[34]

According to the *Visuddhimagga*, meditation begins when the practitioner focuses the mind on the chosen meditation object. In the case of the so-called earth *kasiṇa*, the first method and the only one that describes the process in full, this means a physical object composed of earth, such as a flattened patch of dirt. The meditator stares at this object until able to "see" it even with closed eyes. This mental representation of the meditation object is termed the "acquired sign" (*uggahanimitta*), and by continuing to focus on it the meditator eventually enters "access concentration" (*upacārasamādhi*), a state that, while technically still preliminary to the first *dhyāna*, is described as a momentous achievement marking the first taste of the higher "world of pure form" to which *dhyāna* gives access in this life and the next.[35]

At this moment, we are told, the meditator's mind becomes calm, free of defilements, and purified. At the same time, the meditator's mental object also changes. In place of the acquired sign, a "counterpart sign" (*paṭibhāganimitta*) now appears, described in distinctly visual terms as a purified version of the original meditation object. For the earth *kasiṇa*, originally a patch of dirt, the counterpart sign is "like a mother-of-pearl dish well washed, like the moon's disk coming out from behind a cloud" (Ñāṇamoli 1991, 125). Importantly, the counterpart sign is *not* a perfect, eidetic *visualization* of the initial object in the sense of a mental representation that is phenomenologically equivalent to ordinary vision. Rather, it is something like the purified essence of the object. For the water *kasiṇa*, for example, both the original object and the "acquired sign" have bubbles, froth, and other such details whereas the counterpart sign "appears inactive, like a crystal fan set in space" (ibid., 166). So too the counterpart sign of the fire *kasiṇa*, originally a real fire that flickers and moves, appears "motionless like a piece of red cloth set in space, like a gold fan, like a gold column" (ibid.,

---

34. On the dates of Buddhaghosa, compiler of the *Visuddhimagga*, see Hinüber 1996, 102–103. For an overview of the *Visuddhimagga*'s presentation of the initial steps of meditation practice, see Vajirañāṇa 1962, 103–165; W. King 1980, 31–50; and Shaw 2016.

35. *Visuddhimagga*, 125; Ñāṇamoli 1991, 123–125. Other Pāli commentaries describe the process similarly (Cousins 1973, 129n32). "Access concentration" is known only from the Pāli commentaries, but other schools had comparable notions of a state lying in between ordinary consciousness and the first *dhyāna* (ibid., 118).

167). (The counterpart sign actually brings with it a *loss* of visual "resolution" relative to the acquired sign and the original physical object.) Significantly, the counterpart sign is described in visual terms even when the initial meditation object is not a visual one: in the meditation on the breath, the counterpart sign appears "like a star or a cluster of gems... [or] like a stretched out cobweb or a film or cloud or a lotus flower or a chariot wheel or the moon's disk or the sun's disk" (ibid., 277).

Despite their many differences on matters ranging from the possible objects of meditative attention to the names of the stages of meditative progress, the *Visuddhimagga* and the *Meditation Scripture* make similar claims about the process leading to *dhyāna* and—what I wish to highlight—the semiotics of its attainment. Both assert that the attainment of *dhyāna* (or its immediate precursor, access concentration) will be communicated not only by the arising of the specific attributes that characterize said attainment as a novel state of body and mind, attributes such as bliss, happiness, and mental concentration, but also by an encounter with a new and distinctive *object* of consciousness characterized in visual terms—in less rarified language, a vision. Unlike the descriptions of the attainment of *dhyāna* from early canonical sources, which do not address such questions at all, both the *Visuddhimagga* and the *Meditation Scripture* explicitly frame the significance of these visions in semiotic terms. These visions are valuable not because of what is directly disclosed to the meditator through them, such as the details of Buddhist doctrines or the reality of some external object or being whose existence was in doubt, but rather because their occurrence is a reliable indicator that the meditator has obtained *dhyāna*. For this reason, I shall refer to them as "confirmatory visions."[36]

While the *Meditation Scripture* and *Visuddhimagga* discuss confirmatory visions only briefly, and only in the context of an initial meditative achievement,[37] the topic of confirmatory visions became increasingly important in the *chan* scriptures produced in fifth-century China, particularly those composed or compiled in China, and the range of things the confirmatory visions were said to convey expanded considerably. In the remainder of this chapter, I will chart these developments with respect to three key examples before considering in more general terms the semiotic ideology of meditative experience that all these texts share.

---

36. Visions appearing as signs of the success of ritual or meditative practices is a theme well known in later Tantric Buddhist traditions (Gyatso 2002, 187), and also in the *borān kammaṭṭhāna* (old meditation) traditions of Theravāda Buddhism, which use the same terminology of "acquired" and "counterpart" signs, that have been studied by François Bizot and others (Crosby 2000; 2013; de Bernon 2000; Skilton and Choompolpaisal 2015). As the materials in this chapter show, however, these ideas were evidently widespread in the Buddhist world even in much earlier times.

37. The *Meditation Scripture* also mentions these ideas only in connection with the contemplation of impurity.

The Chan Scripture of Dharmatrāta

Apart from the texts translated by Kumārajīva, the *Chan Scripture of Dharmatrāta* is the only fifth-century *chan* scripture that is of generally unquestioned Indian origin. Its translator, the Gandhāran monk Buddhabhadra, arrived in Chang'an in either 406 or 408 and quickly became famous as a teacher of meditation.[38] As discussed in the previous chapter, he seems to have been the first person in China to bear the title of *chan* master. Moving south in 410, he spent one year on Mount Lu with Huiyuan before settling in the southern capital of Jiankang (Nanjing). According to two early prefaces, it was during his stay on Mount Lu that Buddhabhadra translated the *Chan Scripture of Dharmatrāta*. Introduced to China by an Indian monk who was himself a "meditation master," the *Chan Scripture of Dharmatrāta* differed, in this respect, not only from the *Meditation Scripture* but from all previously known Buddhist meditation texts in China. Indeed, it was as the emblem of a lineage of meditation masters that this text was best remembered in subsequent Chinese Buddhist history.[39]

But for our present purposes, the *Chan Scripture of Dharmatrāta* is significant as an example of a pre-fifth-century Indic Buddhist meditation text whose discussion of confirmatory visions goes well beyond anything found in comparable sources.[40] Though much about the *Chan Scripture of Dharmatrāta* remains uncertain, owing to its cryptic style and the absence of an Indic counterpart to aid in deciphering its unusual technical terminology, structurally it is clearly a compendium of the same kinds of traditional techniques of Buddhist meditation discussed in texts like the *Meditation Scripture* and *Visuddhimagga*.[41] The first method covered, meditation on the breath (*ānāpānasmṛti*), receives the most elaborate attention, which is dispensed under

38. On Buddhabhadra's life, see Chen J. 2014b, 104. Like many foreign *chan* masters in fifth-century China, he hailed from Jibin 罽賓, usually taken to mean "greater Gandhāra" (Enomoto 1994, 265).

39. Later Chinese authors almost never referred to the content of the *Chan Scripture of Dharmatrāta* (a single, anomalous eighteenth-century Japanese commentary only highlights its total neglect in earlier times; see Sengoku 1985 and Mohr 2006). But they often cited its two prefaces, which contain the first examples of the lists of Indian patriarchal masters that would eventually be adopted by the Chan School (McRae 1986, 80–82). The phrase "transmission of the flame" (*chuandeng* 傳燈), the veritable rallying cry of the Chan School denoting the transmission of a lineage of teachers, first occurs with this meaning in Huiguang's preface (Jan 1990, 15).

40. Deleanu 1993 and Yamabe 1999b, 72–76, have both highlighted the text's emphasis on visions. Other brief studies of the text include Satō Taishun 1931, 343–349; Demiéville 1954, 360–363; Andō 1962, 254–255; and Stuart 2015, 1:263–266. See also Chan 2013, who provides a complete though only sparsely annotated English translation.

41. Seven distinct methods are presented: meditation on (1) the breath, (2) impurity, (3) the elements (*dhātu;* 界), (4) the "four immeasurables" (*apramāṇa;* 四無量), (5) the aggregates (*skandha;* 陰), (6) the sense-spheres (*āyatana;* 入), and (7) dependent origination (*pratītyasamutpāda;* 十二因緣). The selection of meditation topics and their ordering are similar to what we find in the *Yogalehrbuch* (Inokuchi 1966, 12).

the four headings "backsliding" (退), "stagnation" (住), "progress" (升進), and "mastery" (決定).[42] Each of these sections is further divided into a preparatory path (方便道) and a superior path (勝道).[43] In the description of the second method, the contemplation of impurity, there is only a preparatory path, suggesting perhaps that the superior path was assumed to be the same regardless of the specific method of meditation. When it comes to the later methods, there is no breakdown into stages or divisions at all. In the end, it is uncertain whether the *Chan Scripture of Dharmatrāta* should be read as a sequential path of meditation or a compendium of different techniques suited for those of differing temperaments (like the *Meditation Scripture* and *Visuddhimagga*, for example), or some combination of the two.[44] A sharp difference in style between the first half of the text, which treats the first three methods entirely in verse, and the second half, which deals with the rest in prose, suggests that the text as we have it is the result of a merging of originally independent sources.[45]

Whatever the details of its textual history, the received *Chan Scripture of Dharmatrāta* is notable, in all its sections, for its recurring claims that visionary experiences will figure prominently among the signs confirming meditative attainment. The first significant discussion of such visions occurs as part of the description of the "progress" stage on the superior path, seemingly a meditator's first taste of attainment:[46]

> Now [the meditator] enters the very subtle stage,
> and he must not follow along with the flow of thoughts.
> The wise person keeps his mind still,
> concentrating it on what he should.
> The marvelous accomplishment in which he now resides
> is pure without stain.
> Becoming fulfilled and not diminishing,

---

42. These appear to correspond to *hānabhāgīya, sthitibhāgīya, viśeṣabhāgīya,* and *nirvedhabhāgīya,* a canonical typology of four aspects of *dhyāna (Abhidharmakośabhāṣyam,* 445.5–16; *Dīgha-nikāya,* 3:277 [cf. Mittal 1957, 64]; *Paṭisambhidāmagga,* 1:35–36), but also a classification of anything that leads to diminution, stasis, progress, and realization along the path (*Aṅguttaranikāya,* 2:167; *Visuddhimagga,* 14–15).

43. These perhaps correspond to *prayogamārga* and *viśeṣamārga* (or *uttaramārga*); see Demiéville 1954, 363n1; Chan 2013, 61n133.

44. Some passages suggest an ordered sequence, with later methods requiring mastery of earlier ones (*DMDL,* T.618:15.317c11–12; 320b20–21). Others align the different methods with different temperaments, suggesting that any method was a possible starting point (*DMDL,* T.618:15.306a26; 318b1–5; 322c27).

45. Demiéville 1954, 363n1; Yamabe 1999b, 73. The unusual title of Huiyuan's preface, "unified preface" (統序; *CSZJJ,* T:2145:55.65b22), suggests he considered the prose and verse sections to be distinct documents. The collective name he gives the text could even been read as two separate names: *Xiu xing fang bian* 修行方便 (*Yogācāra-bhūmi?*) and *Chan jing* 禪經 (see also Huiguang's preface at *CSZJJ,* T:2145:55.66b3).

46. Earlier, the "backsliding" and "stagnation" sections allude to such visions, only to say that at these levels they disappear or fail to develop (*DMDL,* T.618:15.302c16; 304b6).

he abides in purity and calm....
Visible signs then arise in succession.
Many different kinds of signs come forth.
[Because] the meditator is engaged in correct meditation,
his body and mind feel pleasure and joy...
and bodily pleasure having been aroused,
the mind too becomes regulated and peaceful.[47]

While it is left uncertain whether this moment signifies the attainment of *dhyāna* itself, it is clearly meant to be a key first juncture along the path of meditation. Indeed, what this passage describes aligns very closely with the three "signs" that in the *Meditation Scripture* mark the meditator's first entry into the state of *dhyāna*—namely, bodily bliss, a calm and joyful mind, and some kind of vision.[48]

The adequacy of visions alone as proof of meditative attainment seems to have been a topic of debate and perhaps anxiety for the author(s) of the *Chan Scripture of Dharmatrāta:* a latter passage firmly insists that in the absence of bodily bliss and mental calm visions alone are meaningless.[49] Nevertheless, visionary signs were evidently considered very important, and the text goes on to describe possible examples of them in great detail:

The many signs of progress
comprise manifold wondrous images:
lotus flowers, myriad jeweled trees,
fine and beautiful vessels and clothing,
blazing lights,
and innumerable ornamented objects.
O practitioner carefully listen
as I now explain in full detail
the many marvelous signs
that the wise ones say will arise for one
who reaches progress on the superior path.
From the upper disc [of the sky][50]
there will appear many pure signs,

---

47. 將入微妙境，勿隨流注想。慧者攝心住，如應善守持。所住妙功德，澄淨無垢濁。具足無減少，清淨安隱住...色相次第起。種種眾相生。修行正思惟，身心生喜樂...既能起身樂，心亦正安隱。(*DMDL,* T.618:15.307c28–308a10)

48. The triad of body (依; *āśraya;* see Yamabe 2016, 14), mind (念), and object of mind (緣), as the areas where signs of attainment appear, are also mentioned together in a later passage (*DMDL,* T.618:15.322a22–b2).

49. *DMDL,* T.618:15.308b19–23 compares someone who sees visions but experiences no "bodily sensations" (*chu* 觸) to a thirsty person who sees water but does not taste it. This alludes to the canonical story of Mūsila and Nārada (*Saṃyutta-nikāya,* 2.115; La Vallée Poussin 1937, 218).

50. Literally, "on the upper *maṇḍala*" (於上曼荼邏). A "wind-disc" (風輪) is mentioned in a later passage as the lowest realm of the cosmos (*DMDL,* T.618:15.311a22). See, similarly, Schlingloff 1964, 32n1; 87.

a shower of descending light,
clear and pure like glass.
This light fills [the meditator's] body,
making it extremely relaxed.
It then emerges from his body,
and gradually flows downward,
going near or far depending
on the strength of his roots of goodness.[51]

Reminiscent of the *Visuddhimagga*'s account of breath meditation, the break-through moment in the meditator's progress is accompanied not only by unusual bodily sensations and novel mental states but also by elaborate, concrete visions whose content is not related in any obvious way to the original object of contemplation, in this case the breath. Yet there is also here a more expansive understanding of the semiotic potential of the visionary experience, for it can apparently reveal other aspects of the meditator's person as well, such as the strength of his "roots of goodness."[52] This idea that meditative visions communicate a range of conditions, beyond the attainment of *dhyāna* in itself, is a key theme in later Chinese meditation texts, as we will see below.

Confirmatory visions are discussed throughout the remainder of the *Chan Scripture of Dharmatrāta*, in the verse sections but especially in the prose sections, where the imagery becomes increasingly elaborate over a consistent underlying logic.[53] For example, in the "contemplation of the *skandha*s" (觀陰):

> If the practitioner firmly restrains all distracted thoughts, he will be able to give rise to ultimate, perfected wisdom. If toward his original object of contemplation he remains firm and clear, he will give rise to *samādhi*, parting from all confused conceptions and eliminating his defilements. At this time, various wondrous signs will appear, like pieces of marvelously pure beryl or crystal baubles.[54]

---

51. 一切升進相，殊妙種種印[>相?]。蓮花眾寶樹，靡麗諸器服。光炎極顯炤，無量莊嚴具。慧說為勝道，功德住升進，所起諸妙相，我今當具說，修行者諦聽。於上曼茶邏，純一起眾相，流光參然下，清淨如頗梨。其光充四體，令身極柔軟。又復從身出，漸漸稍流下，隨其善根力，遠近無定相。(*DMDL*, T.618:15.308b29–c10)

52. See, similarly, *DMDL*, T.618:15.308b12–18, where the vision appears near or far to the body depending on the meditator's proximity to the fruits of the path, and *DMDL*, T.618:15.308c26–27, where the location of the vision is correlated with the type of *samādhi* achieved.

53. For a survey of the visionary imagery in the prose half of the text, see Deleanu 1993, 6–7. In the verses, see in particular *DMDL*, T.618:15.316b27–c6, describing the "purity liberation" (淨解脫; *śubha-vimokṣa*), on which see Dhammajoti 2009b, 276–281. The image here of "light radiating from the white bones" (白骨流光) recalls the signs of *dhyāna* as described in the *Meditation Scripture* passage discussed above.

54. 攝諸亂意，能起究竟成就智慧。若根本觀處堅固明淨，能起三昧，離諸亂想，滅除煩惱。諸微妙相，於是悉現，如淨妙瑠璃，如水淨泡。(*DMDL*, T.618:15.320b23–28)

Here again, the various concrete objects or scenes are not described as things the meditator should intentionally imagine or "visualize," but as autonomously appearing visions whose occurrence is claimed to correlate with, and thus to confirm, the attainment of a nameable meditative state.

Comparing the *Meditation Scripture* and *Visuddhimagga,* on the one hand, with the *Chan Scripture of Dharmatrāta* on the other, there is little difference in their approaches to either the basic techniques or stages of meditation practice. What distinguishes them is the greater attention paid in the *Chan Scripture of Dharmatrāta* to describing the experiences claimed to constitute the *evidence* of meditative attainment, experiences that it elaborates along increasingly visual lines, as well as the wider range of information about the meditator that it says these kinds of confirmatory visions might convey.

Confirmatory Visions in the *Five Gates*

While we may be confident that the *Meditation Scripture* and the *Chan Scripture of Dharmatrāta* were largely based on Indian or at least Indic-language source materials, the textual histories of many other fifth-century *chan* scriptures are more complex. Of these, the three most important are:

1. *The Five Gates* (T.619)
2. *The Chan Essentials* (T.613)
3. *The Methods for Curing* (T.620)[55]

Although traditional catalogs classify all three as Chinese translations of Indian Buddhist scriptures, each ascribed to a different translator, in actuality the first text is unclear in status, and the second and third are demonstrably Chinese compositions. Their textual histories, moreover, are closely interrelated. It can be shown, for example, that portions (if not the entirety) of the *Chan Essentials* was composed on the basis of a Chinese text very similar to the *Five Gates,* and also that the *Chan Essentials* and *Methods for Curing* first circulated together as a single document.[56] Stylistic and linguistic evidence further reveals a clear link between the *Chan Essentials* and *Methods for Curing* and the larger body of apocryphal fifth-century Chinese Buddhist texts known to modern scholars as the Contemplation Scriptures, a group whose most prominent member, the *Amitāyus Contemplation Scripture* (*Guan Wuliangshou fo jing* 觀無量壽佛經), has since the fifth century been one of the most important scriptures of East Asian Buddhism. All of these texts seem to have been assembled, through a process involving compilation of previously existing material as well as original composition, in a similar time and place—either in south China, where we have the first solid evidence of

---

55. *Zhi chan bing mi yao fa* 治禪病祕要, *The Secret Methods for Curing Meditation Sickness;* cited as *ZCB* hereafter.

56. For more details, see *Secrets of Buddhist Meditation,* chap. 4.

their existence as complete texts, or perhaps the city of Turfan on the Silk Roads, where many of the Indian and Central Asian Buddhist teachers associated with these texts are said to have dwelled for a time before arriving in central China.[57]

Meditation Masters and Students

Although the *Five Gates* is the shortest of the three and, in some respects, the most difficult to make sense of, it will pay dividends to examine it first. Chinese scriptural catalogs dating from the turn of the sixth century claimed that it had been translated by one of the most famous foreign *chan* masters of the fifth century, the Indian monk Dharmamitra. Whether or not this ascription is accurate, as it exists today the *Five Gates* resembles an assemblage of notes more than it does a coherently organized text, and it consists of two types of material, written in two very different formats. For an assessment of how confirmatory visions are treated in the Chinese meditation literature of this era, what I call the A-format sections provide the most interesting and useful evidence. These sections do not make up a single continuous block in the *Five Gates*, but they are readily distinguishable from the rest by the dialog form in which they are cast.[58]

This format first appears early on in the text. After briefly listing, in a slightly different order, the same five methods of practice described in the *Meditation Scripture*, here termed the "five gates" of meditation, the *Five Gates* begins with a detailed exposition of the method of *nianfo*, or "bringing to mind the Buddha" (Skt. *buddhānusmṛti*). The meditator is told to find a statue or other image of the Buddha, contemplate its features until they can be "seen" even with closed eyes, and then, after returning to seated meditation, bring this image to mind until it appears "just as clearly distinct as if facing a real buddha."[59] Then:

> The practitioner should get up, kneel before the master, and say: "Concentrating my mind while in my cell, it is just as if I were seeing the Buddha."
>
> The master should say: "Go back to your seat. Concentrate your mind on your forehead and single-mindedly bring to mind the Buddha."
>
> [Doing this,] images of buddhas appear from the practitioner's forehead, from one up to uncountable numbers.... The buddhas then return close to [the practitioner's] body and make the ground a golden color. The buddhas then

---

57. Concerning the theories about Turfan as the site of origin, see the discussion and notes under "Paintings of Meditative Attainment" below.

58. The other sections of the *Five Gates* follow a simpler, expository style. On the structure and composition of the *Five Gates* and its relationship to the *Chan Essentials*, see *Secrets of Buddhist Meditation*, chap. 4.

59. 對真佛明了無異。(*WMCJ*, T.618:15.325c21). Using a physical image of the Buddha for such meditation is also mentioned at *WMCJ*, T.619:15.327a13–15 and 329a12–13. For other examples of this, see *ZCSM*, T.614:15.276a7–23; *Si wei lüe yao fa*, T.617:15.299a4–13 (see also Yamabe 2009, 50–54).

disappear into the ground. The ground is level, like the palm of one's hand, clear and pure like a mirror....

This is the *jingjie* (境界) of the attainment of the *samādhi* of bringing to mind the Buddha. Having obtained this *jingjie*, [the practitioner should] tell the master.

The master says: "This is a good *jingjie*. This is called the first gate of contemplation."[60]

Again, the basic procedures for meditation in the *Five Gates*, and the criteria proposed for judging success, are similar if not identical to what we have already seen in both the *Meditation Scripture* and the *Visuddhimagga*. Namely, the practitioner, after obtaining a perfect mental image of an initially external object, continues to focus the mind on that object until experiencing a vision whose content goes beyond the original object and whose occurrence serves as confirmation of a nameable stage of attainment. The *Five Gates*, however, describes this process of vision and confirmation not abstractly, but as an unfolding interaction between a teacher and a student. It shows us, therefore, something new: not just how meditation was supposed to be practiced or what its results were supposed to be, but how those results were supposed to be deployed as evidence of meditative progress within a social context.[61]

Jingjie and the Confirmation of Attainment

In the *Five Gates* the vision that confirms the "first gate of contemplation" is called a good "jingjie." This word *jingjie*, which originally denoted the boundary of a physical territory (Han 2011, 12–37), was used in Chinese translations of Indian Buddhist texts to render a startling number of distinct albeit related words, including, to take only the most common ones, *viṣaya*, *ālambana*, *gocara*, *jñeya*, and *nimitta*.[62] Like the base sense of *jingjie* in Chinese, some of these terms have the literal meaning of a purely physical territory, particularly *viṣaya* and *gocara*. But they also have the hierarchical connotation of a domain accessible or suitable only for certain kinds of beings or for those of a certain level of attainment. This implication is related to another common meaning of words like *viṣaya*, *ālambana*, and *jñeya* as the *objects* of

---

60. 即從座起，跪白師言，我房中係念，見佛無異。師言，汝還本坐。係念額上一心念佛。爾時額上有佛像現，從一至十乃至無量...所出佛，還近身，作地金色。此諸佛盡入於地，地平如掌，明淨如鏡...此名得念佛三昧境界。得是境界已，白師。師言，是好境界，此名初門觀也。(*WMCJ*, T.618:15.325c21–326a2)

61. Some Indian Buddhist texts give the direct speech by which a meditation teacher should instruct the student (Shukla 1973, 411–426). More unusual in the *Five Gates* is the inclusion of the practitioner's reports.

62. *Kōsetsu Bukkyōgo daijiten*, 238–239; Hirakawa 1997, 302. These Indic words themselves have many meanings (Cone 2001, 65–66; 327–328; 590; Edgerton 1953, 214; Monier-Williams 1986, 997; Anālayo 2003). The later meanings of *jingjie* in Confucian thought and Chinese aesthetic theory (Han 2014) are likely indebted to the Buddhist usage outlined here.

human perception, thought of as the "territories" or "spheres" proper to each sensory organ, including the mind. In the context of meditation, these words further convey the more specific notion of a "cognitive object" in the sense of the thing, idea, or quality toward which a meditator directs the mind and of which he or she ideally reaches perfect cognition.[63]

In the *Five Gates* the word *jingjie* partakes of all these senses. As the meditator's "cognitive object," however, it primarily points not to the consciously chosen or cultivated objects of meditation but to the object or objects *normatively* correlated with a given stage of meditative attainment, and thus, to those whose appearance, in the experience of the meditator, confirms that attainment. Like the *Visuddhimagga's* counterpart sign or the signs of the *Meditation Scripture* and the *Chan Scripture of Dharmatrāta*, a *jingjie* is therefore what we may call a "confirmatory vision" or, when described under other sensory modalities as occurs occasionally, a "confirmatory experience."[64] Though the "confirmatory" character of a *jingjie* is not semantically encoded in this word, this sense emerges clearly from its usage in texts such as the *Five Gates*, where it most frequently describes an event implied to have a communicative function—a *jingjie*, in other words, is not just any vision but one whose occurrence is relevant for determining the meditative progress (or, in some cases, lack of progress) of the person who experiences it.

The *Five Gates* does not limit confirmatory visions to the initial attainment of advanced states of meditation, as was the case in the *Visuddhimagga* and the *Meditation Scripture*. Instead the dialog sections of the *Five Gates* depict all meditative progress taking place through a continuing series of instructions, visions, reports of visions, and, in consequence, new instructions assigned accordingly:

> [The practitioner] then tells the master what he has seen. The master says: "Good! You have diligently contemplated. This is the sign of the attainment of concentration with respect to the body." The master instructs [further], saying: "Further contemplate within the navel."
>
> Contemplating as instructed, [the practitioner] sees a five-colored light on the crown of his head. Seeing this, he tells the master.
>
> The master says: "Further contemplate the five lights. They contain five auspicious signs." Contemplating as instructed, he sees a buddha in [each] light, sitting in meditation.

---

63. On *ālambana* in particular, see Shi H. 1994; and for *jñeya* 'what is to be known,' see *Śrāvakabhūmi*, 2:42. In the *Yogalehrbuch*, *jñeya* refers to an entire visionary scene (Schlingloff 1964, 80; 103; 105; 107; 109). This seems particularly close to the meaning of *jingjie* in the *Five Gates* and related sources. In the *Chan Scripture of Dharmatrāta* (*DMDL*, T.618:15.324b16–17), we find the very rare *eryan jingjie* 閻焰境界 as a transcription-translation (a "bilingual binome") of *jñeya*, showing clearly that *jingjie* was, here, taken to be its Chinese translation.

64. *Jingjie* of tangible sensations (feelings of bodily or mental pleasure, or perceptions of warmth) or sounds are mentioned at *WMCJ*, T.619:15.326a15; a25; 329b13; 328c2; c14.

[The master then instructs]: "Further contemplate: do the buddhas in the five lights have any auspicious signs?"

[The practitioner] then sees lotus flowers emerging from the mouths of the buddhas, filling the entire world.[65]

In passages such as these, while no specific attainment is declared, the gradually evolving flow of the meditator's visions, occurring after he has directed his attention to the objects that the master has instructed, implies that progress of some kind has been attained and that the visions in question are its sign. In other dialogs this progress is made explicit by assigning to each of the unfolding visions a number within a hierarchical sequence of stages.[66]

The Character of a Confirmatory Vision

The dialog format of these sections of the *Five Gates* is, of course, a literary device, not the trace of an ethnographic report. Yet even though it is still an ideal rather than a descriptive document, because the *Five Gates* does not merely present ideal meditative experiences in the abstract but describes them as events produced, reported on, and evaluated within an interactional framework, it does effectively show us certain assumptions about the nature of those events.

First, inasmuch as the meditator is not supposed to know their content ahead of time, it is apparent that the confirmatory experiences that mark progress in the *Five Gates* are indeed best thought of as *visions* rather than visualizations.[67] Descriptions of visually rich images and scenes never appear in the master's instructions to the meditation student, but only in the student's reports. In the very few cases where the meditator is told to intentionally bring to mind a complex scene—to "visualize" it—success is confirmed only by its spontaneous transformation into something else. We see this clearly in one passage where the master tells the student to "try to remember doing worldly things with your former lover," to which the practitioner eventually responds: "I remember and see this person, but they transform into impure pus and blood, terrible to behold."[68] That the meditator *cannot* control his or her imagination—that even when trying to imagine a sexual encounter the image in the mind's eye transforms into one of impurity—

---

65. 即以所見白師。師言，大善。汝好用心觀，此身成定相也。師教言，更觀齊中。即如教觀，見頂有五色光焰。見已白師。師言，更觀五光，有五瑞相。如教觀已，見有一佛在光明中，結加趺坐。更觀五光中佛有何瑞相，即見佛口中種種蓮花出，出已遍滿大地。(*WMCJ*, T.619:15.326a26–b2)

66. See, e.g., *WMCJ*, T.619:15.329a11–330a20 (thirty numbered stages of the "contemplation of the Buddha") and 330a21–332a11 (sixteen and then twenty stages pertaining to the meditation on compassion).

67. As I have argued elsewhere, "visualization," a concept coined in the nineteenth century by experimental psychologists, implies a degree of willful control that is usually inappropriate in the context of the visionary experiences aimed for in medieval Chinese Buddhist meditation practices (Greene 2016b).

68. 當語，汝本時所愛人，試憶念與作世事。彼觀已，言，我憶念人，見之，但變作膿血不淨，甚可惡見。(*WMCJ*, T.619:15.328a6–10)

serves as a sign that the meditator has in fact eliminated all trace of craving and lust.

The contrast between the master's instructions and the meditator's reports is strictly observed at the level of terminology. The master instructs the meditator to "contemplate" (*guan* 觀), "look at" (*shi* 視), or "bring to mind" (*nian* 念) a given topic, thing, idea, or aspect of an already reported vision.[69] When the disciple recounts to the master what was experienced, it is usually described as what was "seen" (*jian* 見) or, less frequently, "perceived" (*jue* 覺).[70] "See," in short, never means *should see*, and the *Five Gates* depicts the meditator's progress not as something judged by the ability to visualize prescribed scenes or images, but as something revealed by the unanticipated content of what was "seen."[71]

Second, the unanticipated nature of the visions reveals an easy acceptance of what we can call a "phenomenological discontinuity" between meditative techniques and their hoped-for results. Consider the following passage:

> Instruct [the practitioner] to contemplate his body and make it even clearer. Instruct him to contemplate the navel of one of the buddhas [seen previously]. If he says: "I see light emerging from the buddha's navel and reaching to the horizon in all directions, and standing within the light are numerous buddhas," then this is the seventeenth thing.
>
> Instruct him to contemplate along the light. If he says: "I see innumerable people within the light, all experiencing happiness," then this is the eighteenth thing.[72]

Here, as throughout the *Five Gates*, the master instructs the practitioner to "contemplate" (*guan*) a present object (his body) or an aspect of a previous vision (the buddha's navel, and then its irradiated light). Scholars studying the history of Chinese Buddhist contemplative practices have subjected this

---

69. "Contemplate" (*guan*) is the most common verb in the master's instructions. It appears in the practitioner's responses only when restating the assigned practice (*WMCJ*, T.619:15.328a20–21). For "look at" (*shi*), see 325c20, 326a15, 326a17, and 332b1–2; and for "bring to mind" (*nian*), see 325c22–23, 326c3, 327a1–3, 327c11–12, 328a8–10, and 329b12–16. We also find the verbs *yixiang* 憶想 (327c22) and *yinian* 憶念 (328a9) in the instructions, both seeming to mean "imagine" or "remember."

70. *WMCJ*, T.619:15.326a15 and b20, 327c29, 328a15, c2, and c14. This opposition follows normal Chinese grammar, which clearly distinguishes between attempted and completed sensory perception (as does English: *look* versus *see*, *listen* versus *hear*). This is true in literary Chinese (Geaney 2002, 41) and modern vernaculars (*kan* 看 versus *jian* 見 or *kanjian* 看見). Chinese Buddhist texts *translated* from Indic languages, which can mark such contrasts by verbal inflection, often fail to make these distinctions. We find cases, for example, where *jian* and *guan* translate, in the same text, identical underlying phrases (Ōminami 1975, 235–236).

71. The *Yogalehrbuch* presupposes similar ideas about the visionary scenes it describes (Bretfeld 2003).

72. 教觀自身，令復轉明淨。教觀一佛齊中。若言我見佛齊中，光出遍至四方極遠之處，一切諸佛悉上光住。是十七事。教尋光觀。若言我見無量人，於光中現悉受決[>快]樂。是十八事。(*WMCJ*, T.619:15.329c3–7)

verb *guan* to much analysis aimed at clarifying its meaning as a particular kind of mental activity distinguishable from that indicated by similar verbs such as *nian* 念 (bring to mind), which also appears frequently in the instructions in the *Five Gates*.[73] Those seeking the origins of what is imagined to be the distinct approach of "Pure Land" Buddhism in particular have often claimed that *guanfo* (觀佛), a more traditional form of meditation, should be sharply distinguished from *nianfo* (念佛), a distinctly *non*-meditative, devotional practice of intoning the Buddha's name.[74]

Whatever their importance in the doctrines of some later Japanese Buddhist sects, these contrasts have little validity when projected onto fifth-century Chinese Buddhist literature. The *Five Gates*, at least, shows no interest at all in distinguishing the nuances of these verbs of meditative action. Indeed, there is nothing in the text that could falsify any particular English translation of them, be it a seemingly precise psychological term such as "visualize," a verb of unspecified mental action such as "think," or even a word designating a broader mode of action such as "recite."[75] Making such distinctions is not possible because the criterion the *Five Gates* proposes for judging when, say, the action of "contemplating" has been successful is not the generation of a particular psychological state—"contemplating" as opposed to "thinking" or "mentally intoning"—but the subsequent occurrence of a vision, one whose correctness is a matter of its *content*, that is to say, its object. Taking the example at hand, to know if one has correctly "contemplated the navel of the buddha," according to the *Five Gates,* one should attend not to the nature of "contemplating" as a particular form of mental activity, but to the object one then sees in a subsequent vision of light emerging from the navel of that buddha.

The third and most important assumption the *Five Gates* seems to hold about confirmatory visions is that they may be treated as divinatory in character. This is so precisely because the causal connection between these visions and the techniques that produce them was thought to be relatively obscure:

The master should say: "Go to your seat. Concentrate your mind on your forehead and single-mindedly bring to mind the buddha."

When the practitioner does this, images of the buddha appear from his forehead, from one to uncountable numbers. If the buddhas seen by the practitioner emerge from his forehead, go a short distance away from him and then return, the instructing teacher should know that this person is someone who seeks [the path of] the voice-hearer (*śrāvaka*). If [the buddhas] go somewhat far away and then return, he is someone who seeks [the path of] the solitary buddha

73. Yamabe 1999b, 158–184; Yokota 1999.

74. Ōminami 1975; Myōjin 1993a; 1993b; A. Andrews 1993, 18–19.

75. For a consideration of how the verb *guan* might sometimes point to ritual recitation, see Sharf 2001, 166; and Mai 2009, 237–239.

(*pratyekabuddha*). If they go very far away and then return, he is a person of the Great Vehicle.[76]

Here variations in the resulting vision, presumably based on karma from past lives, indicate the meditator's proper path, as did the vision that confirmed the nun Tanhui's affiliation with the Mahāyāna path in the story recounted at the beginning of this chapter. This is precisely the type of information that could be disclosed, according to other contemporaneous sources, by traditional methods of divination, such as by withdrawing a Buddhist sutra at random from a case and judging from its contents.[77] In this passage, the *Five Gates* does not make clear what if any practical consequences the divination will have, but in another passage it suggests that such divinations can determine the initial meditation technique a student should pursue:

> The gate of impurity. When a diligent practitioner comes to the master, before giving him any teachings the master should instruct him to sit in his meditation cell for seven days. One who has affinity [for the contemplation of impurity] will feel, within his body and his navel, a tingling sensation. He will see his own body clearly, and on his left toenail[78] a white drop of water will appear, like a pearl. The practitioner should then get up from his seat and tell the master what he has felt.[79]

Here the meditator's "affinity" (*yuan* 緣)—a term often implying a prior karmic connection—for the contemplation of impurity is divined by means of the visions and bodily sensations experienced after seven days of solitary meditation for which no particular instructions were provided.

That a teacher must in some way divine the appropriate meditation method for the student is a well-known idea in Indian Buddhist literature, and we will see further examples of it in the meditation treatises of Zhyi discussed in the next chapter.[80] What I want to note for now is simply that in relation to how meditative visions are produced, what they are like, and how

---

76. 師言，汝還本坐。係念額上一心念佛。爾時額上有佛像現，從一至十乃至無量。若行人所見多佛，從額上出者，若去去身不遠而還者，教師當知此是求聲聞人。若小遠而還者，求辟支佛人。若遠遠而還者，是大乘人。(*WMCJ*, T.618:15.325c17–326a2). See also *WMCJ*, T.619:15.326a6–7, which is similar.

77. *GSZ*, T.2059:50.344a12–14.

78. The *Yogalehrbuch* similarly mentions the toe*nail* as the starting point for the contemplation of the body (Schlingloff 1964, 86).

79. 不淨門。行者善心來詣師所，未受法時，師教先使房中七日端坐。若有緣者，覺身及齊有瞤動相，自見己身明了，左足大指爪上有白露如珠。行者從座起，以所覺白師。(*WMCJ*, T.619:15.326b19–22)

80. Often, the sign is an element of the meditator's disposition, body, or external behavior, including things like the smell of the meditator's sweat or the texture of his skin (*ZCSM*, T.15:613.271a6–c1; Ñāṇamoli 1991, 101–109). Using features of a practitioner's reported meditative experience to select an appropriate future meditation technique is a less commonly found idea, but we do see a version of it in Buddhaghosa's commentary to the *Vibhaṅga*, albeit

they are interpreted, the *Five Gates* makes no clear distinction between visions taken to be divinatory signs and those understood as marking meditative attainment or progress. That this is so invites a comparison of Buddhist meditative experiences, as understood in texts like the *Five Gates*, with a wider range of religious phenomena in medieval China, including similar forms of "visionary divination" in Daoism (Andersen 1994) or the interpretive practices and strategies surrounding other semiotically charged experiences such as dreams and deathbed visions. I will return to such a comparison later in this chapter and in greater detail in the next chapter.

To sum up, the dialog format of the *Five Gates* instantiates an understanding according to which confirmatory visions provide the metric for all aspects of meditative attainment. This format gives scant attention to practical techniques of meditation per se or to the psychological attributes a practitioner ideally obtains. The *Five Gates* is, certainly, not incompatible with meditation treatises in which such things—how one should meditate or what mental or bodily factors characterize advanced states of meditation—are the main topic of discussion. But its primary concern lies elsewhere. Above all, it asks and then answers the *semiotic* question of *what are the signs* that someone has reached a noteworthy, nameable, or otherwise classifiable level of attainment. While more traditional Buddhist meditation texts such as the *Meditation Scripture* and *Visuddhimagga* do touch on answers to this question in the limited context of the attainment of the first *dhyāna* or access concentration, this concern becomes the main event in the *Five Gates*, where meditation is described primarily as a sequence of obtaining, reporting, and interpreting the many strange visions that will be visited on meditators, on whose basis their achievements can be known.

Confirmatory Visions in the *Chan Essentials*

Of all the fifth-century Chinese *chan* scriptures, it is the *Chan Essentials* and its companion text the *Methods for Curing* that are arguably the most significant for assessing the development of Buddhism in China. This is because these texts were not directly translated from Indic originals but were composed, at least in large measure, by an author or authors whose primary access to the Buddhist tradition was through Chinese-language sources. They therefore help make clear which ideas and norms concerning Buddhist meditation were being actively taken up by the Chinese audiences interested in these topics during this era. Originally circulated as a single document, the two texts reached their present form sometime between 420 and 454. The versions of them we have today were apparently first written

---

only as pertains to a choice between particular sub-methods of "bodily mindfulness" (*Sammohavinodanī*, 250–252; Ñāṇamoli 1987, 310–312).

down, in the year 454, at a nunnery on the outskirts of the southern capital of Jiankang.[81]

Unlike the *Meditation Scripture*, the *Chan Scripture of Dharmatrāta*, or the *Five Gates*, which were rarely cited in later times, the *Chan Essentials* and *Methods for Curing* were frequently consulted when Chinese authors of the fifth through early eighth centuries sought canonical information about the practice of *chan*. Their emblematic significance during this era is well illustrated by a partially surviving sixth-century local Buddhist monastic code that cites passages from the *Chan Essentials* as the primary canonical proof of the necessity and benefits of meditation (Tsukamoto 1975, 295). This text's inclusion among the Buddhist scriptures carved onto cave walls at the Grove of the Reclining Buddha (Wofoyuan 臥佛院) in Anyue county, Sichuan, shows that it retained its prominence well into the Tang dynasty.[82]

That the *Chan Essentials* and *Methods for Curing* enjoyed a more exalted status than the other fifth-century *chan* scriptures is no doubt in part because they, unlike their peers, were written as actual sutras. The opening sections of the *Chan Essentials* even claim that the occasion it records was the first time the Buddha taught his monks to meditate.[83] The desire to bestow this kind of pedigree on understandings of Buddhist meditation that had previously circulated as either the noncodified teachings transmitted by Indian *chan* masters then active in China, or as translations of Indian meditation manuals not themselves framed as the Buddha's own words, was undoubtedly a key motivation for the composition of these texts.

Though the *Chan Essentials* differs from the other texts surveyed above in terms of literary genre, from the perspective of its content it is patently similar to the *Five Gates* in its concern with correlating concrete visions with the attainment of particular states of meditation and other formal milestones on the path to liberation. Unlike the *Five Gates*, however, the *Chan Essentials* also includes detailed information about actual methods of meditation. The most important of these techniques, and one that serves as a convenient place to explore this text's basic approach to the semiotics of confirmation, is the "white bone contemplation" (*baigu guan* 白骨觀), a version of the classical Buddhist contemplation of impurity (*aśubha-bhāvanā*).[84]

The beginning stages of this exercise are set out in the first section of the text, where the Buddha instructs a monk named Kauṣṭhilananda:

---

81. This event is recorded in the colophon collected by Sengyou to the *Chan yao mi mi zhi bing jing* 禪要祕密治病經 (*CSZJJ*, T.2145:55.66a24–b2), a text that I argue originally included both the *Chan Essentials* and the *Methods for Curing*. For more details, see *Secrets of Buddhist Meditation*, chap. 4.

82. For these and other examples, see *Secrets of Buddhist Meditation*, appendix 1. On the Wofoyuan carvings, see "Rewriting the Scriptures at the Wofoyuan" in Chap. 5.

83. *Chan Essentials* 1.1.10 (*CMY*, T.613:15.244b12–13).

84. "White bone contemplation" is a Chinese designation for a form of the *aśubha-bhāvanā* in which the meditator imagines his skeleton emerging from beneath the rotting flesh of his body. This Chinese term does not appear to translate a specific Indic word, but the method itself is well attested in Indian sources (Abe 2014).

Fix your thoughts on the tip of your left big toe. Carefully contemplate one segment of the toe. Imagine it swelling. Carefully contemplate it until it is very clear. Then imagine the swelling bursting open. When you see the first segment [of bone beneath], make it extremely white and pure, as if glowing with white light.[85]

The Buddha then tells Kauṣṭhilananda to "imagine" (*xiang* 想) the flesh stripping away from the white bones of each successive bodily segment, proceeding up the legs to the ribs, chest, and arms.[86] The meditation continues into the interior of the head, passing through the skin, membranes, brain, and brain channels, then down the throat to the viscera, within which lives a mass of bodily worms (*Chan Essentials* 1.1.5). He is then to imagine vomiting up his internal organs, leaving behind only a skeleton.

After a brief narrative interlude in which Kauṣṭhilananda follows these instructions and quickly becomes an arhat (1.1.9–10), the Buddha continues preaching, now to a generic "practitioner." The practitioner must, the Buddha says, repeat the process described previously, ending with a vision of his own skeleton, and then imagine a gradually increasing number of skeletons until he sees them fill the entire world (1.2.1.3). He must then imagine his own body under a number of horrific guises, as a broken, crumbling skeleton (1.2.2.1), as a corpse whose flesh becomes "dark and oozing, like fatty meat scorched by the rays of the sun" (1.3.1), as a bloated corpse (1.4.1), and so on. In contrast to the terse commands of the master in the *Five Gates,* in these and other similar passages the *Chan Essentials* provides elaborate, detailed instructions complete with visually rich descriptions of the forms that practitioners must meditatively imagine their own bodies as taking.

Yet, despite the intricate descriptions, the *Chan Essentials* ultimately subordinates the specific meditative techniques to the same semiotic question— what are the signs that confirm meditative attainment? Consider, for example, the final passage of the section described above in which the meditator, after imaginatively vomiting up his internal organs, is left seeing only a pure white skeleton. Here is the full account of this process, with what I take to be the important junctures numbered:

> (1) Further contemplate your small intestine, liver, lungs, spleen, and kidneys. Make them all liquefy and flow into your large intestine, then out your throat and onto the ground.[87]
>
> (2) When this meditation is complete, you will see (即見) on the ground [a heap of] shit, urine, and bodily worms crawling all over each other. Pus and blood flow from their impurity-filled mouths. When this meditation is complete, you will see yourself as a complete, snow-white skeleton.

---

85. 先當繫念著左脚大指上，諦觀指半節。作泡起想。諦觀極使明了。然後作泡潰想。見指半節，極令白淨，如有白光。(*Chan Essentials* 1.1.1; *CMY,* T.613:15.243b27–29)

86. *Chan Essentials* 1.1.2–3 (*CMY,* T.613:15.243c4–18).

87. In the *Chan Essentials,* "large intestine" (*da chang* 大腸) points to what we would call the "stomach."

(3) If you [instead] see a yellow or black skeleton, you must further repent your transgressions. (3b) Having repented your transgressions, you will see the remaining skin fall from your bones, forming a pile on the ground that grows gradually to the size of a begging bowl. It grows larger still, becoming as big as a large urn, until it is as big as a tower.....

(4) Four *yakṣa*-demons suddenly (忽然) spring out of the ground, their eyes flaming and their tongues like poisonous snakes. Each *yakṣa* has six heads, and each head is different—one like a mountain, the others like the heads of a cat, a tiger, a wolf, a dog, and a rat. Their hands are like those of an ape. The tips of each of their ten fingers are poisonous snakes with four heads, one spraying water, one spraying dirt, one spraying wind and one spraying fire.....Their horrid appearance is truly frightful. These four *yakṣa*s then stand in a line before the practitioner, each bearing on its back the nine kinds of corpses.

(5) The Buddha said to Kauṣṭhilananda: "This is the initial confirmatory vision of the meditation on impurity" (不淨想最初境界).[88]

The opening sections of this passage are clear enough: (1) the meditator actively "contemplates" (*guan*) his internal organs and then imagines them flowing out onto the ground. This meditation will be complete when (2) the meditator "sees" (*jian*) the vomited-out impurities, as well as his own skeleton, now pure white. However, an alternative is also presented. Instead of a pure white skeleton, the meditator might instead see (3) a yellow or black skeleton (i.e., one not yet fully free of its skin). This is a sign that the meditator must now carry out a ritual of repentance, whose successful completion will be marked by further visions in which the skin that clung stubbornly to the skeleton falls off completely. As in the *Five Gates*, this passage presents the meditator's vision of a white or yellow skeleton not as something he calls to mind by "visualizing" it, but as a quasi-divinatory sign indicative of meditative attainment or *lack* of attainment, with the requirement of additional actions (a ritual of repentance) in the latter case. The final passage (4) describes the last vision in similar terms: as an elaborate happening of dramatic proportions, arising suddenly and unexpectedly, that (5) serves as the confirmatory vision (*jingjie*) of the first stage of the contemplation of impurity.

Thus, while the *Chan Essentials* does devote attention to explaining the techniques that meditators should use to direct their minds, its most elaborate passages are not prescriptive in intent but *descriptions* of the many intricate visions that meditators will obtain. These visions, as described in the text, lack any clear phenomenological continuity with the practices that produce them, yet they are nevertheless considered the true signs of the successive, formally named levels of meditative attainment. This logic operates throughout much of the remainder of the *Chan Essentials*. The self-proclaimed tenth contemplation instructs the meditator to first follow the basic white

---

88. *Chan Essentials* 1.1.6–8 (*CMY*, T.613:15.244a5–24).

bone contemplation and then imagine his own body as a detached skeleton whose joints have come undone. But then:

> When he has obtained this contemplation, he will spontaneously see, out beyond all the skeletons, something that resembles a great ocean, calm and pure. His mind being clear and sharp, he sees various multicolored lights in all directions. Seeing these things, his mind becomes spontaneously peaceful and happy. His body and mind become pure, free of distress, and full of happy thoughts.[89]

The experience that certifies this attainment, formally named the "contemplation of the detached bones" in the next section, is again a vision whose content could never have been predicted from the meditative procedure whose success it confirms. We also see, in this passage, an additional element of what we might more broadly call the "confirmatory experience": a sudden feeling of bodily and mental calmness and happiness. This plainly recalls the nonvisionary signs of *dhyāna* in Kumārajīva's *Meditation Scripture* discussed earlier. The *Chan Essentials* does not, then, entirely neglect the more traditional semiotic ideology according to which meditative attainment is to be confirmed by directly experienced states of body and mind, but it does relegate it to a few brief lines here and there.

In the *Meditation Scripture,* only one clear example of a confirmatory vision was given: the previously imagined "white bones radiate light" (白骨流光), indicative of the attainment of the first *dhyāna*. Interestingly, the *Chan Essentials* takes up this same image in the eleventh contemplation. Here the meditator is instructed to first imagine the bones of his skeleton detaching (as in the tenth contemplation), and then to imagine white light radiating from the gaps. This is not the end, however:

> When he attains this contemplation, he will suddenly see a sixteen-foot buddha within this sunlight. Its halo measures eight feet horizontally and eight feet vertically. Its body is golden, radiating white light all over, brilliant and majestic. Its thirty-two major marks and eighty minor marks are each distinctly apparent.[90]

While obtaining this vision is not the end of the meditator's work, it is an initial sign of the attainment of what is eventually named the "contemplation of the radiant light (流光) of the white bones." Once again, we see that the content of the confirmatory vision is distinct from the initial object of contemplation. This example may also illustrate a more general pattern in which something that an earlier tradition had considered to be a confirmatory

---

89. 得此觀時，當自然見諸骨人外，猶如大海，恬靜澄清。其心明利，見種種雜色光，圍繞四邊。見此事已，心意自然安隱快樂，身心清淨無憂喜想。(*Chan Essentials* 1.10.2; *CMY*, T.613:15.247c28–248a2)

90. 得此觀時，當自然於日光中，見一丈六佛，圓光一尋左右，上下亦各一尋，軀體金色，舉身光明，炎赫端嚴。三十二相，八十種好，皆悉炳然。一一相好，分明得見。(*Chan Essentials* 1.11.2; *CMY*, T.613:15.248a12–15)

vision (the radiant light of the bones, in the *Meditation Scripture*) is later incorporated into a set of prescribed practices.[91] The overall logic has not changed, however, for in the *Chan Essentials* the vision that signifies attainment is now something new as well, and there still is a gap between what the meditator is told to do and what must be experienced in order to confirm attainment.

Taken as a whole, the *Chan Essentials* devotes the greatest part of its space and attention to describing the precise content of the visions that confirm the many stages of attainment it names and numbers. By the time we have reached the twelfth contemplation, these visions are of epic proportions. One extended example is worth citing in full, if only to convey a sense of their scope:

> When this meditation is complete,[92] the practitioner will see that within his heart there is a poisonous dragon. The dragon has six heads, and it wraps itself around his heart seven times. Two of its heads breathe out water, two breathe out fire, and two breathe out rock, while wind blows from its ears. From the pores of its body ninety-nine poisonous snakes emerge.... The water spewed forth by the poisonous dragon emerges from the practitioner's feet and flows into the white water. [The water] gradually expands in this manner until he sees a full *yojana*[93] of water. After filling one *yojana*, two *yojana*s are filled. After two *yojana*s, it continues like this until the entire continent of Jambudvīpa is filled. When all of Jambudvīpa has been filled, the poisonous dragon emerges from his navel, slowly crawls upward, and enters his eye. Emerging from his eye, it perches atop the crown of his head.
>
> Then, within the waters, a great tree appears whose canopy spreads in all directions. Without leaving the practitioner's body, the poisonous dragon touches the tree with its tongue. On the tip of its tongue appear eight hundred demons, some of them holding boulders above their heads [ready to throw], with snakes for hands and legs like dogs. There are other demons with the head of a dragon, each of their pores a flame-shooting eye, hundreds of thousands of which cover their bodies. Their teeth are like blade mountains, and they swarm about on the ground. There are other demons, each with ninety-nine heads and ninety-nine hands. Their heads are hideous, like those of dogs, jackals, raccoons, cats, foxes, and rats. Around the neck of each of these demons hangs a monkey. These evil demons play in the waters, some climbing up the tree and leaping about and launching themselves into the air frantically.
>
> There are also *yakṣa*-demons, their heads aflame. The monkeys try to ex-

---

91. Shinohara (2014) has observed something similar in later Tantric ritual manuals, which often instruct practitioners to visualize things that in earlier versions of the same ritual were said to be visions that confirm the ritual's success.

92. This refers to section 1.12.5, in which the meditator was instructed to imagine an image of the buddha within the flames that had appeared in a previous vision.

93. A *yojana* is usually a unit of *length,* on the order of several miles, not area. The sense is perhaps "out to a distance of a *yojana.*"

tinguish these flames with water, but they are unable to control them and instead make them increase. The raging fires approach the crystal pillar within the waters and suddenly flare up, burning the crystal pillar until it is like molten gold. The flames spread, wrapping around the practitioner's body ten times and then rising above him like a golden canopy, like nets spread out across the top of the tree, forming three layers in all.

Suddenly, an evil demon of the four elements appears on the ground, with hundreds of thousands of ears out of which pour water and fire. From the pores of its body small particles of earth rain forth, and it spews a wind that fills the universe. There also appear eighty-four thousand *rākṣasa*-demons, lightning shooting from their pores, each with fangs one *yojana* long. All these creatures romp and play within the waters. From the mountains of fire tigers, wolves, lions, leopards, and other beasts emerge, and they too play within the waters.

When the practitioner sees these things, each of the skeletons, filling the entire universe, raises its right hand. Then the *rākṣasas* stab the skeletons with iron pitchforks and collect them into a pile. At that moment skeletons of nine different colors, in tightly packed rows, come before the practitioner.

There are many other hundreds of thousands of confirmatory visions (*jingjie*). They cannot be described in full.[94]

None of this remarkable scene is said to be anything the practitioner should try to visualize, imagine, or otherwise bring to mind. Rather it is a description—a partial one, as the text ultimately admits—of the visions produced by a meditator's attainment of the "contemplation of the earth, fire, wind, and water elements," which visions are therefore the signs of that attainment.

The appearance of elaborate confirmatory visions in the *Chan Essentials* is not limited to cases in which the prescribed meditative practice involves visually rich acts of imagination. In the twenty-sixth contemplation, the meditator must calm his mind and "vow" (誓願): "May I not be reborn again! May I not undergo any future existence!"[95] A vision then appears of a pond of golden water, in which he sees a tree growing with four fruits on it that seem to represent the four "fruits" (*phala*) of traditional Buddhist soteriology, toward which the meditator has now drawn near. Again the *Chan Essentials* does not explain in any way the forces or mechanisms, psychological or otherwise, that produce this vision. What it apparently wants its readers to think is relevant is rather that *this* is the vision that will appear when the vow to escape rebirth—the making of which is represented as a kind of meditative technique—has been done successfully.

Confirmatory visions also occur in the wake of entirely discursive meditation practices. In the eighteenth contemplation, the meditator reflects

---

94. *Chan Essentials* 1.12.7 (*CMY*, T.613:15.248b26–249a19).

95. 願後世[>不]生，不受後有。(*Chan Essentials* 3.26.11; *CMY*, T.613:15.261b6–7). See also *Chan Essentials* 2.19.2.3 and 3.26.2 for similar examples.

(*siwei* 思惟) on the conditioned nature of anything one might posit as a permanent self:[96]

> As for me, is my hair my self? My bones? Nails? Teeth? Are form, feelings, perceptions, or consciousness my self?...Is the self within the corpse? It is eaten by worms, so how could it be the self? Nor can the living person be the self, since thoughts do not stand still, and in this life no mental state endures permanently.[97]

This kind of meditation on non-self would be stylistically at home in early canonical Buddhist meditation literature. But here in the *Chan Essentials* it is immediately followed by a concrete vision—the meditator sees his own body transformed into a transparent, crystalline substance—that confirms that the meditation has been completed.[98]

Examples such as this occur throughout the *Chan Essentials,* often when the meditator is directed to reflect on the emptiness of a previously experienced vision that is somehow problematic.[99] In the fourteenth contemplation, after seeing the universe filled with skeletons, the meditator experiences great fear (1.14.3). This fear is manifested (we might even say *confirmed*) in a terrifying vision of a horde of threatening demons (1.14.4). At this point, the meditator must contemplate the emptiness of the skeletons and also his own body by way of a typically discursive, doctrinal analysis: he reflects that these things are falsely imagined to be real and are in truth merely the contingent coming together of the four elements or five *skandha*s (1.14.5). Once again, the meditator's success in this exercise is confirmed by a vision, one in which these abstract realizations are given concrete form:

> When he has produced these thoughts, the white skeletons shatter into dust, forming a pile on the ground like a snow-covered mountain. As for the other skeletons of various colors, they are suddenly eaten up by a giant snake. On top of the mound of white snow there is a white-jade person, his body straight and imposing, thirty-six *yojana*s tall, with a neck as red as fire and white light glowing in his eyes. The various white waters and crystal pillars all suddenly enter the crown of the white-jade man's head. The many dragons, demons, vipers, snakes, monkeys, lions, and cats all run in fright.[100]

---

96. In the *Chan Essentials,* the verb *siwei,* a common semantic translation of *chan* in medieval Chinese Buddhist texts, consistently refers to discursive meditation on Buddhist doctrinal truths. See the notes to *Chan Essentials* 1.2.2.2.

97. 如我今者，髮是我耶，骨是我耶，爪是我耶，齒是我耶，色是我耶，受是我耶，想是我耶，識是我耶…若死是我者，諸蟲唼食，散滅壞時，我是何處。若生是我者，念念不住，於此生中，無常住想，當知此生亦非是我。(*Chan Essentials* 1.18.4; *CMY,* T.613:15.252b27–c6)

98. *Chan Essentials* 1.18.4 (CMY, T.613:15.252b27–c27).

99. In addition to the passages discussed below, see also *Chan Essentials* 1.6.3, 1.14.6–7, 3.26.15, 4.31.19–20, 4.31.23–24, and 4.31.28–29.

100. 作是念時，諸白骨人，碎散如塵，積聚在地，如白雪山。眾多雜色骨人，有一大虵，忽然吞食。

Following this vision, the meditator must further reflect on "the emptiness of all *dharmas*" by considering that even the four elements and five *skandhas*— the very categories by which he previously meditated on the emptiness of the skeletons and his own person—arise from causes and therefore lack any substantial essence (1.14.6). This meditation, in turn, is confirmed by further visions that unfold an extended narrative concerning the great tree "whose canopy spreads in all directions," which had first appeared in the long vision cited above (1.12.7), and a herd of black elephants seeking to uproot it (1.14.7). The eventual destruction of the tree of defilements figures prominently in the visions immediately preceding the meditator's final attainment of arhatship.[101]

The Semiotics of Meditative Experience

In proposing that what confirms progress toward Buddhist liberation and sainthood (the destruction of the mental defilements) is a series of visions of a team of elephants uprooting and destroying a giant tree, the *Chan Essentials* deploys a semiotics of meditative experience that I will call *symbolic*. In using this term, my point is not that we need to read the *Chan Essentials* as if it were speaking in code, nor do I suggest that we should construe its references to the destruction of the tree as mere symbols standing in for its true concern, namely, the destruction of the defilements. Rather, by "symbolic" I aim to characterize a key facet of the semiotic ideology that the *Chan Essentials* is both reflecting but also authorizing when it asserts that this kind of experience (a concrete but enigmatic vision) is capable of signaling these kinds of things (meditative attainment).

Specifically, I will use the word "symbolic" in the tradition of Peirce, who distinguished as *icon, index,* and *symbol* the three different "grounds" of signification, that is, the different ways that a sign can be taken, by the one who takes it as meaningful, to relate to its object. An icon, in this understanding, is a sign referring to its object by way of resemblance—for example, a photograph, when viewed as conveying someone's physical appearance. An index is something with a causal, temporal, or spatial connection to its object—a gray hair, when taken as a sign of the age of the person on whose head it grows. Finally, a symbol is a sign produced in conformity with a rule or convention— the word "cow," taken to mean the common domestic animal because it is presumed to have been spoken or written following the conventions of the English language. In keeping with how Peirce has been read by anthropologists,

---

於白雪山上，有一白玉人，身體端嚴，高三十六由旬，頸赤如火，眼有白光。時諸白水并頗梨幢，悉皆自然入白玉人頂。龍、鬼、虵、虺、獼猴、師子、狸猫之屬，悉皆驚走。(*Chan Essentials* 1.14.5; *CMY*, T.613:15.250b5–11)

101. See *Chan Essentials* 1.17.2, 1.17.4, 1.18.2, 1.18.8, 1.18.12, and 1.18.18. In section 1.18.8, the roots and branches of the tree are destroyed leaving only the heartwood. The narrative is taken up again at the end of the fourth sutra (4.31.13, 4.31.27), where the tree is finally destroyed and the meditator obtains arhatship.

I take the trichotomy of *icon, index,* and *symbol* not as objective properties of particular signs but as a way of characterizing how signs are actually used in given communities. In this perspective, signs are not constituted by themselves, but must be taken as such in particular ways (Hanks 1996, 45–48). To investigate "semiotics" in this sense is not, therefore, to subscribe to the idea of a rigid and abstract code of signs or symbols within which the natives remain trapped, unable to see the water in which they swim. Rather, it is to recognize and explore the way that signifying practices—how do we know who is an arhat, after all?—are matters that are brought to bear in real, social worlds and are themselves objects of self-awareness, as well as debate and contestation, on the part of those who use them (Keane 2018, 76).

That the *Chan Essentials* asks us to take meditative experiences as *indexes* is the first thing to note. The vision of the destruction of the tree is claimed to have a real connection to the attainment of arhatship across several dimensions: it is caused by it, it co-occurs with it temporally, and it is linked to it "spatially" as an experience that happens *to* the person who has become an arhat. However, meditative experiences, as the *Chan Essentials* describes them, are not only indexical in this sense. Here the contrast between the "iconic" and the "symbolic" proves a useful tool of analysis: in claiming that the sign of arhatship is a vision of the destruction of a tree, the *Chan Essentials* proposes that the index of arhatship is *symbolic* (but *not* iconic) inasmuch as the relevant experience does not resemble arhatship itself, a state formally characterized in doctrinal literature in terms of internal, psychological qualities like perfect freedom from mental defilements and so forth.

This distinction between the iconic and the symbolic also helps us discern what is at stake in the other accounts of confirmatory visions we have surveyed above. Thus while the *Meditation Scripture* claims that a vision of the glowing light of white bones is a sign of the attainment of the first *dhyāna,* the first *dhyāna* itself is defined not as a matter of white bones and glowing light but as a specific state of the meditator's body and mind comprising bliss, joy, and mental concentration. Here the relationship between the sign (glowing bones) and what it means (the attainment of *dhyāna*) is symbolic to the extent that it is self-consciously obscure to at least some degree. The kaleidoscopic confirmatory visions that fill the pages of the *Chan Essentials,* and to a lesser extent the *Five Gates,* positively revel in a now patently obscure relationship between their content and what they indicate. It is this obscurity that the word "secret" (*mi* 祕) in the full title of the *Chan Essentials* perhaps hints at, amounting to the claim that even if you know what *dhyāna* is in all its details, by having learned its precise characteristics from scriptures or doctrinal compendia, you will not know, without further knowledge or initiation, that *these* experiences are its signs.

In all of the texts surveyed here we do also find examples where meditative attainments are claimed to be signaled in a more "iconic" fashion. Apart from the glowing white bones, the *Meditation Scripture* also proposes two other signs of *dhyāna,* namely, bodily bliss and mental concentration, qualities of the meditator's experience that directly partake of aspects of the state of *dhyāna* itself as it is normatively defined. The *Chan Essentials* too at times says that given attainments will be accompanied by preternatural calm, bodily bliss, mental concentration, or insight into Buddhist truths.[102] Although in isolation such passages might imply that meditative attainment is a matter of indubitably knowing for oneself the bodily or psychological transformations that characterize such attainment, in texts such as the *Chan Essentials* and *Five Gates* they are far outnumbered by the lengthy descriptions of mysterious visions placed within a structured path of progress. The very form these texts take as serial listings of an almost endless variety of visionary experiences is made possible by, and when taken as authoritative could in turn be productive of, a distinctly symbolic semiotics of meditative attainment in which confirmatory experiences are not constrained by resemblance to what they confirm.

In the *Chan Essentials* especially, we can, however, occasionally hazard a guess as to why a particular visionary image may have been thought to indicate a given attainment. Presumably the enormous tree reaching from the bottom of the universe to its summit, whose progressive destruction tracks the meditator's progress, instantiates the mental defilements (*kleśa*) that, according to Buddhist doctrine, bind one to rebirth.[103] (Some doctrinal sources indeed compare the mental defilements to a tree that liberation uproots.)[104] Similarly, when the visions associated with the attainment of stream-entry include an eighty-eight-headed snake being consumed by fire (3.26.14), we may surmise that this image is connected to the Sarvāstivāda doctrine that the stream-enterer permanently severs eighty-eight of the ninety-eight defilements.[105] In these examples, abstract doctrinal claims concerning the ontology of particular stages of the path to liberation seem to have been transmuted, or we might say *objectified,* into concrete visions whose appearance is then asserted to be the true sign that the relevant attainments have occurred.[106] Sometimes, our sources even provide for their obscure images an explicit interpretation. In one passage in the *Five Gates,* for example, the meditator contemplates a skeleton and then has a vision of a "bright star" surrounded by "golden orbs." It is then explained that "the star is the confirmatory vision (*jingjie*) of purity; the golden balls are the confirmatory vision of wisdom," the implication seeming to be that these

---

102. See, e.g., *Chan Essentials* 1.3.3, 1.6.3, 1.15.2, 3.21.11.2, 3.23.1, 3.26.1, and 3.27.4. There are also a few passing references to purely external signs of confirmation such as a pleasant bodily smell (3.21.10) or a peaceful countenance (3.21.11.2; 3.29.2).

103. The first vision of the tree is eventually called the "confirmatory vision of the ninety-eight defilements" (九十八使境界; *Chan Essentials* 1.12.8; *CMY,* T.613:15.249a23; see, similarly, *GFSMH,* T.643:15.657b26–28).

104. *Apidamo da piposha lun,* T.1545:27.238b7.

105. *Apitan ba jiandu lun (Jñānaprasthāna),* T.1543:26.811a2–3; *DZDL,* T.1509:25.300c25–27.

106. Something similar can be found in many Tantric Buddhist rituals (Rambelli 2013, 167–171).

visions are the signs of the meditator's successful development of the named qualities.[107]

Apart from a few isolated cases such as this, however, the import of the visions that fill the pages of these texts remains obscure even as they often seem designed to tempt one's inner hermeneute into action. In the *Chan Essentials*, it would be pleasing to think that the visions of the black elephants— four and then eight in number (1.17.2), they "shake" the tree of the defilements (1.18.17), after which "adamantine beings" burn the tree partially (1.18.18) and then entirely (4.31.27)—have some connection to the claim found in one doctrinal compendium that the *dhyāna*s (four or eight in number) shake the mountain of the defilements while the "adamantine *samādhi*" destroys it.[108] Also, when canonical Buddhist similes for emptiness— wild horses, foam, the leaves of the trunk of a plantain tree—are presented not as similes but as concrete visionary objects in a number of passages, we might suppose that the seeing of these things is a sign that the meditator has gained insight into this fundamental Buddhist principle.[109] The number fourteen, we notice, makes several seemingly significant appearances—a crystal pillar with fourteen levels (1.12.6), a *maṇi* jewel suspended by fourteen threads (1.14.8), fourteen adamantine wheels (4.31.26)—that might have some connection to the "fourteen stages of sainthood" that are mentioned in passing in the *Chan Essentials* but not explained in detail (4.31.3).[110] With

---

107. 星者明淨境界。金丸者智慧境界。(*WMCJ*, T.619:15.326c9–10). In another passage, the student sees a buddha holding a glowing beryl staff, and the master then explains that the staff is the "sign of concentration" (定相) while the light is the "sign of wisdom" (智慧相; *WMCJ*, T.619:15.326a12–13; see also 326c7–8 and 326c15–16). For other explicit interpretation of obscure visionary images, see *Methods for Curing* 1.9.6 and *DMDL*, T.618:15.322c12. These examples where explicit interpretation is given seem similar to the *Yogalehrbuch*'s use of the terms *nimitta* and *adhipatirūpa* ("embodiment," in Schlingloff's translation) to link specific visionary images to doctrinally important categories (Ruegg 1967, 165).

108. *DZDL*, T.1509:25.218b4–8. The defilements are compared to a mountain at *Methods for Curing* 1.14.14 (*ZCB*, T.620:15.340a12). On the adamantine *samādhi* in Chinese sources, see Buswell 1989, 104–115.

109. *Chan Essentials* 1.3.3, 1.15.2.5, 1.16.1, 3.24.1 (see also *Methods for Curing* 1.4.2). "Wild horses" (*yema* 野馬), a term drawn from early Chinese literature, often translated Skt. *marīci* meaning illusion or mirage (Zhu 1990). The *Yogalehrbuch* contains a passage in which similes for emptiness become concrete visions (Schlingloff 1964, 97–98).

110. These may refer to the "seven stages of the worthy (七賢) and seven stages of the sage (七聖)" that Zhiyi says are explained in the "Abhidharma" (*Mohe zhi guan*, T.1911:46.30c28–29). The "seven stages of the worthy," according to this and other explanations, are the well-known sequence of attainments ranging from the five preliminary meditation methods up through the four *nirvedhabhāgīya*s of "heat," "summit," "patience," and "highest worldly *dharma*s" (*Ren wang bore jing shu*, T.1707:33.319c2–5). The "seven stages of the sage," meanwhile, is a classification of the attainments at the level of stream-enterer and above, found in Sarvāstivāda sources (*Apidamo jushe lun*, T.1558:29.131b16–19). These fourteen levels do align, roughly, with the attainments described in the *Chan Essentials*. Pace Zhiyi, I have not found any extant *Indian* Buddhist literature available in Chinese translation that combine these two lists into a single set of fourteen. A different list of fourteen stages mentioned in the writings of Jizang 吉藏 (549–623) includes the ten bodhisattva stages (*Fa hua yi shu*, T.1721:34.461b19–20).

somewhat more certainty, we can surmise that the vision of seven flowers radiating a light that beheads six poisonous dragons (3.26.4) is a sign of the meditator's development of the so-called seven factors of awakening (*bodhyaṅga*).[111] But the cases where we can give even speculative interpretations such as these are in the minority. Far more common, in both the *Chan Essentials* and the *Five Gates*, are visionary scenes whose ordered progression and accumulation of small details carry an aura of greater but unspecified meaning, such as an early passage in the *Chan Essentials* (1.2.1.3–4) where the meditator sees a row of skeletons who each raise their right hand, then both hands, and finally point all ten fingers at the meditator.

It would, of course, be dangerous to assume that imagery that remains obscure for us was intended to be so for the original audiences of these texts. Yet we need not rely only on our own subjective sense: in the master-disciple dialogs of the *Five Gates*, the meditator must tell the master about his vision before its meaning is made clear, giving us reason to think that in fifth-century China, too, it was presumed that meditators would not or should not know the significance of their visions. Given that the confirmatory visions of the *Five Gates* operate similarly to the counterpart sign in the *Visuddhimagga*, it is noteworthy that on one occasion the *Visuddhimagga* suggests a similar understanding of how meditators will come to know the significance of their experiences:

> And when the [counterpart] sign has appeared in this way, the monk should go to the teacher and tell him: "Venerable sir, such and such has appeared to me." But the teacher should say neither "this is the sign" nor "this is not the sign"; after saying "So it has, friend," he should tell him: "Go on giving it attention again and again." For if he were told "it is the sign," he might stop short at that, and if he were told "it is not the sign," he might get discouraged and give up.... [The foregoing] is what the *Dīgha* reciters say. But the *Majjhima* reciters say that he should be told: "This is the sign, friend. Good man, keep giving attention to your meditation subject."[112]

Here we see that attainment of the counterpart sign was considered highly consequential, so much so that some might stop short after having attained it. But more than that, the *Visuddhimagga* also assumes that what counts as the counterpart sign would not be self-evident even to one who truly obtains it.

It is worth clarifying here that the issue is not the problem of *representation*—it isn't that the outside observer cannot know the subjective experience of the meditator. The problem is one of hermeneutics: the significance of a meditative experience whose defining feature is its content, not its qualia, can only

---

111. The *bodhyaṅga* are mentioned explicitly at *Chan Essentials* 3.26.6. Indian Buddhist texts sometimes compare them to flowers (*Da bannihuan jing*, T.376:12.870b7–10; *Shi zhu piposha lun*, T.1521:26.91b13–15).

112. *Visuddhimagga*, 286 (translation by Ñāṇamoli 1991, 278, with slight modifications).

be understood by someone with the requisite knowledge, and that someone need not be the meditator. Notice further that the welter of details that the *Visuddhimagga* had earlier presented concerning the psychological or somatic transformations attendant upon reaching "access concentration" do not here play any obvious role in the interpretive process. Such details were not meant, apparently, to provide prospective meditators with a reliable means of knowing when they had reached this state. Indeed, not only are meditators not assumed to be able to judge their own attainment, but those who can so judge must sometimes hide this fact from the person it concerns. It is, in short, possible to be an accomplished meditator without knowing it.

Although this sketch of how meditative visions are experienced and then interpreted is derived from an analysis of formal meditation texts—documents whose circulation and readership were undoubtedly restricted—these same ideas also informed the way meditation and its results were imagined in genres of literature nominally aimed at a wider audience. According to the biography of the fifth-century nun Tanhui, discussed at the beginning of this chapter, she experienced several unusual meditative visions early in her career. The biography depicts these events as if Tanhui herself were aware of their significance as they occurred. However, an earlier record of Tanhui's youthful meditative attainments, found in the *Records of Signs from the Unseen Realm,* implies a rather different relationship between the meditator, her experiences, and the process through which the significance of those experiences was communicated. In this version, Tanhui had begun her practice of meditation long before she became a nun. At the age of six she was meditating by herself:

> Whenever she meditated, she effortlessly attained confirmatory visions (*jingjie*). However, she did not understand what these were, thinking they were only dreams. Once, when sharing a bedroom with her elder sister, she entered trance (*ding*) during the night. Her sister found her between the folds of a screen, and her body was like wood or stone, drawing no breath. The sister became alarmed and roused the household. Together they shook her, but she did not wake until morning. They hurried to consult various male and female shamans, who all said that Tanhui was possessed by demons. But when Tanhui turned ten, the foreign *chan* master Kālayaśas came to the region of Shu [where they lived]. She asked him about what she had seen [while in trance], whereupon [Kālayaśas] and the nun [Fayu][113] realized that Tanhui already had attainment in *chan*, and so they encouraged her to ordain as a nun.[114]

---

113. Tanhui's later teacher Fayu, mentioned just below, is the likely referent here.

114. 年七歲便樂坐禪。每坐輒得境界，意未自了，亦謂是夢耳。曾與姊共寢，夜中入定，姊於屏風角得之，身如木石，亦無氣息。姊大驚怪，喚告家人，互共抱扶，至曉不覺。奔問巫覡，皆言鬼神所憑。至年十一，有外國禪師罝良耶舍者來入蜀。輝請諮所見，耶舍尼，以輝禪既有分，欲勸化令出家。(*Fa yuan zhu lin*, T.2122:53.453a20–26). For a slightly different translation of this passage, see Campany 2012, 224.

As in the idealized master-disciple dialog of the *Five Gates,* Tanhui's meditation produced *jingjie,* confirmatory visions whose significance she did not
immediately understand, mistaking them for dreams. Only when she describes their content to the famous *chan* master Kālayaśas does she learn of
her own meditative attainment.[115]

Meditation texts such as the *Chan Essentials* and *Five Gates,* together with
stories such as that of Tanhui, claim something more than the proposition
that meditative experiences require external signs of confirmation. Nor is
it merely that we, removed historically and socially from these settings, can
see as culturally, linguistically, or otherwise determined experiences that
our sources present as direct or unmediated. It is, rather, that even ideal
meditative experiences here are overtly *communicative* events. These events
are not valuable because of what they are—the point is not that these are
veridical perceptions that prove the reality of an object whose existence was
previously doubted—but because of what their occurrence is a sign of with
respect to the one who experiences them. That even ideally these signs
require a nontrivial interpretation not governed by mere resemblance—that
they are symbolic rather than simply iconic—is not something these sources
try to hide, but the core of what they actively claim. Indeed this claim arguably serves to justify their own existence, reproduction, and circulation as
repositories of the knowledge necessary for making the appropriate interpretations. Likewise, perhaps, with the *chanshi,* the meditation master who
now appears not primarily as a teacher of meditation techniques but as a
skilled interpreter of reports by others concerning their own meditative experiences. Such a role for the *chan* master is foregrounded in the story of
Tanhui, where it stands in contrast to the mistaken hermeneutics of the
shamans, who judge the case on the basis of Tanhui's external behavior
alone.[116] In this respect, the *chan* master is akin to the authoritative figure in
early Chinese literature whom Steven Van Zoeren (1991, 63–68) calls the
"moral-hermeneutical adept," the ethically or spiritually cultivated person,
Confucius being the archetypal example, whose own status is revealed
through the ability to discern the true, hidden character of other people by
accurately reading the signs of their appearance, speech, or behavior.

The knowledge that a *chan* master must wield in order to be a moral-
hermeneutical adept in this sense is, accordingly, the same kind of information that forms the substance of the *chan* scriptures that emphasize visions,
such as the *Five Gates* and *Chan Essentials.* If, as Sven Bretfeld (2015) cogently
suggests, the classical Buddhist *mārga* treatise is a literary genre that gives
narrative meaning to Buddhist doctrine by setting each aspect of it within a

---

115. Kālayaśas was later remembered as the translator of the *Amitāyus Contemplation
Scripture.*

116. Profound trance from which one cannot be roused (*nirodha-samāpatti*) is disparaged
in many Buddhist doctrinal sources (Sharf 2014a). In Chinese Buddhist hagiography, however,
it is usually a mark of meditative prowess (see, e.g., *BQNZ,* T.2063:50.940b28–c1).

timeless story of meditative progress from ordinary being to liberated saint, texts such as the *Five Gates* and *Chan Essentials* can be said to do just the opposite: they provide the tools that enable the particular, concrete experiences of individual meditators to be deemed instances of something normatively valuable. Rather than explaining where within an ideal meditator's experience each normative doctrinal truth will be realized, these texts explain what normative attainment a given concrete experience is the sign of. Seen in this light, these texts are neither descriptions of the experiences of past meditators nor prescriptions designed to produce or inculcate normatively sanctioned experiences, but something akin to handbooks for the interpretation of meditative experience.[117]

The Affordances of a Semiotic Form

There appears to be a history to the ideology—again, in the sense of *self-reflexivity*—in which Buddhist meditative attainment is communicated through symbolic visions, and to the corresponding need for textual or other repositories in which the meanings of such visions are explained. As we have seen, texts such as the *Chan Essentials* and *Five Gates* assume that symbolic confirmatory visions are the general means of verifying attainment at all stages of the meditative path. The *Chan Scripture of Dharmatrāta* and also the fragmentary Sanskrit meditation manual found in Central Asia known as the *Yogalehrbuch* (though its dating is less clear) show that such ideas were to at least some degree inherited from Indian or Indic traditions that must have been part of the teachings of the many foreign *chan* masters plying their trade in China at this time.[118] But those traditions themselves may not have been particularly ancient. Although the *Meditation Scripture* and the *Visuddhimagga* reveal that similar ideas were known across a wide swath of fourth-century Indian Buddhism, they invoke confirmation by symbolic vision only in the case of the initial attainment of the first *dhyāna*. And it is difficult to find clear traces of these ideas in demonstrably earlier sources. The term "counterpart sign" (*paṭibhāganimitta*) that refers to such visions, for example, is not attested in Pāli sources earlier than the canonical commentaries, whose final compilation was contemporaneous with the composition of the *Visud-*

---

117. Handbooks of this nature are regularly used in the *borān kammaṭṭhāna* traditions of Southeast Asia; see Bernon 2000, and also Jordt 2007, 67–70, in reference to the rather different tradition of Mahasi Sayadaw in contemporary Burma. Fully exoteric, publicly available texts about meditation also can serve this function in practice, as does, for example, the *Amitāyus Contemplation Scripture* in an anecdote reported by Charles Jones (2004, 277) from contemporary Taiwan.

118. On the connections between fifth-century Chinese meditation texts (including the *Five Gates, Chan Essentials,* and Contemplation Scriptures) and the fragmentary Sanskrit meditation text known as the *Yogalehrbuch* (meditation manual) after the title of Schlingloff's 1964 edition, see Yamabe 1999b, 60–72 and 300–352.

dhimagga.[119] There is also some evidence that the *Visuddhimagga*'s approach to the counterpart sign might have been relatively novel, as the *Vimuttimagga*, a key source for the *Visuddhimagga*, uses the word *paṭibhāganimitta* but *not* in connection with the attainment of access concentration.[120] Early Chinese translations may attest to a similarly timed shift. The Indian meditation texts translated into Chinese prior to the turn of the fifth century do not discuss the idea that the initial attainment of *dhyāna* will be confirmed by visions.[121] These sources do not necessarily tell us what kinds of interpretive practices surrounding meditative attainment were in use on the ground. Still, it is significant that only in the late fourth century, judging by the sources we have, does the confirmation of meditative attainment by symbolic confirmatory visions come to be a regularly occurring part of formal Buddhist meditation literature.

But regardless of the precise timing, the emergence of these ideas and their associated practices must be placed against the backdrop of broader trends in the visual and religious cultures of India across the first centuries of the common era. As many scholars have noted, the growing prominence of physical images of deities and their worship during this time, along with other changes in material and literary culture, was paralleled by an increasing presence of visions and visual events in written accounts of higher religious goals and practices.[122] This sea change in religious culture must have been accompanied by new understandings of the aims of even traditional forms of Buddhist meditation. Still, the notion that significant meditative attainments are confirmed by symbolic visions does not necessarily conflict with classical models of the Buddhist path, which as we have seen most often do not explicitly frame themselves in semiotic terms: characterizing the first *dhyāna* as a moment when "the mind is concentrated," they do not tell us if this an account of the ontology of the first *dhyāna* or a description of what

---

119. Cousins 1973, 120. Cousins also tries to locate a canonical precedent for the *paṭibhā-ganimitta* in the *Uppakilesa-sutta* (*Majjhima-nikāya*, 3:152–162; *Zhong ahan jing*, T.26:1.532c9–539b11; see also Stuart 2017, 140–142). Yet the term is not used in that text, and the Pāli commentaries explain the passage with reference only to the "divine eye" gained by mastery of *dhyāna* (Anālayo 2011, 736n251). The issue, as I see it, is not whether pre-commentarial Pāli texts propose that *dhyāna* can sometimes lead to visions—clearly, they do—but whether they also hold up such visions as the key evidence of meditative attainment in general, which I think they do not.

120. On the *Vimuttimagga* (I use the conventional Pāli reconstruction of its title), see Crosby 1999 and Anālayo 2009. In it, the *paṭibhāganimitta* (彼分相) is contrasted with the *uggahanimitta* (取相) as a mental representation of the original external object that can be generated at will, without returning to the original, external object (*Jie tuo dao lun*, T.1648:32.413c19–29). Access concentration is mentioned only later.

121. Greene 2016a, 137–139. I know of only one instance of these ideas within the voluminous Sarvāstivāda and Vaibhāṣika *abhidharma* sources translated into Chinese, from the *Nyāyānusāra* of Saṅghabhadra (fl. late fourth or fifth century) in connection with the contemplation of impurity (*Apidaomo shun zheng li lun*, T.1562:29.672a3–6).

122. Beyer 1977; Kinnard 1999; McMahan 2002; Harrison 2003; Gethin 2006; Rotman 2009; White 2009, 83–121; Gifford 2011; Hatchell 2013; Anālayo 2015.

kind of experience provides evidence of the first *dhyāna*.[123] What sets the literature discussed in this chapter apart relative to earlier Buddhist accounts of meditation is its explicitly hermeneutic focus, its self-reflexivity regarding the question of how one should use meditative experiences as evidence of meditative attainment and its privileging therein of a symbolic, visionary semiotics.

In addition to having a history, the semiotic ideology of meditative experience that texts such as the *Chan Essentials* reflect, endorse, and furnish tools for had certain *affordances*—certain things became possible, though not, surely, inevitable, when the principal evidence of meditative attainment consisted of symbolic visions.

Paintings of Meditative Attainment

One such affordance was a new way of artistically representing meditative attainment and those who reach it. In caves 20 and 42 of the Toyok grottos near the city of Turfan, the Central Asian polity that arguably became the westernmost site of significant Chinese cultural influence (Hitch 2009), we find several sets of murals that depict, in tiered registers along the side walls, meditating monks before whom a variety of unusual objects appear (figs. 2–5).[124] The precise content of these scenes is often obscure. But aided by a few inscriptions and careful textual study, scholars such as Miyaji Akira and Yamabe Nobuyoshi have established their connection to the fifth-century *chan* scriptures that mostly strongly emphasize visions, such as the *Chan Essentials* and *Five Gates,* as well as to the closely related and more famous Contemplation Scriptures.[125] Yet the murals do not precisely match any known text in either their content or arrangement. This could indicate, as Yamabe has proposed, that the paintings and texts both derived, via different routes, from Buddhist traditions local to Turfan, which has long been suspected, based on written historical records, of being the site where these fifth-century texts reached their final form.[126] We do not know why, by whom, or even pre-

---

123. Kate Crosby (2013, 54) has similarly noted that despite their novel elements, the *borān kammaṭṭhāna* meditation traditions do not actually contradict canonical Theravāda treatises such as the *Visuddhimagga.*

124. Cave 1 originally had comparable imagery, and Stein and Grünwedel describe two other similar caves (Miyaji 1995a, 18). A few small images from Stein's cave have been preserved (F. Andrews 1948, plate IX).

125. Miyaji 1995a; 1995b; 1996; Yamabe 1999a; 1999b; 2002; 2004; 2014. See also Lai 2002 and Ning 2007.

126. Yamabe 1999b, 497; 2002, 140–141; 2004, 405. Yamabe, however, must assume without evidence that if the texts *had* been written elsewhere and then imported to Turfan, they would have been authoritative and the murals would have followed them closely. This is debatable. The texts themselves admit to providing only a partial account of the full range of authoritative visions (*Chan Essentials* 1.12.9, 2.19.2, 2.20.13, 3.27.5; *CMY,* T.613:15.249a19, 252b22, 255a1–2, 262b1; *WMCJ,* T.619:15.329a8–9). A community that held these texts as authoritative might have had reasons for producing paintings of similar but different visions. In general, the Buddhism of Turfan owed as much or more to Chinese influence from the east as it did to Indic influence

cisely when these paintings were made, although they are usually dated between the fifth and seventh centuries (Ning 2007). Nor do we know the usage, actual or intended, to which the images, or the caves in which they appear, were put—that the paintings are about meditation does not necessarily mean that they or the caves they ornament were used for meditation practice itself.[127] But we need not answer such questions to find noteworthy what the paintings accomplish simply *as paintings*—that they give objective form to a multiplicity of meditative attainments and by extension a wide variety of accomplished meditators, each confirmed as such by a different concrete vision.

That these are indeed paintings of meditative *attainment* (rather than prescriptions for meditative practice in any straightforward way), and that they are, accordingly, visual counterparts to the descriptions of confirmatory visions in texts such as the *Five Gates* and *Chan Essentials,* is made clear by the partially visible top register on the left wall of cave 20 (figs. 2 and 3) and the well-preserved top two registers on the right wall of this same cave (fig. 5). Here we find images of monks sitting in meditation posture with external displays of miraculous power such as emitting fire or water from their bodies and riding on a variety of flying animals.[128] The images of the meditating monks and their visions in the lower registers are presented together with the miracle-performing monks of the upper registers in a single, coherent grid. These images are thus evidently all meant to show the same thing: monks who have reached some kind of attainment. The upper registers illustrate this with depictions of external miracles, particularly the emission of fire and water that were the standard way of artistically differentiating the realized saint from an ordinary monk (Waldschmidt 1930). But in the lower registers, the Toyok paintings give tangible form to other modalities of accomplishment, to "*chan* masters" experiencing visions of unusual but precisely defined content.[129]

When significant meditative experiences are visionary signs as opposed to realizations of abstract truths or the experience of psychological states, they become translatable into visual form *as such*—a nontrivial point given

---

from the west (Hansen 1998, 37). New traditions and texts created in central China in the early fifth century could easily have been imported to Turfan at a later date.

127. Sharf 2013. Yamabe (2010) argues cogently, on architectural grounds, that only the smaller, side rooms of cave 42 (and *not* cave 20, which has a different layout) could have been sites for seated meditation practice.

128. Miyaji 1995b, 20–21. The motif of monks riding flying animals derives from an episode in the *Sumāgadhāvadāna,* from whose narrative it was eventually divorced, in both art and literature, to become an independent way of depicting meditative attainment (Yamabe 1999a, 42–43).

129. The inscriptions in cave 20 all read "practitioner" (行者), but two inscriptions from Stein's cave read "*chan* master" (F. Andrews 1948, plate IX; Miyaji 1995a, 38). Though of limited thematic diversity, the Central Asian images of monks meditating on skulls, skeletons, or corpses also manage to depict the content of meditation itself (Feugère 1989; Miyaji 1992, 427–430; Greene 2013; Howard and Vignato 2015, 108–109).

Figure 2. Toyok cave 20, left wall, upper registers. Meditating monks experiencing visions of what appear to be flaming or jeweled trees emerging from ponds of water. Line drawing by Miyaji Akira.

that classical Buddhist art never had a means of depicting the precise moment of the Buddha's awakening.[130] And, perhaps more important, it becomes possible to distinguish pictorially a spectrum of possibilities, different in form but equally marks of status-bearing attainment, attributed to individuals who outwardly bear no obvious signs of sanctity. In this connection, we may suspect that at least part of the intention of the Toyok paintings was to hint that the community of monks and nuns conceals a similarly diverse contingent of realized meditators. (While the small distinguishing details in the paintings—the cut of monks' robes, the kind of chair they sit on, and the style of their shoes—surely do not identify specific individuals, they do effectively serve as signs of the specificity that individuals have.) In this way, a symbolically oriented semiotic ideology of meditative attainment affords a diversity of material representations of such attainment, which diversity is available to be made into an icon of the breadth of the attainments of the living monastic community.

The *Chan* Master as Moral-Hermeneutical Adept

When meditative attainment is confirmed by symbolic visions, there is no longer, even ideally, a necessary link between the phenomenology of a given meditative experience and the nature of the attainment it confirms. On the one hand, this means that we cannot necessarily know, from our knowledge

---

130. The defeat of Māra and / or the earth-touching gesture are the usual stand-ins for this moment (Bautze-Picron 1998). Yet strictly speaking the defeat of Māra is not the awakening proper, which occurs only later, when the Buddha realizes the four noble truths or the teaching of *pratītyasamutpāda*, events that do not easily admit visual depiction.

Figure 3. Toyok cave 20, left wall, detail. The partially surviving Chinese inscriptions to the two lower figures describe the meditators' visions using language similar to passages from the *Amitāyus Contemplation Scripture*. Photo courtesy of Miyaji Akira.

Figure 4. Toyok cave 42, right wall. The meditating monks here and elsewhere in cave 42 are shown gazing at a great variety of strange visions. In contrast to cave 20 (figs. 2, 3, and 5), in cave 42 there are no inscriptions, but Yamabe (1999a) has shown that many of the scenes depicted are vaguely similar to visions described in the *Chan Essentials*. Line drawing by Miyaji Akira.

Figure 5. Toyok cave 20, right wall. Each of the three registers shows distinctively rendered images of saintly monks. In the top register, the monks ride flying animals. In the middle register, flames and jets of water emerge from their bodies, revealing their meditative attainment. The two visible scenes in the bottom register show monks experiencing visions associated with the contemplation of impurity: a bloated or blue-colored corpse on the left, and one being picked at by a bird on the right; both corpses appear to be women. *Xinjiang shi ku: Tulufan Bozikelike shi ku*, pl. 170.

of how given meditative attainments are described doctrinally, what kinds of experiences those seeking those attainments might have hoped for or been encouraged to seek or report. But perhaps more important, it also means that meditative experiences can be accepted as events whose occurrence is disclosed only through the first-person report of the meditator, even as interpretive authority over these events is entrusted to someone else.

This kind of separation is entailed by the master-disciple dialogs of the *Five Gates* and is instantiated in the endless variety of unusual visions in the *Chan Essentials*. It also underlies the story of Tanhui in the *Records of Signs from the Unseen Realm*, a tale that not only elevates Tanhui to the status of an accomplished meditator but also construes the ideal *chan* master—Kālayaśas, in this case—as the wielder of unique interpretive skills relative to first-person accounts of meditative experience.[131] This understanding of the *chan* master as a "moral-hermeneutical adept" is also seen in the biography of the fifth-century meditation teacher Sengyin, which records the following interaction between Sengyin and a student of *chan* who "had some attainment" (頗有所得) and reported it to him:

> Sengyin then said to him: "In what you are practicing there should occur an unusual confirmatory vision (*jing*).[132] If you obtain it, then this means you will gain whatever rebirth you wish." Cultivating without cease, [the monk] indeed had an unusual experience. He told Sengyin about it. Sengyin gave him a warning counsel: "With this attainment you will certainly obtain happiness in the future, [i.e., rebirth in the Pure Land,] but unfortunately your present life is slated to come to an end." The monk was delighted, saying, "I have long wished for rebirth in the Western Land [of Amitāyus]!"[133]

In this record, Sengyin's prowess as a *chan* master consists not in his own meditative attainments, which are only briefly noted in the biography's introduction, but in his ability to correctly interpret someone else's meditative experience. Sengyin's prediction of a good rebirth combined with an early death is most peculiar. Narratively, it is clever in that it allows for the prediction to prove true when the monk's death is described in the ensuing lines. But it also shows us that the compilers of his biography did not think their audience would assume that Sengyin was basing his judgment on a personal familiarity with the experience in question.

---

131. For another story in which someone (a ruler) turns specifically to a *chan* master when seeking to assess the sanctity of other monks, see *GSZ*, T.2059:50.392c18–19. That the *chan* master in this story remains nameless suggests that it was this status in particular that was deemed narratively relevant.

132. *Jing* 境 is here seemingly synonymous with *jingjie* 境界, used earlier in the biography in reference to Sengyin's own attainments.

133. 印語之曰，上坐所學，應得異境。若得，便能隨願往生。修之不已，果值異應。即以告印。印戒之曰，此法乃將來美事，然脫不幸大命應終。此僧欣然曰，由來願生西方。(*Meisōden shō*, Z.1523:77.355c24–356a1)

Many similar anecdotes are told about Zhiyi (538–597), whose influential treatises on meditation inherited key ideas from the fifth-century *chan* scriptures, as we will see in the next chapter. According to Zhiyi's early biography, while still a student of the *chan* master Huisi (515–568) he on one occasion entered a deep state of meditative trance (*ding* 定). When he related the details of this experience to his teacher, Huisi replied: "Only you could have witnessed (*zheng* 證) this, and only I could have recognized (*shi* 識) it: the trance you entered is the [so-called] preliminary practice of the Lotus *samādhi*."[134] Although the specific things Zhiyi witnessed are not described, the mechanics of his interaction with Huisi—a first-person report followed by the master's identification of his meditative attainment as a named, canonically sanctioned achievement—tally with the master-disciple dialogs of the *Five Gates*. Zhiyi, after becoming the master himself, is said to have performed a similar interpretive feat when a monk asked him what it means when "someone enters trance and hears Mount She shaking." Zhiyi replies that it is a *bad* state of meditation and the monk, who confesses he was asking about his own experience, marvels that other Buddhist teachers had been unable to explain it.[135] Yet another tale of meditators who "witness" things but do not know their significance appears in the biography of Zhiyi's disciple Facong 法彥 (d. 611).[136] After he had entered a state of trance that lasted seven days, Facong "told his teacher everything he had witnessed" (具向師說所證法相), whereupon someone overhearing his report interjected that these things correspond to the second of the "eight *vimokṣas*," a set of canonical meditative attainments that are described in great detail in Zhiyi's treatises. It would seem that Zhiyi's meditation manuals, like the *chan* scriptures, could also serve as repositories of the information needed by those whose job was to interpret the experiences reported by others and assign them a place within a normative hierarchy of attainments.[137]

Personal Experience and Institutional Authority

Across various kinds of sources from fifth- and sixth-century China we find endorsed a semiotic ideology of Buddhist meditative experience that emphasizes the confirmatory power of symbolic vision and proposes that the signs of meditative attainment are at once personal experiences known only

---

134. 非爾弗證非我莫識。所入定者法華三昧前方便也。(*Sui Tiantai Zhizhe da shi bie zhuan*, T.2050:50.192a5–6). The word I translate as "witness," *zheng* 證, is used in Chinese Buddhist literature from as early as the Han dynasty to render *sākṣāt-karoti* 'to witness,' but also in other contexts connected with meditative or other Buddhist attainment (Karashima 2010, 634–635).

135. *Sui Tiantai Zhizhe da shi bie zhuan*, T.2050:50.192b8–12. Cf. Andō (1973, 438), who takes this as a question by the monk about someone else.

136. *XGSZ*, T.2060:50.571a17–18. On Facong's biography, see Ōmatsu 2016, 200.

137. Later versions of this episode make Zhiyi the one who explains the meaning (*Fa hua zhuan ji*, T.2068:51.59c12–18; *Fo zu tong ji*, T.2035:49.198b4–9).

to the meditator *and* events whose meaning and consequences require authoritative interpretation. The individuals who produced, read, and circulated the documents and artifacts I have discussed in this chapter undoubtedly had their own localized agendas for doing so. But from a more general perspective, the approach to meditative experience these sources articulate can be seen as having the strategic function of maintaining the plausibility of Buddhist meditation as a means of producing living saints in the face of institutional skepticism concerning personal claims to authority and unsanctioned attributions of such authority.

I take it as self-evident that *both* these forces have been in operation throughout Buddhist history—that even as those wielding the levers of institutional authority were, for obvious reasons, reluctant to allow individuals to simply declare their own attainment of what were sometimes called "superhuman states" (*uttarimanuṣyadharma*), to deny meditation all independent authority would have been neither plausible in theory, given the centrality of individual meditative attainment to the mythos of Buddhism, nor sustainable in practice. Indeed, that the authors of normative Buddhist disciplinary literature tried to regulate personal declarations of attainment, making it a transgression to declare one's attainment to laypeople, for example, shows us not the success of the Buddhist church in institutionalizing the charisma of the individual yogi but rather a persistent anxiety about its failure to fully do so.[138]

Given these opposing imperatives, to hold that meditative attainment is communicated by a real, personal, indexical experience while simultaneously proposing that its full meaning is only legible in a symbolic manner unmoored from direct, iconic connection to what it denotes, is to permit—indeed, it is to demand—claims to meditative experience whose content is known only to the person in question while also constraining final authority over the significance of those claims to those with institutionally sanctioned access to the requisite interpretive knowledge. (Let us note, in passing, the parallels here with systematized *kōan* practice, in which the sign read by the master is an utterance or gesture indexically connected to the individual whose attainment is at issue, who must after all speak or perform it, even as it is ultimately judged, implicitly or explicitly, in light of a canon of correct responses codified in texts to which the meditator is not supposed to have access.)

Of course, all of this is so only ideally and in theory. In practice, meditators who reported unusual experiences may have had inklings small or large

---

138. For this reason, it is precisely backward, I think, to read the many episodes in the *vinaya* that depict monks devoted to meditation as buffoons or sexual deviants as meaning that such figures were *actually* held in low esteem when those stories were written, as Gregory Schopen, departing from his more usual against-the-grain hermeneutics, has suggested (2004, 26). Contemporary Buddhist societies certainly have no shortage of wildly popular monks and nuns whose charisma is attributed by their followers to their individual pursuit of meditation (Tambiah 1984; Rozenberg 2010).

as to what was expected or hoped for. The presence of publicly accessible images of significant meditative visions, such as those in the Toyok caves (at least potentially), should also be noted. And, of course, those doing the interpreting could, had they wished, surely have manipulated things based on other factors—it is hard to imagine that medieval *chan* masters did not occasionally use their interpretive authority to read the daydreams of their patrons as signs of spiritual attainment. Yet even given potential vagaries of usage, the normative ideologies concerning the mechanics of meditative experience and its interpretation that I have discussed above may have proven useful because they had the potential to conceal any such manipulation from all interested parties.

At this point it is worth returning to the parallels with divination that I have alluded to throughout this chapter. As a general rule, the results of divination can, of course, be manipulated. But its integrity as a means of communication with extra-human powers requires that such manipulation be concealed, even—perhaps especially—from those doing the manipulating. Most divinatory systems thus take as their sign something whose selection or production can be construed as beyond willful human interference. This can mean a product of chance such as the rolling of dice, or a pre-given aspect of the situation such as the lines of one's palm, or at the very least an object whose selection as the sign is not directly controlled by the interpreter, such as the Tarot card that is chosen not by the reader of the cards but by the one being read for.[139] Sincerity of this kind, however, is harder to achieve when access to the sign is mediated by, or simply is, an individual's own, nominally private experience. This may be one reason that human divinatory mediums are often children: not because children are more likely to have visions (whether they are or not is not the issue), but because their susceptibility to manipulation is concealed by their presumed lack of motive for dissimulation (Johnston 2001).[140]

In a similar way, the semiotic ideology of meditative experience advocated and instantiated in the meditation texts surveyed in this chapter makes possible a measure of sincerity. It makes it possible for meditators themselves, those tasked with evaluating them, as well as any third parties, to genuinely believe that attainment has been reached despite the obviously vested interests of the meditators themselves, whose reports alone disclose the sign.

---

139. As Luhrmann (2016, 6) observes, the Tarot card "is chosen by the one being read for, and that person believes the reading (if he or she believes) precisely because the reader does not control which cards are read." I would add that it is for this same reason that the *reader* believes his or her readings, something of equal importance for the long-term maintenance of the tradition. On the importance of chance in divination, see Morgan 2016 and 2018, 147–160.

140. The suitability of children for visionary encounters with the divine is, of course, not limited to the case of formal divination. Most of the famous Marian visionaries of the past few centuries have been children, to take but one example (Orsi 2016, 48). On child mediums in Tantric ritual, see Strickmann 1996, 217–236.

Because meditators do not know what a given vision means, their claims to have seen whatever they report can be trusted.[141] And because what the master interprets is not something he controls, being based on the meditator's personal report, and because the decoding follows protocols enshrined in texts or traditions that the master has (in theory) not himself invented, his judgments too can be seen as free from bias or manipulation, both by third parties and by the meditator. Both the meditator and the master can *sincerely* claim that meditative attainment has occurred even as both avoid full responsibility for the accuracy of this claim. Since standard tests of Buddhist sainthood, such as the ability to perform miracles, are of uncertain outcome in practice, this deniability may well have come in handy. Here again we may note the parallels with divination, which as anthropologists have sometimes theorized often functions to limit attributions of blame when, in a situation where objective evidence does not provide reliable guidance, groups must make important choices that have the potential to negatively impact the whole community, such as when deciding in which direction to set out on a hunt (LLoyd 1999, 155), or in our present case, deciding who is a master of meditation. A semiotic ideology of meditative experience in which symbolic visions are the currency, one that in early medieval China was given its necessary tools in texts such as the *Five Gates* and *Chan Essentials,* makes it possible for sincere claims of personal experience—those events the having-happened-to-me of which is not a point of dispute—to become socially relevant even while subjecting the implications of those claims to the constraints of a qualified master and canonical text.

---

141. It is noteworthy that the *Chan Essentials* takes a particularly hard line on the punishments that await those who report visions they have not actually experienced. In explicit contrast to the *vinaya,* where false but sincere claims (those made as a result of "pride") are *not* transgressions, the *Chan Essentials* says that even pride is no excuse and that any false report will lead to rebirth in hell (*Chan Essentials* 4.3.29). One reason for this distinction may be that what the *Chan Essentials* is prohibiting is the claim to have *seen some particular thing;* at this level of experience, wrong and insincere claims can only be one and the same.

3

Visions of Karma

THE STORIES OF monks and nuns known for their accomplishments in Buddhist meditation—figures like Sengxian, Daofa, Puheng, and Tanhui—have shown us that meditative attainment, for the authors and audiences of early medieval biographies and miracle tales, was something that could be verified by the experience of unusual visions. The evidentiary power of visions was also assumed by many of the fifth-century meditation texts known as the *chan* scriptures, especially those composed or compiled in China, which depict progress in meditation as a hierarchical sequence of named stages, each stage correlated with a distinct set of visions. These texts presented themselves less as manuals detailing the proper methods of meditation practice than as guidebooks for the interpretation of meditative experience, as repositories of the kind of knowledge that could allow someone to accurately read the enigmatic visionary experiences of individual meditators as signs of specific, normative meditative attainments.

But besides illustrating a particular understanding of what the experiential signs of meditative attainment are, these sources describe meditative experiences as taking place in specific contexts and serving particular ends. Sengxian's vision of the Buddha Amitāyus confirmed not only his status as a master of meditation but also his imminent rebirth in the Pure Land. Puheng's vision was a sign of his attainment of the fire-radiance *samādhi*, but it also "made quite clear to him the retribution of his karma from past lives."[1] Both of the visions attributed to the nun Tanhui—the glowing white light (in her biography) and the vision she mistook for a dream (in the *Records of Signs from the Unseen Realm*)—also seem linked to past karma, and the vision of the layman Liu Yimin was correlated, in an unspecified way, with the curing of his illness. These aspects of the stories point us to further questions concerning the place of Buddhist meditation socially and doctrinally in early medieval China. What, for example, was meditative attainment thought to accomplish? Why would anyone have thought meditation a worthwhile pursuit? And what consequences could have been expected from claims to meditative experience?

---

1. 先身業報頗亦明了。(*GSZ*, T.2059:50.399b22)

In this chapter, I argue not only that these questions can be answered but that we can do so without merely restating abstract doctrinal claims (e.g., that meditation leads to "enlightenment") or ignoring the insider perspective entirely (concluding, for example, that claims to meditative attainment were primarily exercises of social or institutional power). A preliminary sketch of how this can be done emerges from two further stories that show not only the kinds of experiences Buddhist meditation was thought to produce, but also the reasons those experiences might be sought.

Meditation as Divination

The fifth-century Chinese monk Daojin 道進, a disciple of the famous translator Dharmakṣema, was originally from the Northern Liang (北涼) kingdom, based in modern Gansu province. After the Wei invasion of 439, Daojin followed the Liang court west to Turfan and was later remembered as one of the first Chinese monks to receive the so-called bodhisattva precepts, a new and eventually widely popular form of Buddhist empowerment available to both monastics and laypersons (Funayama 1995, 14–21). But according to Dharmakṣema's biography in the *Biographies of Eminent Monks,* Daojin's first attempt to receive these precepts met with certain difficulties:

> Dharmakṣema said: "[To receive the precepts], first repent your transgressions." Daojin then repented assiduously for seven days and seven nights. On the eighth day, when he went to receive the precepts, Dharmakṣema suddenly became angry. Daojin thought: "This must be because my karmic obstructions have not yet been eliminated." He then exerted himself strenuously for three years, *alternating the practice of chan with rituals of repentance. Eventually, while in trance* Daojin saw Śākyamuni Buddha, together with many great beings, bestow the precepts on him.... He then went to Dharmakṣema to report what had happened. As soon as he arrived within ten paces of him, Dharmakṣema stood up suddenly and exclaimed: "Excellent! You have already been granted the precepts!"[2]

Daojin's story, historically important as an early account of the rituals associated with the bodhisattva precepts, also reveals certain assumptions about the practice of meditation.[3] Strenuous, long-term *chan* practice was apparently something one might do in order to purify one's "karmic obstructions" prior to undergoing such a ritual. The practice of meditation, moreover, was not purely incidental to this process of purification, whose mechanisms are

---

2. 讖云，且悔過。乃竭誠七日七夜。至第八日，詣讖求受，讖忽大怒。進更思惟，但是我業障未消耳。乃勵力三年，且禪且懺，進即於定中見釋迦文佛與諸大士授己戒法...進欲詣讖說之。未及至數十步，讖驚起唱言，善哉善哉，已感戒矣。(*GSZ*, T.2059:50.336c19–27)

3. On Daojin's story in the context of bodhisattva-precept rituals, see Yamabe 2005, 19–23. Kuo Li-ying (1994, 57–58) has noted how this story anticipates the systematic combination of meditation and repentance in early Tiantai.

not spelled out, for it is while he is immersed in meditative trance (*ding*) that Daojin eventually experiences the vision in which he receives the precepts.

The biography of Zhiyan 智嚴 (d. 427) shows that *chan* practice could be linked to other kinds of precepts as well:

> Before becoming a monk, Zhiyan had received the five precepts [of a layman] but had not maintained them perfectly. Later, he became a monk and received the full ordination, but he always harbored concerns that he had perhaps not actually obtained the [full monastic] precepts. He was on this account perpetually in fear. Though he practiced *chan* contemplation for many years, he was not able to become clear about this matter.[4]

Continuing to fear that his ordination as a full monk was invalid, owing to his earlier transgressions of the lay precepts, Zhiyan eventually journeyed to India where he met an arhat who helped resolve his doubts by traveling to the Tuṣita heaven in trance and asking Maitreya, who confirmed that Zhiyan did indeed "have" the precepts.[5] Taken as a whole, this story is primarily a testament to the anxieties felt in China in the early fifth century concerning the proper procedures for monastic ordination, anxieties undoubtedly triggered by the relatively recent appearance of full translations of the massive (and not always mutually compatible) Indian Buddhist monastic codes.[6] But the passing reference to meditation also reveals certain assumptions about why someone might carry out this practice: namely, that one might undertake *chan* practice in order to learn if one had the precepts or not. Here, meditation is not an activity that leads to religious purity, as we might have thought, so much as the medium through which the prior establishment of that purity might be revealed.[7]

That meditation might indicate, through its attendant visions, the presence *or* absence of the kind of purity normally procured through the repentance of sins—a purity often described as the absence of karmic obstructions—

---

4. 嚴昔未出家時，嘗受五戒，有所虧犯。後入道，受具足，常疑不得戒。每以為懼。積年禪觀而不能自了。(*GSZ*, T.2059:50.339c5–8). See also *CSZJJ*, T.2145:55.112c21–23

5. On the connection between meditation and the cult of Maitreya during this era, see Demiéville 1954, 378.

6. Funayama 1998, 272–273; Greene 2017a, 440–442.

7. Similar ideas may be implied by Daojin's story as well. Although the role that *chan* plays in his eventual purification is unclear in the version cited, a possibly earlier version of the tale in a different source says that Daojin's three years of strenuous practice was devoted entirely to "repentance" and the vision that confirmed his receipt of the precepts occurred not in meditation, but in a dream (*Pusa jie yi shu*, T.1811:40.568c7–13; see also *Fan wang jing pusa jie ben shu*, T.1813:40.605a24–b2). In other words, in the version of the story that includes meditation, what it replaces is not the process that generates Daojin's purity (the repentance) but the medium through which that purity is communicated (the dream). As Yamabe (2005, 23) suggests, this alternate version may have derived from Daojin's *Ming seng zhuan* biography, which is not extant but whose one-line summary specifically mentions the receipt of the precepts in a dream (*Meisōden shō*, Z.1523:77.362a10–11).

was a fundamental assumption not only of hagiographies and miracle tales but also of the technical Buddhist literature pertaining to *chan* that was composed or compiled in China during the fifth and sixth centuries. As I will suggest, this understanding can be seen as a semiotic instantiation of the foundational Buddhist doctrine that meditative attainment (*dhyāna* or *samādhi*) depends on purity with respect to the precepts (*śīla*). This doctrine is typically presented as a statement about the sequential relationship and mutual dependence of two key steps on the path to liberation. But in fifth-century China, it was additionally understood to sanction certain kinds of interpretive practice: that meditation depended on one's purity did not simply prescribe what was needed before one could meditate; it also meant that the visionary experiences produced by meditation could be *signs* revealing one's purity or lack thereof.

Chan could thus function as a kind of divination, and significant meditative experiences were understood to be occurrences whose phenomenology, as visions, and meaning, as potential signs of karmic purity, were nearly identical to events that could occur in dreams, deathbed rituals, and other domains. These parallels should force us to think carefully about the relationship between meditation and other aspects of Buddhism and the Chinese religious world more broadly. Although meditation was indeed thought of as the elite and normative Buddhist practice par excellence, this does not mean that its fruits pointed exclusively to the transcendent, immaterial, and nonlocalized realm of liberation or nirvana. They could be, and often were, interpreted in relation to materially and temporally instantiated ritual activities such as repentance, which was among the most widely practiced elements of medieval Chinese Buddhism and a space where the goals of Buddhism were articulated in terms compatible with many other forms of Chinese religion as well. This understanding of the social and semiotic functions of *chan* was widely if not universally shared—it was not only how meditation operated on the ground and was imagined in the miracle tales and popular literature of the day; it was also how it was analyzed in theory, both in canonical scriptures and in high-flown tracts of scholastic doctrine.

Zhiyi on Basic Meditative Experience

Arguably the most influential early Chinese writings on the topic of Buddhist meditation were those attributed to Zhiyi 智顗 (538–597). Although he is best remembered as the founder of the Tiantai school, whose identity as such emerged only after his death (Penkower 2000; J. Chen 1999), his meditation manuals were read, used, and adapted by later Chinese Buddhists of all affiliations. Modern scholars have most often approached Zhiyi's writings on meditation primarily as sources for gauging his individual creativity. However, these texts, particularly those dating from the earliest periods of his life, are equally if not more usefully seen as evidence of a widely shared approach to the practice of *chan* that had been developing in China since the early fifth century. Because these texts provide a systematic vocabulary concerning how meditation works and how the experiences it produces should be interpreted, they can help us assess the key moves that were made in the fifth-century *chan* scriptures that preceded them. For this reason I begin with them here even though these early Tiantai meditation texts are chronologically among the last episodes in the story this chapter tells.

Habit and Retribution in the *Sequential Approach*

Zhiyi's first major treatise on meditation was the *Elucidation of the Sequential Approach to the Perfection of Chan* (*Shi chan boluomi ci di fa men* 釋禪波羅蜜次第 法門). Tiantai doxographers and the modern scholars following in their train have tended to view the *Sequential Approach* as the product of a not-yet-mature understanding, a foreshadowing at best of Zhiyi's later, more creative masterworks.[8] Yet the very lack of "mature" Tiantai doctrines that has made the *Sequential Approach* less exciting for those interested in Zhiyi's own intellectual development renders it an invaluable source for an overview of broader, shared Chinese understandings (Fukushima 1965a). Indeed, whatever else it is, the *Sequential Approach* is notable as one of the few surviving treatises on Buddhist meditation authored in China before the seventh century.[9] From this perspective, the text of the *Sequential Approach* gains in interest even though many of its ideas are in fact shared by later Tiantai writings. With an eye to unearthing how Zhiyi drew on the same approach to meditative experience that informs many of the fifth-century *chan* scriptures, let us therefore look not to the abstract, overarching structures of the Buddhist path within which Zhiyi situated meditation and its fruits, but to the comparatively basic, though by no means simple, matter of the nature and meaning of the experiences that initially occur during meditation practice.

Zhiyi addresses this subject under the headings "the practice of calming"

---

8. Zhiyi's early biography encodes this interpretation of the text by dating its composition to several years before the secluded retreat where he supposedly attained awakening (*Sui Tiantai Zhizhe da shi bie zhuan*, T.2050:50.192c19–20; Satō Tetsuei 1961, 40–45; Shinohara 1992, 121). On Zhiyi's biographies, see Yamauchi 1986, 508–542. Important studies of the *Sequential Approach* include Andō 1957; Satō Tetsuei 1961, 103–127; Tada 1976; Asada 1978; Nitta 1981, 26–110; Muranaka 1986, 153–270; Aoki 1989; Ōno 1994, 111–128; and H. Wang 2001 (the only major English-language study). Unlike the *Mohe zhi guan*, which has several well-annotated modern Japanese translations and now a complete English translation (Swanson 2017), the *Sequential Approach* has only a single, essentially unannotated modern Chinese translation (Su S. 2006) and one still-in-progress modern Japanese translation (Ōno 2012).

9. Most of Zhiyi's writings survived only because they were preserved in Japan, from where they were reintroduced to China in the tenth century (Brose 2008). Many other meditation treatises by sixth-century authors were not so lucky, such as the *Zhi guan fa* 止觀法 of Sengchou 僧稠 (480–560) and the *Ci di chan yao* 次第禪要 of Zhiyi's own teacher Huisi 慧思 (*XGSZ*, T.2060:50.554c11; 564a16–17; T.1924, the *Da sheng zhi guan fa men*, attributed to Huisi, in fact dates to the seventh century or later; see Kashiwagi 1980, 235–264; Okimoto 1988, 195–201).

(止門) and "confirming roots of good and evil" (驗善惡根性), both situated in the section entitled "preliminary expedients" (前方便) that is arguably the heart of the treatise.[10] According to what Zhiyi says here, the first step in the practice of *chan* is to "calm" the mind through one of several possible techniques.[11] When successful, the practice of calming leads to "confirming roots of good and evil," an event Zhiyi describes as a sudden experience, good or bad, that is connected in some way to the meditator's deeds and thoughts from previous lives.[12]

With respect to the overall path to liberation, these initial experiences occur at an early stage, but Zhiyi clearly viewed them as being of great practical importance (Ōmatsu 2013). Indeed, in his elaborate ritual manuals for the "four forms of *samādhi*," usually regarded as the summit of Tiantai praxis, he presents exactly these same kinds of confirmatory experiences as what one might hope to obtain at the *conclusion* of the rites.[13] In the *Sequential Approach*, Zhiyi makes it clear that understanding their meaning when these experiences occur is essential for all further practice, and he duly presents a complex classification of their possible varieties.

First are what he calls the experiences that result from "outer" good roots. These, he explains, are the karmic residues of the five kinds of past good action: charity, keeping the precepts, obeying one's parents, venerating and supporting the Buddhist church, and reading the scriptures. These deeds, while good, are called outer because they are performed with a "non-concentrated mind" (*sanxin* 散心) and hence are distinguished from the inner, soteriologically superior good roots of the past practice of meditation. Once the meditator has calmed the mind, the existence of good roots of any kind is revealed by the sudden appearance of either visions or unusual mental states associated with the action in question. For the first of the outer good roots, those associated with past acts of charity:

---

10. *CDFM*, T.1916:46.491c2–505a6. On the structure of the *Sequential Approach*, see Sekiguchi 1969, 26–27. The "preliminary expedients" section, covering the basic practice of meditation and its initial fruits, and the "cultivation and confirmation" (修證) section, detailing the higher stages for each possible method of meditation, together make up the majority of the *Sequential Approach*. "Preliminary expedients" is divided into "external" methods (maintaining the precepts, regulating diet, sleep, and posture, and rejecting material desires), and "internal" ones describing seated meditation itself. The centrality of the "preliminary expedients" section is seen from Zhiyi's own *Lesser Calming and Contemplation* (*Xiao zhi guan* 小止觀), the most influential Buddhist meditation manual in all of East Asia, which is primarily a summary of it (Sekiguchi 1961, 40–42; Andō 1968, 272–279; Nitta 1981, 335–341). For a summary of the "internal" expedients section, see Fukushima 1965b.

11. Zhiyi lists three such methods: (1) "fixing [the mind] to an object" (繫緣), (2) "suppressing the arising of thoughts" (制心), and (3) "realizing the ultimate truth" (體真) of emptiness, which by eliminating false conceptualizations naturally calms the mind (*CDFM*, T.1916:46.492a21–b11).

12. *CDFM*, T.1916:46.494a6–12.

13. *Fa hua sanmei chan yi*, T.1941:46.954c1–955c4 (Stevenson 1987, 526–537); *Fang deng sanmei xing fa*, T.1940:46.947b28–948c9 (Stevenson 1987, 586–593).

It may be that the practitioner, sitting in tranquility, suddenly sees things such as various kinds of clothing, bedding, food and drinks, precious treasures, fields and gardens, ponds and lakes, or carriages and chariots. Or, as a result of this mental tranquility, the practitioner is suddenly able to let go of greed and practice charity, with no remaining stinginess. These are the manifestation of the signs associated with the two kinds of good roots—of habit (*xi* 習) and retribution (*bao* 報)—associated with acts of charity in either the present life or a past life.[14]

Zhiyi then gives similar accounts of the arising of outer good roots associated with other actions. In each case the typology is the same: the meditator experiences either a *vision* of objects or scenes associated with the act in question (in the above passage, these seem to be the objects that one gave as charity) or else the arising of the same wholesome *mental state* that accompanied the original action (a mind of generosity, in the example above). Zhiyi classifies these two modalities—visions versus states of mind—using the terms retribution and habit, respectively.

Although it is unclear what exactly inspired the categories Zhiyi called habit and retribution,[15] the contrast between them expresses a long-standing, variously theorized, and somewhat problematic division found throughout Buddhist systematic thought: the division between good and bad mental tendencies and their serial continuity, on the one hand, and good and bad actions themselves—karma in its primal sense—that linger on unseen until yielding their retribution, on the other.[16] Without unpacking the full history of these concepts, we may say that, for Zhiyi, habit and retribution explain cause and effect within and across lifetimes in two distinct ways: (1) as a mental continuum in which good and bad psychological states give rise to similar ones in the future (habit), and (2) as a different kind of continuum in which good and bad actions produce painful or pleasant objective circumstances (retribution). Elsewhere, he defines the two modes of cause-and-effect in the following way:

---

14. 行者若坐中靜定，忽見種種衣服、臥具、飲食、珍寶、田園、池沼、車乘，如是等事。或復因心靜故，自能捨離慳貪心，行惠施，無所悋惜。當知此是過去今生布施習、報二種善根發相。(*CDFM*, T.1916:46.494b17–20)

15. Fukushima 1974, 280; Stevenson 1987, 709n45; Muranaka 2004. As I suggest below, the categories these terms point to may have derived from certain common analyses of the nature of deathbed experiences.

16. Early Buddhist thought usually sharply distinguishes the "mental defilements" (*kleśa*), the unwholesome mental tendencies of greed, hatred, and delusion, from karma itself. This was in part polemical, as it differentiated Buddhism from rivals such as the Jains, for whom karma was a physical substance, adhering to the soul, whose destruction required painful asceticism. Buddhists, in contrast, claimed that while karma was indeed the "seed" of future rebirth, it would not ripen in the absence of the "moisture" of the mental defilements (craving, aversion, and delusion); hence the painful asceticism needed to purge karma itself could be left alone (Bronkhorst 1986). Later Buddhist thought did not always make these same sharp distinctions. On these issues, see Mizuno 1974.

The present arising of mental defilements is called the habitual cause (習因). [When these mental defilements] lead to action, [i.e., bad deeds], this is the retributive cause (報因). When in the next life [similar] mental defilements arise again, this is the habitual fruit (習果). The pain and suffering [experienced as karmic retribution for the past deeds] is the retributive fruit (報果).[17]

In the *Sequential Approach*, Zhiyi deploys these categories primarily to explain the two modalities of experience—mental states versus visions—that he says will occur to those who sufficiently calm their minds through meditation. "Seeing various forms and objects is a sign caused by retribution," he says. "When good mental states appear, this is the sprouting of good caused by habit."[18]

Though the operation of "habit" is relatively self-explanatory (a given mental state leads to a similar one in the future), Zhiyi depicts the link between meditative visions and the actions whose "retribution" they are as having the potential to be much less straightforward. In the case of past charity (*dāna*) in the example cited above, we may infer with relative ease that the objects seen—bedding, food, and so forth—are those whose donation constituted the act of charity in question. It is much less clear, however, why the sign of having maintained the precepts in a past life, the second category of outer good, would be a vision of "oneself looking beautiful and lovely, or wearing clean, pure, religious clothing."[19]

As with our previous analysis of confirmatory visions in the fifth-century *chan* scriptures, we may view this as a contrast between iconic and symbolic modes of communication. Habit, we might say, signals its origin *iconically*, through a state that resembles it (a given mental state in the past gives rise to a like mental state in the present). Retribution does so *symbolically*, through visions requiring nontrivial interpretation. Though he did not, of course, use these words, Zhiyi recognized that habit and retribution operate in semiotically distinct registers. Manifestations due to habit, he says, are easy to recognize because they replicate the selfsame mental state. Those due to retribution, on the contrary, are difficult to understand and require consultation with a master.[20] The contrast between iconic and symbolic meditative experiences is, from this point of view, a way of describing a difference between experiences in which meditators are presumed to be capable of discerning the significance of what has occurred on their own and those in which the assistance of an external authority is assumed to be required.

During the initial stages of meditation, according to Zhiyi, manifesta-

---

17. 今生煩惱起名習因。成業即報因。後生起煩惱名習果。苦痛名報果。(*Mohe zhi guan*, T.1911:46.112a29–b2). Cf. Swanson 2017, 1366.

18. 見諸相貌，悉屬報因相，現善心開發，皆是習因善發也。(*CDFM*, T.1916:46.494c13–14)

19. 忽見自身相好端嚴，身所著衣清淨如法。(*CDFM*, T.1916:46.494b21–22). That these images would be symbols of moral purity is, of course, not terribly shocking. The point is simply that, in all these cases, a certain amount of hermeneutic work is needed to make this connection.

20. *Mohe zhi guan*, T.1911:46.113b18.

tions of the outer good roots laid down by past wholesome actions may occur, along with others associated with the inner good roots of past meditative attainment. Zhiyi classifies these inner good roots according to the method— based on the five gates of *chan*—by which the past attainment may have been reached. He then divides each of the five methods into three subtypes, yielding fifteen possible inner good roots. The manifestation of the good root associated with past practice of "following the breath" (隨息), the second variety of meditation on the breath (the first gate of *chan*), is typical of how these are then described:

> His mind immersed in either sense-sphere trance or preliminary trance, [the meditator] suddenly feels his breath—going in and going out, long or short, up until [he feels his breath going in and out] through the pores of his entire body. In his mind's eye he sees the thirty-six [impure] things within his body as clearly as if observing the different grains of rice, millet, flax, and beans within a storehouse. He then feels a sudden delight and experiences the joy of tranquility.[21]

Other inner good roots manifest similarly, with correspondingly different content. The good root of past practice of the "nine meditations" (九想)— the contemplation of the nine stages of a decaying corpse—manifests as a sudden feeling of disgust for sense objects, along with sudden visions of one or more of the nine kinds of corpses.[22] The good root of past practice of the white bone contemplation produces a sudden freedom from any grasping at a self, along with a vision of one's own body as a skeleton radiating white light.[23] The good root of past practice of "bringing to mind the buddha" (*nianfo*) manifests as a sudden awareness of the Buddha's many wondrous qualities, together with a vision of the Buddha's form or, alternatively, hearing the Buddha's preaching.[24]

Like the outer good roots, inner good roots manifest when the practitioner has reached an initial state of calm, categorized technically as "sensesphere trance" or "preliminary trance," terms from Indian commentarial literature denoting two levels of meditative concentration just shy of the first *dhyāna*.[25] The existence of these good roots, created in the past when *dhyāna* was obtained in one of the fifteen possible ways, is "confirmed" (驗) by the

---

21. 於欲界未到靜定心中，忽然覺息出入長短，及遍身毛孔虛疎。即以心明見於身內三十六物，猶如開倉見穀粟麻荳等。心大驚喜，寂靜安快。(*CDFM*, T.1916:46.495a20–24)

22. *CDFM*, T.1916:46.495b3–7.

23. *CDFM*, T.1916:46.495b7–12. Zhiyi names this practice the "liberations" (*beishe* 背捨)— that is, the eight *vimokṣa* meditations. However, the content here aligns with what other Chinese Buddhist sources call the "white bone contemplation," which was classified as one of the so-called liberation meditations in some sources.

24. *CDFM*, T.1916:46.496a10–20.

25. In the Indian Buddhist sources available in Chinese translations, sense-sphere trance (欲界定)—a *dhyāna*-like state that remains within the *kāma*—rather than *rūpa-dhātu*—was known from the *Satyasiddhi-śāstra* (*Cheng shi lun*, T.1646:32.367c27–29) and the *Da zhi du lun* (T.1509:25.272a26), while preliminary trance (未到定; *anāgamya-samādhi*) was discussed in

spontaneous occurrence of an experience similar to what one would hope to achieve when cultivating the meditation method in question.[26] Once the existence of a given inner good root has been confirmed, one may then proceed to further develop the specified method of meditation that, it is now known, one has already successfully practiced in a previous lifetime.[27]

Zhiyi and the *Chan* Scriptures

Even from this brief introduction, we can see clear continuities between Zhiyi's understanding of the initial production and interpretation of meditative experiences and the treatment of such issues in the fifth-century *chan* scriptures, such as the *Five Gates* and *Chan Essentials,* where confirmatory visions are most prominent. As observed in the previous chapter, progress through meditation in those texts is marked by visions that are often profoundly *discontinuous* with the practices that produce them and of whose successful attainment they are the sign. Although Zhiyi presents these matters within a set of categories organized far more systematically than anything in the earlier *chan* scriptures, he too insists on a similar discontinuity between the initial techniques of mental calming and the subsequent confirmation of past karmic roots through sudden experiences that can include, as a major component, concrete visions.

It is worth noticing, moreover, that in the case of the inner good roots, the visions that Zhiyi describes are similar if not identical to things that meditation manuals such as the *Chan Essentials* often direct the practitioner to actively imagine or recollect. According to Zhiyi, it seems, even those visions that might elsewhere be the subject of deliberate cultivation, such as seeing one's own internal organs, or imagining one's body as a white skeleton, or bringing to mind the physical form of the buddha, can also occur—and indeed, usually first occur—as spontaneous visions triggered by a state of intense mental calm. In fact, for Zhiyi, at all stages of one's practice of meditation, given attainments can arise without deliberate cultivation when triggered by past "good roots." This is made clear later in the *Sequential Path,* when he discusses the arising of the formal levels of *dhyāna.* Under the heading "the nonfixity of the arising of *chan*" (發禪不定), Zhiyi explains that meditative attainment occurs in two distinct varieties: (1) as the result of the specific techniques (方便) associated with that attainment, *or* (2) as the "sprouting of good roots from past lives" (發宿世善根).[28] He then goes so far as to say that the very word "cultivation" (修), arguably the most basic Chinese

---

Sarvāstivāda treatises (Nakamura 2001, 1291). Both are functionally equivalent to the access concentration (*upacāra-samādhi*) of the Pāli commentaries.

26. Zhiyi says, however, that the visions appearing as confirmation of good roots are more fleeting than those that occur during meditative attainment itself (*CDFM,* T.1916:46.495a1–5).

27. *CDFM,* T.1916:46.505a8–15. Zhiyi also proposes other possible responses, including that one can select a different or opposed method of meditation. The point remains, however, that knowledge of one's past-life meditative attainment informs one's next course of action.

28. *CDFM,* T.1916:46.499a15–23.

Buddhist term for the practice of meditation, has two possible meanings: "cultivation that is obtaining" (*dexiu* 得修)—the deliberate cultivation of new meditative attainments—and "cultivation that is activation" (*xingxiu* 行修)— the spontaneous activation of meditative states, and their corresponding visions, that one had already attained in past lifetimes, triggered in the present by a sufficiently calmed mind.[29]

Zhiyi gives an example of how these two modalities of attainment might work for a given individual:

> Some practitioners, having in past lives cultivated and obtained the contemplation of impurity [up to the stage of] the skeleton radiating white light, give rise in this life, through the practice of calming, to [the manifestation of good roots corresponding to the initial stage of] the contemplation of impurity, but have not yet obtained [the stage of] the glowing white bones. This is called "incomplete." When [the good roots are] fully manifest [and one sees the glowing white bones], it is called "complete." But when the power of their past practice is used up, *they will not make further progress through the cultivation of calming.* [They must now] focus their minds and contemplate the white bones, purifying the skeleton and cultivating without cease, and then they will awaken. Following in accord with their contemplation, their confirmatory visions (*jingjie*) will gradually develop until [the four stages of] contemplation, purification, perfuming, and cultivation[30] associated with the eight liberations are complete. This is something attained through diligent cultivation and practice in the present life, not something connected to the manifestation of good [roots] associated with practice in past lives.[31]

From this description we see that provoking the manifestation of meditative attainments from past lives does require effort, namely, the cultivation of "calm" (止). But it does *not* require deliberate engagement with the specific

---

29. *CDFM*, T.1916:46.500a22–25. In these cases, one's past karma (the past attainment) serves as the "primary cause" (*yin* 因), likened to the seed, for the arising of that state again in the present, while the present practice of calming serves as the "supporting condition" (*yuan* 緣), likened to the water that moistens the seed. Zhiyi may have derived this contrast between "cultivation that is obtaining" and "cultivation that is activation" from theories found in various *abhidharma* texts (Andō 1968, 445).

30. These four stages refer, in Zhiyi's system, to the levels within which "worldly" (世間; Skt. *laukika*) trance reaches its full development in "transcendent" (出世間; *lokottara*) trance (Nitta 1981, 68–77). According to Zhiyi, within the contemplation of impurity the transition from worldly to transcendent occurs at the level of the glowing white bones (白骨流光), the third of the eight liberations (*beishe* 背捨; *vimokṣa*). Zhiyi's point in the passage cited here is that the meditator will now move into the levels of the contemplation of impurity beyond the stage of the glowing white bones (already achieved in a past life).

31. 自有行人，宿世已經修，得不淨白骨流光，今於止中但發得不淨，未得白骨流光。此名不盡。若具足發者，名之為盡。若過去所習，勢分已盡，雖復修止，則不增進。若更專心諦觀白骨，練、薰、修，悉皆具足。此即是今世善巧精勤修習之所成就，非關過去習因善發。(*CDFM*, T.1916:46.500b7–15)

topics or visions associated with the states of meditation in question (such as the white bones in the above example). That becomes necessary only later, after one's past good roots have been exploited to their full extent. This could conceivably take a certain length of time, and it might result in a variety of visions and experiences attesting to increasingly advanced states of attainment.

Karmic Obstructions and Inauspicious Visions

Before taking stock of what we have seen so far, we must discuss the final aspect of Zhiyi's account of preliminary meditation practice: the possibility that calming the mind will lead to the arousing of what he calls "evil roots." As Zhiyi explains it:

> For some practitioners, when they cultivate meditation, owing to the gravity of their defilements and sins, *though they calm their minds and abide in tranquility* none of the inner or outer roots of good described above manifest. Rather, they experience only the arising of defilements.[32]

As this passage makes clear, evil roots are not the obstructions that prevent a practitioner from calming the mind at all. Such hindrances Zhiyi had already discussed earlier, along with the other external preliminaries such as regulation of diet and posture. Evil roots, in contrast, refer to a different class of problems triggered by the *successful* calming of the mind.

Zhiyi classifies the evil roots by means of their opposition to the five gates of *chan*: (1) breath meditation is opposed by distracted thinking, (2) the contemplation of impurity by lust, (3) the cultivation of love by hatred, (4) the contemplation of dependent origination by confusion, and (5) bringing to mind the Buddha by "obstructions of evil karma" (惡業障).[33] Zhiyi further classifies the evil roots as belonging to habit (the first four) or retribution (the last one).[34] Habit and retribution are, of course, the same two categories that Zhiyi deployed to distinguish the two modes in which each of the good roots might manifest: either as the sudden occurrence of positive mental states (habit) or as the sudden appearance of visions (retribution).

Here we should pay particular attention to Zhiyi's inclusion of "obstructions of evil karma" as a hindrance on the same order as mental defilements such as lust, hatred, and confusion, whose purification is more usually the target of Buddhist meditative cultivation. Equated with the mental defilements to the extent that they impede meditation, obstructions of evil karma nevertheless have a distinct etiology:

---

32. 自有行人修禪定時，煩惱罪垢深重，雖復止心靜住，如上所說內外善法，都不發一事。唯覺煩惱起發。(*CDFM*, T.1916:46.501b4–7)

33. Zhiyi's list of the five methods of *chan* and the hindrances they oppose matches the list in Kumārajīva's *Meditation Scripture*, but he changes the order, placing breath meditation first.

34. *CDFM*, T.1916:46.501a19–22.

If one has committed an evil deed in the past for which in the future one is to experience an unpleasant retribution, then [until that time] the evil remains supported [in its existence] by that [past] deed. If a practitioner cultivates good before having experienced the retribution [for that past deed], because good and evil are opposed, the [past] deed will prompt that evil to arise and obstruct the good [that is being presently cultivated]. This is known as a karmic obstruction. . . . It obstructs a practitioner by preventing the arising of meditative trance and wisdom, and for this reason is called an obstruction.[35]

Perhaps inspired by some version of the Sarvāstivāda theory that past entities (*dharma*s) continue to exist even in the present, Zhiyi suggests that past evil karma, even before it fructifies in retribution, retains some kind of existence and can, when opposed by the cultivation of good (in this case, meditation), suddenly arise and cause an obstruction. Classified by Zhiyi as "retribution," karmic obstructions are an impediment to meditation that is categorically different from the evil mental impulses such as lust, hatred, and confusion that he classifies as "habits" and collectively designates as the "obstructions of the defilements" (煩惱障). In Zhiyi's usage, then, karmic obstructions are not the results of bad karma fully arisen in the objective circumstances of one's life, such as illness, misfortune, or a bad rebirth. They are rather something like *premonitions* of yet-to-arrive karmic fruits, which a successful calming of the mind has the power to reveal.[36]

Karmic obstructions also differ from the "obstructions of the defilements," those resulting from habit, in how they manifest. When the evil roots of lust, hatred, confusion, and distracted thinking appear, Zhiyi explains, they are simply a renewed occurrence of the mental state in question: a sudden feeling of lust, for example, is a manifestation of the evil root of lust.[37] Just as with habit in the case of good roots, habit in the case of evil roots denotes for Zhiyi a kind of serial psychological continuity, potentially across lifetimes, in which past unwholesome mental states give rise to similar ones in the future. For karmic obstructions, however, the situation is more complicated, and here Zhiyi enumerates several possibilities. The meditator may suddenly become dull and lethargic, or be filled with the urge to violate the precepts or abandon the monastic vocation.[38] Most interesting is the third possibility—what Zhiyi calls "oppressive visions" (境界逼迫):

---

35. 由過去造惡，未來應受惡報，即以業持此惡。若行者於未受報中間而修善者，善與惡乖，業即扶惡而起，來障於善。故知即是業障 ... 障一切行人禪定智慧不得開發，故名為障。(*CDFM*, T.1916:46.502b5–9)

36. Although "karmic obstructions" (*ye zhang* 業障) is nominally a translation of the Indian Buddhist term *karmāvaraṇa*, that word normally has a very different meaning: the small class of misdeeds that impede further soteriological progress in the present lifetime, usually the five sins of "immediate retribution" (*ānantarya*) that ensure rebirth in hell in one's next life (Mochizuki 1958–1963, 1057).

37. *CDFM*, T.1916.46.501b10–502a15.

38. *CDFM*, T.1916:46.502a17–24.

In this case, when the practitioner cultivates concentration . . . he feels a sudden bodily pain and feels something oppressing him. Externally, he sees visions (*jing* 境) such as [his own body] without head, hands, feet, or eyes, or else he sees torn [monk's] robes, or else [he sees himself] sinking into the earth, or else his body burned by fire, or else he sees himself falling from a high cliff, [or else] two mountains blocking him, or *rākṣasa*-demons, tigers, or wolves.[39]

These oppressive visions parallel the visions that occur as retribution in the case of good roots. But rather than pure or pleasant scenes showing the objects of meditation cultivated in past lives, the practitioner now sees frightening visions whose relationship to the past evil actions that have caused them, and which they by extension signify, is both indexical—the claim is, precisely, that there is a real, causal connection—and *symbolic,* in that it is patently obscure.[40] These symbolic experiences can again be contrasted with the iconic manifestation of the evil roots classified as habit, which take the form of a renewed occurrence of the same mental state, such as the evil root of lust being indicated by a sudden arising of lust.

A Systematic Theory of Meditative Visions

This account of the introductory stages of meditation in Zhiyi's *Sequential Approach* can be summarized under four main points.

First, while Zhiyi was aware of the many canonical techniques of Buddhist meditation, such as meditation on the breath, the contemplation of impurity, and so on, he does not propose that a practitioner should begin by directly engaging with such methods. Instead meditation begins with the comparatively straightforward exercise of mental calming, which when successful triggers, in the form of a spontaneous, unexpected experience, the sudden sprouting of the roots laid down in past lives through either good and evil actions or past meditative attainment.

Second, the so-called inner good roots of past meditative attainment will manifest as experiences nearly identical to those characteristic of the attainment in question, either as the sudden occurrence of the relevant mental state or as a sudden vision of the kind that normatively accompanies the attainment, such as the impure body, the nine kinds of corpses, and so on. Notice how this understanding of the course that meditation practice will initially take justifies the acquisition, reproduction, and transmission of a body of purely theoretical knowledge concerning a wide variety of meditation methods and the normative states to which they lead, information

---

39. 若行人於修定之時 . . . 而身或時卒痛，覺有逼迫之事。見諸外境，或見無頭、手、足，無眼、目等，或見衣裳破壞，或復陷入於地，或復火來燒身，或見高崖而復墮落，二山隔障，羅剎虎狼。(*CDFM*, T.1916:46.502a24–28)

40. The *Sequential Approach* does not explain the precise meaning of any particular vision apart from its being a "karmic obstruction." In the *Mohe zhi guan*, Zhiyi discusses similar visions and at one point describes them as indicative of a transgression of the precepts in past lives (*Mohe zhi guan*, T.1911:46.113a).

provided, not coincidentally, in the later portions of the *Sequential Approach* itself. This knowledge is needed, given Zhiyi's framework, in order to *recognize*, in oneself or another, the appearance of good roots associated with the many different meditative attainments. Such a perspective, needless to say, tallies with what we saw in the previous chapter as one of the defining marks of the *chan* master in early medieval China: the ability to properly interpret the significance of the meditative experiences of others.

Third, the cultivation of mental calm could also lead to bad experiences, understood as the manifestation—often in visions—of evil roots. Beyond the obstructions of the defilements and the karmic obstructions already discussed, Zhiyi also describes two further inauspicious manifestations: the arising of bodily illness, and the interference of demons.[41] Of these, demonic interference is recognized as especially pernicious because it can cause visions nearly identical to those that are the signs of good roots, and consultation with a skilled master is required in such a case to discern the difference.

Finally, the manifestation of both good and evil roots is explained by way of two complementary but distinct forces: habit, which produces internal mental states similar in character to their causes, and retribution, which produces symbolic visions, for good or ill, and other objective encounters.

While scholars have usually identified well-known doctrinal treatises from India as the primary sources for Zhiyi's *Sequential Approach,* it is actually the fifth-century *chan* scriptures in which confirmatory visions play such a large role—the *Five Gates, Chan Essentials,* and *Methods for Curing*—that prefigure Zhiyi's account of basic meditative experience most directly.[42] On a few occasions, Zhiyi cites these texts overtly,[43] but on the whole his debt to them, or to the later ramifications of the traditions that produced them, lies at the level of what was broadly assumed concerning the production and interpretation of meditative experiences. The notion, for example, that the initial practice of fixing the mind to a single object, or "calming," will provoke spontaneous and elaborate visions is a basic presupposition of the master-disciple dialogs in the *Five Gates.* Zhiyi's further claim that the content of those visions might then serve to divine the most suitable method of meditation to undertake next is also found, minus his terminology and explanatory framework, in the sections of the *Five Gates* that deal with explicitly divinatory readings of confirmatory visions.

More striking still is Zhiyi's account of inauspicious meditative experiences, particularly those related to karmic obstructions, for here we see Zhiyi working within the same semiotics of meditative experience that informs the *Chan Essentials* and other fifth-century *chan* scriptures. What he shares

---

41. Zhiyi's inclusion of illness and demonic attack mirrors the themes of the *Methods for Curing,* originally a kind of appendix to the *Chan Essentials.*

42. Kumārajīva's *Da zhi du lun* is the source most often identified by modern scholars as Zhiyi's major inspiration for the *Sequential Approach* (Asada 1978, 25; Andō 1968, 14–16).

43. Zhiyi's citations of the *Chan Essentials* and *Methods for Curing* are listed in *Secrets of Buddhist Meditation,* appendix 1; see also Sengoku 1980.

with those earlier sources, as we will see in detail in the ensuing sections of this chapter, is the assumption that meditative visions can be signs that reveal past karma, understood as something distinct from the meditator's presently active or latent defiled mental tendencies.[44] This same understanding is seen in the stories of Zhiyan and Daojin discussed earlier, who practiced meditation to reveal the presence or absence of the kind of purity usually gained through rituals of repentance, and it comes up again and again in a wide range of sources and literary genres throughout the fifth, sixth, and seventh centuries. The semiotic ideology linking meditative visions to past karma was one in which the experiential fruits of meditation were significant not as inner, cognitive transformations, but as signs to be used to navigate relationships with a wider world of Buddhist ritual practice. These connections were more than incidental—this was not a feature of Buddhism "on the ground" that stood in contrast to the prescriptions of doctrinal texts, nor was it a characteristic of only local or folk Buddhism in opposition to the normative or exegetical tradition. It was instead part of a widely shared understanding of Buddhist meditative experience, one that informed elite meditation manuals such as those of Zhiyi, where it was grounded in a complex doctrinal apparatus, no less than popular, widely circulating miracle tales, which implicitly reveal the same basic paradigm.

Visions of Karma in the *Chan Essentials*

As we saw in the previous chapter, the *Chan Essentials* presents the path of meditation as a continuing series of confirmatory visions that serve to indicate the specific attainment a meditator has achieved in a sequence of named and numbered stages of accomplishment stretching from the beginning contemplation of impurity up through the liberation of an arhat. In this section, I want to unpack the notion of meditative attainment, for the *Chan Essentials*, as we will see, often claims that confirmatory visions point to something more concrete than a merely abstract attainment—namely, the need for (or subsequent success of) the performance of a ritual of repentance (*chanhui* 懺悔).

Although Indian Buddhist meditation manuals frequently discuss the purification of transgressions, they typically present it only as a prerequisite of the practice of meditation. In these formulations, purification of this sort is a preliminary step, something required before getting on with meditation itself, which then proceeds as an entirely internal cultivation. In contrast,

---

44. Previous scholarship has struggled to identify a clear source for Zhiyi's ideas about meditatively produced "signs of karma" (*ye xiang* 業相), as such matters are not discussed in the principal Indian scriptures he drew from. Some scholars point to the ritual traditions associated with the *Da fang deng tuoluoni jing* 大方等陀羅尼經, which Zhiyi of course knew well (Fukushima 1974). But that text does not itself discuss the practice of meditation. What the example of the *Chan Essentials* shows us is that these ideas were indeed linked to the practice of seated meditation in China long before Zhiyi's time.

the *Chan Essentials* posits a situation in which the meditator's need for the ritual purification of transgressions is revealed by the practice of meditation itself. This way of treating the possible meaning of meditative experience foreshadows Zhiyi's *Sequential Approach,* which treats meditation as a site where symbolic visions reveal the presence or absence of karmic obstructions, the particular class of hindrances to progress whose cure is not psychological, in the sense of involving the manipulation of mental tendencies of which one is or could be directly aware, but penitential, effectuated through the rites of repentance that, as a class, were among the most widespread forms of medieval Chinese Buddhist ritual.

In the *Chan Essentials,* the idea that meditative visions can signal the need for repentance is made clear early in the first section of the text, where the meditator, who has begun with the white bone contemplation, has imaginatively stripped the flesh from his body and vomited up his internal organs, leaving behind only a skeleton. Before describing the elaborate confirmatory vision, or *jingjie,* that it says marks the attainment of the first stage of the contemplation of impurity, the text mentions other possibilities:

> When this meditation is complete, you will see yourself as a complete, snow-white skeleton. If you [instead] see a yellow or black skeleton, you must further repent your transgressions.
>
> Having repented your transgressions, you will see the remaining skin fall from your bones, forming a pile on the ground that grows gradually to the size of a begging bowl. It grows larger still, becoming as big as a large urn.[45]

Here a vision of a snow-white skeleton signals the successful completion of the previously described exercise. But there is an alternative possibility: a vision of a yellow or black skeleton, explained as a sign that the meditator must "repent," a word that implies some kind of ritual procedure even though no specifics are mentioned here. Successful repentance results in a further vision in which the yellow or black skeleton becomes purified of its lingering flesh,[46] which segues directly into a long vision of the four *yakṣas* that is eventually identified as the confirmatory vision of the contemplation of impurity.

Let us note three things about the sequence here. First, meditative visions in the *Chan Essentials* are not always *good*—like Zhiyi's claim that the initial accomplishment of meditative calm produces a manifestation of good *or* evil roots, the text here describes visions indicative of success as well as other, alternative visions said to be signs of the presence of obstacles. Second,

---

45. 此想成已，自見己身，如白雪人，節節相拄。若見黃黑，當更悔過。既悔過已，自見己身骨上生皮，皮悉褪落，聚在前地，漸漸長大，如鉢多羅。復更長大，似如瓮堈。(*Chan Essentials* 1.1.7; CMY, T.613:15.244a8–12)

46. The lingering flesh (literally, the "[still] living skin"), which is what makes the bones less than purely white, is perhaps being analogized to the practitioner's lingering impurity. The duality of impure flesh versus pure bones is a common trope in many cultures (Watson 1982).

some of the obstacles revealed by the visions require, for their elimination, not new or alternative methods of meditation but a ritual act of repentance. Third, the success of such a ritual is not guaranteed and is something for which a confirming sign is needed, namely, a subsequent vision.

In stating that meditative visions can signal the need for a rite of repentance, the *Chan Essentials* presents meditation as integrated into a wider ritual context. This integration is not only practical, in the unsurprising sense that those who practice meditation were not imagined as remaining aloof from other forms of Buddhist ritual; it is also *semiotic*—meditative experiences do not pertain only to meditation itself but have consequences for the meditator's relationship with other domains of practice.

Lacking the kind of systematizing impulse that Zhiyi displays in the *Sequential Approach*, the *Chan Essentials* does not attempt to offer a complete account of all possible meditative visions and their causes. We can say, however, that by declaring that some visions signal the need for repentance, it presents these events as analogous to what Zhiyi identifies as the manifestations of evil roots of the "karmic obstructions" type. There are also other cases where it is implied, even though repentance is not explicitly mentioned, that certain visions are caused by or grounded in the meditator's past transgressions. In the second contemplation, for example, the meditator again performs the white bone contemplation (1.2.1) and comes to see many skeletons filling the universe and then crumbling into disconnected bones (1.2.2.1). The practitioner must then reflect on the decay of the skeletons and contemplate the truth of non-self (1.2.2.2). Upon contemplating the scattered bones again, the meditator then has a vision of a blazing fire that builds to terrifying proportions and is accompanied by various physical ailments (1.2.2.3). This frightening vision is to be countered by reflecting on its emptiness. The instructions for carrying this out include information about the origin of the vision itself:

> He must arouse his thoughts and think as follows: "During countless eons in the past I did many things productive of burning anguish. Pulled by the force of that karma, I now see this fire."
>
> He must further think: "This fire comes into existence from the four great elements. My body itself is empty and its four great elements have no master. This raging fire arises adventitiously from emptiness. My own body and the bodies of others are all also empty. This fire is produced by false imagination. What could it burn? Both my body and the fire are impermanent."[47]

By meditating on its emptiness, the vision of terrifying fire eventually dissipates, but only after the appearance of the fire is attributed to the force of

---

47. 當自起念而作是言：我於前世無數劫來，造熱惱法，業緣所牽，故使今者見此火起。復當作念。如此火者，從四大有。我身空寂，四大無主。此大猛火，橫從空起。我身他身，悉皆亦空。如此火者，從妄想生，為何所燒。我身及火，二皆無常。(*Chan Essentials* 1.2.2.4; *CMY*, T.613:15.245b21–26)

the meditator's evil deeds from past lives. Nothing here approaches the subtlety and clarity of Zhiyi's explanation of how it is that karmic obstructions, produced by evil deeds in past lives, generate oppressive visions. But it is nonetheless tempting to see in the *Chan Essentials* the kind of source material that Zhiyi was working with, directly or indirectly, and organizing into his architectonic, doctrinally grounded edifice.

For Zhiyi, it will be recalled, the category of "oppressive visions" describes karmic obstructions that take the form of a vision having a symbolic connection to the transgression that has caused them—a vision of a torn monk's robe as an indication of a violation of the precepts, for example. The *Chan Essentials* occasionally links visionary images to past evil deeds in a similar manner.[48] In the fifth contemplation, after the meditator has quelled his craving for sensual pleasures by imagining his body as a sack of skin filled with pus and worms (1.5.1), an unpleasant vision occurs:

> When this meditation is complete, the practitioner sees a giant *yakṣa,* as big as a mountain, its hair wild and disheveled like a forest of brambles. Its sixty eyes flash like lightning. Its forty mouths each have two fangs, like flaming pillars pointing upward, and tongues like sword trees that reach to its knees. It attacks the practitioner with an iron club that is like a blade mountain. [The practitioner sees] many other things like this. When he sees these things, he becomes terrified, and his body and mind begin to tremble.
>
> These appearances are the evil roots of his past-life violations of the precepts. Supposing what is not the self to be the self, what is impermanent to be permanent, and what is impure to be pure, he gave himself over to indulgence and became stained with attachment, craving all kinds of sensual pleasures.[49]

Here the *Chan Essentials* unambiguously links the terrifying vision, which has emerged in the wake of a successful stilling of the mind in the previous section, to the meditator's past transgressions and furthermore describes it using the same term "evil roots" (惡根) that figures so prominently in the *Sequential Approach.* The content of the vision also seems to encode this relationship symbolically. The "sword trees" and "blade mountains" that describe the *yakṣa*'s tongues and weapons, for example, are standard instruments of torture found in Buddhist hells, as if to say that the cause of this vision is a transgression that will lead to rebirth in that realm.[50]

In many other passages the *Chan Essentials* similarly attributes the sudden

---

48. The specific image of a torn monk's robe is actually mentioned at *Chan Essentials* 2.20.6–7.

49. 此想成時，見大夜叉，身如大山，頭髮蓬亂，如棘刺林。有六十眼，猶如電光。有四十口，口有二牙，皆悉上出，猶如火幢。舌似劍樹，吐至于膝。手捉鐵棒，棒似刀山，如欲打人。如是眾多，其數非一。見此事時，極大驚怖，身心皆動。如此相貌，皆是前身毀犯禁戒諸惡根本。無我計我，無常計常，不淨計淨，放逸染著，貪受諸欲。(*Chan Essentials* 1.5.2; *CMY*, T.613:15.246c6–14)

50. This kind of imagery appears in other passages as well. See *Chan Essentials* 1.6.2; 1.12.7; 1.14.7, as well as *Methods for Curing* 1.8.2; 1.14.2; 1.14.3; 1.14.4.

appearance of inauspicious visions to the practitioner's "sins" (罪) or "evil karma" (惡業) from past lives, with different responses required. Sometimes, as eventually occurs in the passage above, it is said that the practitioner should contemplate the emptiness of the frightening vision. More often, the practitioner is instructed to carry out a ritual of repentance (*chanhui*).[51] In the next chapter, we will look more closely at the concrete procedures that such rituals would have included, but the main point for now is that in taking certain meditative visions as signs of "sin," the *Chan Essentials* portrays meditative progress not as a linear path effectuated by meditation alone, but as a reciprocal process in which meditation provokes visions that sometimes indicate a need for repentance, which, when successful, unleashes previously blocked meditative attainments.

The final sections of the first sutra in the *Chan Essentials* show that this interplay was imagined as continuing into the upper reaches of the path to liberation. Having ascended through the many levels of the contemplation of impurity, the meditator now sees the seven buddhas of the past, who deliver teachings that propel him into a state close to complete awakening. The process that generates this vision is described as follows:

> He should again fix his thoughts and contemplate the suffering, emptiness, impermanence, and non-self of the body and the emptiness of everything.
>
> Having reflected in this way, he no longer sees a body when he contemplates his body, no longer sees a self when he contemplates his self, no longer sees a mind when he contemplates his mind. Then, he suddenly sees the great earth, with its mountains, rivers, boulders, and cliffs, disappear completely. When he emerges from trance, he appears drunk or mad.
>
> He must then, with a mind of utmost devotion, carry out a ritual of repentance, make prostrations, and clean the ground of the sanctuary, setting aside his practice of contemplation.
>
> While making prostrations, even before he has raised his head, he will suddenly see the Tathāgata's true emanation, who touches his head and commends him: "O Dharma child, well done, well done! Today you have properly contemplated the buddhas' teaching of emptiness."[52]

The pattern here is familiar. Having earlier contemplated suffering and impermanence (1.18.11), and in response obtained a favorable vision (1.18.12), the meditator now contemplates emptiness, which leads to a vision of the world disappearing and a stupor akin to madness. To remedy this situation,

---

51. *Chan Essentials* 1.13.3, 1.14.6, 1.14.7, 1.17.3, 1.18.8, and 1.18.14, among others. See also *Methods for Curing* 1.14.7 and the long ritual of repentance in *Methods for Curing* 1.9, discussed in the next chapter.

52. 復還繫念。觀身苦空無常無我，悉亦皆空。作是思惟時，觀身不見身，觀我不見我，觀心不見心。爾時忽然見此大地，山河石壁，一切悉無。出定之時，如癡醉人。應當至心，修懺悔法，禮拜塗地，放捨此觀。禮拜之時，未舉頭頃，自然得見如來真影。以手摩頭讚言：法子，善哉善哉，汝今善觀諸佛空法。(*Chan Essentials* 1.18.13–14; *CMY*, T.613:15.253c22–29)

the practitioner must put meditation aside and carry out a ritual of repentance, whose success is confirmed by the appearance of the Buddha's "true emanation" (真影), who delivers teachings that lead the practitioner to awakening (1.18.19).[53] Here, in effect, the culminating vision and attainment of the first sutra is generated not in the calm of meditation but while prostrating during the performance of a ritual of repentance.[54]

In much of the remainder of the *Chan Essentials*, repentance is similarly presented as a key force effectuating progress on the path to liberation, and meditative visions as the medium whereby the need for or success of such repentance will be indicated. In the second sutra, the opening narrative frames the ensuing teachings as a special meditation method designed for those with grave sins when the Buddha's interlocutor Nandi queries the Buddha as follows:

> Those who have karmic obstructions will not see the confirmatory visions even though they have fixed their thoughts. How should they who have such afflictions and sins, ranging from the violation of the minor transgressions (*duṣkṛta*) up to the gravest of sins, repent? How can they extinguish the signs of their sins?[55]

Nandi asks the Buddha for a method that can help those who are unable to gain confirmatory visions because they have violated the precepts of the *vinaya*. Yet what the Buddha then provides is less a method of eliminating the stain of transgression than a special method of meditation that will accurately *reveal* when such obstructions are present. The meditator must first "contemplate the Buddha" (*guanfo*) by following a step-by-step meditation on the physical components of a statue of a buddha (2.19.1.1–6). This leads to a fantastic vision of glowing buddhas filling the universe within whose lights certain impurities that "occur as retribution for sin" (從罪報得) may appear, thereby indicating that the practitioner must put aside meditation and devotedly carry out a ritual of repentance (2.19.1.9).

As in the first sutra, this sequence, in which meditation produces visions interpreted as signs of the need for repentance, is not a one-time event. Having become pure through repentance, the meditator will see "buddha images seated on lotus flowers everywhere within the four oceans, their august bodies fully endowed with the thirty-two marks" (2.19.1.9). But the practitioner must then go on to consider:

---

53. The "true emanation" is a truly existing, efficacious projection of a past buddha. I discuss this unusual concept, which occurs in this and a few other texts from this era, in "The Bodies of the Buddha" in *Secrets of Buddhist Meditation*, chap. 3.

54. This recalls the way that *chan* masters, in medieval hagiography, are often depicted as reaching liberation not while seated in meditation, but at some other moment. See, e.g., *XGSZ*, T.2060:50.562c26–563a14 (the biography of Zhiyi's teacher Huisi).

55. 有業障者，若繫念時，境界不現在前。如是煩惱，及一切罪，犯突吉羅乃至重罪，欲懺悔者，當云何滅是諸罪相。(*Chan Essentials* 2.0.1; *CMY*, T.613:15.255a9–12)

When the World-honored One was in the world, he carried his bowl and staff, entered villages to beg for food, and traveled everywhere to teach, so as to bring blessings and salvation to living beings. *Owing to what sin from a past life* do I see today only the seated image and not the walking image?[56]

Here it is the *failure* to see the Buddha's movements that signals the presence of sin from a past life. And again, after repenting further, the practitioner returns to meditation and sees the seated images stand, walk, and fly through the air (2.19.1.10). But even this may not be the end, for those with "excessive lust" will be unable to fully benefit from the contemplation of the Buddha and will need to meditate on the breath (2.20.1).[57] Success in this method, which is described in detail, leads to a vision of a cloud-like light that encircles the meditator seven times (2.20.5). But here again another possibility is mentioned:

[If] he has violated any of the minor precepts, even [merely] a *duṣkṛta* sin, this light will appear black, like a wall or like charcoal. Or else he will see the light as similar to an old torn monk's robe.... [He must] not conceal even tiny violations. If he conceals any violation, he will see the many radiant lights as rotten wood. *When he sees this, it will be known that he has violated the precepts.* [In such a case,] he must again arouse a sense of shame and remorse, repent and rebuke himself, sweep the sanctuary, clean the floors, and perform many kinds of menial service. He must then make offerings and pay reverence to his teachers and parents.... After cultivating merit in this manner, with full remorse, he should count his breaths as before. He will again see the light, radiant and exquisite, just as it was before [he violated the precepts].[58]

This passage is noteworthy because it does more than merely state that impure meditative visions are the inevitable consequence of a violation of the precepts; it furthermore treats such visions explicitly as a sign that should be used to inform the meditator himself that such a violation has occurred. Despite Nandi's request at the outset of the sutra, what the *Chan Essentials* has provided is not a novel means of purifying transgressions—indeed, readers are presumed to already know how to carry out the appropriate rituals of repentance. What it outlines instead is a novel way of knowing, through visionary means, when such purification is needed and when it has been successfully accomplished.

In sum, the practice of meditation as taught by the *Chan Essentials* does

---

56. 世尊在世，執鉢持錫，入里乞食，處處遊化，以福度眾生。我於今日，但見坐像，不見行像，宿有何罪。(*Chan Essentials* 2.19.1.10; *CMY*, T.613:15.255c21–23)

57. This is unusual; the antidote to lust is normally meditation on bodily impurity.

58. 於輕戒乃至突吉羅罪，見光即黑，猶如牆壁。或見此光，猶如灰炭。復見此光，似敗故衲...乃至小罪，慎勿覆藏。若覆藏罪，見諸光明，如朽敗木。見此事時，即知犯戒。復更慚愧，慚悔自責，掃兜婆，塗地，作諸苦役。復當供養恭敬師長、父母...如是慚愧，修功德已，如前數息，還見此光，明顯可愛，如前無異。(*Chan Essentials* 2.20.6–7; *CMY*, T.613:15.257a26–b12)

involve (as instructions in this subject usually do) a series of exercises to counteract specific mental defilements such as lust or ignorance by focusing the mind on particular objects—the impurities of the body, an image of the Buddha, the breath, or abstract doctrines such as emptiness. Yet meditation is also more than this. Through the visions that occur to the meditator during its practice, it is also a medium that reveals, to one who can interpret the signs correctly, the meditator's karmic obstructions—the stains of sin from this or previous lives that must be purified not by meditation itself but by recourse to rituals of repentance.

Meditation and Repentance

Although novel in its details, the semiotics of meditative experience laid out in the *Chan Essentials* is arguably grounded in an ancient and pervasive set of Buddhist ideas and practices establishing a reciprocal relationship between meditation, seen as the means of attaining normative soteriological fruits, and rituals for purifying transgressions.

Formally, this connection is expressed through the doctrine of the "three trainings," according to which virtue (*śīla*), meditation (*samādhi* or *dhyāna*), and wisdom (*prajñā*) comprise the totality of Buddhist practice as a hierarchical sequence of steps, each necessary, the latter of which are dependent, in some way, on the earlier. Classical Indian accounts of the Buddhist path give various explanations of what "virtue" might mean in this context, but a large part of it was usually understood to mean adherence to the Buddhist monastic code, the rules of conduct whose acceptance, in a ritual of ordination, defines one's status as a monk or nun (Walshe 1995, 68–73 and 99–100).

The idea that taking on the monastic rules and then following them purely are a necessary precondition for success in meditation practice is mentioned prominently, if briefly, in the key Indian meditation treatises that appeared in China in the early fifth century, such as Kumārajīva's *Meditation Scripture* and Buddhabhadra's *Chan Scripture of Dharmatrāta*. The same idea can be found in earlier and roughly contemporaneous Indian treatises such as the *Vimuttimagga,* the *Visuddhimagga,* and the *Śrāvakabhūmi,* as well as in later sources such as the *Bhāvanākrama*s of Kamalaśīla (ca. 740–795).[59] In some of these texts, furthermore, the principle that one must be "pure" with respect to the precepts is expressed through a concrete requirement: one

---

59. For the *Bhāvanākrama*s, see Tucci 1958, 205; Tucci 1971, 3; and Adam 2003, 192. In the *Śrāvakabhūmi*, the need to maintain pure *śīla* by receiving the precepts and atoning for transgressions is discussed, along with other aspects of *śīla*, in the section on the requisites (*saṃbhāra*) needed before commencing meditation (*Śrāvakabhūmi*, 1:68). Let us also note the *Yogalehrbuch*, which in the opening lines of each section describes the meditator as one "who has completed the preparatory work beginning with *śīla*" (*śīlādikṛtaparikarmaṇaḥ;* Schlingloff 1964, 86 / 128R4); what this means concretely is not specified. The other texts mentioned here are discussed below.

must ritually purify any transgressions before commencing meditation practice. In the *Vimuttimagga*, the need for this purification is explained at the conclusion of the introductory chapter on *śīla*, just prior to introducing the techniques of meditation:

> When a monk first receives instruction in meditation he must examine himself with regard to the seven classes [of the monastic precepts].[60] If he has violated a *pārājika* [the gravest monastic rules], then he has cut off his monkhood and dwells in a state lacking the full precepts. And the elders have said that only one who abides in the full precepts will obtain the higher attainments. If, however, he has violated any of the [lesser but still serious] *saṅghāvaśeṣa* offenses,[61] he should repent by way of the whole community procedures, [as stipulated in the *vinaya*].[62]

Kumārajīva's *Meditation Scripture* opens with an essentially identical admonition:

> When a person desiring to practice meditation first goes to a master, the master must ask: "Have you maintained the precepts purely? Do you have any heavy sins or evil perversions?" If he says he is pure as regards the five classes of the precepts [of the *prātimokṣa*][63] and has no heavy sins or evil perversions, he may be instructed in the practice....
>
> If he says [he has violated] a grave precept,[64] the master must say: "A person with a mutilated face should not look in the mirror. Leave! By chanting scriptures, proselytizing, or doing good deeds, you can plant the conditions for attaining the path in a future life. But in your present life you cannot [reach any meditative attainment], like a withered tree that even if watered will no more sprout flowers, leaves, or fruits." If he has violated any of the other precepts, he should be instructed to repent (*chanhui*) using the appropriate method.[65]

---

60. The rules of the *prātimokṣa* are traditionally divided into either five or seven categories.

61. The *saṅghāvaśeṣa* are the second most serious category of the monastic rules. Purifying a violation of them requires a period of probation followed by a formal readmission (Nolot 1996, 116–136). On the various forms of this word, see Nolot 1987.

62. 若比丘初受禪法，於七聚中觀於自身。若具[>見?]犯波羅夷，斷比丘法，住不具足戒。若住具足戒，當得勝法，是先師所說。若見犯僧伽婆尸沙，以眾事懺悔。(*Jie tuo dao lun*, T.1648:32.404a10–14). Cf. Ehara et al. 1961, 24, whose translation here is problematic. This passage has no parallel in the *Visuddhimagga*. "Whole community" procedures must mean the usual *vinaya* methods for purification of *saṅghāvaśeṣa* transgressions involving a gathering of thirty fully ordained monks.

63. *Wu zhong jie* 五眾戒. The usual term for the five divisions of the precepts is *wu pian* 五篇, but this translation is also attested (*DZDL*, T.1509:25.226a2–3; *Mohesengqi lü*, T.1425:22.396a20).

64. "Grave precepts" here must mean the *pārājika*s (see, similarly, *DZDL*, T.1509:25.226a2–3).

65. 學禪之人，初至師所，師應問言，汝持戒淨不。非重罪惡邪不。若言五眾戒淨，無重罪惡邪，次教道法…若言重戒，師言，如人被截耳鼻，不須照鏡。汝且還去。精懃誦經、勸化，作福，可種後世道法因緣。此生永棄。譬如枯樹，雖加溉灌，不生華葉及其果實。若破餘戒，是時應教如法懺悔。(*ZCSM*, T.614:15.270c28–271a5). For a slightly different translation of this passage, see Yamabe and Sueki 2009, 7.

In short, one who wishes to practice meditation must either be pure already or carry out an appropriate ritual of repentance. Both texts also say that certain grave transgressions exist that cannot be purified, and they, accordingly, will permanently impede one's practice of meditation in the present lifetime.

Although the notion that meditation depends on *śīla* in the sense of maintaining the precepts is well known in principle, there has been a tendency to overlook or ignore it in modern scholarship on Buddhist meditation.[66] Even those who do mention the foundational role of the precepts in Buddhist meditation theory frequently explain it from an exclusively psychological standpoint, thereby reducing the significance of Buddhist ethical practices in relation to meditation to their function as an introductory form of mental training.[67] Yet, as we have already seen, Buddhist meditation manuals themselves do not reduce *śīla* to "ethics," let alone to a condition of merely psychological purity. For these texts, to have pure *śīla* was neither a simple absence of wrongdoing nor a personal commitment to a set of moral guidelines; it was a positive, socially recognized condition generated by initiation into the Buddhist community through a ritual whose core was a commitment to follow a set of ascetic restraints and an agreement to be judged accordingly.[68] The connection between pure *śīla* and ritual practice was therefore ongoing: for Buddhist monks and nuns, it required not only initial ordination but also remaining in good standing thereafter by purifying any transgressions of one's vows through the fortnightly ritual known as the *poṣadha*.

Thus the links between formal rituals of confession and repentance and the initial production or restoration of meditative attainment were longstanding in Buddhism. According to the ritual formula for the *poṣadha* ceremony as preserved in the Pāli *vinaya*—one of the oldest sources for such rites—failure to reveal violations of one's vows is a "hindrance" (*antarāyika*), a word then explained to mean a hindrance to meditative attainment. Revealing (*āvikareyya*) one's wrongs in turn yields "comfort" (*phāsu*), meaning the comfort of *dhyāna* and the higher states dependent on it.[69] That purifica-

---

66. Many compilations of Buddhist primary texts on meditation, for example, mention this relationship only in passing (Conze 1975, 7) or not at all (Bucknell and Kang 1997; Shaw 2006). Even studies of the path to liberation from a pan-Buddhist perspective typically say little to nothing about *śīla* and focus entirely on meditation as *dhyāna*, *prajñā*, or both (see, e.g., Buswell and Gimello 1992). Among other things, this has led to some glaringly inaccurate assessments of the novelty of Daoist ideas about meditation in comparison to Buddhist ones; see Zürcher 1980, 112, and more recently Verellen 2019, 193, who both argue that medieval Daoists *modified* the Buddhist practices they borrowed by connecting meditation to morality.

67. Vajirañāṇa 1962, 79; W. King 1980, 28; Gunaratana 1985, 16; Gethin 1998, 170; and Gombrich 2009, 14.

68. Here I follow Egge (2002, 27), who cogently suggests understanding *śīla*, in the context of the formal monastic rules or the eight fast-day precepts for the laity, not as "ethics" but as "observing a set of ascetic restrictions ritualized by the taking of vows."

69. *Vinayapiṭaka*, 1.103–104; Horner 1938–1971, 4:134–135. These passages have been discussed by Braun 2002, 102. On *phāsu* and its usages, see Caillat 1960, 41–55.

tion of transgressions leads to *samādhi* and other higher states of meditation is similarly discussed in the Mahāyāna ritual traditions that emphasize acknowledging (*pratideśanā*) misdeeds to obtain remission from their consequences, misdeeds now understood not as transgressions of the monastic rules, a topic concerning which Mahāyāna rituals have little to say directly, but evil karma in general.[70] The power of transgression to block meditative attainment seems even to have been formalized in the concept of "remorse" (*kaukṛtya*), one of the five hindrances to *dhyāna*, according to doctrinal formulas, but also what confession is elsewhere said to destroy (Gunaratana 1985, 15).

Janet Gyatso has noted that the meditative practices at the core of the Tantric ritual meditations known as *sādhana*s are not independent programs but are embedded in the communal rituals that authorize those who may participate in them. The requirement that the would-be practitioner of a *sādhana* first be initiated by a master through a ritual of consecration (*abhiṣeka*) means that "individuals are not considered to possess the permission to transform themselves... automatically. Rather, they must first take part in a ritual, a ritual that is controlled by others" (2002, 185). The Tantric practices that Gyatso discusses emerged during a relatively "late" phase of medieval Buddhism. The canonical relationship between "precepts" and "meditation" demonstrates, however, that the link between external rituals authorized by others (what Gyatso calls the "outer" side of self-transformation) and the technologies leading to "inner" transformation (paradigmatically, meditation) is an ancient and fundamental one in Buddhism.

Its dynamics, however, were not always the same. The *Meditation Scripture*, for example, declares that rituals for purifying past transgressions are necessary to attain the fruits of meditation but grants them only a preliminary role—having become pure through repentance, one can successfully practice meditation. In that text, at least, there is not yet any trace of the idea that the fruits of meditation themselves might convey information about the need for further purification, a key feature of the *Chan Essentials* as we have seen. Though a full history of how and when these changes came about may remain out of reach, it is nevertheless instructive in this regard to return to the *Five Gates*, which contains some of the raw materials (or things closely resembling the raw materials) from which the *Chan Essentials* was composed or compiled. It is notable that the master-disciple dialogs in the *Five Gates*, despite their almost exclusive focus on meditative visions, never mention the existence of the frightening, inauspicious visions that the *Chan Essentials* routinely

---

70. The *Upāliparipṛcchā*, a key early source for these rites (which in their fully developed form as the five- or seven-limbed "supreme worship" [*anuttara-pūjā*] became the foundational Mahāyāna liturgy), says that acknowledgment of transgressions allows bodhisattvas to "part from the remorse of their transgressions and [thereby] obtain *samādhi*" (*āpatti-kaukṛtyān niḥsarati samādhiṃ ca pratilabhate;* Bendall 1902, 171; Python 1973, 39).

discusses and interprets as signs indicating the need for repentance.[71] Repentance, moreover, is prescribed in these dialogs on only two occasions: first as a preliminary purification before beginning meditation proper, and then in the wake of an *unsuccessful* attempt to use visions to divine a suitable meditation method:

> [The practitioner] should again contemplate his body. [If he sees] impure pus and blood, then instruct him to perform the contemplation of impurity. If he sees white bones, instruct him to perform the white bone contemplation. If he sees suffering sentient beings, instruct him to perform the cultivation of love. *If he sees none of these things*, he must contemplate the Buddha and single-mindedly entreat him by begging for mercy and repenting.[72]

The bulk of this passage foreshadows Zhiyi's notion that by calming the mind meditators can stimulate visions that indicate the good roots of their past practice of a given method of meditation and hence their present affinity for it. So too, its statement in the final line that those who need to repent must "contemplate the Buddha" (*guanfo*) is reminiscent of the second sutra of the *Chan Essentials,* where this exercise is specifically connected to the purification of sin. But even with these parallels, it is still notable that the need for repentance in this text is signaled by the *absence* of vision, not by the presence of an inauspicious vision as in the *Chan Essentials* and Zhiyi's manuals. The *Five Gates,* in other words, treats repentance as earlier Indian meditation texts typically do—as an initial purification that makes meditation possible at all.

In short, the *Chan Essentials* appears novel, relative to its antecedents and in anticipation of what would follow, in treating repentance as more than a mere preliminary. The purity afforded by repentance is not only something that makes one fit for the "higher" practice of meditation, but also something one comes to know by taking success in meditation as its sign. We have here a new semiotic ideology of meditative experience. In it, the doctrinally posited dependence of *dhyāna* on a repentance-generated purity is construed not as an abstract statement about causality, nor only as a prescription for doing one practice before the other. It is, rather, the grounds for a reciprocal relationship in which the results of meditation, because they depend on ritual purity, are signs of the presence or absence of that purity.

---

71. Some passages, however, do describe visions or experiences to which the master must *not* give approval (*WMCJ*, T.619:15.328c13–20). The format of the *Five Gates* is discussed in Chap. 2.

72. 還自觀身。不淨膿血，即教作不淨觀。若見白骨，即作白骨觀。若見苦痛眾生，即作慈心觀。若不見此事，還觀一佛至心懇惻求哀懺悔。(*WMCJ*, T.619:15.329b2–5). The other passage is *WMCJ*, T.619:15.330a21–22. Outside the dialog sections (and ignoring two cases where the meditator, in his visions, instructs *others* to repent), repentance is mentioned once in the section entitled "Method for the Contemplation of the Buddhas of the Ten Directions" (*WMCJ*, T.619:15.327c13–15; parallels at *Fo shuo guan jing*, T.2914:85.1460a1–2 and *Si wei lüe yao fa*, T.617:15.299c15–16), but here too it is the *absence* of a vision that indicates the need for repentance.

In finding this dynamic expressed in a Chinese-authored (or compiled) text in a newly systematic way, I do not mean to suggest that it was unknown outside Chinese Buddhism. It is likely that this approach to meditative experience was known to and endorsed by at least some of the Indian Buddhist *chan* masters who came to China in the fifth century. Indeed, we can occasionally find hints of similar ideas in properly Indian sources from around this era. One of these is a brief passage from the *Samantapāsādikā*, Buddhaghosa's commentary to the Pāli *vinaya*. The context, interestingly, is not meditation at all but rather how, in a case of doubt, one can determine if a monk or nun has committed a transgression of the monastic rules. If the matter remains unclear even after someone learned in the *vinaya* has been consulted, a real possibility given the legal subtleties of many rules, one may, this passage tells us, instruct the person to practice meditation and attempt to enter the state of *dhyāna*. If this proves impossible, it can be known that a violation did indeed occur.[73] What is striking about this passage is that the familiar principle that purity is a prerequisite for meditation is applied not in answer to the question "What must one do before meditating?" but rather to the issue of how one can know if one is pure.

Like the *Five Gates*, however, the *Samantapāsādikā* still seems limited to saying that it is the *failure* to obtain significant meditative experience that is the relevant sign. A brief but telling passage in the *Chan Scripture of Dharmatrāta* allows us to infer that the next step, in which significance is read not only in the absence of meditative experience but in the content of that experience, was also known in India or, at least, Indic Central Asia. In a section on the "contemplation of the sense gates" (觀入), there is a brief digression concerning the precepts and the way that one's purity with respect to them can be perceived in the course of meditation itself. For those who are pure, it says, what are called the "signs of the precepts" (戒相) will be discernable as a blissful feeling in the body, a happy feeling in the mind, or visions of pure objects such as jewels or gems.[74] However:

> Within the three [locations of body, mind, and object] there are also other signs, which disturb and obstruct.... [Seeing them (?) the meditator] should then seek to repent his transgressions.... [Among the visions he may see] his own body without hands, feet, eyes, ears, nose, or tongue, or with his limbs deformed or missing, or his body sunk into dirt and mud. Or else he inspects his body [and sees it to be] free of all dirt and defilement, cleansed and pure, and dressed in fine clothing.[75]

---

73. *Samantapāsādikā*, 1.236 (see also Huxley 1996, 145; *Shan jian lü piposha*, T.1462:24.717b12–28; Bapat and Hirakawa 1970, 177).

74. *DMDL*, T.15:618.322a22–b2.

75. 復次，三種中更有雜相。嬈亂障礙…請求悔過…或身無手、足、眼、耳、鼻、舌，一切肢節，悉不完具。或身沒塵埃。或觀察自身，離諸塵垢，澡浴塗身，名衣上服。(*DMDL*, T.618:15.322b2–10)

Mentioned only briefly, it is unclear what importance these ideas held within the overall system of meditation articulated in this text, and none of its many other discussions of meditative visions refer to anything comparable.[76] But we can clearly see here the seed idea that the content of one's meditative experience can be construed as a sign of either purity or, conversely, a kind of impurity that necessitates repentance. It is precisely this idea that would be elaborated in the *Chan Essentials* and take form more systematically in the later writings of Zhiyi.

The *Scripture on Meditation Most Sublime*

One and a half centuries lie between the composition of the *Chan Essentials*, in the early to mid-fifth century, and the treatises of Zhiyi in the late sixth. We might therefore wonder to what extent the similarity in these sources' approach to the semiotics of meditative experience and the relationship between meditation and repentance reflects a broadly continuous tradition across this era in China. This is a difficult question to answer because the vast majority of Chinese-authored Buddhist texts (as opposed to new translations of Indian texts) dating from this period have been lost, potentially obscuring the degree to which Zhiyi was drawing on immediately antecedent traditions. One source that does provide evidence for this continuity is the *Scripture on Meditation Most Sublime* (*Zui miao sheng ding jing* 最妙勝定經), an apocryphal sutra composed in the early sixth century that survives only in manuscripts from Dunhuang.[77]

The *Scripture on Meditation Most Sublime* was obviously seen by sixth-century Chinese Buddhists as an important authority on the practice of meditation. It was cited extensively by Zhiyi, by his teacher Huisi, and by other contemporaneous authors, and it even plays a role in an early story that it was upon reading this sutra that Huisi abandoned doctrinal studies in favor of devotion to meditation.[78] The *Scripture on Meditation Most Sublime* aggressively asserts the primacy of *chan* over other forms of Buddhist practice. Entering a state of meditative trance (定) for a single day and night, it claims, is more meritorious than building monasteries, making images, or copying or studying scriptures, and *chan* is "the fastest way to obtain the supreme path of the Buddha."[79]

---

76. The only other substantial discussion of repentance is the opening passage, which says that it must be done before beginning one's practice (*DMDL*, T.15:618.301c17–25).

77. Sekiguchi 1969, 396–402; Fang 1995b; Inosaki 1998 (the most complete edition). There is also a Tibetan translation from the Chinese (Silk 2019, 238), and a modern French translation and study based on Sekiguchi's edition (Magnin 2002). That the text is not mentioned in the *Chu san zang ji ji* but is cited by sixth-century authors (see next note) suggests an early to mid-sixth-century dating.

78. *XGSZ*, T.2060:50.562c26–27. On the citations of the text in Tiantai sources, see Sekiguchi 1969, 380–382. Several citations can also be found in the writings of Xinxing 信行 (540–594), founder of the Three Levels movement (Yabuki 1927, *betsu hen*, 349; Nishimoto 1998, 609).

79. 最是疾得無上佛道。(Inosaki 1998, 321; Fang 1995b, 340)

Meditation is supreme because while the learned but arrogant go to hell, one who practices *chan* "eliminates the evil karma and heavy sins of birth and death."[80] Cultivating *chan* for one to seven days will, in fact, entirely eliminate even the most heinous sins, including the *ānantarya* sins that usually assure rebirth in hell in one's next lifetime, the *pārājika* transgressions that normally entail expulsion from the monastic order, and even the sin of slandering the Mahāyāna scriptures, often considered the one truly heinous crime for which there can be no atonement. *Chan* alone can extirpate these sins, the text explains, because it is only through *chan* that practitioners can perceive their ultimate emptiness.[81] What is telling here is the form of the argument: *chan* is the supreme Buddhist practice because it is the best way to purify past transgressions—because it is, in essence, the best method of repentance.

Though the *Scripture on Meditation Most Sublime* suggests that there are many methods for meditation, it only gives one concrete example, the contemplation of impurity:

> When performing the contemplation of impurity one will see the four elements in one's body—the spleen, stomach, bones, and joints, the blood that flows like turbulent water, the impurities that leek from the nine orifices, and the horribly revolting stinking filth of piss and shit. Immersed in trance one might see all kinds of things, some moving, some still, some blue, some yellow, some white, some black. Such strange sights agitate the mind. Having seen them, one must restrain the mind and bring it back [to its object]. Then the white bones will radiate light.[82]

As in certain fifth-century *chan* scriptures, the *Scripture on Meditation Most Sublime* indicates that successful meditation on the impurity of the body will

---

80. 能除生死惡業重罪。(Inosaki 1998, 322; Fang 1995b, 342). The claim here is reminiscent of a famous story, preserved in sixth-century sources from north China, in which a certain monk visits the underworld and reports back that Buddhist monks devoted to exegesis are routinely sent to hell, while those devoted to "meditation and recitation" (禪誦) are not. The empress, hearing this, supposedly invited "one hundred meditation monks" (坐禪僧一百人) to live in the palace and receive her offerings (*Luoyang qielan ji*, T.2092:51.1005b8–c8; Y. Wang 1984, 73–75).

81. Inosaki 1998, 322–323; Fang 1995b, 342–343. Mahāyāna scriptures often claim that understanding emptiness destroys even the gravest sins. In China, these ideas were often invoked by way of a famous verse from one of the Contemplation Scriptures: "Those who wish to repent / should sit upright and bring to mind the true nature of things, / for sins are like frost or dew / that melt away in the sun of wisdom." 若欲懺悔者，端坐念實相，眾罪如霜露，慧日能消除。(*Guan Puxian pusa xing fa jing*, T.277:9.393b11–12). Zhiyi, among many others, frequently cited this verse (see, e.g., *Mohe zhi guan*, T.1911:46.39c14–16, where he also cites the *Scripture on Meditation Most Sublime*).

82. 若作不淨觀，時見身四大，脾、胃、骨、節、血流，亦如激水，九孔流出不淨之物，屎尿臭穢，甚可厭患。於此定中，見種種物，若動，若住，若青，若黃，若白，若黑。種種異變，令心散亂。見此事已，攝之令還，白骨流光。(Inosaki 1998, 324; Fang 1995b, 344). I punctuate the final line here in light of the parallels with the *Meditation Scripture* (see next note). Cf. Magnin 2002, 286n194.

be confirmed by a vision of the "white bones radiating light."[83] And like the *Chan Essentials,* it also describes alternate, more sinister visions that might occur to those who are stained by transgressions:

> However, if [a monk] has violated the four grave precepts, or if a nun has broken the eight grave precepts, or a laywoman the five precepts[84]... [or if one] steals the property of the Buddha, Dharma, the universal Sangha,[85] one's teachers or parents, or the monastic community, or if one slanders the Mahāyāna scriptures saying that they have no power, then when in trance such people will see their bodies as follows: their breath will be like a black cloud, their blood like a raging fire, their bones like mountains or rocks, their vessels like a forest of trees, their five viscera like poisonous snakes. Their hands [will burn] as if holding a torch against the wind. [They will see] great mountains atop their heads, ready to collapse. Lions will emerge from their mouths, *rākṣasa*-demons from their eyes, cobras from their noses, and jackals and wolves from their ears. An ocean of water will flow out from their big and little holes [for urine and excrement]. If the buddhas of the ten directions have appeared to them, they will all become black.[86]

Sins, rather than impeding meditative experience entirely, lead to the perverted forms of it described here using imagery similar to that found throughout the *Chan Essentials* and related texts.[87] These experiences are, moreover, not merely the inevitable result of trying to meditate when impure, but are furthermore the means whereby one's state of impurity is communicated, information that serves a practical purpose:

> If they see these signs, they should get up from meditation and go to the forest or a deserted place, chant scriptures, and repent their sins. When, after one to seven weeks, their sins have been removed, they should enter trance [again]. If

---

83. The unusual phrase *liu guang* 流光, literally, "flowing light," is the same word that the *Meditation Scripture* uses to describe the radiating light of the bones (*ZCSM*, T.614:15.272a21). The expression "restrain the mind and bring it back [to its object]" (攝之令還) is also very common in the fifth-century *chan* scriptures.

84. Interestingly, the text mentions lay*women* but not laymen, though this absence could reflect an error in the manuscript transmission rather than a feature of the original.

85. *Zhaoti* 招提 (*cāturdiśa* 'of the [Sangha of the] four quarters'), meaning property that belongs to the universal community of Buddhist monks and nuns rather than a particular, local community.

86. 若犯四重性戒，尼破八重，優婆夷破五種戒...盜佛物、法物、招提僧物、師長父母物、大眾僧物，及謗方等經，言無威德。如是之人，於禪定中見自身中氣如黑風，血如猛火，骨如山石，脈如林木，五藏如蛇蚖。見手捉大火，逆風如走。頭戴大山，去如復倒。口出師子，眼出羅刹，鼻出蟒蛇，耳出豺狼。大小便道，流水如海。若有十方一切諸佛，皆悉變黑。(Inosaki 1998, 324; Fang 1995b, 344)

87. Some of the parallels are very close indeed. The vision of water flowing out of the anus, in the passage cited above, may be compared to *Methods for Curing* 1.12, which suggests that diarrhea can result from improper meditation practice, as well as *Chan Essentials* 3.29.2, which says that a meditator with excessive lust will see fire and then water emerge from his penis.

their sins have been weakened successfully, they will gradually see their bodies turning into [pure] mountains of beryl. If they [have been fully purified and thus] are no longer in the condition of being violators of the four grave precepts or any others up to the five grave precepts,[88] the buddhas of the ten directions will appear to them, while in trance, simultaneously preaching the Dharma.[89]

Here inauspicious visions inform meditators that they must carry out a ritual of repentance, and subsequent visions, produced by renewed meditation, reveal the level of purification or degree of access to higher states that the work of repentance has afforded. Just as we saw in certain passages in the *Chan Essentials*, even though the *Scripture on Meditation Most Sublime* begins by stating that the practice of *chan* can destroy the gravest transgressions, it ultimately suggests that this occurs not because meditation itself destroys transgressions, but because it discloses, through visions suitably interpreted, when transgressions are present and when they have been purified.

Meditation and Dreams

As we have seen, throughout the fifth and sixth centuries *chan* was held to be a means of gaining access to an acutely sensitive state in which unanticipated visions of one kind or another might occur. These visions were significant not as direct perceptions of things distant in time or space, or as manifestations of mental power and control allowing one to visualize some pre-given scene or object, or because they were inherently desirable as experiences in themselves. Their importance lay, rather, in being *signs*, occurrences deemed to communicate, in a more or less symbolic way, important information about the person to whom they appeared. A central piece of this information was knowledge about the presence of obstructions caused by past sins or transgressions, or conversely the degree of purification from such hindrances that one had gained by the performance of rituals of repentance. To the extent that meditative experiences were imagined as taking place in this way and as carrying such meaning, they were similar to other forms of prophetic visionary experience that Chinese Buddhists believed could occur under different circumstances and in more commonplace settings—for example, dreams.

Buddhist Dreams

While naturalistic explanations of dreams as the result of bodily illness or demonic or divine possession, or obsessive thinking, were also known in pre-

---

88. "Five grave precepts" (五重性戒) may be an error for "five [lay] precepts" (五種戒), mentioned in the earlier passage; alternatively, it might refer to the final items listed there (slandering the Mahāyāna sutras and so forth).

89. 若見此相，從禪定起，往至林中，空閑之處，讀方等經，懺悔先罪。或以七日、二七、三七、四七、五七、六七、七七日，眾罪已除，便入禪定。罪若薄者，漸見身如琉璃山。若不破四種[>重]乃至五重性戒者，禪定中見十方佛同時說法。(Inosaki 1998, 324; Fang 1995b, 344)

modern India and China, the widespread existence in both Buddhist and non-Buddhist settings of formal typologies of dreams, manuals of dream interpretation, and stories of dreamers and their dreams show that dreams always had the potential to convey true information about the past, present, or future, or even to actually connect the dreamer to another realm or place.[90]

Buddhist texts, of course, often analogize dreams and delusions and liken liberation to an awakening. In this rhetorical mode, dreams are antithetical to the Buddhist ideal of mental control honed through meditation. The so-called dream yoga of Tibetan Buddhism, for example, is an attempt to tame the chaos and passivity of the ordinary dream to turn it into a site of deliberate religious practice (Young 1999, 117–127). At the same time, however, there is a competing Buddhist discourse about dreams in which the fruits of meditation are likened to dreams, not distanced from them. Zhiyi's treatises on meditation, on more than one occasion, suggest that confirmatory visions can occur in meditation or in a dream.[91] The most celebrated example in East Asia of a record that treats dreams and meditative visions as essentially identical is the famous dream journal (*yume no ki*) of the thirteenth-century Japanese monk Myōe (Tanabe 1992; Girard 1990). But similar ideas were expressed from very early on in Chinese Buddhism.

One of the earliest sources to discuss meditation on the physical form of the Buddha, the *Pratyutpannabuddha-saṃmukhāvasthita-samādhi* (*Samādhi of Direct Encounter with the Buddhas of the Present*) first translated into Chinese in the second century of the common era, says that visionary encounters with the buddhas resulting from sustained religious practice will occur either while the practitioner is immersed in *samādhi* while meditating or else during a dream (Harrison 1990, 32). Even when not equating the two as here, other passages in this text continue to analogize meditative visions to dreams. To call something dreamlike, in Mahāyāna philosophy at least, is often a claim about ontology—all things, including the buddhas, are like dreams in that they are empty, produced by the mind, or both. The *Pratyutpanna-samādhi* does sometimes use the dream comparison to make such claims (ibid., 39), but it also deploys it differently, not to suggest that meditative visions lack substantial reality but to explain why meditation, like dreams, creates *actual* contact with faraway things, such as the buddhas presently dwelling in other world systems, in defiance of the normal laws of space and time.[92] This aspect of its dream analogy was highlighted by Kumārajīva in his early fifth-century

---

90. The literature on these topics is vast. On Indian (including Indian Buddhist) approaches to dreams, see O'Flaherty 1984 and Bautze-Picron 2009. On Indian Buddhist typologies of dreams, see Mayer 2006. On dreams and their interpretation in China, see Somiyé 1959; Ong 1985; Liu W. 1989; and Strickmann 1988. On Chinese dream manuals, see Drège 1981 and Drège and Drettas 2003. On dreams in Chinese and Japanese Buddhism, see Strickmann 1996, 291–336; Müller 1992; Faure 1996, 114–143; Struve 2012; and Moro 2012, 144–152.

91. *CDFM*, T.1916:46.485c29–486a3; 505c1; *Mohe zhi guan*, T.1911:46.107b20–23.

92. Harrison 1990, 32; 40. On this aspect of the text's dream analogy, see Akamatsu 2015, 70–72.

letters to Huiyuan, who had feared—wrongly, Kumārajīva assured him—that to call an encounter with the buddhas dreamlike would be to deny their reality.[93] Because dreams were already understood to be potentially revelatory, to liken meditative visions to them was actually a positive statement about their communicative power.

In the fourth- and fifth-century hagiographies of Buddhist monks and nuns we have already glanced at, dreams frequently serve to predict future events, as they so often do in Chinese literature more broadly.[94] In such cases, the eventual verification of the dream is a loose index of the dreamer's saintliness. But some presentations of dreams suggest a more direct affinity with meditative confirmatory visions in particular. For example, the Buddhist dream manuals that became known in China around this time often emphasize the role of dreams in divining not future events but one's own level of spiritual progress, or conversely—in a move that gives such progress or its lack a concrete entailment—the presence of hindrances, caused by past misdeeds, that now require remedial action.[95]

Indian Buddhist scriptures that approach dreams in this way figure among the earliest Buddhist texts translated into Chinese.[96] But the most extensive collection of interpretations of this type is the *Scripture on the Bodhisattva's Dreams* (*Pusa meng jing* 菩薩夢經), first translated into Chinese in the sixth century, which lists 108 different dreams and interprets their meaning as signs indicative of one's progress toward buddhahood.[97] Notably, this collection includes *inauspicious* dreams: one who sees a buddha facing backward has, in a past life, created hindrances for Buddhist monks and their followers and must now make donations to the Buddhist church to "remove this karmic obstruction" (除業障).[98] In a manner reminiscent of the *Chan Essentials*' continuing prescription of repentance even at the higher stages of meditation, the *Scripture on the Bodhisattva's Dreams* sometimes combines signs of progress and hindrance into a single event. Dreaming about the cremation

---

93. *Jiumoluoshi fa shi da yi*, T.1856:45.134c8–15; Kimura 1960, 35. See also Faure 1991, 214.

94. On the narrative role of dreams in Buddhist hagiography in China, see Jensen 2018.

95. Daoist sources too often claimed that violation of the precepts would produce inauspicious dreams; see F. Lin 1995, 103.

96. See for example *Dao xing bore jing*, T.224:8.459b5–c11 (cf. Conze 1973, 227–228), translated into Chinese in the second century. The various translations of the *Karuṇāpuṇḍarīka-sūtra* also contain a long passage on the soteriological significance of specific dreams (*Bei hua jing*, T.157:3.176c20–178a20; *Da sheng bei fentuoli jing*, T.158:3.244a7–245b2; *Bao fan zhi qing ru lai jing* 寶梵志請如來經, cited in *Jing lü yi xiang*, T.2121:53.211a28–c2; I. Yamada 1968, 2:66–77).

97. The *Pusa meng jing* is first listed, as an anonymous translation, in late sixth-century catalogs (*Li dai san bao ji*, T.2034:49.112b19; *Zhong jing mu lu*, T.2146:55.120c3). It was later incorporated into the *Da bao ji jing* under the name *Jingju tian zi hui* 淨居天子會 (*Da bao ji jing*, T.310:11.80c12–91b21; on this, see *Kaiyuan shi jiao lu*, T.2154:55.665b8–9). The eventual attribution of the translation to Dharmarakṣa (fl. ca. 300) has nothing to support it. The extant Tibetan translation suggests an original Sanskrit title of *Svapnanirdeśa* (Harrison 2003, 135–138; Esler 2012, 320–324).

98. *Da bao ji jing*, T.310:11.82a2–4.

of the Buddha is thus a sign of reaching the first stage of the bodhisattva path but *also* an indication of the lingering obstruction caused by the past sin of having spoken ill of Buddhist teachers, purification of which requires a seven-day ritual of repentance carried out in front of a stupa.[99]

Meditation and Dreams in the Contemplation Scriptures

The fifth-century *chan* scriptures themselves almost never mention dreams.[100] Yet the potential semiotic equivalence of dreams and meditative confirmatory visions is frequently implied in another set of apocryphal scriptures associated with the foreign *chan* masters of the fifth century: the so-called Contemplation Scriptures.[101] These texts give various instructions for contemplating (*guan*) the Buddhist deity with which each is concerned. Usually, practitioners are directed to contemplate or imagine (*xiang*) the physical form of the deity and possibly the land or heaven in which he dwells, all of which is described in rich, visually evocative language. Such contemplation will, the texts say, destroy a vast quantity of sin (*zui*) and ensure rebirth in the heaven or pure land in question. As a typical example, consider the seventh section of the *Amitāyus Contemplation Scripture,* historically the most famous and widely used member of the group and the one through which modern scholars have most often considered these practices:

> If you wish to contemplate that buddha [Amitāyus], you must arouse your mind and imagination and imagine a lotus flower upon the seven-treasure ground [of the Pure Land], making each leaf of the lotus the color of a hundred gems, with eighty-four thousand veins [as exquisite as in] a heavenly painting, each vein radiating eighty-four thousand lights.... Make everything extremely clear, like viewing one's own face in a mirror. When these meditations are complete, sins leading to five hundred million *kalpa*s of rebirth will be destroyed, and your future rebirth in the Land of Bliss will be assured.[102]

---

99. *Da bao ji jing,* T.310:11.82b14–18.

100. The one exception to this is *Methods for Curing* 1.9.5 (*ZCB,* T.620:15.337a24).

101. These texts, first identified as a distinct group by Mochizuki Shinkō (1946, 283–298), are the (1) *Ocean-Samādhi Contemplation Scripture* (*Guan fo sanmei hai jing;* T.643); (2) *Maitreya Contemplation Scripture* (*Guan Mile pusa shang sheng Doushuai tian jing;* T.452); (3) *Samantabhadra Contemplation Scripture* (*Guan Puxian pusa xing fa jing;* T.277); (4) *Ākāśagarbha Contemplation Scripture* (*Guan Xukongzang pusa jing;* T.409); (5) *Medicine King Contemplation Scripture* (*Guan Yaowang Yaoshang er pusa jing;* T.1161); and (6) *Amitāyus Contemplation Scripture* (*Guan Wuliangshou fo jing;* T.365). On my reasons for translating their titles as *X Contemplation Scripture* rather than *Scripture on the Contemplation of X,* as well as the relationship between these texts and the *chan* scriptures, see p. 14n25 and passim in *Secrets of Buddhist Meditation,* chap. 1. On these texts as a group, see Yamabe 1999b, 25–58, and Mai 2009. Mochizuki also noted the *Avalokiteśvara Contemplation Scripture* (*Guanshiyin guan jing* 觀世音觀經), mentioned in medieval catalogs, as a lost example. On another possible member of the corpus, see Quinter 2010.

102. 欲觀彼佛者，當起想念，於七寶地上作蓮花想，令其蓮花一一葉作百寶色，有八萬四千脈，猶如天畫，一一脈有八萬四千光...皆令分明，如於鏡中自見面像。此想成者，滅除五百億劫生死之罪，必定當生極樂世界。(*Guan Wuliangshou fo jing,* T.365:12.342c22–343a15)

Not unreasonably, passages such as this are typically read as having been intended to prescribe what Richard Payne calls a "soteriology of visualization" in which "seeing the Pure Land . . . [serves] as a means of being reborn there" (Payne 1996, 250).

The *Amitāyus Contemplation Scripture* is unusual relative to the other Contemplation Scriptures, however, in failing to describe any of the contexts—practical, ritual, or interpretive—in which the "contemplation" it proposes should be carried out. Information of this sort is provided in the other Contemplation Scriptures. The *Ākāśagarbha Contemplation Scripture,* for example, describes a similar practice of imagining (*xiang*) the physical form of the deity but goes on to also explain the ritual and hermeneutic setting in which success will later be confirmed by way of a meditative vision or a dream:

> Having first given rise to shame, prostrate to the buddhas of the ten directions for one to seven days, chanting the names of the thirty-five buddhas and the name of the greatly compassionate Ākāśagarbha bodhisattva. [Then] bathe, burn precious incense . . . and imagine the bodhisattva Ākāśagarbha, with a wish-fulfilling jewel at the crown of his head. This jewel is the color of purple gold. Seeing this jewel, you then see his divine headdress, within which appear the images of the thirty-five buddhas. Within the jewel the images of the buddhas of the ten directions appear. The body of Ākāśagarbha bodhisattva is twenty *yojana*s tall . . . and he sits in the cross-legged posture, his hands holding a mighty wish-fulfilling jewel. . . .
>
> This bodhisattva, because of his pity for sentient beings, will appear in the guise of a monk or some other form and *either in a dream or while you are sitting in meditation* will use a *maṇi*-jewel seal to stamp your arm with the characters "sin removed."[103]

As the text explains, one who wishes to purify his sins must imagine the deity Ākāśagarbha in a precisely stipulated way. Yet as in the *chan* scriptures, success is confirmed only later, by a vision whose content is not restricted to what the aspiring practitioner was directed to imagine, so that the precise phenomenology of the initially prescribed "imagining" is evidently not what is of crucial importance. The semiotics of confirmation here is therefore just the same as that in the *Chan Essentials.*

There is, however, a key difference: in the *Ākāśagarbha Contemplation Scripture,* seated meditation (*chan*) is mentioned *only* as a site of the later confirmatory vision. The activity of "imagining," in contrast, takes place in a separate ritual in which the deity is venerated and entreated, incense

---

103. 既慚愧已，一日乃至七日，禮十方佛，稱三十五佛名，別稱大悲虛空藏菩薩名。澡浴身體，燒眾名香 . . . 當起是想：是虛空藏菩薩，頂上有如意珠，其如意珠作紫金色。若見如意珠，即見天冠。此天冠中，有三十五佛像現。如意珠中十方佛像現。虛空藏菩薩身長二十由旬 . . . 此菩薩，結加趺坐，手捉如意珠王 . . . 若此菩薩，憐愍眾生故，作比丘像及一切像，若於夢中若坐禪時，以摩尼珠印，印彼人臂，印文有除罪字。(*Guan Xukongzang Pusa jing,* T.409:13.677b25–c9). This passage is one of the earliest known references to the ritual use of seals (印) in a Chinese Buddhist context.

burned, and so forth. As I have argued elsewhere, the Contemplation Scriptures were originally thought of as providing methods of practice that were associated with the famous fifth-century *chan* masters while being more accessible than the teachings classified under the name *chan* itself.[104] Rhetorically, they offered users a way to obtain some or all of the benefits associated with *chan* without having to claim mastery of *chan,* and this framing extends within the texts themselves: instructions that in the *chan* scriptures were commonly associated with formal, seated meditation practice, such as imagining or contemplating the physical form of the deities, are in the Contemplation Scriptures turned into what we might call a liturgy.[105] In both sets of texts, however, confirmation of one's attainment still takes place via a subsequent vision—in the case at hand, a vision of the bodhisattva Ākāśagarbha coming to stamp one's arm with the words "sin removed," which can occur, the text tells us, either in a meditative vision or in a dream, a medium of visionary encounter accessible to anyone in principle.

In the other Contemplation Scriptures, dreams are similarly mentioned as a site of confirmatory visions occurring in parallel with meditative or waking visions or substituting for them. On some occasions, hierarchies of value are implied to exist between these options. A passage in the *Ocean-Samādhi Contemplation Scripture,* for example, says that confirmation by dream vision will substitute for waking visions only in those of weaker faculties.[106] A text containing portions of the otherwise lost *Avalokiteśvara Contemplation Scripture* also says that those with particularly strong sins will experience dream visions rather than meditative visions.[107] The *Medicine King Contemplation Scripture* explains that confirmatory visions will first appear during a dream as a sign that karmic obstructions have been removed, followed by further visions during meditation.[108] Sometimes, however, dreams alone are mentioned as the site where visions attesting to purification will occur.[109]

---

104. See *Secrets of Buddhist Meditation,* chap. 1.

105. Cuong Mai cogently suggests that the word "contemplate" in the titles of these texts can be understood as implying something like "instructions for rites of concentrated recitation before a central cultic image" (2009, 294). If we take the Contemplation Scriptures as liturgies, another salient contrast between them and texts such as the *Chan Essentials* is that they almost never describe *inauspicious* visions, though occasionally they allude to their possibility (*Guan Puxian pusa xing fa jing,* T. 277:9.393c4–5). The one exception is the *Ocean-Samādhi Contemplation Scripture,* which briefly describes one example (*GFSMH,* T.643:15.691b12–14) and also discusses negative deathbed visions (I discuss these below). This text, however, is exceptional among the Contemplation Scriptures: ten times as long as any of the others, it cannot have itself been a common liturgy (excerpted versions of it, suitable for that purpose, exist among the Dunhuang manuscripts; Yamabe 1999b, 513–558).

106. *GFSMH,* T.643:15.663a10.

107. *Qing Guanshiyin pusa xiao fu du hai tuoluoni zhou jing,* T.1043:20.37b2–3. On this text as the presumed lost *Avalokiteśvara Contemplation Scripture,* see Greene 2012, 328–336.

108. *Guan Yaowang Yaoshang er pusa jing,* T.1161:20.663a19–21. See similarly *Guan Puxian pusa xing fa jing,* T.277:9.390b27–c4.

109. *GFSMH,* T.643:15.665c29–666a4; 666b12–16; c9–11; c26–29; *Guan Puxian pusa xing fa jing,* T.277:9.391b1–2.

One particularly telling passage in the *Ocean-Samādhi Contemplation Scripture* notes that by following the prescribed practices the relevant visions will occur "even if you do not practice seated meditation" (雖不坐禪).[110] Here a semiotic potential the reader is assumed to already attribute to meditative visions is argued to also be available in the more accessible form of a dream. The claims that dreams will be the site of confirmation for those with weak faculties or sins should probably be read similarly—not as a statement that the dream sign is inferior, but as an argument that it is available even to ordinary men and women.

While the Contemplation Scriptures often seem motivated by a desire to offer efficacious alternatives to *chan,* their highlighting of dream visions also reveals certain background assumptions about meditation and meditative visions. First, they show us what we have already seen elsewhere: that *chan* was a privileged site where confirmatory visions attesting to the meditator's purity were expected to occur. But second, by repeatedly invoking dreams as a potential alternative to them, the Contemplation Scriptures show us that meditative confirmatory visions were assumed to be *similar* to dreams. That this was so, and that for this reason the untutored might mistake a real meditative vision for a dream, was a key element in the story of the nun Tanhui, discussed in Chapter 2, who had taken a spontaneous liking to *chan* as a child and had effortlessly obtained "confirmatory visions" (*jingjie*) even while regarding them as mere dreams, until the Indian master Kālayaśas, the putative translator of the *Amitāyus Contemplation Scripture* no less, tells her they are actually signs of meditative attainment.[111] Thus even true or authoritative meditative visions were dreamlike. If they were more than dreams (though even dreams were not all to be dismissed), their status as such did not lie in their experiential quality but in their meaning, which only a qualified interpreter could know.

Deathbed Visions

As dreamlike experiences that symbolically communicate information about karmic obstructions or the lack thereof, meditative confirmatory visions were also much like deathbed visions. As with dreams, the connections between Buddhist meditation and death or deathbed ritual comprise a vast topic that goes well beyond the few, hesitant steps we can take here.[112] It is well known that in many Buddhist traditions the ideal death is described as a "meditative" one in which negative emotions such as fear and craving do not impinge on serene acceptance and total concentration on the Buddha.

---

110. *GFSMH,* T.643:15.667a23–25.

111. *Fa yuan zhu lin,* T.2122:53.453a20–26.

112. On deathbed ritual in Chinese Buddhism, see Satō S. 1988 and Shinohara 2007a and 2007b. On deathbed visions associated with the pure land, see Becker 1984 and Stevenson 1995a. The most comprehensive study in English on Buddhist deathbed ritual, focusing on Japan, is now the magisterial Stone 2016. On Buddhist death rituals in contemporary Southeast Asia, see Davis 2016 and Langer 2007 (who also treats classical Pāli sources).

For our purposes, what is noteworthy here is how these links could also be traversed in the opposite direction. The claim that the ideal death was meditative did not just serve to prescribe and enforce normative ideas and practices in relation to death; it also helped to explain what meditation and meditative experiences were like, and what they could mean, by analogizing them to a class of experiences that touched on everyone—the semiotically charged visions, good *and* bad, made manifest at the moment of death.

The Theory of Deathbed Visions

Buddhist ideas about deathbed visions are closely linked with the widespread belief, whose reach goes well beyond Buddhism, that the character of one's last moment of consciousness has an outsized influence on one's postmortem fate (Edgerton 1927). As critics ancient and modern have pointed out, assigning such importance to the final moment of life is not necessarily compatible with the usual view of karma, in which it is good and bad deeds over the course of a lifetime that determine rebirth, and reconciling these positions occupied much Buddhist commentarial labor (Stone 2016, 14). Similar issues were germane to the question of meditative attainment. For Buddhist theories also claimed that certain meditative achievements would have necessary consequences for one's next life: full liberation and the attendant freedom from subsequent rebirth, of course, but also other meditative attainments such as the *dhyāna*s, which were usually held to ensure one's rebirth in the heavens of the "world of pure form" (*rūpa-dhātu*), the cosmic realm with which *dhyāna* was associated. There thus exists a basic point of commonality between meditative attainment and the moment of death in that they both have the potential to be singular events powerful enough to override, as far as one's immediately subsequent rebirth is concerned, even a lifetime of contrary deeds.

Given such ideas, it is easy to see why some technical Indian Buddhist accounts of the moment of death would also say that those with meditative attainment will experience deathbed visions whose content mirrors the meditative visions they obtained during life. According to the Pāli commentaries, a dying person will experience, at the last moment, either a "sign of karma" (*kamma-nimitta*), described as an object that the mind seized on at the moment of carrying out the particular deed now impelling one's rebirth, or a "sign of rebirth destiny" (*gati-nimitta*), a premonitory vision of the location of rebirth, such as a vision of the fires of hell or the palaces of heaven.[113] A third possibility, the manifestation of karma itself (rather than its "sign"), is also mentioned—instead of experiencing a vision, one simply relives the

---

113. *Visuddhimagga*, 549–550 (Ñāṇamoli 1991, 562–563); *Sammohavinodanī*, 156–160 (Ñāṇamoli 1987, 191–195). See also Stuart 2017, 147–148, discussing a similar account in the *Saddharma-smṛtyupasthāna-sūtra*. On the *kamma-* and *gati-nimittas*, see Langer 2007, 57. They are also discussed in the *Vimuttimagga* (*Jie tuo dao lun*, T.1648:32.451a10–29; Ehara et al. 1961, 264–265).

mental state that was active at the moment of the original action (Gethin 1994, 23). What these possibilities could entail is spelled out in multiple scenarios: for those going from a good state of rebirth to a bad, and from a bad to a good, and so forth. Included as a special case are those who will be reborn in the world of pure form associated with the attainment of *dhyāna*. In their case, the dying person will see the sign associated with the object on whose basis *dhyāna* was obtained in life (such as the earth *kasiṇa*). Although the commentaries use the word "sign" (*nimitta*) without elaboration, this likely refers to the "counterpart sign" that indicates to the meditator his attainment of access concentration, as we saw in Chapter 2. In other words, the deathbed visions of dying meditators will be the same visions that confirmed their initial attainments during life. In the context where it appears, this claim is phrased as an explanation of the character and meaning of certain kinds of deathbed visionary experience. Yet indirectly it also amounts to an assertion about the nature of confirmatory visions experienced in meditation—that they are, in a sense, deathbed visions experienced before the moment of death.

The Mirror of Karma

Meditative visions and those experienced at death were linked in Buddhism because each offered a privileged window onto normally hidden aspects of a person's past karma. A frequent image for this function was that of the mirror, which appears in the earliest known Chinese Buddhist source to discuss deathbed visions, An Shigao's second-century translation of the *Yogācārabhūmi* of Saṅgharakṣa.[114] A complete, late third-century translation of this same text by Dharmarakṣa, the *Scripture on the Stages of Cultivation,* was held by later Chinese Buddhists to be the most comprehensive scripture on *chan* available in China prior to the early fifth century. According to this version, this is what occurs at death:

> [At this moment] all the good or evil that [the dying person] did during life suddenly comes to his mind,[115] and he becomes aware of the way that evil and good in this life lead to blessing and misfortune in the next. Those who have done good will have a relaxed and happy countenance, while those who have done evil will appear unhappy....
>
> It is just like an old person who looks in a mirror and sees all the features of his body—the white hair, wrinkles, missing teeth, boils or stains, dour expression, flabby skin, hunched back—and trembles at his advanced years. Seeing these things, he feels ashamed, and putting away the mirror [thinks]: "I have left youth behind,[116] old age is upon me!" His heart grieves, and he no longer

---

114. *Dao di jing,* T.607:15.233b11–26.

115. 即心念本. An Shigao's version is clearer: "He *then sees in his mind* the good and evil deeds he originally performed [in life]" (是人本所行好醜罪福心便見; *Dao di jing,* T.607:15.233b13).

116. 吾已去少. That *shao* 少 here means "youth" is confirmed by *Dao di jing,* T.607:15.233b18.

feels at ease, for he has reached the end. So it is that just as when an old person peers into a mirror and seeing himself knows he has reached decrepitude, so too one who has habitually done evil becomes fearful and dejected by the evil visions he sees [at the moment of death],[117] and he deeply reproaches himself: "Surely I am going to a miserable rebirth!"[118]

Here, with this moment depicted much as it is in the Pāli commentaries, evil visions that are harbingers of a bad rebirth are said to appear to the dying person within a mind that is mirrorlike in its revelatory power. A very similar analogy is deployed in several of the fifth-century *chan* scriptures, the only difference being that the topic is not death but meditation. As we saw earlier, the opening passage of Kumārajīva's *Meditation Scripture* states that *pārājika* violations make one unfit for instruction in meditation, because "a person with a mutilated face should not look in the mirror."[119] The *Chan Scripture of Dharmatrāta*, just before explaining that meditative visions can reveal the purity of one's precepts, notes that meditators require such purity because "just as one with a severed nose would not delight upon gazing into a mirror, so too a monk with broken precepts, upon inwardly examining himself, will not delight."[120] This trope of a disfigured person gazing into a mirror was evidently a common way for Indian Buddhist meditation texts of this era to explain how transgressions impeded meditation or rendered it unpleasant— that mutilation was a criminal punishment in India no doubt made this a compelling analogy.[121]

That meditation practice makes the mind mirrorlike and therefore capable of discerning things as they really are is, of course, an image found throughout the Buddhist tradition (Demiéville 1973; Wayman 1974). The familiar analogy is straightforward: like a (metal) mirror, the mind properly reveals its object only when untarnished or—in an often interchangeable image, that of the surface of water—when calm and still. The image of the mirror appears with this meaning in Chinese writings on Buddhist medita-

---

117. 所見惡變. On *bian* 變 (transformation) meaning a vision, particular an evil or inauspicious vision, see *Zheng fa hua jing*, T.263:9.76c8; *CMY*, T.613:15.248a29; *ZCB*, T.620:15.339b8. These examples show, pace Mair (1986, 24), that *bian* came to mean "vision" as early as it did "painting," a usage first attested in the fifth century (Karashima 2016), or even earlier.

118. 其生存時所為善惡，即心念本。殃福吉凶，今世後世，所可作為，心悉自知。奉行善者，面色和解，其行惡者，顏貌不悅⋯如有老人而照淨鏡，皆自見形。頭白、面皺、齒落、瘡痍、塵垢、黑醜、皮緩、脊傴、年老戰疫。設見如是，還自羞鄙，閉目放鏡。吾已去少，衰老將至。心懷愁憂，已離安隱，至於窮極。素行惡者，臨壽終時，所見惡變，愁慘恐怖，深自剋責：吾歸惡道，定無有疑。亦如老人照鏡，見身知為衰至。(*Xiu xing dao di jing*, T.606:15.186a1–13)

119. *ZCSM*, T.614:15.270c28–271a5.

120. 譬人截鼻照鏡，不自喜樂，破戒比丘亦復如是，內省其身，心不自悅。(*DMDL*, T.618:15.321c27–29)

121. Some *vinaya*s, for example, prohibit the ordination of mutilated individuals, seemingly on the grounds that it implied a criminal background (*Mohe sengqi lü*, T.1425:22.418b14–c27; *Wu fen lü*, T.1421:22.119a29–b9).

tion as early as the third century,[122] and it was often used this way in the fifth-century *chan* scriptures, those translated from Indic languages as well as those composed in China.[123] Like the image of seeing to the bottom of a pool of clear water familiar from the early Buddhist scriptures, the reflective capacity of mirrors and still water expresses the fundamental principle of Buddhist meditation theory: that wisdom arises only in a calm, purified mind—that is to say, when the conditions of *śīla* and *samādhi* are both present.

Yet as we have seen, in fifth-century Chinese *chan* scriptures such as the *Chan Essentials* as well as in the meditation treatises of Zhiyi from the late sixth century, a mind stained by transgressions does not simply fail to reflect anything, as a dirty mirror or windblown water would. As the *Methods for Curing*, the companion text to the *Chan Essentials*, puts it:

> Precept breakers...though they do practice meditation, falsely claim that the confirmatory visions of breath counting appear to them. But from the very beginning, they see [only] a blackened buddha like the leg of a black elephant, or like a person covered in ash; they see monks with smashed heads and broken legs, and nuns adorned in flower garlands; they see divine elephants transforming into monkeys with flaming hair that approach and cause disturbance; or else they see wild foxes or wild jackals with a hundred thousand tails, within which are innumerable insects and other assorted vile things; or else they see starving camels, pigs, or dogs; or they see a monk being attacked by *kumbhāṇḍa*-demons, evil *yakṣa* spirits, and murderous *rākṣasa*s each wielding an assortment of weapons and vicious fires.[124]

Far from being locked out of the acutely sensitive mental state in which visions can spontaneously occur, those who are impure—because of violating the precepts or karmic obstructions from past lives—*clearly* see impure things.[125]

The mind that arises in meditation, then, functions as a mirror in the same way as the mind at the moment of death. The issue here is not the optical properties of reflecting surfaces but the divinatory powers so often attributed to mirrors in India, China, and elsewhere in the ancient world.[126] Like the famous "karma mirror" that reveals one's good or evil deeds upon

---

122. *CSZJJ*, T.2145:55.43a21–24 (Kang Senghui's preface to the *Anban shou yi jing*).

123. *DMDL*, T.618:15.319c23–26; 323c15–16; *Chan Essentials* 1.17.5 (*CMY*, T.613:15.252a21). See also *GFSMH*, T.643:15.650a2; 654c7; 660a27–28; 692b20–21; *Guan Wuliangshou fo jing*, T.365:12.341c20–21; 343a15.

124. 此破戒人...雖行禪定，偽現數息所見境界。始初之時，見黑色佛，如黑象脚，見如灰人。見諸比丘，頭破脚折，見比丘尼，莊嚴花鬘。見諸天象，化為獼猴，毛端火然，來觸擾已。或見一野狐，及一野干，有百千尾，一一尾端，無量諸蟲種種雜惡。或見羸瘦駝驢、猪、狗。鳩槃茶等，諸惡夜叉，羅剎魁膾，各持種種武器惡火，打撲比丘。(*Methods for Curing* 1.9.2; *ZCB*, T.620:15.337a2–15)

125. In the *Mohe zhi guan* (T.1911:46.112a6–8; Swanson 2017, 1365), Zhiyi explains that it is by making the mind mirrorlike that concentration enables the manifestation of signs of either good or evil karma. See, similarly, *Fang deng sanmei xing fa*, T.1940:46.946b24–29 (Stevenson 1987, 137), which, interestingly, calls for a mirror to be placed on the altar during the rite.

126. Kaltenmark 1974; Orofino 1994; Strickmann 2002, 277.

arrival in the purgatorian courts of King Yama, and like the hagiographical trope of a physical mirror that shows past evil deeds or premonitions of one's future rebirth, the mind of the meditator and the mind of the dying person alike become mirrors capable of revealing either purity *or* impurity.[127] Meditation, like death, was a moment of great possibility productive of visions confirming liberation, while at the same time something that might engender more sinister encounters.[128]

Confirmatory Visions and Deathbed Experience

Many of the Buddhist scriptures that became popular in China from the fourth and fifth centuries onward promise their devotees auspicious deathbed visions, typically of a buddha or bodhisattva understood to be an envoy from the pure land or heaven of one's impending rebirth (Fujita 1970, 566–567). The famous "nine grades of rebirth" section of the *Amitāyus Contemplation Scripture* became the most widely cited source of these ideas, but the other Contemplation Scriptures also mention such things in passing.[129] The *Ocean-Samādhi Contemplation Scripture,* uniquely among them, discusses inauspicious deathbed visions as well, specifically the visions visited on those destined for hell, whose many subrealms this text describes in exquisite detail.[130]

Scriptural sources usually portray deathbed visions, good or bad, as what inevitably occurs based on one's karma. But the theoretical link between the last moment of consciousness and one's rebirth destiny also translated into (or was itself the doctrinal translation of) a practical interest in manipulating this moment to bring about the right state of mind, the right vision, and hence the desired rebirth. In the Buddhist deathbed procedure that eventually became the standard one in medieval China and elsewhere in East Asia, the dying person was placed before an image of the Buddha and connected to it

---

127. For physical mirrors as revealers of evil deeds, see *XGSZ*, T.2060:50.461b4–6. A section of the *Methods for Curing* draws on this idea when it directs the meditator to generate shame by imagining a mirror in which his kinsman can see his previously concealed evil deeds (*Methods for Curing* 1.2.2; *ZCB*, T.620:15.333b8–13). Some of the Contemplation Scriptures discuss the idea that premonitory visions will appear within a physical mirror at the moment of death (*GFSMH*, T.643:15.672b3–11). The karma mirror (*yejing* 業鏡) as an instrument of judgment in purgatory is first attested in eighth-century sources (Teiser 1994, 175), but it could derive from an earlier use of this word to mean a physical mirror in which deathbed visions appear, a meaning seen in Chinese-authored texts from the seventh century (*Ji shen zhou san bao gan tong lu*, T.2106:52.421b24) and, even earlier, in Chinese translations of Indian Buddhist texts (*Zheng fa nian chu jing*, T.721:17.177c7–15).

128. As Jacqueline Stone notes, the doctrine that a single moment of proper devotion at the time of death could save even a grave sinner was not a simple promise of salvation for all, since it was "shadowed by the corollary possibility" that a single moment of *wrong* thought could lead one to a bad rebirth despite a lifetime of good (2016, 22).

129. *Guan Wuliangshou fo jing*, T.365:12.344c8–346a26; *Guan Yao wang Yao shang er pusa jing*, T.1161:20.661c18–19; *Guan Mile pusa shang sheng Doushuai tian jing*, T.452:14.420b11–13; *GFSMH*, T.643:15.693b29–c2. All the Contemplation Scriptures show at least some effort to ritualize and control the deathbed moment (Mai 2009, 375–390).

130. *GFSMH*, T.643:15.669a5; 669b13–14; 670a7–10; 670b4–5, and passim.

with a five-colored string, with the image facing west, as if leading the way to the pure land, or east, as if coming from that realm in welcome.[131] These sensory stimuli in the deathbed chamber were, on the one hand, thought to help maintain the dying person's focus on wholesome things and prevent the arising of negative mental states such as fear or attachment, which could lead to a bad rebirth. At the same time, the entire arrangement was itself a ritual enactment of the ideal deathbed vision of a welcoming or guiding buddha. It was as if, by a kind of sympathetic magic, such a ritual could bring about the desired visionary sign confirming a good rebirth—confirmation that we know was important not just for the dying but for the living too, who had personal and institutional interests in discerning, and being able to prove, the good rebirth of the departed (Stone 2016, 182–220). In any case, the dual character of the moment of death—as both a confirmation of an already determined destiny *and* a locus where such destiny could be manipulated—closely parallels the possibilities attributed to meditative confirmatory visions, which for authors such as Zhiyi, as we have seen, could occur either as the manifestation of good roots from past lives, triggered by initial mental concentration, or as a new attainment, the result of present meditative effort.

But even more to the point, both deathbed visions and meditative confirmatory visions were not just revelatory but also *diagnostic*. The *Chan Essentials,* as we saw, treats inauspicious meditative visions not only as carriers of information about the existence of past transgressions, but also as signs directing one to carry out a ritual of repentance to eliminate the obstruction, a ritual whose success is to be confirmed by a new vision. An essentially identical process was envisioned in the case of deathbed visions by Shandao 善導 (613–681) in his *Method for the Samādhi of Bringing to Mind the Buddha Based on the Pratyutpanna Sutra,* a key source for later deathbed ritual practices in China and Japan as well as one of our best early windows onto the ritual contexts in which the Contemplation Scriptures and their teachings were applied.[132] This text outlines the general procedure for a seven-day ritual of "bringing to mind the Buddha" (*nianfo*). After arranging the ritual space, one endeavors to bring to mind the Buddha for seven days, while either sitting or standing, with the aim of obtaining a *jingjie,* a confirmatory vision. Though he does not give any examples, Shandao makes clear that the resulting visions could be good *or* bad, with bad ones necessitating a separate ritual of repentance.[133] Shandao then says that these exact same procedures should also be followed in deathbed rituals:

---

131. Cole 1996, 324–328; Shinohara 2007a, 116–122; Stone 2016, 17–22; 148–156. There also is some evidence of an alternative procedure in which a dying person was shown images of corpses or skeletons in order to contemplate impermanence or achieve *dhyāna* (Greene 2013, 286–289).

132. Shandao's ritual manual is preserved in the *Guan nian Emituo fo xiang hai sanmei gongde fa men* (T.1959), translated in full by Inagaki 1999–2001. See also Stevenson 1995b and Stone 2016, 19.

133. *Guan nian Emituo fo xiang hai sanmei gongde fa men,* T.1959:47.24b15–16.

A practitioner who is about to die, whether sick or not, must also rely entirely on the previously described method.... He should face west and focus his mind on contemplating and imagining Amitāyus Buddha. His thinking and chanting in harmony, with each unceasing utterance he should resolutely imagine being reborn in the Pure Land and a host of holy ones, atop their lotus pedestals, arriving to lead him there.

If the sick person sees such visions (*jing*), he must tell his caregiver, who should write them down. If the sick person is unable to speak, the caregiver must repeatedly question him about what *jingjie* he sees. If he says that he sees signs [attesting to] sin, those in attendance must bring to mind the Buddha on his behalf and aid him in repentance in order to eliminate the sin. If the sin is successfully eliminated, the host of holy ones atop their lotus pedestals will then appear as soon as he brings them to mind.[134]

Shandao directs the dying person to intentionally generate, through an act of focused, meditative imagination, the kinds of visions that would naturally arise for one destined for an auspicious rebirth, yet he does not describe the action as a manipulation—he does not say that visualizing the Buddha *causes* rebirth in the Pure Land. Rather, he treats the procedure as a tool for generating diagnostic visions that either confirm a favorable rebirth or indicate a problem requiring an intervention, whose success is then marked by the replacement of the tainted vision by a good one.

Could the widespread Buddhist understanding of deathbed visions as revelations of rebirth destiny or past karma have helped shape the way that texts such as the *chan* scriptures came to construe significant meditative experience as visionary signs revelatory of karmic purity or impurity? Although the evidence does not allow us to draw so firm a conclusion, it is difficult to avoid the impression that there was a great deal of interpenetration between the two domains, in both of which the meaning of such visions was not merely a question of abstract doctrine but also a matter of the specific interpretations carried out by given communities as they struggled to make sense of what had happened to particular individuals either in their final moments of death or their meditative séances.

We might, for example, consider again the categories of habit and retribution which Zhiyi used to classify confirmatory meditative experiences, the former a manifestation of the mental state associated with a good or bad past deed or meditative attainment, the latter a sudden vision linked to the past karma in question. Tiantai scholars ancient and modern have never identified a precise canonical precedent for Zhiyi's use of these categories.[135] Yet they

---

134. 又行者等，若病不病，欲命終時，一依上...迴面向西，心亦專注，觀想阿彌陀佛。心口相應，聲聲莫絕，決定作往生想、華臺聖眾來迎接想。病人若見前境，即向看病人說。既聞說已，即依說錄記。又病人若不能語者，看病人必須數數問病人見何境界。若說罪相，傍人即為念佛，助同懺悔，必令罪滅。若得罪滅，華臺聖眾念現前。(*Guan nian Emituo fo xiang hai sanmei gongde fa men*, T.1959:47.24b21–28). I have benefited from Stevenson's translation of this passage (1995b, 377–379).

135. The lack of unanimity among commentators as to where these terms come from

are, as we can now see, strikingly similar to the Pāli commentarial contrast between the two kinds of deathbed experience: visions of the objects associated with past actions and of the impending realm of rebirth itself, on the one hand, and the reliving of the state of mind that was active when the original action was performed, on the other. We need not conclude that Zhiyi based his theories of meditative experience on an explicit model of deathbed experience. More likely, he was simply drawing on the presuppositions of a long-standing and evidently widespread tradition—one seen in fifth-century *chan* scriptures such as the *Chan Essentials,* in the Contemplation Scriptures, and in the later writings of Shandao—in which the visions that occurred in meditation and those characteristic of the moment of death were seen as having been generated in similar ways, as carrying similar meanings, and as similarly implicated in decisions about the need for rituals to deal with the effects of karma.

To reiterate, there is nothing unexpected in the notion that a good Buddhist death is "meditative," broadly speaking—the idea that mastery of meditation allows for the mastery of the moment of death is close to being a universal Buddhist ideal, canonically expressed in the biography of the Buddha himself, who both achieved liberation and also died while immersed in the state of *dhyāna* (Walshe 1995, 271). What is less obvious, and what the sources we have examined have shown us, is that these connections did not operate only in one direction, with death transformed, for the enlightened, into an exemplary final moment of meditation. In fifth- and sixth-century China, at least, this analogy also cut the other way: meditative experiences were understood to be similar, in nature and meaning, to the experiences of someone at the moment of death, which was obviously an event of potential relevance to everyone, not just a few elite meditators. To enter a state of meditation was to voluntarily put oneself into a condition of exquisite visionary sensitivity analogous to what was thought to be achieved automatically, though no less significantly, in the final seconds of one's life when visions of karma, good and bad, come to one and all.

Meditation and the Hermeneutics of Purity

In this chapter I have traced a number of instantiations of a widely shared Chinese understanding that Buddhist seated meditation—*chan*—leads to experiences, paradigmatically visionary, that communicate information about the presence or absence of karmic obstructions, the as-yet-unripened fruits of one's past transgressions. This understanding was equally presumed in narratives such as those of Daojin and Zhiyan, who practice *chan* not merely to become enlightened (whatever that would have meant to them) but to gauge their purity with respect to past transgressions; in apocryphal (but in their time fully canonical) scriptures on meditation in which the se-

---

and how they should be understood is reflected in Swanson's translation of the *Mohe zhi guan,* which is not consistent in its treatment of them (2017, 410 and 1366).

miotic links between meditative experience and purifying rites of repentance are discussed at length; and in the meditation treatises of Zhiyi, which despite their formalized vocabulary and systematizing tendency are grounded in similar assumptions about meditation, its practice, its results, and, especially, the hermeneutics of those results.

To understand meditative experience as a divinatory medium for revealing otherwise hidden information about past transgressions is by no means incompatible with basic Buddhist doctrines. The ancient Buddhist notion that *dhyāna* depends on purity with respect to one's vows (*śīla*) already contains (or can be seen to contain) the germ of these ideas, although the sources of the impurity that medieval Chinese sources intended meditation to reveal did go well beyond violations of the monastic rules to include transgressions in past lives and past evil karma in general. While hinted at in Indian sources such as the *Chan Scripture of Dharmatrāta*, it is not until the fifth-century *chan* scriptures that were composed or compiled in China that we first see a systematic exposition of the idea that past transgressions do not simply prevent significant meditative experience but also cause particular forms of it. The potentially abstract doctrinal claim that meditation depends on purity was there translated into a semiotic relationship in which significance flowed in the other direction—down from the nominally higher sphere of meditation to questions relating to karma, sin, and purification, questions that meditation was not intended to transcend (as some modernist interpretations of the implications of normative Buddhist doctrine would have it) but to answer, in a better, more powerful way.

The authors and compilers of these fifth-century Chinese meditation texts thus seem to stake out new ground, relative to classical Buddhist models, in claiming that purification of the type associated with the repentance of transgressions was something far more than a preliminary step onto the path of liberation. Texts like the *Chan Essentials* imply that meditators will be plagued by so-called karmic obstructions all the way up to the highest levels of attainment, and that while the signs of such obstruction would be revealed in meditation, its effective treatment would lie elsewhere, in a cleansing ritual of repentance. In providing the interpretive tools for navigating the connections between meditation and repentance, the fifth-century *chan* scriptures were thus the direct precursors of Zhiyi's more systematic meditation treatises and ritual manuals, in which meditation and repentance are so often conjoined into a single, overarching form. As Daniel Stevenson recognized over thirty years ago, the early Tiantai integration of meditation into a wider ritual and cultic program was not the *ex nihilo* creation of Zhiyi's unique genius (as so much traditional scholarship on him tends to imply), but the systematization of Indian Buddhist liturgical forms that first became widespread in China during the fifth and sixth centuries.[136] Texts such as the

---

136. Stevenson 1987. See also B. Williams 2002, who examines other ritual traditions relevant to this question.

Chan Essentials fill in this story by showing us not the liturgical structures that Stevenson studied (although these are discussed too), but the understanding that went along with those structures concerning what seated meditation is, what kinds of experiences it will produce, and what those experiences have the potential to mean and point to in the world for the one who experiences them. This was an understanding that linked seated meditation to broader ritual programs not only in practice but also in theory.

I stress that this was also so in *theory*—that this understanding was an integral part of what constituted and was accepted as canonical Buddhist doctrine in fifth- and sixth-century China. According to one influential strand of contemporary scholarship on Buddhism, we should not expect what is propounded in the elite doctrines of canonical texts to match the way Buddhism is instantiated "on the ground." Given its normative centrality in Buddhist doctrine concerning the path to liberation, and the undeniable fact that only a small minority of Buddhists ever had the inclination or the luxury of time to devote themselves to it intensively, meditation is most often placed by scholars on the elite or normative rather than the popular or lived side of things. For this reason, postcolonial and post-Orientalist criticisms have insisted—and rightly so—that Buddhism is not, and was not, merely a religion of "otherworldly asceticism," in Weber's famous if flawed characterization; that most Buddhists were not inwardly focused meditators intent on psychologically efficacious mental training aimed at a world-transcending spiritual goal. As this revisionist stream of scholarship so often tells us, even if those methods and aspirations were indeed valued by a small cadre of Buddhist virtuosos and then by "intercultural mimesis" (Hallisey 1995) ended up becoming the orthodox account of Buddhism's true purport among Western scholars and practitioners, such matters were never the main concern of the vast majority of Buddhists. Most Buddhists—monastic and lay, educated and not, at the apex of society as well as at the bottom—had interests that were more localized, embodied, and practical, and they approached Buddhism as a religion that used efficacious rituals and the assistance of gods, buddhas, and bodhisattvas to secure concrete benefits for oneself, one's family, and one's country in this world and the next.

What the material surveyed in this chapter demonstrates, however, is that even on the level of elite doctrinal texts and normative injunctions—at least in China during the time period under consideration—meditation was never reduced to an inner, mental cultivation alone. Neither in its means nor in its ends was meditation even *supposed* to be different in kind from a host of other, nominally lesser forms of Buddhist practice. At the same time, to challenge in this way a purely psychological reading of Buddhist meditation does not require that we disassociate it from the pursuit of extraordinary "experiences" in the sense of happenings to which the subject has privileged access. Indeed, the evidence gathered in this chapter and the last shows that, contrary to what some have argued (Sharf 1995), Buddhists in medieval China did indeed aspire to such things. But if personal meditative experience was thought to be a privileged site of knowing, this does not mean that it was believed to remove all uncertainty. More so than perceptions, meditative experiences, as signs, were in fact recognized as lacking transparent meaning, because they were not thought to resemble or correspond to what they were held to confirm or possibly confirm. As signs understood to operate symbolically, in the sense of being linked to their referents in a nonobvious way, these experiences did not always point inward to the mind of the practitioner or upward to the transcendent realm of nirvana. They also (if not usually) pointed outward and down to the concrete, shared world of rituals, prayers, and karma that all Buddhists inhabited. In respect of both their phenomenology, as spontaneous visions of varied and obscure content, and their meaning and semiotics, as signs revealing karmic purity and the success or failure of rituals of repentance, the experiences that medieval Chinese Buddhists hoped to attain through meditation, and imagined others so obtaining, were more or less continuous with the miraculous happenings that could occur in any number of other circumstances, such as dreams, deathbed visions, or any of the many other types of divine encounter that Buddhist piety of all kinds was thought capable of producing. Meditation may well have been a practice into which only a chosen few might ever have hoped to be initiated. But there was no radical disjunction between the aims of those who gained access to its mysteries and what was sought by Buddhists of less exalted abilities, ambitions, or circumstances.

4

Repentance

To JUDGE FROM the meditation manuals and other texts examined in the previous chapter, carrying out a ritual of *chanhui* (懺悔)—usually translated as repentance or confession—was an undertaking of considerable importance and power for Buddhists of all types. As the ritual cleansing of violations of the Buddhist precepts, *chanhui* was a precondition for successful meditation. But along the road to Buddhist salvation it also was far more than a mere preparatory rite. The meditation practice for which *chanhui* made one fit was itself a means of obtaining visions that could indicate a need for further *chanhui* rituals. And within those rituals, amazing things might happen. In the instructions for meditation that in the fifth century were compiled into the *Chan Essentials* (1.18.13–14), it is during a ritual of repentance, while prostrating to the Buddha, that the practitioner encounters the Buddha's true emanation and hears it preach the Dharma for the first time, an event that quickly lifts him to an advanced meditative attainment and the assurance of final liberation.

The following tale, recounted in a late fifth-century text on monastic discipline composed by the otherwise unknown Chinese monk Fadu 法度, illustrates this evidently widespread idea that repentance has the power to directly trigger the highest normative soteriological achievements:

> There was once a monk named Saṅghavastu,[1] who violated his vow of celibacy. Realizing what he had done, he set aside his staff and robe and donning only his underrobe went about crying: "I am a thief who steals from the buddhas of the ten directions of the past, present, and future!" He traveled widely seeking a means of repentance until at last he found a *vinaya* master. Knowing that Saṅghavastu's transgressions were grave, the *vinaya* master magically created a giant firepit. Saṅghavastu shackled himself and then hurled himself into the fire, which instantly transformed into a pool of water. Then the *vinaya* [master]

---

1. The reconstruction of this name is hypothetical (but see *Fan fan yu,* T.2130:54.1013a20).

said: "If this is your mind, then your precepts have returned to you." Free of the sin of having violated the precepts, Saṅghavastu immediately became an arhat.[2]

With a seemingly Buddhist spin on the Brahmanical idea that death by fire is the only punishment that can purify the gravest infractions, this tale implies that breaches of celibacy, normally a cause for expulsion from the monastic order, can in fact be expiated using special methods.[3] But the claim also goes farther: Saṅghavastu's profound expression of contrition, followed by a self-inflicted punishment that he believed would lead to his own death, not only purifies his sin but immediately propels him forward to arhatship.

The notion that repentance itself can effectuate liberation also informs a story told in several early sixth-century sources concerning the monk Fahui 法惠 (d. 499–501). As the supervisor of nuns in the Gaochang (Turfan) region, Fahui once traveled farther west to the oasis city of Kucha, where he had been told a certain Zhiyue would grant him a great teaching. Fahui finds Zhiyue, who only offers him a large serving of grape wine. Reluctant to break the precepts by drinking, Fahui refuses at first, but when Zhiyue threatens to leave, he acquiesces. Quickly becoming drunk, he passes out. And upon waking:

> Fahui felt great shame, knowing he had violated the precepts. He hit himself and in his remorse blamed himself for his conduct to such an extent that he wanted to end his life. But then, as a result of these reflections (*siwei*), he obtained the third fruit [of sainthood, becoming a non-returner]. Zhiyue returned and asked: "Did you get it?" To which [Fahui] replied: "Yes!"[4]

Chinese Buddhist hagiography often tells of monks (and less frequently nuns) who by their very flouting of the normative rules for ascetics show their transcendence of them (Kieschnick 1997, 51–63). Saṅghavastu and Fahui, however, neither purely maintain the precepts nor transcend them. Their

---

2. 有比丘名僧伽婆藪，遂犯婬，便自覺悟，捨錫杖、法衣，著小舍勒，出入大唱云，我是十方三世佛賊。徧求自悔，至持律所，知其犯重，即化作一大火坑。僧伽婆藪便束身，走投火，火即變成涼池。律云汝心如是，戒還得之。無破戒罪，即得羅漢。(*Apiba lü* 阿毗跋律, cited in *Si fen biqiuni chao*, Z.724:40.761c22–762a3). The *Apiba lü* was supposedly written by Fadu, about whom nothing else is known, between 483 and 494 (*CSZJJ*, T.2145:55.13c7; *Zhong jing mu lu*, T.2146:55.141a4). It survives only in fragments. The name *Apiba* 阿毗跋 (or *Piba* 毗跋 in some sources) is of unclear meaning; it may be a pseudo-Indic transcription.

3. On these Brahamanical ideas, see Kāṇe 1930–1962, 2:924–928. Some Indian Buddhist sources explicitly repudiate this idea of purification through fire (Silk 2007, 277–280). Zhiyi's explanation of repentance, to be discussed below, also mentions the idea of being willing to throw oneself into fire.

4. 自知犯戒，追大慚愧。自搥其身，悔責所行，欲自害命。因此思惟，得第三果。直月還問曰，已得耶。答曰，然。(*BQNZ*, T.2063:50.946b24–27; see also Fahui's biography at *Meisōden shō*, Z.1523:77.358b1–9). This tale vaguely recalls a story told in the *Pānīya-jātaka* where reflection on a wrong deed allows someone to immediately enter a state of meditation and attain liberation (*Jātaka*, 4:114; Cowell 1895, 4:71, no. 459).

stories promote a different model of Buddhist excellence in China—that of the *penitent* monk.[5] Even though Fahui's transgressions do not stem from a lack of restraint per se, this story still emphasizes the power of remorseful repentance, self-castigation, and even physical self-punishment for real sins. The profound nature of penitence is also highlighted lexically: Fahui's remorse is itself a kind of "reflection" (*siwei*), a word often used as a semantic translation of *chan* (meditation), and it brings about the kind of attainment that meditation texts and other sources described as the normative goal of the Buddhist path.[6]

In the previous chapter, a connection between repentance and meditation was seen in the way that certain meditative experiences were understood to be signs revealing the presence or absence of the kind of purity gained through repentance. In this chapter, we consider repentance itself as a key part of the wider ritual and cultic worlds within which the practice of Buddhist meditation occurred in medieval China and in reference to which its fruits were understood. We turn, in other words, to a final aspect of the semiotic ideology of meditative experience and attainment: people's understandings and assumptions about the *consequences* of sign reading, a topic that will take us well outside the practice of meditation itself.

Directing attention to these things, however, aims at something more than just illuminating the broad cultural setting within which meditation happened to have taken place. As we saw in the previous chapter, and are reminded by the stories of Saṅghavastu and Fahui, repentance was connected to meditation, the Buddhist soteriological practice par excellence, not solely as a matter of practice but also in theory. Even in formal, canonical expositions of meditation, the practical and semiotic connections between meditation and repentance arguably privilege the latter. In these sources, practicing meditation is still an inner, mental cultivation carried out in the seated, cross-legged posture. But this activity is enabled by repentance, done to reveal when repentance is necessary, and potentially yields its final fruits in a ritual of repentance. In other words, the inner cultivation of meditation cannot be separated from its ritual contexts not just on the a priori historicist grounds that context matters, but rather because those ritual contexts are already part of how the import of meditation is presented to us in our sources.

The questions this chapter pursues, then, are as follows: What was "repentance" (*chanhui*) in early medieval China? What did a ritual of repentance involve, and what kind of activity was it thought to be? How was it theorized

---

5. We might mention as another penitent monk the famous sixth-century *chan* master Xinxing, founder of the Three Levels (*sanjie* 三階) movement, who is said to have renounced the full precepts (but to have retained a rank superior to the novices), carried out manual labor, and required his followers to live in separate cloisters, apart from the other monks and nuns, as "mute sheep" who remained silent when spoken to (Hubbard 2001, 3–30). These activities are similar to aspects of the *vinaya* penance of probation, discussed below.

6. On *siwei* as a translation of *chan*, see *DZDL*, T.1509:25.185b16.

as a category in relation to other Buddhist practices such as meditation? And how did the ways that this theorization took place relate to wider religious ideas that had currency outside Buddhism as well? As we will see, the activities encompassed by the Chinese term *chanhui* all had precedents in India, but the way they came to be understood in Chinese Buddhism was deeply informed by a ritual world that pre-existed Buddhism's arrival in China, one in which pleading for mercy from sin through a formal declaration of repentance (*hui* 悔) had long been a primary vehicle for obtaining religious benefits.

Chanhui

During the fifth century, different activities going by the name of *chanhui* emerged as a dominant form of Chinese Buddhist ritual.[7] *Chanhui* rituals were part of the daily monastic liturgy and also became the most important component of the activities carried out by both clergy and laity on the "abstinence" (*zhai* 齋) days that occurred six times a month and structured the Buddhist calendar. Through these rituals, patrons and participants hoped to obtain immediate as well as future benefits, including salvation for the souls of the dead, the ordering of the state, and rebirth in heaven.[8] The efficacy of *chanhui* is discussed in many of the Buddhist texts translated into Chinese in the second, third, and fourth centuries (Shi D. 2000, 25–27), and rites going by this name were undoubtedly practiced throughout this time. Still, the fifth century clearly marked a turning point of sorts, and most later forms of Buddhist *chanhui* rituals draw to at least some extent on scriptures and ritual manuals translated or composed in the early fifth century.

Traditional Definitions of *Chanhui* and Its English Translations
Before looking at these rituals in some detail, we might first consider the question of what the term *chanhui* meant to Chinese Buddhists, and secondarily how it has been rendered in English. The words most often used to translate it—"repentance," "confession," "confession and repentance," and "confession and contrition"—are all problematic in certain ways,[9] so let us begin instead with the definition provided in modern Japanese and Chinese dictionaries

---

7. Several books have treated the topic of Buddhist *chanhui* in early medieval China in recent years: Ri 1982; Kuo 1994; Shi D. 2000; Shengkai 2004; Wang J. 1998 and 2008; and Yang M. 2007. These studies are all indebted to the voluminous Japanese scholarship on this subject, above all the works of Shioiri Ryōdō, the most important of which have been recently collected in Shioiri 2007. In English, see B. Williams 2002; Hong 2014; Stevenson 1987 (esp. 401–418) and 2007; Chappell 2005; McGuire 2014, 53–80; and Adamek 2015.

8. Concerning the popularity of *chanhui* rituals among the southern aristocracy in the fifth and sixth centuries, see Vande Walle 1979; Nakajima 1991.

9. These translations are standard in scholarly writing on Chinese Buddhism and also in contemporary dictionaries of modern and classical Chinese (Mathews 1996, 18; *A Chinese English Dictionary*, 132; DeFrancis 2003, 97; Kroll 2015, 40 [who adds: "to ask forgiveness"]; *Le Grand Ricci,* entries for *chan* 懺 and *chanhui* 懺悔).

of Buddhist terminology, which say that *chanhui* means "to remorsefully apologize for transgressions so as to thereby request mercy."[10] This by all accounts is a traditional definition, and it is notable in several ways.

First, *chanhui*, by this understanding, is not primarily a matter of *confession*, if by this word we mean the revelation of specific, hitherto hidden transgressions. The scripts that Chinese Buddhists used (and to this day still use) to conduct *chanhui* rituals usually do contain lists of sins, but the lists are almost always formulaic and inclusive; what they enumerate are not the specific misdeeds that the ritualist is conscious of having committed but all possible transgressions that one might be guilty of in this or even previous lifetimes.[11] Indeed, it is the nonspecific nature of such a script that allows it to be used as a communal liturgy.[12] In fact, the transgressions for which one carries out a ritual of *chanhui* need not even be one's own and hence can include the sins of family members, among others (Chappell 2005), something also true of medieval Daoist repentance rituals (Bokenkamp 2013). It would be a mistake to take the formulaic nature of such scripts, and the fact that the ritual can be performed on behalf of others, to mean that *chanhui* was an unusual or deficient form of "confession," a charge first leveled by early Christian missionaries in China, who did *not*, we should note, use the word *chanhui* in their translation of Christian confessional terminology (Zürcher 2006, 118). The point here, rather, is that the concept of confession fails to capture the kind of action *chanhui* was thought to be.[13]

Second, *chanhui* is not a purely internal act, as the word "repentance"—which is arguably the most appropriate translation from a semantic point of view, and the one I mostly use—might suggest. Rather, to engage in *chanhui* is in some manner to *express* one's remorse to another person or to a divine presence.[14] It is, accordingly, a necessarily social and ritual act. By synecdoche, then, the word *chanhui* typically denotes the entire rite within which such declarations are made, rites that invariably include offerings, worship, and other formal invocations. Moreover, *chanhui* is not merely descriptive of

---

10. 謂悔謝罪過以請求諒解。 (*Fo guang da ci dian*, 6772). See, similarly, *Bukkyō daijiten*, 6.1493. This definition has been directly adapted from medieval lexicons (*Yi qie jing yin yi*, T.2128:54.448b9 and 700c12; cf. 408b2, which is different and probably influenced by Yijing's comments, which I discuss below).

11. There are some isolated exceptions to this characterization. From the early medieval era, perhaps the most famous of these is the personal repentance liturgy attributed to Shenyue 沈約 (441–513), in which he describes his own youthful indiscretions in detail (*GHMJ*, T.2013:52.331b16–c26).

12. Zürcher 2006, 113, suggests the communal confession of sins during a Catholic mass as an analogy.

13. "Confession" may also not be the right idea in the case of Daoism; see "Repentance in Early Daoism" below.

14. Tada 1981, 45–48. As Tada notes, modern dictionaries often obscure this point. The *Han yu da ci dian* (11.466), for example, defines *chanhui* as: "to *recognize* one's past errors or sins and *feel* regret."

such rituals; it also has a function within them. The famous stanzas on repentance from the *Golden Light Scripture,* translated in the early fifth century and a source for many later Chinese repentance liturgies, provides a typical example:

> I now *repent* (*chanhui*) all the myriad sins of my karma accumulated through evil acts of body, speech, and mind. / I now *repent* all the myriad sins of having failed to honor the Buddha, Dharma, or Sangha. / I now *repent* all the myriad sins of having failed to honor bodhisattvas and *pratyekabuddha*s. / I now *repent* all the myriad sins of having, out of ignorance, slandered the true Dharma, as well as those of having failed to honor my parents, teachers, and elders.[15]

Here *chanhui* is not a mere description of what someone must do through other means—it is itself a word meant to be used. To express remorse for one's transgressions involves actually saying, "I *repent*." The word is therefore illocutionary, in Austin's sense (1962), and in this capacity forms a key component of almost all *chanhui* liturgies.

Third, and most important, the act of *chanhui* is not a merely self-expressive gesture; it is rather the expression of remorse for the particular end of requesting remission from the expected consequences of the transgressions in question. In liturgical texts of the Mahāyāna variety, upon which the general structure of medieval Chinese Buddhist *chanhui* rituals was based (Stevenson 1987, 432–462), one who repents the named transgressions typically goes on to request that their negative effects, in the form of bad karma, be eliminated. In the *Golden Light Scripture* this request occurs just after the verses cited above.

Writing in the late sixth century, Zhiyi highlights this aspect of *chanhui* in the first of his widely cited explanations of the meaning of the word:

> As for the meaning of *chanhui, chan* means to ask pardon[16] of the Three Jewels and all sentient beings, while *hui* means to seek indulgence by expressing shame and pledging to correct one's wrongs. [One declares]: "If this sin of mine can

---

15. 身口意惡，所集三業，如是眾罪，今悉懺悔。或不恭敬，佛法聖眾，如是眾罪，今悉懺悔。或不恭敬，緣覺菩薩，如是眾罪，今悉懺悔。以無智故，誹謗正法。不知恭敬，父母尊長。如是眾罪，今悉懺悔。(*Jin guang ming jing*, T.663:16.337a17–23). Here *chanhui* translates *deśyāmi* 'I declare' or 'I acknowledge' (Kuo 1994, 25; Nobel 1937, 27–28).

16. "Ask pardon of" translates *chanxie* 懺謝. Note that Zhiyi's definition is circular: he glosses *chan* 懺 via a compound that includes this character. He seems not to have been trying to define the word *chanhui* so much as explaining the significance of doing *chanhui*. Western scholars, in this passage, have sometimes rendered *chanxie* as "confess" (Stevenson 1999, 468; Kuo 1994, 62), but this cannot be correct and is probably influenced by the idea, derived from Yijing's comments discussed below, that *chanhui* must include the meaning of "confession." *Chanxie* surely has the same meaning in Zhiyi's comments here as the Chinese word *xie* 謝, "ask pardon of" or "apologize to." There are many clear examples in medieval Buddhist texts where *chanxie* can only be construed this way (see, e.g., *Shi song lü*, T.1435:23.188b24–25; *Da fang bian fo bao en jing*, T.156:3.146b5; *DZDL*, T.1509:25.71a21–25).

be destroyed, then in the future I would rather lose my life than to again perform this deed, which is productive of suffering." Giving rise to a state of mind like that of the monk who said to the Buddha that he would sooner throw himself into a mass of fire than to transgress the Buddha's pure precepts, one prays that the Three Jewels will confirm their acceptance [of this prayer]. This is what is called *chanhui*.[17]

For Zhiyi, it is a plea for remission from a merited punishment, effectuated by the sincere expression of remorse and a vow to exercise future restraint.

Chanhui as a Plea for Mercy for Oneself or Others

Zhiyi's emphasis on *chanhui* as a *plea for mercy* matches closely how the word was deployed by early Chinese translators of Indian Buddhist literature. We can see the usage and meaning attributed to this word particularly clearly in the translations of narrative literature, where the context of the story shows us what *chanhui* was thought to accomplish and how and by whom it could be carried out. In one early collection of tales, for example, a group of ministers, realizing that they have wrongly imprisoned a forest hermit (*pratyekabuddha*) and mindful that wronged ascetics in India often use their magic to enact swift vengeance, turn to him to "perform obeisance and do *chanhui*, [saying]: 'We were fools for having wrongly imprisoned you, O sage. Have compassion and pardon us this transgression! Let us not, in the future, be punished [for it].' "[18] Here, just as Zhiyi suggests, to render *chanhui* is to declare that one's actions were wrong and to beg for remission from any retribution.[19]

That the request for remission is the central element comes out clearly in another relatively early translation of an Indian text, a telling of the famous story in which Devadatta tries to kill the Buddha using a herd of wild elephants. After this misadventure, Devadatta's disciple, King Ajātaśatru, is

---

17. 夫懺悔者，懺名懺謝三寶及一切眾生，悔名慚愧改過求哀。我今此罪，若得滅者，於將來時寧失身命，終不更造如斯苦業。如比丘白佛，我寧抱是熾然大火，終不敢毀犯如來淨戒。生如是心，唯願三寶證明攝受，是名懺悔。(*CDFM*, T.1916:46.485b16–23). In his commentary to the *Golden Light Scripture*, Zhiyi gives a similar explanation: "*Chan* means 'surrender to,' while *hui* means 'submit to.' It is just as in the secular world when one has committed a crime against the ruler, [to avoid punishment] one submits to and then fully obeys [the ruler], daring not to go against him.... One thus submits oneself at the feet of the Three Treasures and obeys the teachings without daring to commit [further] wrong, and hence it is called *chanhui*." 懺者首也，悔者伏也。如世人得罪於王，伏欵順從不敢違逆...伏三寶足下正順道理，不敢作非，故名懺悔。(*Jin guang ming jing wen ju*, T.1785:39.59a8–11). "To surrender to" (*shou* 首) was a secular Chinese legal principle by which those who turned themselves in before their crimes had been discovered obtained a reduced sentence (Rickett 1971).

18. 作禮懺悔。我等愚癡，無故枉困道士，當以大慈，原赦我罪，莫使我將來受此重殃。(*Xing qi xing jing*, T.197:4.165b1–3). This text is listed as an anonymous translation in the *Chu san zang ji ji* (T.2145:55.21.c23). It uses the older sutra introductory formula (聞如是) typical of pre-fifth-century texts (Funayama 2007a, 244; Nattier 2014, 41–44).

19. Although in this and the next case the original Indic term is unknown, both would fit with a causative form of √kṣam; see n. 26 below.

described as rendering *chanhui* to the Buddha by saying: "It was not my wrong-doing, it was that of Devadatta!"[20] Notice here that Ajātaśatru *denies* that he is responsible for what has happened. No clearer example could be found to demonstrate that the central meaning of *chanhui*, as this word was employed by the translators and authors of these texts, was to *plead for remission*, not confess.

Hence we need not appeal to a distinctly "Chinese" modification of Buddhist principles, as some scholars have done (Chappell 2005), to explain why *chanhui* so often became a means of redressing not only one's own transgressions but those of others. Even in early translations of Buddhist literature into Chinese we find many examples where *chanhui*, in the sense of *plead for mercy*, operates in this fashion. While some are relatively prosaic, involving the delivery of an apology by a third party,[21] in other cases what transpires is equivalent to a full-fledged *chanhui* ritual. In a story from the early Chinese translation of the *Avadānaśataka*, for example, a certain monk encounters a hungry ghost who beseeches him to "make offerings to the Buddha and his monks *and do chanhui on my behalf*, for then I can surely escape [confinement in] this body of a hungry ghost."[22]

As a plea for remission, the performance of *chanhui* is prompted in many stories by the initial appearance of the punishment one wishes to avoid in full. Commenting on the famous passage in the *Amitāyus Contemplation Scripture* where Queen Vaidehī, imprisoned by her evil son, renders *chanhui* to the Buddha, Huiyuan 慧遠 (523–592) poses the question: "How does Vaidehī know that she has sinned in the past such that she now seeks to perform *chanhui*?" The answer is that her unjust imprisonment is the evidence of a past-life sin that she seeks to destroy through *chanhui*.[23] The idea that it is an encounter with hardship that motivates a person to carry out *chanhui* is a staple trope in medieval Chinese Buddhist stories (Campany 2012, 74, 181, 242). One performs *chanhui* not merely out of an inward feeling of guilt, though

---

20. 非是我過，提婆達多耳。(*Da fang bian fo bao en jing*, T.156:3.147c2–7). This eclectic text was compiled in China sometime in the fifth century (Funayama 2007b, 9).

21. *Da banniepan jing*, T.374:12.594a2–3.

22. 今若能為我設供施佛及僧，為我懺悔，我必當得脫餓鬼身。(*She ji bai yuan jing*, T.200:4.225b1). The parallel passage in the extant Sanskrit version, for the Chinese 為我懺悔, reads *deśanāṃ ca kāraya* (Vaidya 1958, 117). If this is the same reading the Chinese translators saw, they must have interpreted it to mean "make [on my behalf] a declaration [of sin]," taking *deśanā* as implying *pāpadeśanā*, "declaration of sins," which the Chinese word *chanhui* often translated. In the extant Sanskrit *Avadānaśataka*, however, *deśanā* in this passage seems more likely to mean *dharmadeśanā*, preaching the Dharma, with the idea being that by hearing a Dharma discourse the hungry ghost will be able to gain a better rebirth. The Chinese translation, which also later includes a scene of the hungry ghost appearing himself and repenting, may have been based on a slightly different version. Stories in which those in unfortunate destinies ask the living to perform *chanhui* on their behalf are common in later Chinese Buddhist literature (see, e.g., *Shen seng zhuan*, T.2064:50.1014.b22–24), as are those in which Buddhist monks are asked to do *chanhui* for someone who is still alive (Yanagida 1969, 220; Faure 1986a, 131; Wu 1979, 13).

23. *Guan Wuliangshou fo jing yi shu*, T.1749:37.177c24–178a2 (K. Tanaka 1990, 145–146).

a sense of remorse is certainly not excluded (as in the story of Fahui above), but because of an objective circumstance that, in accordance with the principles of karma, is a *sign* of a past sin for which remission can now be sought. This logic, needless to say, is identical to the way fifth-century meditation texts such as the *Chan Essentials* treat certain meditative visions as signs of a karmic obstruction that must be purified through repentance.

Chanhui as Repentance

From the standpoint of a performative, illocutionary act, to do *chanhui* is to plead for remission from punishment. But to understand the place of this concept and its attendant practices in the medieval Chinese world, simply translating *chanhui* as "pleading for remission from punishment" is not enough. We must also take into account the fact that, semantically, the Chinese character *hui* 悔, forming the second half of the word, does mean *remorse*. And indeed, in Chinese Buddhist literature, *chanhui* was often used interchangeably with the fully Chinese term *huiguo* 悔過, literally meaning "to express remorse for wrongdoing." *Huiguo* was actually the more common expression until the turn of the fifth century, and it too was something one could do on behalf of others.[24] With this in mind, while we may continue to translate *chanhui* as "repentance," we must remember that it pointed to a recognized form of social action. *Chanhui* did not mean the expression of remorse full stop, but an expression of remorse in a context where that was how one could plead for remission from the merited consequences of bad actions either for oneself or for another. As we will see in a moment, such conventions were common in pre-Buddhist China, where "expressing remorse for wrongdoing" (*huiguo*) or "blaming oneself" (*zize* 自責) had long been the usual way of asking for mercy from both human sovereigns and divine forces.

The translators who rendered the ritual formulas of Indian Buddhism into Chinese were clearly aware of these conventions, and they took into account not just the semantic meaning of the words, but also the pragmatic question of what kind of language was used in China to do similar things. This awareness helps explain the creation of the word *chanhui* itself, long a source of controversy among commentators ancient and modern.

Lexically, *chanhui* appears at first glance to be a bilingual binome, a single term that combines both a transcription and a semantic translation of a foreign word.[25] Many early Chinese commentators, beginning with Jingying Huiyuan and Jizang 吉藏 (549–623), explained the word in this way: as a combination of *chan* (懺), the sound of the Indic verb √*kṣam*, with its Chinese

---

24. For a clear example, see Dharmarakṣa's 284 translation of the *Avaivartikacakra-sūtra*, in which the audience "expresses remorse for wrongdoing" (*huiguo*) in order to beg for mercy for those who in later generations might slander the sutra (*Aweiyuezhishujing*, T.266.9.225a18–21). The later Chinese translations of this text (T.267 and T.268) use the word *chanhui*.

25. On this class of terminology in Chinese Buddhist texts, see Chen S. 2000, 379–384.

meaning *hui* (悔), "express remorse."[26] Yet things are not quite so simple. As was later pointed out by Yijing 義淨 (635–713), a frequent critic of mainstream Chinese Buddhism in light of his firsthand knowledge of India, the verb √*kṣam*, in its causative or imperative forms, actually means "request pardon" (*ren* 忍), a concept with "no connection at all" to the idea of remorse. Moreover, he noted, the ritual texts that Chinese Buddhists typically use to purify themselves of transgressions are in fact translations of Indian texts that use the term *āpatti-[prati]deśanā*, which, Yijing explains, means "speak one's sins" (說罪). From this analysis, Yijing concludes that the Chinese word *chanhui* is a bad translation, since "repentance" (*hui*) means neither "speak one's sins" nor "request pardon."[27]

Yijing's intention here was normative and polemical. He believed that *chanhui* expressed an idea that was not in accord with proper Buddhist understanding. And his polemic failed inasmuch as Chinese Buddhists did not stop using this term. But his philological analysis was not without merit, as modern scholars have noted (Hirakawa 1990). The Chinese word *chanhui* does indeed often translate the expression *[prati]deśanā*, "to acknowledge [sins]," which, as Yijing noted, is what many Indian Buddhist ritual formulas say one should do with one's transgressions.[28] (It is this term that *chanhui* translates in the passages from the *Golden Light Sutra* cited earlier.) Still, we should not conclude

---

26. *Guan Wuliangshou jing yi shu*, T.1749:37.177c25–27 and *Jin guang ming jing shu*, T.1787:39.162b28–29, respectively. The commentaries of Daoxuan 道宣 (596–667) are thus not where this explanation first appears, as many scholars have claimed (Shengkai 2004, 16; Hirakawa 1990, 434; Tada 1981, 58n6). Most Chinese commentators say the *chan* of *chanhui* corresponds to the Indic *chan-mo* 懺摩; since *chanhui* is done by the person who has transgressed, this can only imply a second-person imperative ("please forgive") or third-person causative ("ask forgiveness of") form of √*kṣam* (in the indicative, "to be patient"), both common in Indian literature (Cone 2001, 753; Hiraoka 2002, 258–260). Jizang alone gives *chan-mo-pi* 懺摩毘, clearly trying to represent a causative verbal or participial ending (*kṣamāpayati, kṣamāpita*). Some modern scholars (Hirakawa 1990), agreeing with Yijing (discussed below), have suggested that *chanhui* cannot be a translation of √*kṣam* because *chanhui* usually takes a single object—the transgressions—while causative √*kṣam* takes the *person whose forgiveness is sought* as a direct object (when √*kṣam* is in the imperative, the person being forgiven is an indirect object usually in the dative). Yet even though Hirakawa is right that, later, *chanhui* most commonly translated other words, there are early instances, anomalous relative to later usage, where *chanhui* does follow the Indic grammar of causative √*kṣam*: "some bowed their heads and begged *the prince* for forgiveness" (或有叩頭懺悔太子; T.172:3.427b6); "I now beg *the Buddha* for forgiveness" (我今懺悔如來尊; T.120:2.543b4). There is therefore no reason to doubt that *chanhui* began as a translation of (causative or imperative) √*kṣam*, meaning "request mercy."

27. *Nan hai ji gui nei fa zhuan*, T.2125:54.217c18–22. See also *Gen ben shuo yi qie you bu pi'naiye*, T.1442:23.706.a8–10.

28. *Vinayapiṭaka*, 1:126 (Horner 1938–1971, 4:167). For a survey of this formula and others, see Haskett 2010, 91–115. Mahāyāna rituals use multiple synonymous verbs in sequence, including "I do not conceal" (*na pracchādayāmi*) and "I reveal" (*āviṣkaromi*). *[Prati]deśanā* is often translated as "confession." Yet, as in Chinese *chanhui* rituals, the Indian Buddhist scripts for doing *pratideśanā* are often formulaic, not personal (Crosby and Skilton 2008, 14–19). Thus whatever its semantic meaning, the action denoted by the word *pratideśanā* does not always have the character of what we would call the act of *confessing*.

from this that *chanhui* simply means "to speak one's sins," that is, to confess—not, at least, if the point is to understand what this word meant to Chinese Buddhists. Indeed, by the turn of the fifth century, *chanhui* regularly translated multiple Indic words, not only *pratideśanā* 'to acknowledge [sins],' but also causative or imperative forms of √*kṣam* 'request pardon,' as well as the verb *pratikaroti*, a common term in Indian religious texts for a formal declaration of guilt and plea for mercy.[29] Searching for a single Indic equivalent of *chanhui* is thus a red herring: *chanhui* was, or at least by the turn of the fifth century had become, a fully Chinese concept, one that was seen as the appropriate rendering of multiple different Indic words, many (if not most) of which did not explicitly carry the semantic weight of "repent" or "remorse."

Yijing was, then, essentially correct: the Chinese word *chanhui* introduces a semantic component, the idea of remorse, that was lacking, at least overtly, in the Indic words or phrases it was most commonly made to translate. This is not to say that all such ideas were necessarily absent from the Indian practices collectively designated in China as *chanhui*. But in terms of the categories by which these forms of social and ritual action were represented, there is nonetheless a significant difference between the Indian and Chinese terminology. This difference came about in part because the translators of Chinese Buddhist literature were not just producing philologically correct glosses on Indian words. They were producing language intended to accomplish speech acts—specifically, pleading for remission from punishment—for which there already were conventional forms of expression in China. Grasping the meaning and role that *chanhui* came to have in Chinese Buddhism, the powers that were attributed to it, and the intellectual work that was accomplished by making typologies of it, requires that we take these points into consideration. But before proceeding to that assessment, it is time to examine a concrete ritual of Buddhist repentance—one connected to the fifth-century meditation texts we have been studying—in greater detail.

Repentance for Meditators

Although most of the fifth-century Chinese *chan* scriptures examined in the previous chapters say that rituals of *chanhui* are a necessary accompaniment

---

29. The Jain *paḍikkamaṇa* (Skt. *pratikramaṇa*) was used in a nearly identical meaning (Caillat 1965, 155–157). Dundas's description of Jain *pratikramaṇa* is an equally apt summary of the Buddhist rituals that in China were called *chanhui:* an "inner examination and self-criticism conjoined with a predetermined liturgical recitation which acknowledges transgressions towards other creatures and provides an expiation for these in the form of a request for forgiveness" (Dundas 2011, 330). *Chanhui* often translates *pratikaroti* in the Chinese translations of *vinaya* and Āgama literature (Mori 1999), where it means the procedures specified in the *vinaya* to restore a violator to purity (*Manorathapūraṇī*, 3.216), hence the term *appaṭikamma* 'for which there can be no atonement,' referring to the *pārājika* transgressions (*Aṅguttaranikāya*, 1.20; *Manorathapūraṇī*, 1.94; *Samantapāsādikā*, 7.1319). Some explanations of the word stress the ritual act of acknowledging the transgression and requesting the community's acceptance; in these cases, it is nearly synonymous with √*kṣam* (*Manorathapūraṇī*, 2.170).

to the practice of meditation, they provide few details concerning how such rites are to be carried out or what they are intended to accomplish.[30] Readers of these texts were evidently assumed to already know about such matters or to have access to that information elsewhere.[31] However, we do find one comparatively rich set of instructions for a repentance ritual in the *Methods for Curing*, which includes, among its many methods for "curing" meditators of problems such as physical illness and demonic attacks, a long section called Method for Curing Violations of the Precepts (治犯戒法).[32] We cannot say if this rite was ever actually employed by Chinese Buddhists. But at the very least it shows us how some fifth-century Chinese Buddhists chose to imagine the benefits and procedures of repentance—how, that is, drawing on Indian Buddhist models, they were working with the category of "repentance" in the context of the forms they thought relevant for practitioners of meditation.

Method for Curing Violations of the Precepts

The instructions begin with a general claim that meditators who transgress the Buddhist monastic code will be led into harm.[33] Precept breakers, we are told, will falsely report to their teachers that they see the proper confirmatory visions (*jingjie*) while meditating when in fact they see only inauspicious visions, such as monks with smashed heads and broken legs. These negative visions will soon lead them into madness, causing them to "dance and sing, lie on the ground in filth, and perform various evil actions."[34] To cure these problems, a multifaceted ritual is required, divided into three main parts, each beginning with *chanhui*, an act of repentance, followed by a final section in which the results are announced to the monastic community.

In the first segment of the ritual (*Methods for Curing* 1.9.3), the transgressor repents his misdeeds to his personal teacher and then brings to mind (*nian* 念) and venerates a litany of deities and other objects of worship: the seven buddhas of the past, including Śākyamuni Buddha, followed by the thirty-five buddhas, numerous bodhisattvas, and the Great Vehicle. He then contemplates emptiness (觀於空法) and imagines these deities pouring water over his head. He further imagines himself as having fallen into hell, where he prays to be rescued by the Buddha. Although the Method for Curing Violations of the Precepts gives only a few details concerning these steps, it makes

---

30. In most cases, no procedure at all is described (*ZCSM*, T.614:15.271a5; *Chan Essentials* 1.1.7, 1.2.1.5, 1.13.3, 1.18.8; *WMCJ*, T.619:15.329b5; 330a21; *DMDL*, T.618:15.322b4). Others provide only rudimentary instructions (*Chan Essentials* 1.14.6, 1.17.3, 1.18.14, 2.19.1.9, 2.19.2.4).

31. A passage from the *Ocean-Samādhi Contemplation Scripture* even explicitly states that the procedure for repentance is found "in another text" (*GFSMH*, T.643:15.655b6–24).

32. *Methods for Curing* 1.9.1–12; *ZCB*, T.620:15.336c16–337c17.

33. The transgressions to be treated are described as those "ranging from the *duṣkṛta* (突吉羅) to the *pārājika* (波羅夷) offenses" (*Methods for Curing* 1.9.1; *ZCB*, T.620:15.336c20–21), which suggests the monastic *prātimokṣa*. Later it is also assumed that the practitioner will have a monastic robe. Laymen and laywomen are, however, mentioned in the introduction to the ritual.

34. 或歌，或舞，臥地糞穢，作種種惡。(*Methods for Curing* 1.9.2; *ZCB*, T.620:15.337a15–16)

perfectly clear the criterion for judging their success: the practitioner will
have an auspicious dream in which the buddhas he has prayed to "will, from
the white tuft of hair between their eyebrows, emit a light that relieves his
hellish suffering."[35]

In the next part (1.9.4), the toilet-cleaning penance, attention shifts to
a community-focused set of tasks. The transgressor must remove his outer
robe (saṅghāti) and appear before the full monastic community, where "he
must cast his body to the ground like a great mountain collapsing. His heart
filled with shame, he must repent all his sins, and for eight hundred days
perform menial services for the other monks [such as] cleaning and emptying the toilets."[36]

In the third part (1.9.5), the practitioner returns to his preceptor after
the eight hundred days of menial service and again repents. He is then instructed in meditation:

> The wise teacher must say to him: "O monk, you must now contemplate your
> body as a golden vase filled with four poisonous snakes, two of which go up while
> two go down, each spewing poison most dreadfully. Next contemplate a dragon
> with six heads that encircles the vase and spews poison that drips into the mouths
> of the snakes. A great tree [covering] the four directions emerges from the
> golden vase and fills the triple world. The black elephants approach and try to
> uproot the tree. On all four sides fire springs forth."[37]

Many of these images—the black elephants uprooting a tree, the six-headed
dragon—appear among the confirmatory visions identified in the *Chan Essentials*. Here in the Method for Curing Violations of the Precepts, the preceptor explains their symbolic meaning to the penitent monk (1.9.6) before
instructing him to again clean the sanctuary and "contemplate the Buddha"
(*guanfo*) until he sees the Buddha radiate light and touch his head with his
hand. Then he must perform the contemplation of impurity until he has
completely mastered it with no remaining obstacles.

As a final step, the practitioner—using language typical of the legal proceedings of the *vinaya*—declares his or her purity to the community and asks
for permission to "recite the precepts" (說戒), that is, to formally rejoin the
Sangha as a member in full standing:

> I, the monk so-and-so (or, the nun so-and-so), have finished eight hundred days
> of menial service, have performed the contemplation of the poisonous snakes,
> have completed the meditation on hell, have further contemplated a single

---

35. 放白毫光，救地獄苦。(*ZCB*, T.620:15.337a24)

36. 五體投地如大山崩，心懷慚愧懺悔諸罪。為僧執事作諸苦役，掃廁擔糞，經八百日。(*ZCB*,
T.620:15.337a26–28)

37. 智者應當告言。比丘。汝今自觀汝身，猶如金瓶盛四毒蛇，二上二下，吐毒可畏。復觀一龍六頭
繞瓶，龍亦吐毒毒，滴蛇口中。四方大樹，從金瓶出，遍三界。黑象復來，欲拔此樹，四面火起。(*ZCB*,
T.620:15.337b2–6)

buddha, recited the repentance text, and in the contemplation of impurity I have again reached the stage of the nonexistence of self and other, where I have had a confirmatory vision of the Buddha pouring a pitcher of water over my head. And in my dreams a god appeared and told me I was pure. That I am now fully humble is something I know for certain. Please permit me [to rejoin the Sangha].[38]

Following this declaration, which is notable for including a public claim to meditative attainment of some kind, the penitent is deemed to have "regained the state of being no different than a pure monk."[39] The connection between the ritual and the restoration of meditative power is then reiterated by declaring that those who fail to properly repent for even minor violations of the precepts will, in their present lifetime, never attain liberation *even if* they practice meditation (1.9.10).

Grave Transgressions and Their Purification

Later Chinese Buddhist exegetes often cited the Method for Curing Violations of the Precepts as the most effective way to purify violations of the *pārājika* transgressions, the most serious infractions of the monastic rules, which nominally entail the permanent loss of status as a monk or nun.[40] The promise to completely heal such transgressions is indeed a distinctive feature of this ritual. That it addresses this question at all, however, is not unprecedented. The question of how and to what extent one could become free of the consequences of *pārājika* transgressions was in fact a fertile site of commentary, where medieval Buddhist analysts, both Indian and Chinese, thought through the relationship between transgressions, purity, institutional status, and matters of soteriology.

As we saw in the previous chapter, the foundational Buddhist doctrine of the three trainings postulates that meditative attainment depends on having pure *śīla*. While the term *śīla* encompasses various modalities of ethical practice and ascetic restraint, it also refers specifically to taking on, through ordination, and successfully following thereafter, the many rules of training for Buddhist monks and nuns contained in the *prātimokṣa*. The notion that only those who follow an ascetic discipline can obtain final liberation was shared throughout the Indian religious milieu in which Buddhism arose. Even though Buddhists distinguished themselves relative to this background by denying that *severe* ascetic discipline was necessary (Freiberger 2006), they still agreed that one had to take on some restrictions in

---

38. 欲說戒時，應唱是語：某甲比丘，某甲比丘尼，已八百日，行於苦役。七日觀佛眉間白毫，作毒蛇觀，地獄想成，復觀一佛，說懺悔法，不淨觀門無我人鏡[>境]，還復通達。境界中，佛以澡罐水，灌比丘頂，天神現夢，說已[>己]清淨。今已慚愧。我所證知。唯願聽許。(*Methods for Curing* 1.9.8; *ZCB*, T.620:15.337b15–20)

39. 然後方與如淨比丘得無有異。(*ZCB*, T.620:15.337b22)

40. *Si fen lü shan fan bu que xing shi chao*, T.1804:40.97a7.

order to become a monk or nun, and that only those who possessed this status could reach the highest religious goals.[41]

The link between one's formal status as a monk or nun and the possibility of higher religious attainment is what was at stake when Indian Buddhist meditation manuals claimed that *pārājika* transgressions, which cannot be atoned for in the manner of other violations of the monastic rules, produce permanent obstacles to meditative achievement. Thus, according to the *Vimuttimagga*, anyone who transgresses a *pārājika* has "cut off his monkhood" and will therefore be incapable of meditative attainment.[42] This idea must have been reasonably widespread in middle-period Indian Buddhism, and it is alluded to in other post-canonical Pāli sources.[43] It is also mentioned in some of the Indian meditation manuals introduced to China in the early fifth century. Kumārajīva's *Meditation Scripture* says that a *pārājika* violator, like a "withered tree" that will not produce leaves or fruit even when watered, must renounce meditation for the present lifetime in favor of other forms of practice such as the recitation of scriptures.[44] Similar statements appear in Kumārajīva's *Explanations of Meditation*.[45]

The *Vimuttimagga* and the *Meditation Scripture* both presume a monastic audience. Although denying *pārājika* violators the ability to successfully meditate, these texts also seem to assume that they might well be found within the Buddhist monastic community.[46] This was not an unreasonable assumption because Indian Buddhist monastic codes do provide methods of purification that allowed such people, specifically those who had violated the vow of celibacy (the first *pārājika*), to remain within the clerical fold, albeit in a position of reduced status commonly known as a *śikṣādattaka* (one who has been given the training).[47] As we will see, the authors of the Method for Curing Violations of the Precepts were clearly engaging with Indian debates about the soteriological and meditative potential of the *śikṣādattaka*. Because

---

41. There did eventually develop a concept of a layperson's *śīla* as the five precepts or the eight fast-day precepts (Agostini 2002). And even early scriptures do allow that laypeople could attain *some* of the highest Buddhist fruits. But the famous doctrine that a layperson who becomes an arhat will either become a monk or nun or die within twenty-four hours (*Milindapañho*, 264–266) shows the reluctance to extend such ideas indefinitely (Gombrich 1988, 75–76).

42. *Jie tuo dao lun*, T.1648:32.404a10–14.

43. *Samantapāsādikā*, 1.236.

44. *ZCSM*, T.614:15.271a3–5.

45. *Chan fa yao jie*, T.616:15.287a27–b3.

46. The *Chan fa yao jie* comments that such a person should "preach the Dharma and spread the teachings" (說法教化; T.616:15.287b3) rather than meditate. This seems to presume an official, clerical position.

47. On the *śikṣādattaka*, see La Vallée Poussin 1927, 208; Hirakawa 1964, 246–254; Satō Tatsugen 1986, 146–152; Schopen 2002, 262; and Clarke 2009. José Cabezón (2017, 188) has suggested that the *śikṣādattaka* option was "rarely" employed in practice in South Asia, but his only evidence for this claim is that the formal requirements are stringent. Of the extant *vinaya*, only the Pāli does not discuss these procedures explicitly. Pāli commentaries, however, do say that one in this situation can return to the novitiate, a functionally similar result (Kieffer-pülz 2018, 41n58).

these debates centered on the nominally unpardonable *pārājika* transgressions, those who participated in them were obliged to theorize otherwise unstated assumptions about the relationship between meditation, rituals of purification, and institutional status.

To see how the Method for Curing Violations of the Precepts engages these debates, it will be helpful to first review how the Indian monastic codes introduce the *śikṣādattaka* position and what they say are its promises and limitations. These sources all do so through the story of a monk named Nandi.[48] The story has many variants but all seem to share its main features: seduced by a goddess while meditating in the forest, Nandi breaks his vow of celibacy but immediately confesses, and for this reason the Buddha allows him to become a *śikṣādattaka*. Institutionally, the *śikṣādattaka* retains part of his monastic identity but must occupy, in perpetuity, an institutionally liminal space, one similar to that held by those undergoing the temporary probation required after transgressing lesser but still grave rules.[49] Those in this condition take on a special monastic rank below that of fully ordained monks or nuns but above the novices. They also must abstain from certain ritual prerogatives of the fully ordained—they may not, for example, accept food served by other monks, have their feet washed by other monks, or participate in the fortnightly communal recitation of the precepts.[50]

Though its practical details are clear, it is less obvious what the liminality of this state implies for the binary, all-or-nothing link between monastic status and meditative-soteriological potential. (That the stories describe Nandi specifically as a *meditator* suggests some awareness of this issue even in the earliest sources.) One Indian tradition of monastic law, that of the Mūlasarvāstivādins, eventually argued that, in theory, a *śikṣādattaka* completely retains his meditative and soteriological potential. In this version of Nandi's story, he is explicitly told to continue his meditation practice, and eventually he becomes an arhat (Clarke 2009, 29–30). But this understanding was not universal and may even have been something of an anomaly.[51] That meditation manuals of diverse origins such as the *Vimuttimagga* and the *Meditation Scripture* both make a point of refusing instruction to anyone who

---

48. See Clarke 2009 for a thorough survey of the different versions. Chinese sources all imply "Nandi"; the *Mūlasarvāstivāda-vinaya* gives "Nandika." The *Mahāsāṅghika-vinaya* adds the epithet "the meditator" (禪難提; *Mohe sengqi lü*, T.1425:22.232a17). "Nandi the Meditator" is the protagonist of the second sutra of the *Chan Essentials;* see *Secrets of Buddhist Meditation*, appendix 4, no. 2.

49. *Mānatva* (P. *mānatta*) is the basic six-day period of punishment; *parivāsa* refers to additional days of punishment required if the offense was concealed (Nolot 1996, 116–136). I use the term "probation" loosely to refer to this condition in general.

50. Nolot 1996, 116–136; Satō M. 1963, 411–432; Hirakawa 1964, 246–254; the precise restrictions vary somewhat between the different *vinaya* traditions (Clarke 1999, 212–215).

51. Even in the Mūlasarvāstivāda version, when Nandika (Nandi) becomes an arhat, the Buddha declares that he then also automatically regains his status as a full monk (*Gen ben shuo yi qie you bu pi'naiye za shi*, T.1451:24.246.a9–11). Thus the two categories are here still mutually exclusive, maintaining the bond between the institutional and the soteriological.

has transgressed a *pārājika* is one indication of this. Even more relevant, given the subject of this study, is that all of the Indian *vinaya* texts translated into Chinese in the late fourth and early fifth centuries (the time when such texts were first introduced systematically) either remain silent on this issue or else explicitly deny that Nandi, and those like him, had the ability to gain higher soteriological fruits during the remainder of their present lifetime.[52]

The *Exposition of the Sarvāstivāda Vinaya,* an Indian *vinaya* commentary either translated into Chinese in the early fifth century or composed around this time by an Indian teacher living in China (Funayama 1998, 280–282), is categorical in saying that one who breaks celibacy will, no matter what, be unable to reach fruition in the present lifetime:

> When crops are crushed by hail, they do not then yield fruit. Similarly, one who violates this precept [of celibacy] will not obtain any of the four stages of sainthood [stream-enterer, once-returner, non-returner, and arhat]. When a seed has been burnt, even though one might plant it in fertile soil, provide it with fertilizer, and irrigate it, it will neither sprout nor bear fruit. Similarly, one who violates this precept, even while striving diligently, will never be able to produce the sprouts and fruits [consisting in] the fruits of the path.... [All this is so] for one who violates this precept, *even one who remains a member of the pure clerical assembly.*[53]

That one who breaks celibacy might still "remain a member of the pure clerical assembly" would seem to allude to some version of the provisions for the *śikṣādattaka*. If so, this passage, even while acknowledging that such people might gain some measure of *institutional* remission from the consequences of their transgressions, insists that they will nevertheless remain permanently hobbled from a soteriological point of view. This conclusion is made even more explicit in the *Vinaya-mātṛkā-sūtra* (*Pini mu jing* 毘尼母經), an Indian *vinaya* text of uncertain lineage also translated into Chinese around the turn of the fifth century.[54] This text, after telling Nandi's story and describing the *śikṣādattaka* role, provides the ritual and legal utterances (*karmavācanā*) for reincorporating the transgressor into the monastic community:

> This monk, from today forth, having performed this legal act, is to be known as one who holds the precepts purely. Despite this, in this lifetime he will not be able to transcend birth and death through the attainment of any of the four stages of sainthood. Nor will he be able to attain any undefiled merit. It is merely

---

52. The *Mūlasarvāstivāda-vinaya*, which Clarke takes as his primary focus, was not translated into Chinese until the late seventh century.

53. 復次如好田苗，若被霜雹摧折墮落，不得果實。犯此戒亦爾。燒滅道苗，不得沙門四果。復次如焦穀堆，雖種良田，糞治溉灌，不生苗實。犯此戒亦爾，雖復懃加精進，終不能生道果苗實。如斷多羅樹，不生不廣。犯此戒亦爾，不得增廣四沙門果。復次如斷樹根，樹則枯朽。若犯此戒，道樹枯損...若犯此戒，雖在出家清淨眾中 ... (*Sapoduo pini piposha,* T.1440, 23:515b4–15)

54. On the *Vinaya-mātṛkā-sūtra* (the Sanskrit title is hypothetical), see Hirakawa 1960, 263.

that his obstruction will not cause him to fall into hell. That is all. Just as a leaf fallen from a tree does not grow again, so too is it utterly impossible for someone who has violated a precept of the first category [a *pārājika*] to attain the four stages of sainthood or accumulate any undefiled merit.[55]

Here there can be no question: the potential for reaching future soteriological attainments is denied to the *śikṣādattaka* even as he is acknowledged to have again become "one who holds the precepts purely."

Karma, Community, and Meditation

The *Vinaya-mātṛkā-sūtra* distinguishes between the question of institutional purity, which a violator of celibacy can regain, and soteriological potential in the present lifetime, which is denied. But a third domain is also invoked: the karmic consequences of the transgression, namely, rebirth in hell, a destiny the transgressor is first threatened with before being granted remission thanks to the methods provided.

To attribute to a *vinaya* ritual of purification the power to prevent rebirth in hell is unusual. Indian Buddhist literature usually suggests that *vinaya* rituals for the atonement and purification of violations of the monastic rules only restore one's legal and institutional purity without removing the post-mortem, karmic consequences of the wrongdoing, if any there be.[56] This distinction reflects, on the one hand, the fact that many monastic rules—such as not eating after noon—are not general ethical principles but contingent laws, applicable only to those who have vowed to follow them, whose violation should not normally have karmic consequences at all.[57] From a different and potentially inverse perspective, however, the separation of the domains of karma and monastic discipline (as a training that leads to higher meditative attainments) expresses a key normative claim of early Buddhist thought: that liberation does not result from destroying bad karma directly, through the painful austerities that rival ascetic groups argued were neces-

---

55. 此比丘從今得羯磨已，名為清淨持戒者，但此一身不得超生離死，證於四果。亦不得無漏功德。然障不入地獄耳。喻如樹葉落已，還生樹上，無有是處。若犯初篇，得證四果，獲無漏功德，亦無是處。(*Pini mu jing*, T.1463:24.813b12–17). This text also tells of a different monk, who after breaking his celibacy tried to atone by throwing himself into a pit of fire, only to be caught beforehand by Ānanda (*Pini mu jing*, T.1463:24.813a28–b11). This story is very similar to that of Saṅghavastu, discussed at the beginning of this chapter.

56. *DZDL*, T.1509:25.395c11–15.

57. The Pāli tradition marks this as the contrast between *lokavajja* (faults for everyone) and *paṇṇativajja* (faults by stipulation), and explicitly notes that even arhats sometimes transgress the latter (*Milindapañho*, 266; Horner 1963, 2:83). Sarvāstivāda sources make a similar distinction (La Vallée Poussin 1988, 2:605). Seemingly for such reasons, *vinaya* texts rarely discuss the karmic consequences of transgressions (Jaini 1992, 197–198). Yet, pace Jaini, this taboo was not universally respected (see, e.g., Hirakawa 1993–1994, 2:51 and 3:10–12). The evident tension and ambiguity here reflects the Buddhist tendency to embrace the principles of karma while also claiming that the highest Buddhist fruits offer transcendence of them (see Egge 2002).

sary for this, but by using the Buddhist path of precepts, meditation, and wisdom to become free of the mental impurities (*kleśa*) in whose absence past karma lacks the power to cause rebirth.[58]

For the authors of the *Vinaya-mātṛkā-sūtra*, however, the making of such distinctions was not a priority. The violation of celibacy, not itself a universal ethical mandate but a rule applicable only for ascetics,[59] is posited as having negative consequences in each of three distinct domains: karma (unpleasant rebirth), community (damage to one's status as a monk or nun), and meditation (obstacles to advanced soteriological attainments), with purification pointedly offered only for the first two.

To return now to the Method for Curing Violations of the Precepts, this text can be seen as yet a further argument in this conversation concerning the scope of both transgression and purification. Acknowledging that transgressions cause problems in the same three domains discussed by the *Vinaya-mātṛkā-sūtra*, it offers, in contrast, complete purification. These three areas of benefit—which together constitute a schematic map of the power of repentance—align with the three main parts of the ritual as outlined above.

In the first part (1.9.3), after repenting to his teacher, the practitioner imagines being rescued from hell by the Buddha's light. In addition to this dramatization, that the purpose of this section of the ritual is to gain relief from the negative karmic consequences of one's transgressions is further seen by its clear debt to the liturgical traditions of the Mahāyāna, shown primarily in the objects of worship the practitioner calls on: the Great Vehicle itself, as well as the thirty-five buddhas that frequently appear in Mahāyāna repentance rituals whose stated aim is invariably the destruction of negative karma.[60] The contemplation of emptiness, also mentioned prominently, is likewise often presented in Mahāyāna scriptures as a means of destroying the negative karmic effects of even the most grievous sins (Harrison and Hartmann 2001, 189–190).

The second part of the ritual (1.9.4) engages with, and attempts to supersede, the *vinaya* procedures for purification of *pārājika* transgressions. The transgressor now goes before the monastic community "wearing only his underrobe (*antarvāsa*)," where he repents.[61] The outer robe was considered

---

58. Bronkhorst 1995 and 1998. Bronkhorst connects this claim to the Buddhist (re)definition of "karma" as intention (*cetanā*) rather than mere physical action.

59. That breaches of celibacy are not by nature *ethical* violations is made clear by the frame story in the *vinaya* for this rule, which involves a monk who was persuaded by his parents to impregnate his wife in order to ensure the continuity of his family line. The act of sexual congress that motivates the Buddha to make a rule about monastic celibacy is thus explicitly one that is both licit (intercourse with one's spouse) and unmotivated by lust.

60. The thirty-five buddhas are the key objects of worship in the liturgical sequence known as the *triskandha*, one of the earliest and most important Mahāyāna ritual forms. On the *triskandha* rite, which forms the core of the typical Chinese *chanhui* ritual, see Shizutani 1974, 133–147; Shioiri 2007, 281–288; Barnes 1999, 1993; B. Williams 2002, 57–66; Nattier 2003, 117–121.

61. 脫僧伽梨著安多會。(*ZCB*, T.620:15.337a25–26)

emblematic of monkhood, and having to remove it, as Nandi did after breaking celibacy, appears to have been understood as a symbolic declaration that
one is fit for expulsion.[62] The Method for Curing Violations of the Precepts
then stipulates that the penitent must carry out the "menial service" of cleaning and emptying the toilets for eight hundred days. These tasks correspond
to, or at least invoke, the low-status duties that *vinaya* texts assign to the
śikṣādattaka (or anyone undergoing probation), duties similar to those expected of novices, whom they now outrank only marginally.[63] Toilet cleaning
in particular was emphasized in the accounts of these chores that became
known in China at this time.[64] The *Vinaya-mātṛkā-sūtra*, which later became
something of a locus classicus for these duties, says that probationers:

> must live in a separate dwelling and must not lodge with the other monks. They
> must sit in a lower position than all other fully ordained monks, whose mats,
> when eating, their own mats must not touch. Moreover, they are to perform all
> kinds of menial service for the other monks, such as sweeping the sanctuary and
> the monks' quarters, and they must thoroughly clean the toilets. Further, when
> they go among the other monks, they must not be addressed. If they are asked
> questions, they must not answer.[65]

The expression "menial service" (*kuyi* 苦役)—or perhaps "ascetic" service—
that characterizes the janitorial tasks of the probationer is the same word
the Method for Curing Violations of the Precepts uses to describe the eight-
hundred-day penance of service and toilet cleaning, a penance that we might
interpret as a middle ground between the lifelong sentence of the *śikṣādattaka*
and the short probation that *vinaya* texts prescribe for lesser but still serious
transgressions.[66]

Though less severe than the lifelong *śikṣādattaka* penance, the procedures in the Method for Curing Violations of the Precepts also offer benefits
far greater than anything discussed in the Indian *vinaya* texts available in
China in the fifth century. First, because they are said to work for all violations of the monastic precepts, they potentially apply to other *pārājika*s

---

62. *Shi song lü*, T.1435, 23:3a12. In one version, Nandi removes *all* his clothes and goes
before the other monks naked (*Mohesengqi lü*, T.1425:22.232b6).

63. The duties of both novices and junior monks are often described in terms comparable to those of the *śikṣādattaka* or probationer (*Sapoduo pini piposha*, T.1440, 23:514b28–c1;
Si fen lü, T.1428, 22:801c5–6). This similarity was noted by Chinese commentators (*Si fen lü
shan fan bu que xing shi chao*, T.1804, 40:98c27–99a4).

64. The *Mūlasarvāstivāda-vinaya* version similarly mentions the chore of changing the
water or leaves used for toilet hygiene (Schopen 1998, 158).

65. 不得與僧同處。一切大僧下坐不得連草食。又復一切眾僧苦役，掃塔及僧房，乃至僧大小行來
處，皆料理之。又復雖入僧中，不得與僧談論。若有問者，亦不得答。(*Pini mu jing*, T.1463:24:811a29–
b5). Later Chinese commentators often cited this text when discussing the duties of probationers (*Si fen lü shan fan bu que xing shi chao*, T.1804, 40:97a27–b1).

66. The *śikṣādattaka* punishment itself is a kind of middle ground between temporary
probation and total defrocking (Clarke 2009, 28).

beyond the breach of celibacy.[67] And second, because the penance of toilet cleaning lasts for only eight hundred days, not a lifetime, and afterward one is "no different than a pure monk"—specifically permitted to recite the precepts with the community, a privilege denied to a *śikṣādattaka*—they restore monastic status completely.

The focus of the third part of the Method for Curing Violations of the Precepts (1.9.5) is meditative attainment, whose derangement was cited in the introduction to the ritual as a key negative consequence of transgression. Having completed eight hundred days of humbling servitude, the practitioner is now assigned a series of meditations and other ritual practices. Although the meditations are discussed in a cursory manner, the unusual imagery here patently invokes the same methods that are discussed in great detail in the *Chan Essentials*. The final practice mentioned is the contemplation of impurity, and the ability to attain it "without further obstacles"—an attainment that the penitent must formally lay claim to at the conclusion of the ritual—is taken to be the final sign of successful purification.

Restoration of meditative ability is thus the final promise of the ritual. Once again it is as it pertains to the fate of those who violate the gravest transgression, the *pārājika*s, that this promise contrasts most sharply with the Indian sources known in fifth-century China, which either fail to mention or else explicitly reject the possibility of future meditative and soteriological attainment for a *śikṣādattaka*.

The Scope of Repentance

The Method for Curing Violations of the Precepts is one of several fifth-century Chinese Buddhist texts in which new rituals of repentance were introduced that spoke directly to concerns expressed in the *vinaya* literature that was at this time becoming available in translation. In their incorporation of *vinaya*-style penances (toilet cleaning and menial service) and their reconstitution of the relationship between transgressions and monastic status (and by extension, meditative potential), the new rituals contrasted sharply with the repentance rituals of Indian Mahāyāna scriptures such as the *Golden Light Scripture,* which claimed only to purify negative karma. That traditional Mahāyāna rites failed to address the connection between transgression and monastic status was noted explicitly in some of these new Chinese texts, which offered themselves as a solution to this oversight (Greene 2017a, 388–389).

We can easily understand why fifth-century Chinese Buddhists would have had *vinaya* on the mind. During a comparatively short span of time in

---

67. Chinese commentators struggled with this point. Zhiyi, for example, argued that the Method for Curing Violations of the Precepts should be interpreted in light of other *vinaya* literature, and hence as valid only for violations of celibacy. Daoxuan, in contrast, took it as proof that purification was possible for all *pārājika* violations (Greene 2017a, 374n34).

the early fifth century, hundreds of fascicles of Indian *vinaya* texts were translated into Chinese, stemming from at least four distinct schools of Indian
monastic law. Previously, only a tiny amount of comparable literature had
been available in China (Hirakawa 1960, 155–162). These enormous sets of
new rules, regulations, and legal procedures were never fully put into practice in China. But there was a clearly growing sense that ideally they should
be taken into consideration. During the early years of the Song (420–479)
dynasty, the imperially supported Qihuan monastery in the southern capital
attempted to implement many new rules from the recently translated
Mahāsāṅghika-vinaya. Controversy ensued when a major patron of the temple
objected to practices that offended local sensibilities, such as eating with the
hands in what was seen as an ungainly squatting posture (Chen Z. 2015).
Chinese Buddhists of the early fifth century were, it seems, becoming aware
that their customary practices did not always live up to the norms of Indian
vinaya law. This is also clear from the records of a controversy that erupted
when the nun Huiguo 慧果 (364–433), after reading an unspecified Indian
"text on monastic rules," realized that the ordination lineage of Chinese
Buddhist nuns might be invalid owing to irregularities in the first ordination of Chinese nuns a century earlier.[68]

The validity of ordination touches on the core issue of Buddhist monastic
identity. Yet so too does the question of the proper means of purifying transgressions of the rules whose maintenance defines this status. The extent to
which Chinese Buddhists ever followed the *vinaya* rules for purification is an
open question. But the early fifth-century translation of the copious *vinaya*
literature on this subject seems to have led, at the least, to a certain anxiety
on this point. We detect in literature from this era a growing fear that one's
legitimacy as a member of the clergy, eventually reified as a metaphysical
entity known as the "precept essence" (*jieti* 戒體), could easily become lost,
without one's knowledge, owing to transgressions unknown or purifications
insufficiently or incorrectly performed. This is the anxiety evident in the story
of Zhiyan, discussed in the previous chapter, who feared that his failure to
purify his violations of the precepts while a layman, many years prior, might
mean that, despite all other indications, he was not really a monk after all.

Whatever the historical circumstances motivating its creation may have
been, the ritual of repentance presented in the Method for Curing Violations of the Precepts incorporates a typology in which the act of *chanhui* provides remedial benefit across the three domains of karma, community, and
meditation. Repentance, according to this text, eliminates the threat of
negative rebirth, (re)creates status as a pure Buddhist monk or nun in the

---

68. *BQNZ*, T.2063, 50:937b27–28 (Tsai 1994, 37–38). See also *GSZ*, T.2059, 50:341a28–b7;
Heirman 2001. These sources insist that the original nuns' ordination *had* been valid, owing
to exceptions in the *vinaya* for ordinations in distant lands. Yet they also record that a contingent of nuns from Sri Lanka was eventually brought to China to assist in performing new ordinations for Huiguo and others, an undertaking that would hardly have been necessary had
there not been, at the time, serious doubts and concerns.

present life, and helps one (re)gain the meditative power that is the first step on the path of higher soteriological attainment. This model assigns to "repentance" a great deal of power, making it a framework in which both this-worldly and other-worldly goals have a place.

The Method for Curing Violations of the Precepts comes to us within a document, the *Methods for Curing*, whose aim, broadly stated, is the treatment of problems that arise during meditation. These methods are presented as having a particularly close connection to that form of training specifically and may well constitute the kind of repentance ritual that *chan* scriptures such as the *Chan Essentials* recommend for meditators at various stages in their practice. Yet what we might call the theory of repentance proposed by the Method for Curing Violations of the Precepts cannot be limited to this context alone. Many other fifth- and sixth-century Chinese sources exhibit the same classificatory impulse to make of repentance—a concrete ritual replete with offerings, prostrations, and pleas for mercy—a stage on which multiple modalities of efficacy are mapped onto an inclusive hierarchy of religious goals.

A few examples of this kind of theorizing may suggest how widespread the tendency was in fifth- and sixth-century Chinese religious thought to treat repentance not as one practice among many but as the meaning of religious activity as a whole, in its broadest possible terms. Fittingly, the famous typologies of repentance offered by Zhiyi in the late sixth century conclude the discussion, seen now not as the products of his singular genius, as traditional Tiantai scholarship so often has, but as variations on a theme whose antecedents, both in Buddhism and in Daoism, stretched back into the early years of the fifth century, if not long before.

Great Vaipulya Dhāraṇī Scripture

The text known as the *Da fang deng tuoluoni jing* 大方等陀羅尼經, the *Great Vaipulya Dhāraṇī Scripture*, was widely used in the fifth and sixth centuries as an important compendium of rituals for the destruction of sins (罪). Centered on the power of its eponymous spell (*dhāraṇī*), it attributes to repentance the capacity to bring benefits across the same three domains of karma, community, and meditation.[69]

---

69. For a study of the content and structure of the *Great Vaipulya Dhāraṇī Scripture*, see Ōtsuka 2013, 225–278. Bibliographic records claim the text was translated in Turfan by a certain Fazhong 法眾 in the early fifth century (*CSZJJ*, T.2145:55.12a15–17). Fazhong is unmentioned apart from this single bibliographic reference, and even the *Li dai san bao ji*, which often inflates the records of earlier translators, links him only to this one text (T.2034:49.83a19). This suggests that, like other texts supposedly translated in Turfan in the early fifth century (such as the Contemplation Scriptures), the *Great Vaipulya Dhāraṇī Scripture* may be a Chinese compilation or partial composition. It is best known as the canonical source for Zhiyi's *Fangdeng Repentance*, the only surviving example of a full ritual manual based on it. Epigraphic evidence from north China (Kuramoto 2016, 279–306), as well as literary records from south China (*GHMJ*, T.2103:52.334a22–b12), show that repentance rites based on the text were widespread during the fifth and sixth centuries. Dunhuang manuscripts of *Great Vaipulya Dhāraṇī Scripture* show some small but interesting differences with the received versions (Kuo 2015).

The core narrative of the scripture introduces three different modes of purification, presented through three episodes concerning a monk named Leiyin 雷音 and a bodhisattva named Huaju 華聚.[70]

1. Leiyin is meditating and about to enter *samādhi* when he is disturbed by demons.[71] He prays to the Buddha, who directs Huaju to teach Leiyin a powerful spell for taming demons.
2. Leiyin and Huaju go to the Buddha, who tells a story about a certain Vasu, presently residing in the Avīci hell. Vasu is revealed to have entered hell only as a skillful means to show living beings how they can realize the ultimate emptiness of sin and become free from negative rebirth.
3. The Buddha narrates the past lives of both Leiyin and Huaju. Here the issue is the power of the spell to purify violations of the precepts, meaning the monastic precepts, the precepts for novices, and the bodhisattva precepts.

The three episodes each present a slightly different understanding of the power of the main *dhāraṇī*, and they may well have originated separately (Shinohara 2010, 273). However that may be, we can still note the motivation for and effect of their combination. Taken together, the episodes form a coherent unit in which the purification of sin through repentance eliminates: (1) obstructions to the practice of meditation, (2) evil karma that leads to rebirth in hell, and (3) transgressions of one or more sets of status-defining precepts. Though their ordering is different, these are the same promises made by the Method for Curing Violations of the Precepts.

Divine Spells of the Seven Buddhas and Eight Bodhisattvas

A differently structured but similarly inclusive categorization of repentance can be found in the *Divine Spells of the Seven Buddhas and Eight Bodhisattvas* (*Qi fo ba pusa suo shuo da tuoluoni shen zhou jing* 七佛八菩薩所說大陀羅尼神咒經). This text is a collection of spells and rituals that appeared in China during the late fourth or early fifth century. It is unknown whether it was translated from an Indian source or assembled or partially composed in China, but like the *Great Vaipulya Dhāraṇī Scripture* it was an important resource for later Buddhist repentance literature.[72]

---

70. *Da fang deng tuoluoni jing*, T.1339:21.641c18–647a23. I here follow Shinohara's (2010, 255–266) detailed summary of each section. Kuo (1994, 101–102) also implicitly recognizes these three episodes as the key narratives of the text.

71. *Da fang deng tuoluoni jing*, T.1339:21.641c21–24.

72. Zhiyi, for example, mentions the existence of repentance manuals based on the *Divine Spells of the Seven Buddhas and Eight Bodhisattvas*, and hagiographies mention fifth-century figures who practice these rites (Stevenson 1987, 228–229). On the structure of the text and its relationship to other medieval *dhāraṇī* collections, see Shinohara 2014, 4–10.

The *Divine Spells of the Seven Buddhas and Eight Bodhisattvas* presents many different spells, and in some cases includes a description of the ritual in which they are to be recited. In almost all cases the destruction of sins (罪) is a principal benefit, and when the ritual procedures are described they most often center on repentance. Across the various spells, the different benefits that are listed can thus be read collectively as a loose typology of the power of repentance.

The first seven spells, linked to the seven buddhas of the past, provide one such scheme. The first spell promises to eliminate natural disasters, such as floods, crop failure, invasions, rebellions, epidemics, or demonic infestations.[73] The second spell, in contrast, causes all living beings in the world to arouse the aspiration for awakening, purifies them of their sins, and heals their illnesses, and frees the one who recites or copies it from the obstructions caused by their grave sins committed in past lifetimes.[74] The third spell causes those who hear it to be reborn in the land of Akṣobhya Buddha and never again enter the lower realms of rebirth.[75] The fourth spell promises the attainment of the "*samādhi* of the adamantine banner" (金剛幢三昧), the eradication of all mental defilements, and the permanent end of suffering.[76] These first four spells present a hierarchy of benefits ranging from the comparatively mundane up through the highest normative goals of Buddhism. The benefits promised by the many subsequent spells consist of different combinations of these four levels.

The seventh spell is the first to give a detailed account of the repentance ritual in which it should be used.[77] According to the instructions, the practitioner must make offerings to the Buddha and then, standing before a relic-containing stupa, "prostrate to the ground, repent his transgressions, and rebuke himself" (五體投地悔過自責) while chanting the spell eighty-one times. This is to be repeated six times a day for twenty-one days. After the twenty-first day, he will receive a vision of a great light, and deities such as Indra will descend and "bestow upon him [confirmation of (?)] the four stages of sainthood" (授與四沙門果).

The soteriological benefits of the spell and ritual in which it is embedded are explicitly described here as attainment of the stages of sainthood. In other sections, similar benefits are promised in relation to meditation (*chan* 禪). A spell from the second fascicle, associated with a bodhisattva named Lord of Trance Power (定自在王) promises, for those who wish to practice meditation but find themselves disturbed by demonic forces, to "remove the obstructions to meditation," to "bestow the waters of meditation," and to "plant the seed of liberation."[78] The ritual that releases these

73. *Qi fo ba pusa suo shuo da tuoluoni shen zhou jing*, T.1332:21.536b21–536c1.

74. Ibid., T.1332:21.536c14–18.

75. Ibid., T.1332:21.537a4–18.

76. Ibid., T.1332:21.537b6–8.

77. Ibid., T.1332:21.538a26–b7.

78. 除禪定障…賜其禪定水…種以菩提芽。(Ibid., T.1332:21.545b11–13)

benefits is full of the florid pleas for forgiveness and remission of sin that are typical of Buddhist repentance rites:

> The practitioner must at this time rebuke himself: "I have acted wrongly. I have been entangled by Māra. Full of shame, I rebuke myself, and lower my head in shame. O buddhas and sages! In previous ages I fell into the hells and the realm of beasts or the hungry ghosts. Battered by the waves of rebirth I was again and again reborn. I have now obtained a human body, but owing to my weak capacities and scant wisdom, even though I try to practice meditation I am unable to reach any attainment, as I am covered over by the defilements. But I would sooner have my body smashed to dust than ever again be obscured by these defilements.… [Addressing the buddhas]: Pardon me my errors and transgressions! Destroy and expunge my sins! Cleanse my eye of wisdom and make it pure! Scour the impurities of my mind with the water of your compassion!"[79]

The practitioner must then prostate and chant the spell, say the name Lord of Trance Power three times, and then "concentrate his mind in meditation, and in each moment express remorse for his transgressions and rebuke himself."[80] This combined activity of meditation and repentance will destroy the practitioner's sins and the Lord of Trance Power will himself then appear so as to confirm this.

The Daoist Abstinence Ceremony

In early medieval China, the notion that the repentance of sins could generate a normatively inclusive range of religious benefits was shared across a wide spectrum of Chinese society. It was true not only among Buddhists and in Buddhist forms of ritual; it was articulated in similar ways in medieval Daoism as well.[81] Of particular note for this study are certain fifth-century accounts of the purpose and meaning of the Daoist *zhai* 齋 or "abstinence ceremony," as Campany (2012, 51–52) cogently suggests this polyvalent word is best translated in the context of early medieval China.

The word *zhai* originated in the early Chinese ritual tradition, where it referred to the presacrificial period of mental purification and physical abstinence—from meat, alcohol, sex, fine clothing, and other sensual pleasures—that made the ritualist fit to communicate with the ancestors

---

79. 行人爾時應當自責：我為不善。為魔所縛。慚愧自責，低頭愧恥。諸佛及眾賢聖。我於往劫，墮大地獄、畜生、餓鬼。洄波六趣，數受生死。今得人身，鈍根少智，欲修禪定而不能得，為諸結使之所覆蔽。我今寧當碎身如塵，終不為此結使所蔽…赦我您咎滅除我罪。洗我慧眼令得明淨。以慈悲水蕩滌心垢。(Ibid., T.1332:21.545b24–c3)

80. 一心禪思，於一一時，悔過自責。(Ibid., T.1332:21.545c7–8)

81. My brief treatment of Daoist ideas about sin and repentance is intended only to suggest some ways that Buddhist approaches participated in broader, shared Chinese religious ideals. For a thorough treatment of medieval Daoist ideas about sin and redemption, see Verellen 2019.

or other spirits.[82] Chinese Buddhists adopted the word, from an early date, to denote the general abstemiousness of Buddhist monks and nuns, as well as the Buddhist rituals of communal merit-making involving both the clergy and the laity, modeled on the Indian *poṣadha* ritual, that took place six times a month and on other special occasions (Hureau 2010, 1213–1227; Campany 2015).[83] By the fourth century if not earlier, the repentance of sins was seen as central to, perhaps even synonymous with, the Buddhist abstinence ceremony.[84] The abstinence days were believed to be those days of the month when celestial envoys descend and inspect the conduct of humans and report any transgressions to the divine authorities, making them the most opportune moments for carrying out such practices (F. Chen 2013, 62–65).

In the late fourth century, a number of new Daoist groups began promoting a regularly scheduled abstinence ceremony. Although the new rites drew on earlier Daoist liturgical forms, they first appeared among Daoist movements strongly influenced by Buddhism—the so-called new Celestial Masters tradition of Kou Qianzhi 寇謙之 (363–448) in north China, and, somewhat earlier, the Lingbao movement in south China.[85] The codification of the Lingbao ritual tradition by Lu Xiujing 陸修靜 (406–477) during the mid-fifth century made the abstinence ceremony a central element of Daoist ritual, a status it long retained.

As laid out in the *Instructions for the Performance of Abstinence Ceremonies,* one of the original Lingbao texts of the late fourth century, abstinence ceremonies are to be performed on ten appointed days each month.[86] To begin,

---

82. Tada 1981, 49–52; Yamada T. 1999, 176–178; and Brashier 2011, 209–212. The *zhai* was also linked to mental purification through the reduction of emotions and desires, as in the "fasting of the mind" (*xinzhai* 心齋) of Zhuangzi (*Zhuangzi ji shi,* 1:146–147).

83. Fifteen *zhai* days occurred in each of the three "long" abstinence months (Forte 1979; Liu S. 2008, 75–114).

84. Funayama 1995, 60–63. Xi Chao's 郗超 (336–377) *Feng fa yao* 奉法要 mentions repentance as a principal activity on abstinence days (*HMJ,* T.2012:52.86b13; Zürcher 1972, 164). So too the *Mouzi li huo lun* (*HMJ,* T.2012:52.2a1). In China, Buddhist abstinence ceremonies were associated with repentance from an early date. The word *chanhui* itself first appears in such a context, in translated Buddhist texts from the third century (*Liu du ji jing,* T.152:3.19a22). The term *zhaichan* 齋懺 (abstinence repentance), common in Chinese-authored texts during the fifth and sixth centuries and seemingly synonymous with *chanhui,* is a further indication that abstinence ceremonies and repentance were tightly intertwined (see, e.g., *GSZ,* T.2059:50.325a1; 356c25; 362a5; *GHMJ,* T.2013:52.334a22; 334b13; 334c7).

85. Lü 2008, 233–240 and Yamada T. 1999, 101–117. On the development of Daoist ritual in general during this era, see, additionally, Yamada T. 1995 and Lagerwey 2009. On the mutual borrowing between Buddhist and Daoist ritual practices during this time, see Strickmann 2002 and Mollier 2008.

86. *Tai ji zhen ren fu Lingbao zhai jie wei yi zhu jing yao jue* 太極真人敷靈寶齋戒威儀諸要訣 (HY 532; Ōfuchi 1974, no. 24; Bokenkamp 1983, 484). On this and other Lingbao texts that treat repentance, see Hsieh 2010, 753–758, and Bokenkamp 2013. Other early Lingbao texts give similar procedures for the abstinence ceremony (Lü 2008, 142–167; Yamada T. 1999, 219–227).

the head ritualist summons the various spirits and gods whom his status empowers him to command, and who will assist him in presenting prayers to the higher divine officials, and then supplicates a host of higher gods with offerings of incense. He then prepares scriptures for chanting and asks for pardon for previously committed sins, events described as follows:

> Set out the scripture table and incense burner. Place a high seat among them. Facing the seat, pay reverence to the scriptures three times and then say:
>
> "We now entrust our fate to the Supreme Ultimate, the Great Dao Most Perfected.... Burning incense and chanting scriptures, we long for the salvific benevolence of the Supreme, and we pray that may be pardoned and expunged the grave sins and terrible transgressions leading to rebirth, committed in this or past lives, of our parents back for seven generations, of all living beings from the emperor down to the common people, of ourselves and all the people of our households, [sins such as] having killed our lords or fathers, having failed to be filial to our parents, having disobeyed our teachers or abused our friends, having discarded truth and clamored after falsity, having robbed and plundered, having engaged in armed conflict against our own country or another country, having killed living beings and taken pleasure in it, having had sexual relations with the wives of others, [etc.] ...
>
> "All these many great sins, *which we cannot even remember*, have over the generations solidified and become embedded. We are now bound up by them without release and suffer for them without respite. We pray, by burning incense and practicing the path, that we will be saved and released from them. We now repent (改悔) them. We submit to and obey the precepts and prohibitions. We will not dare transgress them. We now, of our own will, take responsibility and apologize [for these past sins]."
>
> Then everyone in unison, with utmost earnestness, strikes their head to the floor.[87]

As in typical Buddhist repentance rituals, here too there is no confession of specific sins. The sins at issue are indeed too numerous even to remember. It is rather a matter of *pleading*, on behalf of oneself and one's family, ancestors, and retainers, for remission from any and all possible sins committed in this life or lifetimes past, sins laid out in a scripted list of intentionally broad generality. Similar liturgical scripts are found in many Lingbao texts, which by the mid-fifth century had adopted the Buddhist term *chanhui* to denote this kind of pleading.[88]

---

87. 羅列經案香鑪，施安高座於其中也。次向高座禮經，都三拜。言。臣等今歸命太上無極大道至真...今燒香轉經，希仰太上濟度之恩，乞七世父母，以及帝王民人，一切眾生，臣等身及家門太小，願得赦除前世今世生死重罪惡過。或弒君父，或不孝二親，或背師欺友，或廢真就偽，或爲劫賊攻伐家國，或伐他國，或殺害眾生以爲快樂，或淫犯他妻...諸如此等，莫大之罪，不可憶識，積世結固，纏綿不解，冤對不已。乞今燒香行道，以自度脫，於是改悔，伏從禁戒，不敢又犯。亦任意所首謝。皆一時頭腦頓地，心中欣欣。(HY 532, 7b8–8b10)

88. According to Bokenkamp (2013, 127–129), neither the Shangqing nor *early* Lingbao

For this study the *Instructions for the Performance of Abstinence Ceremonies* is a useful example of Daoist repentance because it also presents the benefits of the abstinence ceremony, and hence the power of pleading for remission from sins, in broad and more theoretical terms that readily show its alignment with the parallel claims made for repentance in the Buddhist examples discussed earlier. The following passage, which Lu Xiujing himself would later cite in his own sermons, is particularly notable in this regard:

> [Through the abstinence ceremony,] on the highest level one can ascend to the ranks of the transcendents and attain the Dao. At the middle level, one can make one's home peaceful and the nation secure, extend one's lifespan, keep one's name upon the registers of the blessed, and obtain the way of non-action. Finally, at the lowest level, one can expunge the crimes of past lives, obtain pardon for present-life transgressions, obtain rescue from danger and trouble, dispel disasters, cure illnesses, release the dead from suffering, and bring salvation to all living beings. There is thus nothing for which the abstinence ceremony is not suitable![89]

The *Instructions for the Performance of Abstinence Ceremonies* here classifies the benefits of the Daoist abstinence ceremony into three domains of decreasing normative exaltedness: (1) transcendence and the Dao, (2) long life for oneself, one's family, and the state, and (3) salvation for the souls of the dead and the resolution of immediate troubles such as illness and natural disasters.[90] Although these three levels do not line up precisely with the Buddhist typologies of repentance discussed earlier, a similar impulse animates them. Here, as in the Buddhist examples, a suite of religious goals are positioned with respect to a canonical hierarchy of value that is formally respected—transcendence is a higher goal than saving one's ancestors from after-death punishment—even as it is muddied by the claim that all of the goals can be reached by a single, communal ritual of pleading for mercy from sins.

Zhiyi on the Three Kinds of Repentance

The most sophisticated medieval Chinese Buddhist expositions of the modalities of repentance occur in the works of Zhiyi, dating to the late sixth century. The most famous of these is found in the *Sequential Approach*, whose treatment of basic meditation practice was examined in the previous

---

scriptures use the word *chanhui*. It seems to have become common in Daoist texts only during the fifth century.

89. 上可昇仙得道。中可安居寧國，延年益壽，保於福祿，得無爲之道。下除宿罪，赦見世過，救危難，消災，治病，解脫死人憂苦，度一切物，亦莫有不宜矣。(HY 532, 10a4–8). Lu Xiujing cites this passage in his *Dongxuan Lingbao zhai shuo guang zhu jie fa deng zhu yuan yi* 洞玄靈寶齋說光燭戒罰燈祝願儀 (HY 524, 10b6–11a1), a compilation of his writings (Schipper and Verellen 2004, 254).

90. The link here between appeasing the dead and ending illness makes sense given the tendency of the unquiet dead to trouble the living in this way.

chapter.[91] (That Zhiyi would discuss repentance at length within what is
nominally a meditation treatise should come as no surprise.) Here Zhiyi classifies *chanhui*, or repentance, into three types:

1. Procedural repentance (作法懺悔)
2. Repentance based on the contemplation of signs (觀相懺悔)
3. Repentance based on the contemplation of non-arising (觀無生懺悔)

These categories, Zhiyi explains, encompass all the varieties of repentance
discussed in the Buddhist scriptures. Procedural repentance refers to the
methods in the *vinaya* for purifying transgressions of the monastic precepts.
Repentance based on the contemplation of signs refers to methods of repentance in which purification is confirmed by visions obtained in trance. (Zhiyi
cites the third part of the Method for Curing Violations of the Precepts as a
key example.) Finally, repentance based on the contemplation of non-arising
is the contemplation of the ultimate truth of emptiness. This permanently
dispels karmic obstructions, whose ultimate source is false conceptualiza-
tion, as readily as the morning sun disperses frost and dew.[92]

It is evident—Zhiyi says as much—that these three categories align with
the three trainings of precepts, meditation, and wisdom, respectively, that
form the canonical typology of the totality of Buddhist practice.[93] Zhiyi
further aligns these categories with three categories of sin (罪): (1) the
breaking of the precepts and attendant loss of monastic status, (2) evil karma
that leads to negative rebirth, and (3) the sin that is the defilement of
ignorance, the ultimate root of the others.[94] Elsewhere, Zhiyi likens the
purification of sin by the three kinds of repentance to three increasingly
powerful medicines that (1) cure illness without further strengthening the
body (purification of monastic status), (2) cure illness and also increase
health (purification of evil karma), and (3) cure illness and grant immortality
and the Dao (the purification of ignorance).[95] It is of some note that these
analogies, at the level of illness and the body, line up remarkably well with
the Lingbao classification of the three grades of benefit of the Daoist *zhai*.
Zhiyi's classification is also very similar to the benefits of repentance with
respect to community, karma, and meditation in the Method for Curing
Violations of the Precepts.

Zhiyi also devised other ways of classifying repentance, notably a twofold
distinction between "phenomenal repentance" (*shi chan* 事懺), meaning the

---

91. *CDFM,* T.1916:46.485b6–486c29. This passage has been discussed by many scholars;
see, among others, Kuo 1994, 62–70; Shi D. 2000, 64–80; Shengkai 2004, 94–99; Chi 2008,
315–322; Kobayashi 1993, 347–352; and Stevenson 1999.

92. *CDFM,* T.1916:46.486a17–19; here Zhiyi cites one of the Contemplation Scriptures,
the *Guan Puxian pusa xing fa jing,* T.277:9.393b10–12.

93. *CDFM,* T.1916:46.485c1–3.

94. *CDFM,* T.1916:46.486c4–14.

95. *Jin guang ming jing wen ju,* T.1785:39.60c28–61a4.

concrete forms of cultic worship comprising actual rituals of repentance, and "repentance at the level of principle" (*li chan* 理懺), referring to the meditative discernment of emptiness that is supposed to lie at the heart of all such ritual forms.[96] This contrast between the "phenomenal" and the "principle" evinces a tension characteristic of Tiantai writings on ritual and meditation as a whole, the tension between an emphasis on the correct performance of specific forms of worship, on the one hand, and the claim that true benefit comes only from the meditative realization of the ultimate truth of emptiness, on the other (Stevenson 1993). With ancient roots in Buddhist systematic thought, this tension was essentially covalent with the endlessly worked over dichotomy of conventional versus ultimate truth, and more broadly, can be seen as a doctrinal sublimation of Buddhist social organization in which the laity gain better rebirth by materially supporting a class of renunciate ascetics questing for a rebirth-transcending ultimate goal.[97]

Repentance, for Zhiyi, is thus an eminently inclusive category, just as, in practice, the rituals that went by this name were in the early Tiantai community, where they served equally as daily liturgies for the monastic community, as intensive and often long-term individual retreats for virtuoso practitioners, and as larger, occasional ritual gatherings in which the laity too participated.[98] Zhiyi's typology of the categories of repentance is, we might say, an intellectual or theoretical refraction of the different domains in which rituals of repentance actually took place. These categories do take into consideration normative Buddhist hierarchies of value. They differentiate the mundane gaining of good karma, leading to immediate relief from suffering or better rebirth, from the final liberation of nirvana reached only by the destruction of ignorance and the other mental defilements. They similarly distinguish between doing good and avoiding evil in order to gain happiness in this life and the next and, at a higher level, the meditative discernment of emptiness, in which even rebirth in hell is but a mental projection. Yet all sides of these equations are, for Zhiyi, forms of repentance that eliminate sin.

Scholars of early Tiantai have often argued that Zhiyi's approach to repentance was distinctive relative to the Chinese Buddhist mainstream of his day in that he chose to treat it as an explicitly soteriological practice, a step on the "transcendent" (*lokottara*) path to enlightenment rather than merely

---

96. *Mohe zhiguan*, T.1911:46.13c22–25. These categories were widely used by later Chinese Buddhist exegetes; see Kuo 1994, 71–79; B. Williams 2002, 156–158.

97. Collins 1998. In practice, of course, the contrast between ultimate and conventional does not always or even usually line up with the distinction between monastic and lay attitudes or practices. But Collins's point, as I understand it, is well taken: that the concept of nirvana as an unconstructed realm transcending rebirth is the doctrinal correlate of a social institution consisting of individuals who have (nominally) renounced the ordinary world of productive work and sexual reproduction.

98. Stevenson (1987, 346) identifies these as the three settings of repentance rituals in early Tiantai.

a vehicle for gaining "worldly" (*laukika*) benefits such as the curing of illness. This is said to have found quintessential expression in Zhiyi's claim that the highest form of repentance is the meditative contemplation of emptiness. In this reading, then, Zhiyi's unique genius was to reconceptualize repentance as something whose true benefits emerge only when it becomes a form of meditation (Shioiri 1959, 448), to which end he then included seated meditation as a formal step in some of his repentance manuals (Kobayashi 1993, 365).

Yet, as others have recognized, Zhiyi's position that repentance could be a transcendent rather than merely worldly practice was hardly unprecedented in Chinese Buddhism.[99] More broadly, the purification of transgressions, as discussed earlier, has *always* had soteriological import in Buddhism—at the very least, in endowing one with, or restoring one to, a status conceived of as the necessary precondition for the highest attainments. But even leaving aside the historical revisions that show him to have been less unique than often thought, traditional sectarian scholars of Tiantai have arguably erred at a more fundamental level by reading Zhiyi's theoretical apparatus as having served to subordinate repentance, with its connotation of rituals aimed at gaining worldly benefits, to meditation, as the highest Buddhist practice. For one could equally conclude just the opposite—that by classifying the canonically freighted practice of meditative contemplation of emptiness as the highest form of repentance, Zhiyi was subordinating meditation to repentance. Indeed, in the end it is the category of repentance that Zhiyi uses to encompass all these forms of Buddhist practice. Zhiyi's theoretical system, from this point of view, does not construe repentance as the first step toward enlightenment so much as turn enlightenment into the culmination of repentance. It *sanctifies* the concrete rites of repentance that in fact lay at the core of Chinese Buddhist ritual life on the ground, for all classes of people, by declaring that the normatively highest goals of Buddhism can, under the right conditions, be found within them.

And in this too Zhiyi was not original. Although his novel mapping of repentance onto the canonical division of the three trainings speaks to a sophisticated doctrinal creativity, repentance had already been a wide frame for a long time in China, embracing all possible forms of religious benefit.

Repentance in the Formation of Chinese Buddhism

Scholars have often observed that repentance became more important in Chinese Buddhism than it had been in Indian Buddhism. Rather than a vehicle for personal purification, as it supposedly was in India, repentance came to be seen in China as a means for saving the souls of one's ancestors, if not all beings in the world, a development that was perhaps influenced by Chinese legal ideas concerning familial rather than individual responsibil-

---

99. Stevenson 1987; B. Williams 2002; Shi D. 2000.

ity (Chappell 2005).[100] Yet to some degree this thesis rests on the faulty premise that a single thing called Buddhist repentance existed in India and then was applied to new ends in China. As we have seen, the situation was more complicated than this. The word *chanhui*, which combined a partial transcription of an Indian word with the semantic meaning of "express one's remorse" and the pragmatic meaning of "plead for mercy," was used from early on in Chinese Buddhism to translate a multiplicity of distinct Indian terms, including some that pointed to ritual activities that one might do on behalf of others. By the fifth century, when it became the most common way to talk about these things in Buddhist literature, *chanhui* was a fully Chinese word with its own range of meanings not bound by any single Indian Buddhist concept. Quickly adopted by other religious groups to describe their own forms of repentance, *chanhui* in Buddhism was a broad category that encompassed the methods and goals of a number of facets of Buddhist practice. In short, the significance of repentance in Chinese Buddhism is less a matter of understanding how a given Indian ritual form was transformed in China than of grasping why and how the notion of repentance proved to be a productive category for Chinese Buddhists, one with such deep and powerful resonance that even the highest normative practices such as meditation were brought within its orbit. Although the word *chanhui* was a Buddhist neologism, repentance was in fact a fundamental constituent of Chinese religious thought long before the arrival of Buddhism, and it provided early Chinese Buddhists with a powerful framework through which they could and did understand what Buddhism as a whole was and what it could offer.

Models of Repentance from Ancient China

Before *chanhui* became the most prevalent term, early Chinese Buddhists used a variety of expressions to describe how one should remedy misdeeds and propitiate the buddhas, including "express remorse for transgression" (*huiguo* 悔過), "blame oneself" (*zize* 自責), "take responsibility for transgression" (*shouguo* 首過), and "apologize for transgressions" (*xieguo* 謝過).[101] The specific Indian terminology that these terms were used to render in early translations is not always clear. But what we can say with certainty is that all of this language invoked long-standing Chinese ideas about the power

---

100. The Chinese legal principle of collective, familial punishment is attested as far back as the fifth century BCE (C. Williams 2011). There was also collective *remission:* one could exchange a portion of one's own noble rank to free relatives from punishment for their crimes (Loewe 2010, 299).

101. All these terms appear in translations firmly dated before the year 280 (Nattier 2008). See, for example, *Fa jing jing*, T.322:12.18c28–29; *Za ahan jing*, T.101:2.495a17; *Liu du ji jing*, T.152:3.19a13–14; *Zhong ben qi jing*, T.196:4.158c28; 160b17. The history and early usage of the word *chanhui* itself needs more investigation. It does appear in known pre-280 texts, but only rarely: we find it but once, for example, in the voluminous *Liu du ji jing* (T.152:3.19a22). Only in the late fourth century does it replace expressions like *huiguo* 悔過 as the typical word used in Buddhist texts.

of public declarations of guilt and remorse to elicit remission from divine punishment.[102]

Perhaps the best known traditional Chinese story instantiating ideas of this sort is that of King Tang 湯, the legendary founder of the Shang dynasty (ca. 1600–1050 BCE), who was remembered for offering his own person in sacrifice to the gods after a severe drought. The *Annals of Lü Buwei* (ca. 239 BCE) recounts these events as follows:

> Tang thereupon offered a prayer at Sanglin using his own body as the pledge, beseeching: "If I, the One Man [the emperor] have sinned, let this not reach the myriad people. If the myriad people have sinned, let it rest on me, the One Man. Do not let my lack of diligence cause the Lord on High and the ghosts and spirits to harm the lives of the people." Thereupon, he cut his hair, put his hands in manacles, and had himself prepared in lieu of the usual animals as the offering in a sacrifice to beseech the blessings of the Lord on High. The people were overjoyed, and the rains came as in a deluge.[103]

In other early versions of the story, Tang's admission of guilt takes the form of a list of searching questions about his possible misdeeds as ruler: "Is my government not properly regulated? Does it cause the people grief?...Are the palaces and chambers too glorious? Are the women of the harem too numerous?"[104] Thus, while invoking the old and persistent notion that divine powers are appeased through sacrifice, Tang's story is also infused with the moral economy of the mandate of Heaven, according to which divine disapproval of the ruler's conduct manifests in natural disasters (Allan 1984).

By the Han dynasty, it had become a widely accepted idea that natural disasters were signs that Heaven wished the ruler to repent (*hui* 悔) his transgressions.[105] Han emperors regularly issued edicts on such occasions expressing remorse for whatever wrongs they had done.[106] And during hard times, the precedent of Tang's having ritually "blamed himself" (自責) was

---

102. In this section I draw in part from a number of previous studies of repentance in pre-Buddhist China, including Pettazzoni 1932, 2:23–54; Wu 1979; Tada 1981; Kuo 1994, 7–11; Shioiri 2007, 125–178; Ōfuchi 1991, 159–163; Tsuchiya 1994; Shi D. 2000, 12–23; Nakajima 1991; Hong 2014, 24–55.

103. 湯乃以身禱於桑林曰，余一人有罪，無及萬夫。萬夫有罪，在余一人。無以一人之不敏，使上帝鬼神傷民之命。於是翦其髮，酈其手，以身爲犧牲，用祈福於上帝，民乃甚說，雨乃大至。 (Knoblock and Riegel 2000, 210, with slight modifications to the translation).

104. Knoblock 1988, 3:223–224. On the various versions of Tang's story, see Tsuchiya 1994, 280.

105. Thus, according to the *Bai hu tong yi* 白虎通義 (traditionally dated to 79 CE): "Why does Heaven cause disasters? In order to warn the ruler of men and make him aware of his conduct, out of a desire to make him repent transgressions, cultivate virtue, and deeply ponder [his errors]." 天所以有災變何。所以譴告人君，覺悟其行，欲令悔過修德，深思慮也。 (*Bai hu tong yi*, 4.19b1–20a1).

106. See Zheng Z. 1986, 85–112, who has compiled a list of all the examples in the *Han shu* 漢書 (see also Ōfuchi 1991, 162).

cited by remonstrating officials brave enough to chastise their lords (*Hou han shu*, 41.1408). In the idealized rituals of repentance that were recorded as then taking place, the ruler would refrain from various pleasures (the standard presacrificial "abstinence ceremony"), make offerings to the gods, and present to them a declaration of his guilt.[107]

Tang's sacrificial offer, however, is not a matter of personal repentance, let alone confession. Whether the relevant sins are his *or* those of his people, he declares himself willing to take responsibility for them, a willingness he expresses in words but also through his appearance in the guise of a shackled prisoner. Although it is difficult to know with any precision the symbolic valence this gesture would have had at any given time, it became a much-imitated model. The most famous iterations were the "mud and ashes" (*tutan* 塗炭) abstinence ceremonies of fifth- and sixth-century Daoism, in which those seeking remission for the transgressions of their ancestors presented themselves before the gods with bound hands and hair disheveled (Bokenkamp 2005). An explicit identification between ritual supplicant and condemned criminal appears in the later popular rituals in which the penitent dons a symbolic or even actual cangue, practices that still occur in parts of the Chinese world to this day (P. Katz 2009, 105–115). In sum, the notion was that one could gain a reduced sentence or a pardon by willingly submitting one's guilt before the relevant authority. This was a principle that had been established in secular Chinese law from ancient times (Rickett 1971), and the parallels between the domains did not escape the notice of ancient and medieval Chinese writers.[108]

Repentance in Early Daoism

Tang knows he must repent not out of a feeling of guilt but because of external circumstances that were understood to be a divine punishment. The aim of repentance, in this view, was not to relieve an inner anxiety but to remove

---

107. According the *Zuo zhuan* 左傳, "When mountains collapse or rivers dry up, the ruler abstains from meat and elaborate food, reduces the splendor of his apparel, rides carriages without decoration, banishes music, and leaves his usual abode. The diviner displays objects to be sacrificed to the gods while the scribe reads appropriate words with which to supplicate them." 山崩川竭，君為之不舉、降服、乘縵、徹樂、出次，祝幣，史辭以禮焉。(*Shi san jing zhu shu*, 1902; after Durrant, Li, and Schaberg 2016, 753, with modifications). Although this passage does not reference repentance, the commentary of Du Yu 杜預 (222–284), which gives us some sense of how what is described here was understood during the later Han era, glosses the words "the scribe reads appropriate words" (史辭) as "[the ruler] holds himself guilty" (自罪責).

108. In his *Lun heng* 論衡, Wang Chong 王充 (27–ca. 100) makes this point when observing that the blindness of Confucius's disciple Zi Xia 子夏 could not have been a punishment from Heaven, as some people suppose, because Zi Xia remained blind even after conceding that he had transgressed: "Heaven punishes people as rulers punish their subjects. When the one to be punished concedes guilt, the ruler pardons him. Zi Xia conceded his transgression and making a prostration he expressed his remorse. In this case, it would be fitting that Heaven, whose virtue is most excellent, would have healed his blindness. But since it was not, in fact, a punishment given by heaven, Zi Xia remained blind." 且天之罰人，猶人君罰下也。所罰服罪，人君赦之。子夏服過，拜以自悔，天德至明，宜愈其盲。如非天罰，子夏失明。(*Lun heng jiao shi*, 273).

overt misfortune. The curing of sickness, accordingly, was a key area where the power of repentance was widely appreciated in the era before the arrival of Buddhism. The religious movements of the Eastern Han that constituted the first germs of organized Daoism were known to have drawn on these ideas with particular fervor.[109] Followers of the *Taiping dao* 太平道 movement were remembered for a method of treating the sick that consisted of making them "strike their heads to the ground and think deeply about their transgressions" (叩頭思過).[110] The *Scripture on Great Peace* (*Tai ping jing* 太平 經), which may preserve the teachings of this group, enjoins its followers to repent (*hui* 悔) and beg forgiveness by "striking their heads to the ground and slapping themselves" (叩頭自搏). This act of submission, it was claimed, would motivate Heaven to forgive the transgression and spare one's descendants any further punishment. (The *Scripture on Great Peace* is much concerned with the inheritability of sins across generations.)[111] The command to slap oneself that became a part of many later Daoist rites has been interpreted by some scholars as a ritualized, self-administered punishment intended to substitute for the more severe ones nominally due.[112] To strike one's head to the ground, the ubiquitous kowtow, carried similar connotations and was taken by at least some commentators to be a ritual imitation of the ancient method of execution by head smashing (Fujino 1976).

The so-called Five Pecks of Rice movement, the earliest form of Celestial Master Daoism, was remembered for similar practices. Those who were sick would first ponder their transgressions within a chamber of quietude (*jingshi* 靜室), a name that may derive from the chamber of interrogation (*qingshi* 請室) in which Han-dynasty magistrates questioned suspects (Yoshikawa 1987). Then a priest would write out a petition with the sick person's name and an account of their "intention to accept guilt" (服罪之 意), copies of which would be sent to offices of the heavenly bureaucracy.[113] According to one early account of these practices, one needed to write down "all sins committed since birth" and then make an oath to never again transgress on pain of death (Kleeman 2016, 58).

---

109. On these movements, see Stein 1967. During the Han dynasty, however, the curing of illness by repentance of transgressions was not limited to these groups (Shioiri 2007, 160).

110. *San guo zhi*, 8.264, citing the commentary's citation of the third-century *Dian lüe* 典略.

111. Concerning these ideas in the *Tai ping jing*, see Tsuchiya 2002; Ōfuchi 1991, 119–123; Yoshikawa 1998, 77–81; and Espesset 2002 (see especially nn. 214 and 215 on p. 41).

112. Tsuchiya 2002, 47. Self-slapping, together with prostrations and pleas for mercy, was a part of many fourth- and fifth-century Daoist rites (Lü 2008, 52–54, 74, and 103–104). See also Yamada A. 2004. Beating, self-administered or otherwise, is also mentioned as a means of repentance in some fifth- and sixth-century Buddhist sources (Yang L. 1961; Moretti 2016, 306), as well as in Buddhist stories such as the tale of Fahui discussed at the beginning of this chapter.

113. *San guo zhi*, 8.264 (see also *Hou han shu*, 71.2299). These accounts are discussed in Kleeman 2016, 59. Requesting remission from sins was also part of the daily prayer ritual of the early Celestial Masters, according to the *Hanzhong ru zhi chao jing fa* 漢中入治朝靜法 (Lü 2008, 20–21; Kleeman 2016, 248).

These Daoist petitions have frequently been described in modern scholarship as "confessions" (Wu 1979). Certainly, the notion of writing down a list
of one's sins—a common part of the ideal prescriptions for Daoist petition
rituals later in the medieval era (Verellen 2019, 58–60)—could be interpreted
in this way. Interestingly, however, the few surviving examples of the actual
content of early petitions suggest that, as with King Tang, "confession" may
not be the most apt description.[114] One example, preserved in the *Declarations
of the Perfected* (*Zhen gao* 真誥), is the petition written by Xu Hui 許翽 (ca. 341–
370) to the goddess Wei Huacun 魏華存 as part of his effort to heal the illnesses
of his elder brother and father:

> The divine mother is a humane protectress and always willing to pardon. Thus
> today, with intense apprehension, my inner organs churning, I search within
> and contemplate my transgressions. There is no repairing the faults of the past.
> Were I to lay them all out before you, they would be extremely numerous.... With
> fear and trembling, I, Yufu [Xu Hui], with full sincerity beg to make the follow-
> ing oath: from today, I will make a new start. Cleansing my heart, with sincerity
> I make a covenant with heaven and earth.... I beg that you absolve my father Mu
> and elder brother Huya of interrogation for crimes great and small. Though I
> am of no account, I beg that I personally receive the punishment, so that you
> can absolve and [grant] amnesty [for all their] great and small [crimes]. If the
> divine mother accordingly shows compassion, I, Yufu, will contemplate my trans-
> gression and repair my faults so that the whole family might equally receive your
> grace.[115]

Xu Hui's petition, like the prayer of King Tang, is simultaneously an acknowledgment that one is guilty of a multitude of sins, a plea that others should
not be punished for one's own misdeeds, and a request to bear oneself the
punishment due for the sins of others. Although the possibility of Xu Hui's
"laying out" all his specific misdeeds is touched on, it is ultimately not required. Confession of sins—to the extent we take this word to mean the unearthing and revealing of specific, previously concealed misdeeds—is clearly
secondary to the pleading for mercy and remission, for oneself and for others,
that lies at the heart of this ritual form.

Repentance as a Chinese Translation of Buddhist Renunciation
These Chinese topoi concerning the appropriate performance, power, and
scope of repentance were clearly available to the early translators and exegetes in China who sought to cast Buddhist forms of worship and ritual in

---

114. Both Strickmann (2002, 48) and Bokenkamp (2005, 44–45) have stressed the inap-
plicability of the concept of confession to these rites. Indeed, even the claim that one has been
punctilious in reporting one's sins does not necessarily mean that what is at stake is an inner
soul searching; it could be seen equally well as a conventional aspect of the bureaucratic idiom
used to communicate with Daoist divinities.

115. Bokenkamp 2007, 147, translating from HY 1010, 7.12b–13a.

more familiar terms. In gauging the kinds of cultural translation that this effort involved, it is instructive to observe how the story of Tang was sometimes used when presenting the ascetic and renunciatory aspects of Buddhism. A tale in the third-century *Liu du ji jing,* a much-read collection of stories about the Buddha's past lives, shows an early example of this. The story begins as a typical account of the Buddha's past-life sacrifices—first offering his body to feed hungry fish, he is reborn as a giant fish and then gives up his life again to save the inhabitants of a kingdom suffering from drought, to be reborn as the human ruler of that same kingdom. The narrative then takes a decidedly Chinese turn:

> With the country still suffering from drought, [the king] purified his mind through abstinence and solemnity, refraining from food and refusing gifts. Striking his head to the ground, he repented: "Let the blame for the misdeeds of the people fall upon me! I resolve to sacrifice my life so that the people might be granted rain!"[116]

Moved by his sincerity, five hundred *pratyekabuddha*s appear within his kingdom, and the king then entreats them:

> Casting his body to the ground, [the king] lowered his head and struck it to the ground. Tears flowing, he said: "My mind is soiled and my conduct impure. I have failed to conform to the teachings on the four kinds of benevolence. I have been cruel to the people, and by rights the punishment for this should be mine. Yet it inflicts the lowly and the weak, who have endured years of withering drought. O how the hunger of the common people pains me! Take away the disaster that afflicts them and let this misfortune punish me instead!"[117]

His wish granted, the *pratyekabuddha*s bless the king, and there is abundant rain and good harvest.

The tropes here of drought, kingship, and self-sacrificial repentance would have been instantly recognizable to any educated Chinese reader of the third or indeed any century.[118] Not knowing his exact sources, we cannot say to what extent Kang Senghui, the purported translator of the *Liu du ji jing,* had to work to bring the story into line with the example of King Tang. But whether through minor or substantial narrative changes or merely judicious choice of vocabulary, the self-sacrificing bodhisattva of Indian Buddhist lore appears here as none other than the model Chinese ruler who

---

116. 然國尚旱，靖心齊[>齋]肅，退食絕獻，頓首悔過曰，民之不善，咎在我身，願喪吾命惠民雨澤。(*Liu du ji jing,* T.152:3.2a15–17). I have benefited from the translation of Chavannes (1910, 1.11–14).

117. 五體投地，稽首叩頭。涕泣而曰，吾心穢行濁，不合三尊四恩之教，苦酷人民，罪當伐己。流被下劣，枯旱累載，黎庶飢饉，怨痛傷情。願除民灾，以禍罪我。(*Liu du ji jing,* T.152:3.2a21–25)

118. The appeal of this story to later generations can be seen by its citation in the sixth-century *Jing lü yi xiang* (T.2121:53.60c14–61a81).

relieves a drought by repenting and willingly (if only ritually) shouldering the blame for the sins of his people.[119] The illustrious precedent of Tang would prove useful again to those encouraging the performance of Buddhist rituals in China. In a story in the *Biographies of Eminent Monks*, when the emperor Xiaowu 孝武 (r. 454–464) asks what crime he, the emperor, is guilty of that requires him to do Buddhist *chanhui* (that is, to repent), the monk Tanzong 曇宗 replies that it is King Tang's willing self-sacrifice that shows repentance to be proper even for the pure, since "sage-kings take responsibility for the faults of others" (聖王引咎).[120]

It is, of course, monks and nuns who in theory serve as the models of long-term renunciation in Buddhist societies. In China, this renunciation too may have been viewed in light of the self-sacrificial aspect of public repentance. We know that Buddhist monastics were sometimes employed by Chinese rulers to perform rituals of repentance on occasions when the classical Chinese ritual tradition prescribed this role to the emperor himself. When Emperor Jianwen 簡文 (r. 371–373) asked the monk Fakuang 法曠 to respond to the appearance of a baleful star, an omen of Heaven's disapproval, Fakuang urged the emperor to cultivate his own virtue before eventually agreeing to perform an "abstinence-ceremony repentance" (*zhaichan* 齋懺) that quickly made the star disappear.[121] In the Taiyuan 太元 (376–396) era, another inauspicious star appeared, and this time the court ordered all virtuous monks throughout the land to carry out those rituals.[122] Buddhist monks, for whom abstinence was a permanent condition, were evidently well suited to serve as emperor substitutes repenting on his behalf for the benefit of the state.[123]

Monastic renunciation was an element of Buddhism that was frequently singled out for censure by early Chinese critics, and modern scholars too, using these criticisms as the evidence, have often seen it as the aspect of the Buddhist religion the Chinese public was initially most reluctant to accept.

---

119. The trope of drought resulting from the sins of the king, who must then expiate them to restore the rains, is well known in Indian lore (Goldman 2005, 57–59), as is the idea that the sins of either the king or the people must be "appeased" (*śānti*) to avoid the wrath of the gods (Geslani 2018). The potentially Chinese element in this story is the notion that the king purifies the sins of his people by taking them upon himself. In the only other known version of the tale translated by Kang Senghui, the Buddha is a prominent householder rather than a king, and the only repentance is done by the local farmers, whose earlier slander of the five hundred *pratyekabuddha*s had caused the drought (Shi Y. 1989, 206; *Xian yu jing*, T.202:4.386a5–387a27).

120. *GSZ*, T.2059:50.416a21–26. The many repentance scripts (懺悔文) attributed to Chinese emperors from the southern dynasties during the fifth and sixth centuries (*GHMJ*, T.2103:52.330b29–335a25) show that a Buddhist version of the public repentance ritual that Chinese emperors had long been expected to carry out became common during this era.

121. *GSZ*, T.2059:50.356c19–26.

122. *GSZ*, T.2059:50.396b8–11.

123. According to the *Mouzi li huo lun* 牟子理惑論, an important early apologetic tract, Buddhist monks "carry out abstinence every day" (日日齋; *HMJ*, T.2102:52.2a1–3). This may refer specifically to the restricted diet of the clergy, but also seems to link the word "abstinence" to the monastic lifestyle more generally.

Yet the repeated complaints that monasticism runs contrary to traditional Chinese values need not be taken at face value. On the contrary, they may in fact gesture to the very cultural spaces where such practices could be accommodated and the reasons for their appeal. Anti-Buddhist Chinese writers routinely claimed, for example, that shaving one's head in the manner of a Buddhist monk or nun was not a noble act of renunciation, but a deeply unfilial gesture that violated the injunctions of the *Classic of Filial Piety*, which said that one's body and hair, bequeathed by one's parents, must be protected.[124] But, for precisely these reasons, head shaving, or *kun* 髡, the word initially used in China to describe the bald head of a monk or nun, had long been a potent sign associated with crime and punishment. In the Han dynasty, head shaving was dispensed by the state as the lowest grade of punishment by mutilation and was mandated for all household slaves and forced-labor convicts, of whom it became an identifying characteristic.[125] Parents too used head shaving to discipline children or servants.[126] Even the spirits, whose legal bureaucracy mirrored that of the living, could mete it out to their descendants as punishment.[127]

In the early years of Chinese Buddhism, the bald heads of Buddhist ascetics were complemented by the red robes they wore, and by a remarkable coincidence this was the same color long worn by convicts in China.[128] Chinese critics seized on this visual analogy to depict Buddhism as being, in essence, an undeserved punishment, with the "shaven heads and red [convicts'] garb" (髡首赭衣) of its clergy linked to other areas where this religion supposedly encouraged needless ascetic self-harm, such as self-immolation.[129] The famous anti-Buddhist polemic the *Scripture on the Conversion of the Barbarians* (*Hua hu jing* 化胡經) used these charges to construct an entire mythos in which

---

124. *HMJ*, T.2102:52.2c16–3a6 (*Mouzi li huo lun*). For later examples of a similar criticism, see Michihata 1968, 66–68. On head shaving in Indian asceticism, see Olivelle 1995, 203–207, and Olson 2015, 14–15.

125. Hulsewé 1955, 128–132; 1985, 15–16. The Zhangjiashan 張家山 legal texts now suggest that head shaving may not have become ubiquitous until the later Western Han (Barbieri-Low and Yates 2015, 199). For *kun* as the Buddhist tonsure, see *Qianrimoni bao jing*, T.350:12.192c18–19 (a translation of Lokakṣema or a close follower) and *Wu shi jiao ji jing* 五十校計經 (in *Da fang deng da ji jing*, T.397:13.401c14–17), written in China in the late second or early third century (Greene 2017b).

126. Xu F. 1993, 266–271. Head shaving as a private, family punishment (*si xing* 私刑) was still a recognizable trope well into the early centuries of the common era, as seen in the anecdote concerning Chen Shi 陳寔 (104–187) recorded in the *Shi shuo xin yu* 世說新語 (Mather 1971, 226).

127. On the head shaving dispensed by vengeful spirits, see Bokenkamp 2007, 39 and passim, translating a story from the *Jin shu* 晉書 concerning Wang Yin 王隱 (fl. 318).

128. Red (*zhe* 赭) clothing as a "symbolic mutilation" (*xiang xing* 象刑) is mentioned by Xunzi (*Xunzi ji jie*, 18.327), and is discussed in the Qin statutes (Hulsewé 1985, 68; 72). The *Mouzi li luo lun* says that Buddhist monks wear red (*chi* 赤) clothing (*HMJ*, T.2102:52.4c1–4). According to later accounts, Buddhist monks in the Han wore red, but this was later changed to a "neutral" (雜) color (*Wei shu*, 114.3029; Tsukamoto 1974, 136).

129. *HMJ*, T.2102:52.20b11–13 (Ziegler 2015, 115).

Buddhism was said to have begun as a set of punishments that the Chinese sage Laozi, after traveling to the West at the end of his life, imposed on the Indians who worshiped him.[130] One version of this text cited in a fifth-century source says that Laozi was called the "superficial executioner" (*fu tu* 浮屠) in India, an intentional misreading of an early Chinese transcription of the word *buddha,* because rather than executing the Indians for their crimes he merely shaved their heads.[131] A surviving fragment of a possibly different version makes explicit the implied connection between Buddhist asceticism and criminality, punishment, and repentance:

> When the [Indian] barbarian king did not have faith in Laozi, Laozi manifested his divine power to make him submit. The king begged to be allowed to repent his misdeeds. Shaving his hair and beard, he pleaded for mercy for his crimes and his sins. Lord Laozi was compassionate and took pity on the king's foolish ignorance. So he taught an expedient teaching that would bind and restrict [the Indians] in accord with their capacities. They were all made to practice austerities and beg for food to curb their obstinate hearts, to don red clothing and one-sided robes [that expose the right shoulder] so as to crush their proud demeanors, to cut their bodies and faces [by shaving their hair and beard] so as to display bodies with the mutilated nose and tattooed face [of a criminal], and to abstain from wife and sex so as to make an end to their rebellious seed.[132]

Thus "great criminals are restrained only by stern punishments," explains the seventh-century anti-Buddhist author who cites this passage, whereas for the Chinese, who have never doubted Laozi, to become a Buddhist would be like "willingly wearing the cangue even though free of fault or crime."[133]

Though obviously intended as a criticism of the ascetic aspects of Buddhist monasticism, we might wonder if this rhetoric did not underestimate the religious power of what it condemned. While the critic here suggests that Buddhist clerics should be ashamed to wear robes that expose their right shoulder (and there was indeed a debate in the fourth and fifth centuries about the propriety of such dress for Chinese), the ritual act of exposing bare flesh was also a long-standing element, in theory if not in practice, of Chinese rituals of self-sacrifice.[134] Buddhist apologists were keen to note the analogy,

---

130. On the complicated history of the *Hua hu jing* and its surviving fragments, see Fukui 1965, 256–320; Zürcher 1972, 288–320; Li 2005, 94–240; Liu Y. 2010, 1–116.

131. *San po lun* 三破論, cited in Liu Xie's 劉勰 (fl. 500) *Mie huo lun* 滅惑論 (*HMJ*, T.2012:52.50c4–6). Cf. Ziegler 2017, 20.

132. 胡王不信老子，老子神力伏之。方求悔過。自髠自剪，謝愆謝罪。老君大慈，愍其愚昧。為說權教，隨機戒約。皆令投陀乞食，以制兇頑之心，赭服偏衣，用挫強粱之性，割毀形貌，示為剝劓之身，禁約妻房，絕其悖逆之種。(*Bian zheng lun*, T.2110:52.535a10–15). See also Jülch 2014, 2:371.

133. 深罪約以嚴刑... 可謂身無疵而樂著杻械。(*Bian zheng lun*, T.2110:52.535a24–b8)

134. On early Chinese rituals of bodily exposure, see Schafer 1951. The debates about Buddhist dress in the fifth and sixth centuries are preserved at *HMJ*, T.2012:52.32b12–33b8.

observing that exposing the skin was a sign of reverence in India and a laud-able gesture according to Chinese custom as well, specifically when one pleads for mercy for transgressions.[135] More broadly, "wearing the cangue even though free of fault or crime," as the critic suggests being a Chinese Buddhist would amount to, could easily describe King Tang, whose cut hair and shackled hands, to which he submitted to expiate the sins of others, gave him the appearance of a convicted criminal as well.

The power of repenting and then suffering (or submitting to) punish-ment for crimes even if they were not one's own was, in short, a powerful religious ideal even in pre-Buddhist China. It was also one that Chinese Bud-dhist devotees themselves happily embraced. According to her biography, authored by Shenyue 沈約 (441–513), the nun Jingxiu, who was known to be a great practitioner of meditation, once feared that she had violated the pre-cepts by sitting alone in the meditation hall without any companion.[136] In-quiring with a *vinaya* master, she was told that this was not a transgression. Still unsure about herself, she observed that many local nuns were deficient in the rules:

> She then lamented: "Alas, though the great discipline was [set down by the Buddha] not long ago, its sacred traces have already begun to decay. If one does not lay blame upon oneself for the faults of others, how can one be a leader?" She then did *chanhui* and also carried out the [*vinaya* penance of] probation (*mānatva*). The nuns and monks of the capital all sighed admiringly and said: "Even though her conduct is faultless, and her discipline conforms with the rules, still she thinks deeply about her transgressions. How then can we, who have faults of all kinds, not feel shame?" At that, everyone without exception followed her in doing *chanhui*.[137]

Jingxiu's self-imposed penance of probation—which in theory would involve the same kind of temporary loss of status and submission to menial chores invoked in the eight-hundred-day toilet cleaning regime of the Method for Curing Violations of the Precepts—is explicitly framed as a matter of taking responsibility for the sins of others in the manner of King Tang,[138] affirming the principle that to do such things, even or perhaps *especially* when not guilty oneself, is an act of great power that brings benefit to others.

---

135. *Fa hua wen ju ji*, T.1719:34.356c8–10; *Da banniepan jing shu*, T.1767:38.54b27–28.

136. On Jingxiu, see also Chapter 1, "The Spaces of Meditation."

137. 乃喟然歎曰。嗚呼鴻徽未遠，靈緒稍隤。自非引咎責躬，豈能導物。即自懺悔，行摩那埵。於是京師二部莫不咨嗟云。如斯之人，律行明白，規矩應法，尚爾思愆。何況我等，動靜多過，而不慚愧者哉。遂相率普懺無有孑遺。(*GHMJ*, T.2103:52.271a1–9). Cf. *BQNZ*, T.2063:50.945b3–8, which differs slightly.

138. The word used in Jingxiu's biography—*yinjiu* 引咎, literally, to "draw the faults of others [to oneself]"—is the same term that the monk Tanzong uses to analogize Buddhist *chanhui* to the sacrifice of Tang in the story of Emperor Xiaowu cited earlier.

Asceticism, Attenuated Retribution, and the Destruction of Karma
Given the evident power that was attributed to abstinence and self-sacrificial
punishment in China, it is perhaps not surprising that Chinese Buddhists,
in their retorts to the arguments made in the *Scripture on the Conversion of the
Barbarians*, were seemingly content to reject the specific historical claim that
Laozi was the founder of Buddhism without contesting the notion that Buddhist practices were harsh austerities that were necessary because Buddhists
had many sins to atone.

Asceticism was in fact arguably a less problematic feature of Buddhism in
China—where Buddhists positioned themselves as the ascetics par excellence—
than it had been in India, where ideologically Buddhism occupied a moderate
middle ground, less extreme in these matters than others such as the Jains.
Many canonical presentations of Buddhist doctrine thus *reject* the idea that
one can or should purge oneself of past sins through harsh austerities, a position embodied in the Buddha's own quest for enlightenment, in which he
pointedly gave up such practices as unproductive (Bronkhorst 1986). Given
the frequent efforts of Indian Buddhists to describe their religious goals as
something different than the destruction of sin by way of austerities, it is interesting that Buddhist repentance rituals in medieval China often characterized
themselves as involving, or simply being, an ascetic endeavor of some kind.
The Method for Curing Violations of the Precepts thus describes the required
chore of toilet cleaning as *kuyi* (苦役), literally, "painful service,"[139] a term used
in fifth-century Chinese translations of Indian Buddhist texts to describe the
fasting and other harsh austerities that the Buddha abandoned prior to his
enlightenment.[140] The *Ākāśagarbha Contemplation Scripture*, whose ritual of repentance also prescribes eight hundred days of toilet cleaning, makes the causality even more explicit, declaring that it is *"owing to the power of this ascetic
practice (kuxing 苦行) that this person's sinful karma is now removed forever."*[141]
Whether in reference to this rite or another, it was with similar ideas in mind
that the biography of the nun Huiyu 慧玉 notes that in the year 437 she carried
out an abstinence ceremony for seven days as a means of doing ascetic practice
(*kuxing*).[142] In other sources as well, Chinese Buddhists lauded asceticism as
an ongoing form of repentance and celebrated the power of self-sacrifice—
even the dramatic self-immolation that so bewildered critics—as a means of
redressing past sin.[143]

Free of the need to distinguish themselves from the Jains and other

---

139. The same word is used in the *Chan Essentials* on several occasions when discussing
rituals of *chanhui* (*Chan Essentials* 2.19.1.9; 2.20.7; 4.32.3; *CMY*, T.613:15.255c19; 257b7;
268a3–4).

140. *Chang ahan jing*, T.1:1.48a2–3; 103c13.

141. 此人因苦行力故，罪業永除。(*Guan Xukongzang pusa jing*, T.409:13.677c22–23)

142. *BQNZ*, T.2063.50:937c28 (cf. Tsai 1994, 39).

143. See, for example, *Ji shen zhou san bao gan tong lu*, T.2106:52.406c16–23, where the
inability of an onlooker to see the famous tooth relic in the Famen temple is attributed to his
past sins. After he burns off his finger, the relic appears to him.

hard-core renunciants, Buddhists in China arguably understood the relationship between asceticism, repentance, and the purification of sin somewhat differently than most Buddhists in India. But there were Indian Buddhist precedents, known in China from the fifth century on, for seeing a connection between suffering and expiation. Kumārajīva's translation of the *Daśabhūmika-vibhāṣā* (*Shi zhu piposha lun* 十住毘婆沙論), whose chapter on repentance provided a script for the daily liturgy of some Buddhist communities in China, links *increased* suffering to the expiation of sins in what amounts to a theory of the efficacy of karmic repentance.[144] After worshiping the buddhas and repenting all sins from this and past lifetimes, one must, according to this text, pray that "any retribution for these sins that I am to receive in the three lower realms be experienced in my present lifetime instead."[145]

Karma, in this view, is eliminated not by destroying it outright—impossible, according to traditional Buddhist doctrine—but by preemptively experiencing it in *attenuated* form. As Enomoto Fumio has pointed out (1989; 2002), this idea had already appeared in the Pāli canon as a Buddhist alternative to Brahmanical rituals of purification. The notion of attenuated retribution also explained why some already liberated individuals suffer a heavier-than-expected retribution: being free from future rebirth, their most weighty karma has no outlet apart from an attenuated consequence in the present.[146] It was further argued, again in the very earliest Buddhist texts, that one could attenuate bad karma on purpose, through the meditative cultivation of love (*maitrī*), compassion (*karuṇā*), joy (*muditā*), and equanimity (*upekṣā*), which dilute (but do not destroy) the efficacy of karmic retribution by making the mind "unlimited," just as the water of the Ganges floods a pinch of salt.[147] These canonical examples of attenuated retribution were explicitly cited later in the *Daśabhūmika-vibhāṣā*.[148]

It is unclear if the logic of attenuated retribution was thought to explain why "ascetic" (*ku*) practice or service purifies sin, as was argued by fifth-century Chinese repentance texts such as the *Ākāśagarbha Contemplation*

144. For an introduction to the practice of repentance as outlined in this text, see Ri 1982, 102–120. The daily liturgy of the early Tiantai community was based on this text (*Guo qing bai lu*, T.1934:46.794a18–795b14; Ikeda 1982, 143–145).

145. 於三惡道中，若應受業報，願於今身償。(*Shi zhu piposha lun*, T.1521:26.45a28–29). This passage is included in the early Tiantai liturgy that draws from this text (*Guo qing bai lu*, T.1934:46.794c26–27).

146. The classic example is the serial-killer-turned-monk, and then arhat, Aṅgulimālya (*Majjhima-nikāya*, 2.104; Ñāṇamoli and Bodhi 1995, 715; *Apidamo da piposha lun*, T.1545:27.100a17–21; *Zeng yi ahan jing*, T.125:2.693c3–6). That by the principle of attenuated retribution a liberated being might suffer *more* in their present lifetime than they would have otherwise is to be distinguished from the more common statement that liberated beings, while still alive, continue in general to experience the fruits of past karma (see Cutler 1997).

147. See the *Loṇakapalla-sutta* (*Aṅguttara-nikāya*, 1.249), discussed by Enomoto 1989, 48–50.

148. *Shi zhu piposha lun*, T.1521:26.48c–49a.

Scripture or the Method for Curing Violations of the Precepts. But these ideas were clearly used in a related context: to explain the penitential power of inauspicious meditative visions. In fifth-century meditation texts such as the *Chan Essentials,* unpleasant and frightening visions often appear and are usually interpreted as signs indicating the need for a ritual of repentance. This is also the case, more systematically, in Zhiyi's treatises from the late sixth century. But as a Tiantai commentary to Zhiyi's early meditation treatises, probably from the seventh century, explains it, such visions are themselves a kind of attenuated retribution:

> When visions appear during preliminary meditation, this means that prior to experiencing a certain retribution [one experiences] visions of things such as tigers, wolves, lions, government officials, or a cangue. [When such visions appear,] you must bear them and imagine giving up your life. If your mind fully resolves [in this manner], then the obstacle will be transformed, *and one will not have to experience it later.* Indeed, even shamans, through rituals for transcending sorrow, can avert misfortune. How much more can misfortune be extinguished by accepting the retribution when one's mind has entered trance! This is like the way, in secular law, that one is not punished twice [for the same crime]. If while meditating one resolves to accept the retribution, then the suffering of this karma will not come again. The meditation on death in the eight recollections is undertaken with precisely this intention.[149]

In this understanding, inauspicious meditative visions are not just signs of the need for repentance but the very vehicles of repentance, opportunities to willingly submit to and preemptively suffer one's future karmic punishments, thereby rendering them inert. Although not explicitly mentioned in the Method for Curing Violations of the Precepts, this idea can be seen as already implicit in the technique within that ritual by which contemplating one's own rebirth in hell serves to eliminate this punishment.[150]

This later Tiantai view of the function of inauspicious meditative visions

---

149. 定法不立相現者，於未受報前，或虎、狼、師子、縣官、枷理等相起。即當忍受，作捨身命心。心若成，郭得轉，後不受。譬如巫師度厄，尚能禳災，何況定心受報而不消滅。亦如國法不重害人，若禪中作受報意，業福[>禍]亦不再至。故八念中有念死，其意在此。(*Chan men zhang,* Z.907:55.658b9–16). Attributed to Zhiyi since the eighth century (*Dengyō daishi shōrai taishū roku,* T.2159:55.1055c18), the *Chan men zhang* is a commentary to portions of Zhiyi's *Sequential Approach.* It cites passages from later Tiantai texts authored by Guanding 灌頂 (561–632), and a seventh-century dating is thus likely (Satō 1961, 273–276).

150. See "Method for Curing Violations of the Precepts" above. Similar ideas can be found in Indian Buddhist literature. In the *Koṭikarṇa-avadāna* (Rotman 2008, 39–70), Koṭikarṇa speaks harshly to his mother, but then apologizes to her (*kṣamapitā*). Later, he has a vision of hell and the Buddha explains this to be the retribution for his act of harsh speech. Elsewhere in the *Divyāvadāna,* from where this story comes, "harsh speech" is usually punished severely. We may infer that Koṭikaraṇa's mere vision of hell is because he had properly asked for forgiveness, something that in the *Divyāvadāna* frequently reduces karmic punishment (Hiraoka 1991).

was not a universal understanding. But it serves as another example of the widespread tendency of Chinese Buddhist thinkers, from the third to the seventh centuries, to understand repentance—to plead for mercy by willingly accepting guilt and submitting to the merited punishment—as the core of what Buddhist practices were ultimately about, be they imperial prayers for the safety of the realm, monastic asceticism and renunciation in general, or the practice of seated meditation.

5

From chan to Chan

BUDDHIST MEDITATION, *chan,* first came to be regularly practiced in China during the early fifth century. In the previous chapters of this book we have seen that a relatively stable understanding of Buddhist meditative experience and meditative attainment prevailed from that time until the middle of the seventh century. To be sure, the social and cultural field of Chinese Buddhist meditation was not uniform in any simplistic way during those two and a half centuries. Across space and time there was undoubtedly significant diversity concerning scholastic theories about meditation, the meditative techniques commonly prescribed, and the institutionalization of meditation practice itself, even though the details of those variations are not always visible given our limited sources. With even greater certainty we can be sure that any specific reports or attributions of Buddhist meditative attainment were, on the ground, contested and debated in the way that claims to religious status and authority always are. But this diversity, debate, change, and contestation was not all encompassing; it proceeded according to a shared set of expectations and norms about what kind of evidence could even potentially count for what kind of claim, and what consequences the making of such claims might entail—in the language I have been using throughout this book, there was a shared semiotic ideology of Buddhist meditative experience and attainment. Over the course of this formative period of Chinese Buddhist history, concrete visions, of the kind described in meditation guides such as the *Chan Essentials,* were the sort of sign to which one looked for confirmation of meditative attainment, either for oneself or for others.

Yet this consensus was eventually challenged. The making of this challenge was a key part of what was at stake in the earliest writings of the so-called Chan School, which appear beginning around the year 700 and constitute our first gleanings of this distinctive tradition of Chinese and eventually East Asian Buddhism. The argument of this chapter is that early Chan School presentations of meditation contrasted most dramatically from previously accepted norms in claiming that concrete visions, and indeed tangible meditative experience of any kind, are *never* signs of consequential attainment and hence never valid evidence that someone is a true "master of meditation" (*chanshi*). Early Chan did not promote new techniques of meditation so much as it argued for a new way of understanding the relationship between meditative experience and meditative attainment.

There are two important caveats to this story. First, even though the Chan School proposed a new semiotic ideology of meditative attainment, and even though it succeeded in popularizing it to the extent that the word *chan* itself came increasingly to be associated with this new understanding, the approach to Buddhist meditation and its fruits recounted in the previous chapters of this book never went away. During and after the rise of the Chan School, and down to the present day, Chinese Buddhists continued to engage in activities that by the standards of earlier (though not necessarily their own) centuries would have been recognized as *chan* with the hope of obtaining visionary signs. A glimpse of this later history is provided in the epilogue. Here it is important to emphasize that the historical movement from early Chinese *chan* to the Chan School, even as we trace it, should not be construed as the complete replacing of one ideology of meditation by another. That, indeed, would be to replicate, in altered form, the Chan School's own historical teleology. Rather, what occurred during the development of the Chan School during the eighth century—long noted as a historical moment of important and perhaps even fundamental intellectual change across many areas of Chinese culture and thought—was the opening up of a domain of previous consensus. A new model for the semiotics of Buddhist sanctity was introduced that would, ever after, be available to compete with the old one.

The second caveat concerns the limitations of recounting the early history of the Chan School from the sole perspective of its approach to meditation. Indeed, despite its name, the Chan School cannot be reduced to the "meditation school" any more than the Orthodox Church can be called the form of Christianity most interested in orthodoxy. Modern scholars, therefore, rightly distinguish between *chan,* the activity of seated meditation common throughout Chinese Buddhism, and Chan as the proper name of the distinctive Chinese Buddhist movement that began in the mid-Tang dynasty.[1] The Chan School emerges as a historical object around the year 700, primarily as a set of claims about spiritual genealogy (the self-applied label "Chan School" would only be used later). Through these claims, certain living or recently deceased Chinese Buddhist masters were imagined as the heirs of an elite spiritual lineage stretching from the Buddha down to the Indian patriarch Bodhidharma, who supposedly brought it to China in the early sixth century—a "separate transmission outside the scriptures," as it would eventually be called. These were not the first lineage-based claims to authority in Chinese Buddhist history. But the self-proclaimed heirs of Bodhidharma articulated this decla-

---

1. East Asian scholars often signal this by contrasting *changuan* 禪觀 (meditation) with *chanzong* 禪宗 (Chan School). But both Western and East Asian scholars have overlooked this distinction at times.

ration in a newly compelling way, through vivid and dramatic stories and novel literary forms. Over the past several decades modern scholars have explored the early controversies associated with these claims and ensuing counterclaims, and much of the most interesting recent work on the rise of the Chan School situates it not with respect to meditation per se but as a new and influential chapter within the history of Chinese Buddhist ideas about lineage and authority (Adamek 2007; Cole 2009; Morrison 2010).

The novelty of the Chan School was, indeed, about much more than meditation. Yet it was also about more than just a concern for lineage. The first generations of Chinese Buddhists who claimed descent from Bodhidharma held other distinctive ideas about doctrine and practice in common. This shared heritage need not have been the *source* of the notion of the Bodhidharma lineage, as if claims to this lineage were the mythologized expressions of a real genealogical connection grounded institutionally, doctrinally, or by some other means. (The central conclusion of contemporary Chan studies is that the Chan lineage was not historical in this sense.) But it also was not the case that the mantle of the Bodhidharma lineage was claimed by sundry promoters of any and all understandings of Buddhism.[2] It would seem instead that successive claims to the Bodhidharma lineage, when they managed to endow given individuals with a measure of status and authority, made other aspects of what those individuals taught or wrote—elements of style, doctrine, and even practice—available for imitation by parallel, rival, or subsequent claimants. While this did not create uniformity among those purporting to be Bodhidharma's descendants, either synchronically or diachronically, it did mean that there was an identifiable family resemblance between Chan factions at any given time, even strongly antagonistic ones. And one thing the early Chan factions shared was a distinctive set of ideas about *chan*, a word that in their writings still points most often to the concrete practice of seated meditation. Early Chan texts frequently discuss this topic and criticize, in recognizable and patterned ways, what they say are wrong approaches to it. And those who first claimed Bodhidharma as their spiritual ancestor purported to be (and were described by even their critics and rivals as) *chanshi*, meditation masters, among other things.[3] Again, while early Chan was never solely a matter of a new approach to meditation, it very often was also this.

---

2. At least, not in the heyday of the Chan School in the late Tang and Song dynasties. Without subscribing to the hackneyed narrative of Chan's inexorable decline after this time, or the equally mistaken notion that in its prime the Chan School was a distinct institution separate from the rest of Chinese Buddhism, it is still not wrong to note that the Chan lineage *qua* lineage was eventually divorced from the doctrinal and rhetorical concerns that animate most Chan writings of the Tang and Song dynasties. In contemporary China, for example, essentially *all* Buddhist teachers, regardless of anything else about them, claim to be heirs of one or more Chan lineages.

3. In a gradual process, underway to at least some degree by the mid-eighth century (Chappell 1986), the traditional title "*chan* master" eventually came to mean Chan master.

Yet as we have seen, the practice and mastery of *chan* had long been a source of prestige and authority in Chinese Buddhism. To understand what was novel about the approach to meditation promulgated by the earliest Chan partisans in the 700s, we must therefore sidestep both their own claims to represent the Buddha's original or highest teachings and the inverse claims of modern scholars who have seen in Chan a rejection of Indian methods in favor of distinctly Chinese ones.[4] That we cannot take at face value Chan's own claims to Indian authenticity seems obvious, but by the same token it would be equally wrong to explain Chan-style meditation as novel for being more "Chinese" than its predecessors. If early Chan had something new to say about Buddhist meditation, it was new not in relation to purely Indian forms of practice but relative to what was by then the centuries-old Chinese tradition pertaining to *chan* examined in the earlier chapters of this book.

In this chapter, the story of *chan* before Chan comes to a close by situating the early Chan of the mid-Tang dynasty not as the first chapter in the saga of the later Chan School, but as a new episode in the story of early *chan*, a story in which, as we have amply seen, questions about the authority of meditation and the appropriate means for certifying meditative attainment had long been an ongoing concern. Focusing on these matters in particular will allow us to see that the key moves in early Chan discussions of meditation constituted challenges to previously unquestioned ideas about the semiotics of meditative experience. Eighth-century Chan partisans did not invent the idea that mastery of *chan* was the source of a particular kind of authority. Rather, they grafted their new notion of lineage onto an earlier model, one they tried to supersede but did not ignore, and this required dealing with widely held expectations and norms concerning the kind of evidence that such claims require.

Rejecting the *Chan* Scriptures

The literature of the early Chan School often describes its approach to Buddhist meditation in sweepingly superior terms. Those in Bodhidharma's lineage teach, practice, and have mastered "true" *chan*, or "Mahāyāna" *chan*, or the *chan* of the "supreme vehicle" (最上乘).[5] Since these titles frame Chan-style meditation in terms of values that most if not all Chinese Buddhists would have professed, they do not help us understand what contemporary

---

4. The influential theory according to which Chan was a distinctly "Chinese" reformulation of Indian Buddhism goes back to Hu Shih (1937).

5. The frequent claim that Bodhidharma transmitted the "Buddha mind" (佛心) may also imply a superior form of meditation since "mind training" (心學) was a common term for meditation practice in the early Tang dynasty (*XGSZ*, T.2060:50.592b14; 596a18; 614a5; 696a6). This word likely derived from the technical expression "training in higher forms of mind" (*adhicitta-śikṣāpada; zengshang xinxue* 增上心學), an Indian commentarial explanation of *dhyāna* and / or *samādhi*.

audiences would have seen as the possible alternatives. Occasionally, however, early Chan texts do distinguish themselves from something more specific: the teachings of the fifth-century *chan* scriptures.

In the earliest Chan School document of all, the well-known funerary epitaph for master Faru 法如 (638–689), we can already see a desire to negate or transcend the authority of the fifth-century *chan* scriptures in particular. Faru's epitaph, which survives to this day at the Shaolin temple, is the first known source to link a living or recently deceased person to a semi-secret lineage stretching from the Buddha to Bodhidharma. It invokes the fifth-century *chan* scriptures by citing a brief passage from a preface to one of them—Lushan Huiyuan's preface to the *Chan Scripture of Dharmatrāta*—as proof that a transmission that "did not involve words" existed in India, of which Faru is the heir.[6]

In citing Huiyuan's preface, however, Faru's epitaph invests the idea of lineage with a significance exactly contrary to what was implied in that preface. There Huiyuan had presented it as a secret teaching that Ānanda, compiler of the Buddhist sutras, received from the Buddha but did not include in the canon. Passed on by later Buddhist masters, this secret teaching was eventually threatened with corruption during the age of the decline of the Dharma, compelling its remaining true heirs to compose the *chan* scriptures to preserve it.[7] Huiyuan's preface, in other words, uses the trope of a secret lineage, one transmitting information absent from the canonical scriptures, to authorize not a lineage of living patriarchs but a lineage of *texts*—the *chan* scriptures, an admittedly post-canonical corpus whose authority was thereby equated with that of the sutras (Barrett 1990, 93). In taking only the trope of a secret, oral lineage from its avowed source, the earliest known claim to the authority of the Bodhidharma lineage pointedly negates the authority of the *chan* scriptures themselves.[8]

In the Faru epitaph we can see the outline of a claim concerning the nature of the *chan* of Bodhidharma—namely, that it is *not* the same as what is discussed in the meditation scriptures of the fifth century, heretofore the canonical authorities on this subject in China. This same idea is expressed in a somewhat later text bearing on the Chan lineage, the *Record of the Dharma Jewel through the Generations* (*Li dai fa bao ji* 曆代法寶記). A product of the

---

6. For translations of the relevant sections of the epitaph, see McRae 1986, 85, and Cole 2009, 100. For a transcription of the original text, see Yanagida 1967, 487–488.

7. On Huiyuan's preface, see also "The *Chan* Scriptures" in Chap. 1.

8. When Faru's epitaph was composed, the idea of "*chan* scriptures" would have remained closely identified with the fifth-century *chan* scriptures in particular, since few if any new texts of that type had appeared in China since that time. In fact, as far as historical memory is concerned, only in the early fifth century was China rich in foreign *chan* masters who also transmitted putatively canonical texts pertaining to this subject. None of the foreign Buddhist monks in China during the sixth and seventh centuries who were remembered as *chan* masters (of which there are only a handful) were ever linked to such texts (Mutō 2005a, 65; see also Mutō 2005b, 2006, and 2007).

Sichuan-based followers of Wuzhu 無住 (714–774), the *Record of the Dharma Jewel* claims that the then-contested Bodhidharma lineage was inherited by Wuzhu alone and that it transmits the most perfect understanding of *chan* (Adamek 2007, 136). A passage situated just after the biographies of the first six Chan patriarchs ending with Huineng makes this claim concrete by differentiating Bodhidharma's *chan* from specific examples of supposedly inferior methods:

> The names of these [inferior] forms of meditation are the contemplations of the white bones and the breath, the nine meditations on decaying corpses, the five ways of stopping the mind, the contemplations of the sun, the moon, the towers and ponds [of the Pure Land], and the Buddha, or [the meditation practices] in the *Chan Essentials* that direct a person afflicted by a heat illness to perform the contemplation of cold, one afflicted by a cold illness to perform the contemplation of heat, and one with thoughts of carnal desire to perform the contemplation of poisonous snakes and the contemplation of impurity.[9]

Like Faru's epitaph, the *Record of the Dharma Jewel* attempts to distinguish Bodhidharma's *chan* from that of the specific texts and practices long since considered to be the most authoritative expositions of Buddhist meditation in China. Singled out for censure here are general techniques of meditation associated with both the fifth-century *chan* scriptures, such as the white bone contemplation, and the closely related Contemplation Scriptures, such as the sun contemplation and the pond contemplation.[10] One fifth-century *chan* scripture is even mentioned by name: the *Chan Essentials*.[11]

In addition, the *Record of the Dharma Jewel* proposes an alternative to those texts in the form of the *Scripture on the Gate of Chan* (*Chan men jing* 禪門經), a seemingly apocryphal Chinese sutra that it claims was translated into Chinese by Bodhidharma.[12] When it cites that text in a passage immediately following its denunciation of the *chan* scriptures, we can begin to see what it thought differentiated superior from inferior understandings of meditation:

---

9. 列名如後，白骨觀、數息觀、九相觀、五停心觀、日觀、月觀、樓臺觀、池觀、佛觀。又禪祕要經云，人患熱病想涼冷觀，患冷病作熱想觀，色想作毒蛇觀、不淨觀…諸餘三昧觀等。(Adamek 2007, 326, with slight modifications). See also Yanagida 1971b, 107–108.

10. The "sun contemplation" points to the *Amitāyus Contemplation Scripture* in particular. As we will see below, some early Chan texts prescribe this practice too, suggesting that among the targets of the *Record of the Dharma Jewel* were what it perceived as the wrongheaded meditation practices of rival Chan factions.

11. Although the *Record of the Dharma Jewel* uses the name *Chan mi yao jing* 禪祕要經, nominally the *Chan Essentials* (T.613), the content it cites matches the *Methods for Curing* (T.620) instead. The latter indeed sometimes circulated under the name *Chan Essentials;* see *Secrets of Buddhist Meditation*, appendices 1 and 3.

12. The complete *Chan men jing* survives in several Dunhuang manuscripts (Yanagida 1999b; Inosaki 1998b; Senda 2004).

The *Scripture on the Gate of Chan* says: "If while doing seated meditation one sees an image of the Buddha's form, his thirty-two marks brightly shining, flying through the air performing miracles, is this true or is this a delusion? The Buddha replied: Viewing emptiness while seated in meditation means not seeing any particular thing. If you see the Buddha with thirty-two marks... your own mind is confused, and you are caught in a demon's net. To see such things amid empty quiescence is nothing but delusion."[13]

In linking Bodhidharma to the *Scripture on the Gate of Chan*, the *Record of the Dharma Jewel* is in part rejecting earlier traditions that had associated him with the *Laṅkāvatāra Sutra*, a text that by the late 700s was far too conventional to be a plausible wellspring of Chan understanding.[14] At the same time, however, the *Scripture on the Gate of Chan* is positioned as a canonical meditation text, putatively transmitted from India but bypassing the fifth-century *chan* scriptures in particular. (That its title apes those of the fifth-century *chan* scriptures suggests that its original author may have had a similar idea.)[15]

When the *Record of the Dharma Jewel* cites the *Scripture on the Gate of Chan* as rejecting concrete visions of the Buddha as "delusion," this is, firstly, a rejection of the specific meditation techniques mentioned earlier, such as the white bone contemplation and the contemplations of impurity and the breath. But we should also note the context of this rejection: it is in answer to a question about the status of extraordinary meditative visions. These visions, it asserts, are not *true* (實)—far from evidence of meditative attainment, they are signs that one has been ensnared by demons. This claim stands in sharp contrast indeed to the fifth-century *chan* scriptures, where concrete visions are the signs of attainment even when the object of meditation is emptiness. Indeed, that the evidence of meditative attainment is generally to be found in concrete confirmatory visions was, as we have already seen, an uncontroversial understanding up through the middle of the seventh century. The *Record of the Dharma Jewel* posits the superiority of Bodhidharma's *chan* precisely in its rejection of this hitherto normal understanding. And as we will see, claims to this effect echoed throughout a variety of early Chan School texts.

---

13. 禪門經云，坐禪觀中，見佛形像，三十二相，種種光明，飛騰虛空，變現自在，為真實耶。為虛妄耶。佛言，坐禪見空無有物，若見於佛三十二相，種種光明...皆是自心顛倒，繫著魔網，於空寂滅見如是事，即虛妄。 (Adamek 2007, 326, with slight modifications). See also Yanagida 1971b, 108.

14. Chan's eventual ideological rejection of the *Laṅkāvatāra Sutra* is expressed most dramatically in the Dunhuang version of the *Platform Sutra*, where in one scene the fifth patriarch Hongren changes his mind about having illustrations from that sutra painted on the walls of his temple (Yampolsky 1967, 130).

15. The *Scripture on the Gate of Chan* even refers to itself as the "Secret Essentials of the Gate of Chan" (*Chan men mi yao* 禪門祕要) at one point, perhaps attempting to supersede the earlier *Chan Essentials*. Internally, it also uses the name *Chan yao jing* 禪要經, a title under which one of Kumārajīva's meditation texts (T.616) circulated during the Tang dynasty (*Da tang nei dian lu*, T.2149:55.252c18).

Meditative Attainment in East Mountain Texts

Early Chan writings rarely contrast their claims about meditation with those of other traditions or texts directly, but such contrasts were often implied. We can see this in the meditation instructions contained in the writings attributed to Daoxin 道信 (580–651) and Hongren 弘忍 (600–674), later lionized as the fourth and fifth patriarchs of the Chan lineage and known in their day as the key teachers of the so-called East Mountain tradition from which all early Chan lineages claimed descent. The treatises of Daoxin and Hongren, which strictly speaking cannot be dated earlier than around the year 700, contain some of the earliest instructions for Chan-style meditation. Although largely ignored by the later Chan tradition, whose increasingly radical rhetoric about "sudden" awakening made discussion of concrete methods of meditation taboo, they have been much studied by modern scholars and credited with a novel and seemingly characteristically Chan effort to strip meditation of its accustomed hierarchies of contemplative techniques and its ethical, philosophical, and even institutional contexts, perhaps with the aim—though this is less clear—of making the practice of meditation accessible to a newly widened audience.[16]

Without claiming that these readings are wrong, I suggest that a somewhat different perspective emerges when we carefully compare these texts to contemporaneous accounts of largely similar practices and to the earlier sources on which they clearly drew. In trying to discern what it was in Daoxin and Hongren's instructions for meditation that would have seemed novel and unexpected to their real or imagined audiences, what we find is that while the specific techniques they prescribe are quite similar to those given in many earlier sources, what is different is that they either reject or fail to mention at key moments the confirmatory power of visions and other concrete meditative experiences. Compared with their antecedents and contemporaries, Daoxin and Hongren offered above all a new semiotics of meditative experience, a new argument, that is, about the kinds of experiences that could or could not serve as grounds for claiming meditative attainment.

Daoxin's *Essential Techniques for Calming the Mind*
Two sections in Daoxin's treatise the *Essential Techniques for Calming the Mind* give relatively concrete instructions for meditation practice.[17] The first of

---

16. McRae 1986, 134–147; Bielefeldt 1988, 83–87; Faure 1986b, 111; Sharf 2014b; and Poceski 2015, 81–85.

17. Daoxin's treatise *Ru dao an xin yao fang bian fa men* 入道安心要方便法門 survives only in the *Lengqie shi zi ji* 楞伽師資記, an early Chan history datable to 712–716 (Barrett 1991). For the Chinese text, notes, and a modern Japanese translation of Daoxin's treatise, see Yanagida 1971a, 186–268. For complete English and French translations, see Chappell 1983 and Faure 1989, respectively.

these contains directions for the so-called one-practice *samādhi* (*yi xing sanmei* 一行三昧), and the second is a long, famous passage on what Daoxin calls "guarding the one without moving" (守一不移), one of the most detailed accounts of meditation in all of early Chan literature.

One-Practice Samādhi. Toward the beginning of his treatise, in the context of a discussion on how one can properly meditate on the buddhas, Daoxin cites and then comments on a well-known scriptural passage that describes the "one-practice *samādhi*." This short passage states that one wishing to do this practice should free the mind from distraction, concentrate attention on a single buddha, and then chant that buddha's name. One then sits in meditation posture, faces the direction of that buddha's land, and by "continuously bringing this buddha to mind in each moment of thought," one will eventually "see all the buddhas of the past, present, and future."[18]

Any informed reader of Daoxin's text would have been familiar with the "one-practice *samādhi*," an essentially generic designation for seated meditation based on the venerable method of "bringing to mind the buddha" (*nianfo*).[19] But not only was this kind of meditation practice familiar, so were its expected results. Indeed the original scriptural passage exemplified, in miniature, the common understanding of what had counted as significant meditative attainment in Chinese Buddhism since the fifth century: by focusing the mind intently on a chosen object (a particular buddha), one eventually obtains a concrete vision (the appearance of many buddhas) that goes beyond the initial object to at least some degree, a vision that, as the normative fruit of the practice, confirms one's attainment.

Daoxin's subsequent comments amount to a commentary on this familiar sequence of technique (bringing to mind the Buddha) and attainment (seeing the buddhas of the past, present, and future). He first reproduces part of the scriptural passage exactly (italicized below), before adding his own words:

> If you [as the scripture says] *continuously bring to mind the Buddha in each moment of thought,* then, suddenly, all will be clear and still and you will no longer have any object of mind. The *Greater [Prajñāpāramitā] Sutra* says: "Being without an object of mind is called 'bringing to mind the Buddha.'" What does "being without an object of mind" mean? The very mind that brings to mind the

---

18. 念念相續…見過去未來現在諸佛。(Yanagida 1971a, 186; *Lengqie shi zi ji,* T.2837:85.1287a1–2). For ease of reference, I below cite the line numbers of T.2837, but in all cases I have relied on Yanagida's superior edition.

19. Formalized by Zhiyi as the first of his "four forms of *samādhi*" ritual-meditative programs (Stevenson 1986, 54–58), the one-practice *samādhi* was much discussed by seventh-century Pure Land authors who emphasized the call to chant the Buddha's name (Faure 1986b, 103–104).

Buddha is called "without an object of mind." Apart from the mind, there is no other Buddha. And apart from the Buddha, there is no other mind.[20]

Daoxin's interpretation of the one-practice *samādhi,* whatever else it might do, intervenes in the original scriptural passage at a particular point.[21] After reproducing the instructions to "continuously bring to mind the Buddha," Daoxin describes the ideal results not as "seeing all the buddhas of the past, present, and future," as in the original passage, but as a sudden *absence* of any cognitive object at all. The doctrines Daoxin uses to justify this interpretation—doctrines concerning the ultimate emptiness of the Buddha, or the equality of mind and Buddha—are in and of themselves uncontroversial, or at least were uncontroversial in China at this time. What is novel is the way that these doctrines, for Daoxin, now dictate the phenomenology of the meditative experience that signifies attainment.[22]

Slightly later, Daoxin repeats these ideas concerning the practice of *nianfo* and its results, presenting them now simply as part of his own instructions:

> When you constantly bring to mind the Buddha without giving rise to distractions, there will not be any concrete signs at all, just equanimous nonduality. When you have reached this stage, the mind that is thinking about the Buddha will itself cease. Beyond this there is no need for any confirmation. Just to gaze at this equanimous mind is [to see] the true, Dharma-body nature of the Buddha.[23]

No reader of Daoxin's text would have been surprised to learn that an effective form of *chan* is the method of *nianfo,* or bringing to mind the Buddha. This method had long been recognized as one of the "five gates of *chan*" informing both the *chan* scriptures and later Chinese manuals such as those of Zhiyi. Daoxin's claim that this technique, by focusing the mind intently on a single object, leads to a state of intensive calm in which the mind becomes imperturbable is equally consonant with how earlier Chinese Buddhist sources typically presented the basic practice of meditation. But those sources also maintain—as we have seen in earlier chapters—that it is exactly

---

20. 念佛心心相續，忽然澄寂，更無所緣念。大品經云：無所念者是名念佛。何等名無所念。即念佛心名無所念。離心無別有佛。離佛無別有心。(*Lengqie shi zi ji,* T.2837:85.1287a9–14). I have benefited from the translations of this passage by Sharf 2002, 304; Chappell 1983, 108; and Faure 1989, 142–143, and the discussion of it by Ibuki 1998, 26–27.

21. Daoxin's instructions for the one-practice *samādhi* have been variously seen as prefiguring the later Chan claim that everyday actions can be sites of awakening (Faure 1989, 140n12), as evidence that early Chan did not reject the practice of *nianfo* (Ibuki 1998, 26; Sharf 2002, 304), and as showing Chan's debt to Tiantai meditation methods (Sekiguchi 1969, 320–337; Poceski 2007, 135).

22. In the sermons of Shenhui we find two very similar descriptions of the one-practice *samādhi* as normatively leading not to a vision of the buddhas but to the absence of any "cognitive object" (*jingjie*) whatsoever (Yang Z. 1996, 39; 73).

23. 常憶念佛，攀緣不起。則泯然無相，平等不二。入此位中，憶佛心謝。更不須徵。即看此等心，即是如來真實法性之身。(*Lengqie shi zi ji,* T.2837:85.1287a15–17)

at that moment, when the mind reaches a state of profound tranquility and attention, that some kind of concrete experience will occur, a confirmatory vision or other tangible encounter that serves as a sign of either progress or karmic obstruction that must then be purified through repentance. For Daoxin, however, nothing like this takes place at all, and meditation is successful when there are *no* concrete signs to speak of, when "the mind thinking about the Buddha will itself cease." Daoxin furthermore clearly anticipates that his readers, accustomed to that earlier understanding, might find his description of meditative attainment underwhelming, and he immediately emphasizes that, indeed, "beyond this there is no need for any confirmation."[24] Again, what is provided here is not a new technique of meditation but a new statement about the kind of experience that is to be taken as evidence of meditative attainment.

Guarding the One. Daoxin's most detailed instructions for meditation occur in a later section of the *Essential Techniques for Calming the Mind* under the rubric "guarding the one without moving."[25] Here too we can assess the novelty of Daoxin's directives by comparing them to the earlier, widely known sources on which he has plainly drawn—the meditation treatises of Zhiyi.

To "guard the one without moving," Daoxin says, one must first reflect on sensory and mental objects as lacking in any intrinsic substance, appearing in the mind only as reflections in a mirror. By remaining constantly aware of the emptiness of all impressions, one "becomes tranquil, hearing and seeing nothing" (寂爾無聞見). Turning within, one is "constantly empty and pure" (常空淨).[26] Then, with a calm and purified mind, one "gazes upon a single object with focused attention" (注意看一物)—what object is not stated—and keeps one's attention "tied" (繫) to it, like a flighty bird kept in check by a string tied to its legs.[27] Doing this without pause, eventually "the mind will become wholly and completely concentrated" (泯然心自定).[28] Here, having

---

24. 更不須徵. Cf. Yanagida's free rendering "and it is not even then necessary to point to this as 'Buddha'" (1971a, 194), an interpretation followed by Faure and Chappell. (The Tibetan translation of the *Lengqie shi zi ji* ends just before this line, unfortunately; Van Schaik 2015, 97.) *Zheng* 徵 and *zheng* 證 are interchangeable in medieval Chinese writings. The two words are related etymologically and phonetically, and both were often glossed as *yan* 驗, "confirmation" or "verification" (*Wang Li gu han yu zi dian*, 1298; Ping and Deng 2006, 261).

25. Daoxin's account of "guarding the one" has been much studied by scholars of early Chan, who have noted this term's use in contemporaneous Daoist cultivation literature (McRae 1986, 140–142; Buswell 1989, 137).

26. *Lengqie shi zi ji*, T.2837:85.1288a22–b16.

27. *Lengqie shi zi ji*, T.2837:85.1288b17–19.

28. *Lengqie shi zi ji*, T.2837:85.1288b19–20. *Minran* 泯然 ("wholly and completely") is taken by McRae as "completely" (1986, 141), by Faure as "imperceptibly [insensiblement]" (1989, 153), and by Chappell as "[disturbance] eliminated" (1983, 116; see also Yanagida 1971a, 243). However we translate it, *minran* here seems to point to the moment of entering *samādhi* or *dhyāna*. It also has this meaning in the section on the one-practice *samādhi* discussed earlier (*Lengqie shi zi ji*, T.2837:85.1287a15).

reached a momentary conclusion, Daoxin ends by insisting that these teachings are not his own but are based entirely on the scriptures.[29]

Daoxin was not wrong about his lack of originality. His instructions so far track closely, at times nearly to the letter, with the introductory section of Zhiyi's meditation primer the *Lesser Calming and Contemplation* (*Xiao zhi guan*).[30] The twofold movement in the first part of Daoxin's instructions—first viewing mental and sensory objects as empty reflections, then turning attention back upon the perceiving mind itself to see it too as empty—is nearly identical to what Zhiyi calls "calming the mind by realizing the truth [of emptiness]" (體真止), the third of three methods of "calming" (止) that he presents as the preliminary steps of meditation proper.[31] Daoxin's next instructions—for "gazing" at a single object and fixing the mind to it without cease—are likewise similar in language and content to the first of the three methods of calming, described as "calming the mind by tying it to an object and keeping it there" (繫緣守境止).[32]

So far, Daoxin's "guarding the one without moving" appears to be little more than a mildly idiosyncratic summary of the basic methods of calming from Zhiyi's treatise. In the immediately ensuing section, Daoxin exposes his debt even further by invoking the simile of an archer gradually learning to hit a target by repeated practice, the same figure that Zhiyi uses to conclude his introductory section on the three methods of calming.[33] And, as if simply moving along in Zhiyi's text, Daoxin goes on to provide directions for "contemplating and investigating" (觀察) all things as empty and nondual, directions that easily parse as a summary of Zhiyi's methods for contemplation (觀) that follow next in his manual as well.[34]

If these parts of Daoxin's account of "guarding the one without moving" amount to a summary of known meditation techniques, its next passage, describing the possible results, begins to depart from earlier sources:

---

29. *Lengqie shi zi ji*, T.2837:85.1288b23–26.

30. It is not necessary to suppose that Daoxin was drawing on Zhiyi's treatise directly. The point is merely that Daoxin, in these passages, follows what at the time would have been a widely accepted model for basic meditative practice. On Daoxin's use of Zhiyi here, see Faure 1997, 50–51. Cf. Sharf 2014b, 940, who I think attributes more originality to Daoxin's prescriptions than is warranted.

31. *Xiao zhi guan*, T.1915:46.467a11–29; see also 468b28–469a14. These passages are missing in two manuscript versions of Zhiyi's text that may represent the earliest form of it (Sekiguchi 1961, 339). However, even in these versions, similar passages occur elsewhere (Sekiguchi 1961, 340, 344). This twofold process—first realizing the emptiness of outer sensory objects and then grasping the emptiness of the inner perceiving mind itself—occurs in many early Chan School accounts of meditation and may originally derive from Yogācāra literature (Yamabe 2014b, 279–288; Greene 2020).

32. In the *Sequential Approach*, this method is named "calming [the mind] by tying it to an object" (繫緣止; *CDFM*, T.1916:46.492a6). Daoxin's instructions borrow the common images of "tying" (繫) and "guarding" (守) to describe how the mind remains fixed on its object.

33. *Lengqie shi zi ji*, T.2837:85.1288b27–c2; *Xiao zhi guan*, T.1915:46.467a29.

34. *Lengqie shi zi ji*, T.2837:85.1288c12–22.

[1] If any *strange objects* appear to your mind, be aware of their arising and immediately contemplate the place from whence they arise. Ultimately, they do not [actually] arise.... [In this way] just constantly contemplate [as empty] any disturbing mental objects, mental cogitation, false awareness, conceptualizations, imaginations, or random thoughts.

[2] Such distractions of mind will then not arise, and you will obtain the state of *coarse concentration*. If you can concentrate your mind [in this way], then there will be no more *hankering after objects of mind* at all. To the extent that you can do this, you will become calm and fixed, and to a similar extent you will be able to quell all your defilements. Getting rid of the old ones and not then producing any new ones, this is called liberation.[35]

To understand the novelty of what Daoxin says in this passage, as well as how it differs from what a Tang-era audience might have expected, we must first see how the ghost of Zhiyi still looms large here, just as it did earlier.

In the second paragraph (I will return to the first in a moment), Daoxin posits a sequence of accomplishments: (1) the quelling of mental distractions → (2) "coarse concentration" (*cu zhu* 麁住) → (3) the elimination of all "hankering after objects of mind" (*yuan lü* 緣慮).[36] Done fully, this is, or quickly leads to, "liberation." Daoxin's choice of words here is not random. The two terms I have emphasized are technical concepts drawn from Zhiyi's meditation treatises, where they describe what Zhiyi calls "sense-sphere trance" (欲界定), the first classifiable *dhyāna*-like meditative attainment.[37] In his *Sequential Approach* (of which the *Lesser Calming and Contemplation* is a summary), Zhiyi describes this moment as follows:

> The signs confirming sense-sphere trance...are three: the mind of *coarse concentration,* the mind of subtle concentration, and the confirmation of sense-sphere trance proper. Coarse concentration occurs when one's mind, by practicing the methods described earlier for breath meditation, gradually becomes empty and still, *with no further hankering after objects of mind.* Subtle concentration occurs when one's mind, following upon this, gradually becomes more and more attenuated. At the moment when you attain either coarse or subtle concentration, or when you are about to, an "uplifting bodily experience" will necessarily arise.[38]

---

35. 心緣異境，覺起時即觀起處。畢竟不起...常觀攀緣、覺觀、妄識、思想、雜念，亂心不起，即得麁住。若得住心，更無緣慮，即隨分寂定，亦得隨分息諸煩惱。畢故不造新，名為解脫。(*Lengqie shi zi ji*, T.2837:85.1288c17–1289a6)

36. Reading as adjective-noun: mental hankering (慮) concerned with sensory or mental objects (緣), which is how Zhiyi seems to use the word.

37. On the concept of sense-sphere trance, see Chap. 3, n. 25.

38. 證欲界定相...中自有三。一麁住心，二細住心，三證欲界定。一麁住相者，因前息諸道方便修習，心漸虛凝，不復緣慮。名為麁住。細住相者，於後其心泯泯轉細，即是細住心。當得此麁細住時，或將得時，必有持身法起。(*CDFM,* T.1916:46.509b24–c2)

The close similarity between Zhiyi's description of the attainment of sense-sphere trance and Daoxin's account of where the practice of "guarding the one without moving" leads is quite apparent. Both describe a state reached when intense concentration on a single object has yielded "coarse concentration" first, followed by a state free of all "hankering after objects of mind." Yet there are two crucial differences in how they characterize what will (or should) be the results of the practices they describe. First, what Zhiyi classifies as the lowest of the nameable meditative attainments is proclaimed by Daoxin to be liberation itself. And second, Daoxin conspicuously fails to present this attainment as being confirmed in the usual way.

For Zhiyi, even though sense-sphere trance is an entry-level meditative attainment, it is also the first moment of significant confirmatory experience. It is by attaining sense-sphere trance, he says, that the visions and other experiences will occur that confirm one's store of good or evil roots and allow the divination of information about one's past good deeds, past meditative attainments, or past sins. In the passage cited above, Zhiyi does not discuss these events in detail, having already done so thoroughly earlier in his treatise.[39] But he does mention a different kind of confirmatory experience, an "uplifting bodily experience" (持身法), that he goes on to describe as small, sudden jolts of bodily energy that deepen, when sense-sphere trance ushers one into the first *dhyāna* proper, into the bodily sensations that he calls the "contacts" (*chu* 觸), produced by the infusion into the meditator's body of physical matter (*rūpa*) from the higher "world of pure form" (*rūpa-dhātu*).[40] Such occurrences, Zhiyi says, must be carefully scrutinized and discussed with one's meditation teacher so that they can be distinguished from signs of illness and demonic interference, which are subjectively very similar and can mislead a practitioner into believing that meditative attainment has occurred. Upon attainment of the first *dhyāna* itself, a confirmatory vision (*jingjie*) associated with the meditation technique being pursued will also appear.[41]

Read against Zhiyi, whom he otherwise follows closely, Daoxin's failure to discuss anything remotely like this is striking. Just at the moment in the story when the meditator is described by Zhiyi, and the tradition he channeled, as necessarily undergoing a sudden irruption of elaborate visionary and bodily occurrences, Daoxin says precisely nothing. In fact, he rejects any need to pay attention to concrete visionary or bodily experiences whatsoever. In the first paragraph of his description of the possible results of "guarding the one without moving," he notes that the meditator should dismiss as empty any "strange objects" (*yijing* 異境) encountered while meditating. This appears to be a reference to unusual visions and other concrete meditative

---

39. Namely, in the "internal expedients" chapter, to which Zhiyi here explicitly refers the reader, as discussed under "Zhiyi on Basic Meditative Experience" in Chap. 3.

40. *CDFM*, T.1916:46.510a17–511a9. On the "contacts," see H. Wang 2001, 150–165. They are analogous to the various forms of "bliss" (P. *pīti*) that Theravāda treatises link to the attainment of *dhyāna*.

41. *CDFM*, T.1916:46.510a27.

experiences.[42] That this is Daoxin's meaning becomes inescapable when we realize that this entire section draws, at times verbatim, from the *Awakening of Faith* (*Da sheng qi xin lun* 大乘起信論), the famous sixth-century apocryphal treatise whose doctrine of "original awakening" was so influential among early Chan authors.[43] In the line immediately preceding his invocation of "strange objects," Daoxin had in fact just cited, indirectly, the *Awakening of Faith*'s instructions for "calming" (止) meditation.[44] The next passage in the *Awakening of Faith* goes on to describe a number of possible inauspicious meditative visions:

> Some people, lacking the power of roots of good, may be disturbed by demons, heretics, ghosts, or spirits. If, when sitting in meditation, frightful forms or things resembling attractive men or women should appear, one must bring to mind that they are all only [one's own] mind, and then these visions (*jingjie*) will disappear, no longer able to bother you. Or else they may appear in the form of gods, bodhisattvas, or buddhas fully possessed of all the bodily marks.... Diligently maintain correct mindfulness, without grasping, and you will be able to dispel all these karmic obstructions.[45]

Thus, Daoxin's mention of the need to dispel "strange objects" from the mind is evidently his concise summary of this passage from the *Awakening of Faith*.

In rejecting the significance of unusual meditative experiences or visions, Daoxin may have thought that he was accurately representing the *Awakening of Faith*. Indeed, the passage in question clearly says that visions of buddhas and so forth are karmic obstructions, not signs of attainment. Yet Daoxin's reading was atypical when compared with other Tang-dynasty commentaries on the *Awakening of Faith*, which did not interpret this passage as a wholesale rejection of concrete meditative visions. The commentary of Wŏnhyo 元曉 (617–686), the earliest to discuss this passage in detail, marks

---

42. Yanagida 1971a, 253, agrees that this is the meaning of "strange objects" here (see also Faure 1989, 156, and Chappell 1983, 118). Cf. McRae 1986, 141.

43. On the importance of the *Awakening of Faith* for the early Chan School, see Buswell 1989, 78–104. Long considered a Chinese composition rather than a translation, the status of the *Awakening of Faith* as an assemblage of material derived from earlier Chinese Buddhist texts has now been shown definitively by Ōtake Susumu's exhaustive study (2017).

44. *Da sheng qi xin lun*, T.1666:32.582a28–29, whose wording is invoked nearly verbatim at *Lengqie shi zi ji*, T.2837:85.1288c24–1289a1. Seventh-century commentaries to the *Awakening of Faith* (discussed below) invariably cite Zhiyi's meditation manuals when discussing this passage. That Daoxin has drawn closely on both the *Awakening of Faith* suggests that his proximate source might have been such a commentary rather than Zhiyi's treatise itself. The *Awakening of Faith*'s presentation of "calming" (within its larger account of "calming and contemplation") is broadly similar to both Zhiyi's and Daoxin's. On the "calming and contemplation" section of the *Awakening of Faith*, see Takemura 1985.

45. 或有眾生無善根力，則為諸魔外道鬼神之所惑亂，若於坐中現形恐怖，或現端正男女等相，當念唯心，境界則滅，終不為惱。或現天像、菩薩像，亦作如來像相好具足 ... 當勤正念不取不著，則能遠離是諸業障。(*Da sheng qi xin lun*, T.1666:32.582b4–23)

the words "lacking the power of roots of good" as the key to understanding.[46] He then asks: "Seeing visions such as images of bodhisattvas and so forth *can also be the result of the arousing of roots of good* from past lives. How can these be differentiated?"[47] Wǒnhyo answers his own question with an extended *homage* to Zhiyi, citing long passages from the *Sequential Approach* that explain how to distinguish the meditative visions indicative of past good roots from those that are "false" (邪) or caused by "demons" (魔). Fazang's 法藏 (643–712) commentary to the *Awakening of Faith* follows Wǒnhyo's example nearly exactly. Even more interesting is the *Shi moheyan lun* 釋摩訶衍論, an anonymous eighth-century commentary, two scrolls of which are devoted to the passage on meditative visions.[48] Here this commentary provides a number of methods for countering demonic interference. But it also notes that *some* of the visions encountered are the result of real gods and goddesses visiting meditators as confirmation of their attainment, and strategies are additionally provided for discerning the difference (real gods, for example, always wear ten pearls among their jewelry).[49]

Tang-dynasty commentators, then, generally saw this passage of the *Awakening of Faith* as being consistent with the understanding that informs both Zhiyi's meditation manuals and the earlier *chan* scriptures. While meditators do risk obtaining visions that manifest their "roots of evil" or are signs of the interference of demons, such visions were only a subset of the totality that might occur, some of which always had the potential to confirm positive meditative attainment. Daoxin's instructions for "guarding the one without moving" reject that possibility, and it is this rejection that makes them novel, not their meditation techniques per se, which were drawn from the common lore of Chinese Buddhism. The approach to meditation that Daoxin proposes was new, and was indeed intended to be seen as new, in virtue of its semiotically disenchanted landscape, one where visions and other concrete meditative experiences can only ever be "strange objects," the signs of mental distraction or false thinking, and nothing more.

Hongren, Shandao, and the *Amitāyus Contemplation Scripture*

The second principal example of instructions for seated meditation from surviving East Mountain sources is contained in two sections of the *Treatise*

---

46. *Qi xin lun shu*, T.1844:44.224a4–225b6.

47. 問。如見菩薩像等境界，或因宿世善根所發。云何簡別。(*Qi xin lun shu*, T.44:1844.224a4–5). Jingying Huiyuan's earlier commentary is largely concerned with structural issues and does not add any significant commentary here (*Da sheng qi xin lun yi shu*, T.1843:44.201a17–29). Commentary on this section of the text is not included in the surviving portions of either the commentary attributed to Tanyan 曇延 (516–588), the *Da sheng qi xin lun shu* (Z.755), or the recently discovered and seemingly very early Dunhuang manuscript commentary from the Haneda 羽田 collection (no. 333v, *Tonkō hikyū*, 5:11–19; Kongō daigaku Bukkyō bunka kenkyūjo 2017).

48. *Shi moheyan lun*, T.1668:32.655b1–663c10. Some scholars have suggested that this text was written in Korea (Ishii 1988), though this is not universally accepted (Endō 1996).

49. *Shi moheyan lun*, T.1668:32.662a10–12.

on the *Essentials of Cultivating the Mind* (*Xiu xin yao lun* 修心要論), attributed to the fifth patriarch Hongren.[50] The first of the two sections is especially noteworthy because here Hongren names not only the method he is outlining but its source: the "sun contemplation" (日觀), from the *Amitāyus Contemplation Scripture*. The fact, first of all, that a Chan text would propound a method drawn from a key Pure Land scripture reminds us that no clear line divided these traditions in Hongren's day (Sharf 2002). Even more relevant for our present purposes is that we can compare Hongren's directions for the sun contemplation to Shandao's 善導 (613–681), preserved in his commentary to this same passage of the *Amitāyus Contemplation Scripture*.[51] It is worth remembering that Shandao, despite his later status as a "Pure Land" patriarch, was considered a *chan* master in his time,[52] and his instructions therefore give us an alternate yet contemporaneous example against which we can discern what would have been seen as most distinctive in an early Chan School take on this particular meditation method.

Sun Contemplation. The sun contemplation is the first of the sixteen contemplations of the western paradise of Amitāyus in the *Amitāyus Contemplation Scripture:*

> Sitting upright, face west and contemplate the sun. Focus your thoughts and single-mindedly imagine it, without interruption. You will see the setting sun, its form like a floating drum. Seeing the sun, make it clearly apparent whether your eyes are open or closed.[53]

The subsequent sections of the scripture direct the practitioner to imagine other features of the Pure Land: the waters, landscape, and trees—all described in vivid detail—followed by the physical forms of the Buddha Amitāyus and his attendants. One who can perform these contemplations correctly (正), it is said, will be freed from vast quantities of sin and assured of rebirth in the Pure Land.

In their respective versions of this contemplation, Hongren and Shandao both make explicit that the sun contemplation is a method of seated meditation, begun once the practitioner has assumed the formal meditation

---

50. Like Daoxin's text, the *Xiu xin yao lun* cannot be dated with certainty to before the year 700 (McRae 1986, 120). It is known from over fifteen different manuscripts and late printed editions. Critical editions include McRae 1986, 1–16 [r] and Tanaka R. 2009, 41–60; for an English translation see McRae 1986, 121–132.

51. These parts of Shandao's commentary have been discussed by Pas 1995, 183–188, who translates many of the relevant passages. See also Shibata 2006, 436–446. The earlier commentaries on the *Amitāyus Contemplation Scripture* by Jingying Huiyuan (T.1749) and Jizang (T.1752), and the commentary attributed to Zhiyi (T.1750), do not give any concrete instructions for meditation in the manner of Shandao's commentary.

52. *Shi jing tu qun yi lun*, T.1960:47.50c14.

53. 正坐西向，諦觀於日。令心堅住，專想不移。見日欲沒，狀如懸鼓。既見日已，閉目開目，皆令明了。(*Guan Wuliangshou fo jing*, T.365:12.341c30–342a2)

Hongren (Tanaka R. 2009, 53–54)	Shandao (T.1753:37.261c14–262b14)

[1] Beginners learning to practice seated meditation should rely on the *Amitāyus Contemplation Scripture*. Sit upright, straighten your posture, close your eyes and mouth. Looking straight ahead in front of your chest, imagine a single sun at a suitable distance and keep it there (作一日想守之), moment after moment without cease. Keep your breath well balanced so that it does not sound alternately heavy and then light, which will cause illness.

[1] To inform living beings of the extent of their karmic obstructions, [the Buddha] taught them to concentrate the mind by contemplating the sun. When you first wish to concentrate the mind, you should sit in the upright, cross-legged posture.... Close your mouth and do not gnash your teeth. Push your tongue against your palate so that the breath flows freely through your nose and throat. Contemplate the material elements of your body as empty, devoid of anything.... When your distracted thoughts are eliminated and your mind has become concentrated, gradually turn it toward the sun and carefully contemplate it. Those of sharp faculties will see its bright form appear before them right away.

[2] When doing seated meditation at night, you might see all kinds of good or evil visions (善惡境界). Or you might enter the blue, yellow, red, or white meditative trances (三昧) [in which you see these colors]. Or you might see a bright light radiating from your body and then entering back into it. Or you might see a buddha, endowed with all the bodily marks, performing all kinds of miracles. If you become aware of any of these things, restrain your mind and do not let it become attached. All these things are empty; they only appear to you because of false thinking. A scripture says: The lands of the ten directions are all empty. It also says: The triple world is illusory, made only by the mind.

[2] When the vision (境) appears, it will be as big as a coin or a mirror. On its bright surface signs will appear indicating the extent of your karmic obstructions (業障輕重之相): either (i) a black obstruction, like a black cloud shading the sun, (ii) a yellow obstruction..., or (iii) a white obstruction.... If you see these things, you must prepare a ritual space....

[*Shandao briefly describes the required repentance and explains that its success will gradually purify the obstructions obscuring the vision of the sun.*]

Hongren (Tanaka R. 2009, 53–54)	Shandao (T.1753:37.261c14–262b14)
[3] If you do not obtain trance (定) and do not see any visions (境界), do not worry. While walking, standing, sitting, or lying down, just continue to perfectly keep hold of the true mind. False thoughts will arise no more and any notion of self will also disappear (妄念不生我所心滅).	[3] When you first see the sun while immersed in trance, you will obtain the bliss of *samādhi*, and your body and mind inside and out will feel unimaginably agreeable. When you see the sun, you must thoroughly restrain your mind and make it firm; do not give rise to craving or grasping. If you give rise to craving, the waters of your mind will stir and the pure vision will disappear (淨境即失) or become unstable, moving, becoming dark, or turning black, blue, yellow, red, or white. If you see any of these things…calm your mind with correct mindfulness and resume from the beginning. When all movement is eliminated, the calm mind will again appear.…
	[4] In all the remaining contemplations [of the sutra], this is what is meant by "incorrect" (邪) and "correct" (正), by "attaining" and "losing." If when contemplating the sun you see the sun (觀日見日), mind and vision correspond (心境相應), so this is "correct" contemplation. If when contemplating the sun you do not see the sun, but see other visions, then mind and vision do not correspond, so this is "incorrect."

posture, closed the eyes and mouth, and settled the mind.[54] Following the original scripture, Hongren and Shandao then direct the meditator to "imagine" (*xiang*) or "contemplate" (*guan*) an image of the sun.

What happens next is discussed in radically different ways. Shandao's understanding, in its broad pattern, is consistent with what we found in the

---

54. Shandao's instructions, which I have abridged in the accompanying table, are more detailed than Hongren's and include a long preliminary exercise for calming the mind by imagining the material elements of the body scattering into the four directions, a method vaguely reminiscent of certain procedures in texts such as the *Chan Essentials*.

fifth-century *chan* scriptures, the writings of Zhiyi, and other Buddhist sources from that era: intensive mental focus leads to a state of visionary sensitivity in which "signs" may appear attesting to the presence of "karmic obstructions." According to Shandao (in paragraph 2), the signs will appear as cloud-like obscurations (black, yellow, or white) on the face of the sun. Seeing them means the meditator must perform a ritual of repentance, which Shandao goes on to describe in some detail (omitted in the table) before resuming seated meditation. The repentance will have succeeded if the pure sun now appears. But it is also possible that the obscurations have merely been weakened—the black cloud turning yellow, for example—and this means further repentance is needed. This process of purification must continue until the meditator can see the unobstructed sun.[55] In the final passages (paragraphs 3 and 4), Shandao recognizes some of the ways the vision of the sun can be affected when the mind becomes distracted or beset by craving, but he does not go into the full range of unusual symbolic visions that populate *chan* scriptures such as the *Chan Essentials*. Yet his fundamental agreement with those texts is clear in his assumption that the meditator's visionary experience has a *communicative* function—indeed, the purpose of the sun contemplation, as he explains it, is to provide information about the extent of one's karmic obstructions so that one can respond accordingly.

Hongren's instructions deviate from this understanding just as Daoxin's did in comparison with Zhiyi's. First, with respect to framing: the sun contemplation, for Hongren, leads to an advanced attainment, signaled in the final lines by the words "false thoughts will arise no more and any notion of self will disappear"—an expression he uses elsewhere to describe a realized or awakened person.[56] Like Daoxin, Hongren takes an entry-level attainment—in this case, the first of the sixteen contemplations described in the *Amitāyus Contemplation Scripture*—and implies that it is equivalent to completing the journey. This seeming reclassification of a preliminary meditative attainment into a much greater accomplishment is accompanied by a substantially different claim about the semiotics of visionary meditative experience. In the second paragraph of his exposition, Hongren raises the possibility of such visions at the same moment in the process that Shandao does and furthermore describes them as "good or evil." Hongren, in other words, assumes that his audience will be expecting an explanation of the meaning of such visions akin perhaps to what Shandao provides for the multi-colored clouds that obscure the sun.[57] But Hongren quickly cuts off that line of

---

55. *Guan Wuliangshou fo jing shu*, T.1753:37.262a8–21.

56. It also appears to have been a catch phrase, with this meaning, in certain strands of early Chan literature; see, for example, *Da sheng kai xin xian xing dun wu zhen zong lun* 大乘開心顯性頓悟真宗論, a mid-eighth-century Chan treatise (Tanaka R. 2009, 167). The expression "false thoughts will arise no more" probably derives from Guṇabhadra's translation of the *Laṅkāvatāra Sutra*, an important text for most early Chan School lineages, where it occurs over twenty times (*Lengqieaboduoluo bao jing*, T.670:16.492b19; 494b24; 495b2, etc.).

57. Hongren also speaks of miracle-performing buddhas as among the possible visions,

thought by saying that all such visions are only illusions of the mind, products of false thinking. They occur, he implies, primarily at night and are the same as dreams and hallucinations. In the next paragraph, he makes the further point that there is no need to obtain "trance" (*ding*) or gain access to "confirmatory visions" (*jingjie*) at all.

In the end, what makes Hongren's account of the sun contemplation different from Shandao's is not the claim that meditative visions are ultimately produced by one's own mind or that meditators must avoid attachment to them. Shandao would agree with this, and doctrinally there is little daylight between them.[58] Nor is it that Shandao is "pro" while Hongren is "anti" on the question of visions. The point of divergence lies rather in two starkly different claims about the communicative value of meditative experiences. For Shandao, as had long been the understanding in China, meditative visions are always potentially signs. Under the right circumstances, they can *matter* in a way that Hongren claims they never can. Indeed, the whole point of the sun contemplation, as Shandao understands it, is to generate such signs. What Hongren rejects—and what he assumes his readers will assume—is the entire notion that the content of concrete meditative experiences can or should be interpreted as the sign of either meditative attainment or the outcome of rituals of repentance.[59]

Visions of Chan and Visions in Chan

As we have seen, the writings attributed to Daoxin and Hongren, among the earliest that modern scholars have associated with the nascent Chan School, pointedly rejected the previously uncontroversial understanding that concrete, visionary experiences are to be taken as potential signs of significant meditative attainment. Traces of similar ideas can be found in many other samples of early Chan literature.[60]

Treatise of the Chan Master Bodhidharma of India
One example is the *Treatise of the Chan Master Bodhidharma of India*, an early Chan School text organized as an extended discourse on "methods of *chan*"

---

and this might also be seen as alluding to the more elaborate visions that populate the later sections of the *Amitāyus Contemplation Scripture*.

58. Again, the Buddhist doctrines Hongren relies on here were uncontroversial. What is novel is that he deploys them not simply as ontological claims about the true nature of the world of appearances, but as guidelines for the interpretation of meditative experience.

59. Hongren was not necessarily rejecting the need to carry out rituals of repentance, even if he was denying that meditative experiences could be signs pertinent to them. For other considerations of the way that early Chan authors sometimes framed their teachings as a rejection of the need for repentance, see Adamek 2015.

60. In addition to the examples I discus below, see also the so-called *Chou chan shi yi* 稠禪 師意 (Jan 1983, 94), the untitled Tibetan Chan text translated by Van Schaik (2015, 67–69), and some further, fragmentary examples from the Tibetan Chan documents (Gómez 1983, 121).

(禪門之法)。[61] In addition to its many gnomic assertions about the nature of true "chan," we find a few, seemingly more specific efforts to reject what are presented as wrongheaded approaches to meditation practice. Among these are "Lesser Vehicle" meditation, defined as any method of meditation in which "there is something one seeks, something one sees, and something one attains."[62] This formula of *seeking, seeing,* and *attaining* would seem to characterize the normal Chinese Buddhist understanding of meditation as proceeding from a given practice to a concrete vision that is either the sign of its attainment or an indication of some other condition. In the next passage, the *Treatise of the Chan Master Bodhidharma of India* names meditation on the breath, one of the standard five gates of *chan*, as an example of one such "lesser" practice that must be rejected in favor of the "five gates of contemplation" (五門觀法) known only to followers of the Mahāyāna.[63]

In a later section of the text, the contrast between methods of meditation that lead to "seeing" something concrete and those that do not is taken up again. "Correct contemplation," it says, means "contemplating oneself" (自觀), while "incorrect contemplation" (邪觀) means "contemplating what is other" (他觀) by "focusing on a cognitive object (*jingjie*) outside yourself." The danger of incorrect contemplation is that "one might then come to see things like buddhas, bodhisattvas, or green, yellow, red or white lights." All such things, because they are "falsely seen through the imagining mind," are called incorrect contemplation.[64]

At the very end of his discussion of the sun contemplation, Shandao comments on the recurring phrase "to perform this contemplation is *correct contemplation;* any other (他) contemplation is *incorrect contemplation*" from the *Amitāyus Contemplation Scripture*, a refrain that the *Treatise of the Chan Master Bodhidharma of India* also seems to be addressing.[65] For Shandao,

---

61. *Tianzhu guo Putidamo chan shi lun* 天竺國菩提達摩禪師論. I use Fang Guangchang's critical edition based on BD no. 15054 (北新 no. 1254 in the old classification system) and Pelliot no. 2039 (Fang 1995a, 34–44). For the Pelliot manuscript alone, see Tanaka R. 1983, 199–200.

62. 即有所求，即有所見，即有所得。(Fang 1995a, 43). This section occurs only on the Beijing manuscript.

63. These are not explained, but presumably it means those privy to the *Treatise of the Chan Master Bodhidharma of India* itself. A somewhat different redefinition of the "five gates" of meditation appears in the *Da sheng pusa ru dao san zhong guan* 大乘菩薩入道三種觀, an apocryphal treatise of probably Tang date, known from a single manuscript from Nanatsudera (Makita and Ochiai 1994–2000, 5:316).

64. 謂身心之外，別取境界，惑[>或]見諸佛、菩薩、青黃赤白光明等事，並是相[>想]心妄見…故名邪觀. I here follow the Pelliot manuscript (Tanaka R. 1983, 200).

65. 作此觀者名為正觀，若他觀者名為邪觀。(*Guan Wuliangshou fo jing*, T.365:12.342a21–22 and passim). The *Treatise of the Chan Master Bodhidharma of India* introduces its discussion of the difference between contemplating "self" (自) and contemplating "other" (他) by citing a nearly identical phrase from the *Vimalakīrti Sutra* (*Weimojie suo shuo jing*, T.475:14.555a23–24), changing the wording slightly but significantly by making "contemplating *like this*" (以斯觀者) into "if one contemplates *oneself*" (若自觀者). This makes "other" (他) construe as the opposite of "self," rather than as "different than this."

"correct" contemplation means coming to see the pure sun, the correct object, whereas "incorrect" contemplation occurs when one sees some other object instead. Shandao's reasoning is in keeping with the semiotic ideology characteristic of pre-Chan approaches to meditation, in which meditative visions are judged as good or bad based on their *content,* which must be scrutinized so that one can know what if anything the vision is a sign of. In contrast, the *Treatise of the Chan Master Bodhidharma of India* opens a more profound gap between what is correct and what is incorrect. Encounters with *any* cognitive objects or *jingjie*—the word now stripped of semiotic potential and thus no longer translatable by "confirmatory vision"—are the result of "incorrect" contemplation. By definition, meditative visions possessed of content can *never* be signs of meditative attainment. Only "contemplating oneself" is correct, although what this means and how one might judge if it has occurred are not specified.

Treatise on Severing Cognition

While the *Treatise of the Chan Master Bodhidharma of India* seems to reject any meditation technique that focuses attention on an external object of cognition, other early Chan texts are more accommodating of such practices even while insisting that any unusual visions they produce are never to be taken as signs of attainment. In the *Treatise on Severing Cognition* (*Jue guan lun* 絕觀論)—a text usually associated with the late eighth-century Ox Head lineage of early Chan—the classical Buddhist visualization exercises on pure colors (the *kasiṇa* exercises of the Pāli tradition) are explained as methods taught by the Buddha for "stilling the mind" (住心). However, as this text then insists, one must also know that the visions thereby produced are all "unreal" (不實), and that "people these days who [see themselves] emitting a bright light and take it to mean that they have become a saint are greatly mistaken."[66]

Once more, the Chan criticism is aimed with precision. The ontological claim that meditative visions are mind produced is, again, uncontroversial. The authors of the fifth-century *chan* scriptures would have readily agreed on this point and might even have insisted that this is what ensures they are true signs of the meditator's attainment, something normatively defined, after all, as a special state of mind or consciousness. Where the *Treatise on Severing Cognition* stakes out novel ground is in rejecting the semiotic potential of visionary experience—in claiming not only that a meditative vision is ontologically unreal, but that its occurrence is not a real sign. This argument was more than a merely abstract or doctrinal one. If a vision of radiant light streaming from one's forehead is not a sign of sanctity, then the "people these days" who think that it is must also include those who edited the biography

---

66. 如今人將放光明作聖，大誤也。(Yanagida 1999a, 131–132). This passage is found only in the versions from Pelliot nos. 2074 and 2885. The meditations on pure colors are also mentioned by Hongren; see above table, paragraph 2.

of the monk Puheng discussed in Chapter 2, where precisely this vision was recognized as a sign of his attainment and hence his status as a master of meditation.

Essential Formulas for Sudden Awakening

A final example comes from the *Essential Formulas for Sudden Awakening*, whose discussion of the interpretation of concrete meditative experiences is the most extensive to be found in early Chan literature.[67] Drawing on a famous passage in Kumārajīva's translation of the *Diamond Sutra*, to which it is in some sense an extended commentary, the *Essential Formulas for Sudden Awakening* proposes a relatively simple meditation technique: the practitioner must continually "gaze" (看) at the "place of nothingness" (無所處). The instructions begin in the Madhyamaka register typical of many early Chan treatises, with much handwringing about how one can gaze at "nothing" if it is not a thing. But these more abstract concerns eventually give way to a relatively concrete method of practice when the "place of nothingness" turns out to be a specific location in the body upon which one can focus the mind:

> The place of nothingness lies three inches above your heart. It is empty; there is nothing there. It is called the receptacle (*zang*) and is also called the mind's eye. It is where your spirit-consciousness resides. The sutras call this the "receptacle of the Buddha" (*rulai zang*). Carefully contemplate it and gaze at it for a long time.[68]

Playing on the word *zang* (藏), this passage invokes not only the idea of the "receptacle of the Buddha" (*tathāgata-garbha*), that is to say, the Buddha nature, but also the notion of a physical organ wherein one's spirit-consciousness "resides." Meditating on one's Buddha nature is likened here to the common medieval Daoist practice of meditating on, and then coming to see in a vision, the body gods who dwell in precisely defined anatomical locations.[69]

But in contrast to both Daoist meditation and pre-Chan *chan*, any concrete vision one might obtain by "gazing at the place of nothingness" is to be ignored:

---

67. The full title of this text, *Dun wu zhen zong jin gang bore xiu xing da bi an fa men yao jue* 頓悟真宗金剛般若脩行達彼岸法門要决, seems to mean "Essential Formulas and Teachings for Reaching the Other Shore by Practice of the Diamond Prajñā [Scripture] of the True Lineage of Sudden Awakening." It is known from several fragmentary Chinese manuscripts and one complete Tibetan translation of the Chinese original. One of the Chinese manuscripts has a preface dating itself to 712. For a bibliography of studies of this text, see Tanaka and Cheng 2014, 117–122. Below I rely on the manuscripts of Pelliot nos. 2799 and 3922, and Stein no. 5333, together with the editions of Ueyama 1976 and Huang 2008, 391–400.

68. 諦聽諦聽，無所處在汝心上三寸，虛空無物，名之為藏，亦稱為心眼。如[>汝, Pelliot no. 3922] 神識在中居。經名如來藏者也。汝當諦觀看熟，即是本性清淨。(Huang 2008, 394; Ueyama 1976, 98)

69. Schipper 1995; Lagerwey 2004, 149–164; Robinet 1993, 64–82; Andersen 1979; Lévi 1986.

Question: When gazing...what does one see? *Answer:* Anything possessed of distinguishing signs is empty and false.[70] Just quietly gaze at the place of nothingness. This is correct.

Question: When sitting, sometimes one sees the bodies of bodhisattvas or venerable monks. Sometimes one hears a disembodied voice preaching the Dharma. Sometimes one hears a voice that confers a prophecy of future Buddhahood upon the practitioner.... Are these true [signs]?

Answer: This is just the great demon king who wishes to come grab hold of you. Do not be seduced by these things. They are merely the products of your false mind.... If you take the Buddha to have eyes, distinguishing features, or the thirty-two marks, and with such an understanding see the Buddha, then you are truly ensnared by demons. Just gaze, carefully, for a long time. You might see light within the room, or you might see various things within the light.... You might even see a great light radiating above your body, or colored lights appearing before your eyes. None of this is real. When gazing inward, it may at times be like a cloud, or smoke, or a star, or tangled thread, or a flame, or a human eye, or a human head, or a tree, or water, or the five colors. There are many such appearances. But they are all endowed with distinguishing signs, and thus they are not real.

If you see these things, do not be alarmed or fearful. Diligently practice in the clear light of day. At night, do seated meditation together with others. Do not sit alone. Do not fall asleep while sitting. If you are tired, go to bed.[71]

This, then, is what we may now take to be a typical Chan pronouncement—that meditation, carried out by intensively concentrating the mind on an object, may well lead to unusual sensory experiences, but such things are not, despite what some wrongly believe, ever signs of meditative attainment.[72]

The *Essential Formulas for Sudden Awakening* then takes this line of reasoning to an even more extreme conclusion. Not only are concrete visions never signs of attainment, they are not signs at all. They are, as the final section of this passage explains, nothing more than nighttime hallucinations or

---

70. This is a citation of the *Diamond Sutra* (*Jin gang bore boluomi jing*, T.235:8.749a22–24).

71. 問曰，看時…見何物。答曰，凡所有相皆是虛妄，但靜看無所處即是。問曰，坐時或見菩薩師僧身，或空中聞說法聲，或聞語聲與弟子授記…此是真不。答曰，此是大魔王欲來攝汝，莫愛著，亦是汝妄心所作…汝若將如來有眼有相貌有卅二相，作此解見如來時，真是著魔人也。汝但熟看細看。或見屋中明，或見明中種種物…或是[>見]汝身上放大光明，或眼前種種光色，並不是實。若內看時，或如雲，或如烟，或如星，或如亂絲，或如火，或似人眼，或似人頭，或如樹，或如水，或五色，有種種變現，皆是有相，不實。見此莫驚，莫怕。了了白日用功，夜中共人同坐，莫獨自坐，莫和睡坐，有睡即臥。(Ueyama 1976, 98–99; Huang 2008, 394–395)

72. The *Essential Formulas for Sudden Awakening* does eventually present a positive account of attainment, described as "constantly seeing a pure *jingjie*, undifferentiated inside and out, all of one kind" (常見清淨境界，無邊內外，皆一種; Ueyama 1976, 99). This is a rare example of an early Chan text using the word *jingjie* in a positive sense, but this *jingjie*, notably, is a formless, undifferentiated purity, quite different from the visions described earlier in the text that consist of nameable objects and scenes and which, to this extent, resemble the confirmatory visions identified in earlier Chinese meditation manuals.

dreams, a claim reminiscent of Hongren's hint that visions occur primarily to those who meditate at night. The frank suggestion that one should go to bed if sleepy is a particularly interesting contrast to the more typical ideal of the virtuoso practitioner who meditates long into the night. Semiotically, the problematic here is the precise opposite of that in the story of the nun Tanhui, who meditates at night while others are asleep and where the issue is not the risk of believing a dream to be a true sign, but the possibility that the untutored might mistake a true sign for a mere dream.[73]

Rewriting the Scriptures at the Wofoyuan

Early Chan School proponents saw (and wanted others to see) their new approach to meditation not as a new way to practice meditation, but as a new semiotic ideology of meditative experience. They rejected as meaningless an entire class of such experiences, the concrete visions that had long been reported by meditators and recognized as at least sometimes being the signs of meditative attainment. This reorientation of meditation arguably worked in concert with the notion of the Bodhidharma lineage, which provided a way to legitimize the authority of a new line of *chan* masters without requiring them to claim or be attributed with meditative visions or indeed concrete meditative experiences of any kind.

Yet it was not only partisans of the Bodhidharma lineage who rejected the confirmatory power of concrete meditative experiences during this era. By the turn of the eighth century, others were also experimenting with similar ideas, and to this extent we should see Chan as but one stream of a broader trend in Chinese Buddhism that challenged previously long-standing norms concerning mastery of "meditation" and who might claim it—norms whose canonical sources were still identified in most cases as the *chan* scriptures of the fifth century. In this section and the next, we will consider evidence for this trend in the form of inscriptions carved at the Wofoyuan 臥佛院 (Grove of the Reclining Buddha) cave complex in Anyue county, Sichuan, along with some tentative theories about why these new ideas might have risen to prominence in this era.[74]

The *Chan Essentials* at the Wofoyuan
In the spring of 735, under the sponsorship of a single patron, extracts from two Buddhist scriptures were carved onto the walls of cave 59 of the Wofoyuan: a selection of excerpts from the *Chan Essentials* and a single passage from the *Scripture on the Ten Wheels,* also bearing on the topic of meditation (fig. 7).[75] This carving, besides demonstrating that the *Chan Essentials* retained

---

73. See "The Semiotics of Meditative Experience" in Chap. 2.

74. Portions of this section and the next have been adapted from Greene 2018.

75. On the Wofoyuan complex and the scripture carving project of the early 700s, which filled many caves and featured dozens of different texts, see Sonya Lee 2009; and Ledderose and Hua 2014, 17–37. This carving is dated by a colophon at the end of the *Chan Essentials* section (Greene 2018, 76).

Figure 6. Wofoyuan 臥佛院, Anyue county, Sichuan. Photo by April Hughes.

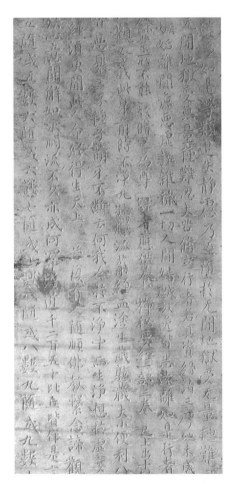

Figure 7. Wofoyuan cave 59. Densely packed inscriptions of sutras cover all the walls of this cave. Shown here are the opening passages of the carving of the *Chan Essentials*. Heidelberg Academy of Sciences.

its status as an authoritative exposition of Buddhist meditation well after the fifth and sixth centuries, is valuable as a historical source precisely because it is an edited and otherwise unattested version of the text in which disparate passages from the original have been woven together into a coherent whole. It is, in effect, a curated version of the *Chan Essentials*, giving us a glimpse of how, at a particular historical moment, the text was understood and what parts were considered important. Here we can see firsthand, as it were, how the understanding of meditation typical of an earlier era of Chinese Buddhism was taken up and transmitted, at least in this one instance, in the eighth century.

At first glance, the excerpts from the *Chan Essentials* seem to be representative passages cited from each of the text's four sutras, including snippets from the narrative introductions, meditation instructions, and some stern warnings about the dangers of false claims to attainment from the text's conclusion. But on further inspection it becomes clear that what the carving has *excluded* is significant: the excerpts, it turns out, include almost no passages pertaining to the elaborate visions that the original text repeatedly presents as the fruits of meditation and the signs of its success. This pattern seems neither to be random nor the result of confining the extracts to portions of the original text that do not give prominent mention to visions. Rather, talk of meditative visions was carefully edited away,[76] and the result is a new document, one that tells a story about meditation and its fruits starkly different than the original.

These interventions commence in the first passage. Here the text of the carving appears straightforward: the Buddha, saying he will explain the method for "bodily mindfulness" (身念處), gives the following instructions for contemplating the impurity of the body:

> Carefully contemplate: "This body of mine has ever been impure. Pus flows from its nine openings. Bound by tendons and smeared with blood, [within it] lie the receptacles of undigested and digested food, urine, feces, and eighty families of worms, each accompanied by eighty million smaller worms. What purity could there be in such a body? ... How could I imagine what is so impure as pure? This false, empty thing as made of adamant?"[77]

As it appears in the carving, this passage is unremarkable, similar to countless other introductory instructions for the contemplation of bodily impurity found throughout the Chinese Buddhist canon. In the original text of the *Chan Essentials*, however, these lines are not mere directives for basic medita-

---

76. As I have shown elsewhere, the carving of the *Chan Essentials* excerpts was based on a pre-existing text, created in the Sichuan region, in which the excerpts had already been selected and arranged (Greene 2018, 81–83). Whether this text was created especially for the carving, or if it had existed locally for some time, remains unclear.

77. Bemmann and Hua 2018, 101–102; *Chan Essentials* 1.18.10–11 (*CMY*, T.613:15.253b19–22; c6–7).

tion practice but an account of what the meditator must do in the eighteenth numbered contemplation, a stage he has reached only after having passed through many earlier levels of attainment, each accompanied by progressively more elaborate visions. And even in the eighteenth contemplation, the excerpted passage is not the meditator's first task, but what he must do after having already traversed a number of preceding steps, including a contemplation of his body with subsequent visions of it as pure white jade, then gold, then adamant (*Chan Essentials* 1.18.1), a further attempt by a herd of black elephants to uproot the tree of the defilements (1.18.2), a vision of music-playing goddesses (1.18.3), in whose wake he must contemplate non-self to resist temptation (1.18.4), a further vision of adamantine mountains with a host of demons trying to destroy them (1.18.6), and a vision of his own body as a mountain of gold (1.18.9). The instructions for meditation on bodily impurity that make their way into the cave 59 carving begin only at this point. But in addition to skipping over these earlier steps, even in the sections it does include the carving omits any of the results of the practices—namely, a further set of dazzling visions that include an encounter with the seven buddhas of the past and the witnessing of the near destruction of the tree of the defilements (1.18.11–18). The carving, in short, has severed the instructions for contemplating bodily impurity from the complex narrative of visionary production and confirmation within which they originally occurred, a narrative that by any measure is the major focus of the *Chan Essentials* as a whole.

After the opening instructions, the cave 59 carving proceeds directly to the following passage, originally from a much later part of the *Chan Essentials:*

> When the Buddha preaches the Dharma, he preaches the four bases of mindfulness, the four right efforts, the four bases of magic power, the five faculties, the five powers, the seven factors of awakening, and the eightfold holy path. He analyzes each of these thirty-seven things and explains them to the practitioner. When he has explained them, he further teaches the contemplations of suffering, emptiness, impermanence, and non-self. Having been taught these things, because he has seen the Buddha and heard the marvelous Dharma, the practitioner's mind will be liberated, and he will soon become an arhat as surely as water follows its course.[78]

In the carving, this formulaic list of higher attainments along the path to liberation reads as a generic account of the Buddha's teaching and the things that someone practicing "bodily mindfulness" will realize. This, however, is a drastic reframing of the passage's original import. In the *Chan Essentials,* the words "when the Buddha preaches the Dharma" introduce the teaching spoken by the visionary buddha who has appeared to the meditator after

---

78. Bemmann and Hua 2018, 102–103; *Chan Essentials* 2.19.2.3 (*CMY*, T.613:15.256b15–20).

earlier meditations and the performance of a ritual of repentance (*Chan Essentials* 2.19.1.1–12), the same visionary buddha who, before consenting to preach, first anoints the practitioner's head with water (2.19.2.2). The carving also omits the subsequent passages, which explain that should the practitioner merely see this buddha without also hearing him preach, he must further repent his sins until he succeeds in gaining another elaborate vision (2.19.2.5).

The next sections of the carving even more blatantly exclude the visionary framework of the *Chan Essentials*. Here, in a discussion of meditation on the breath, we can almost watch as the compiler of the text included in the carving (underlined) edits away all reference to concrete visions:

The Buddha said to Ānanda: One with much lust, even after obtaining this *samādhi* of the contemplation of the Buddha [in which the visions described previously appear], will gain no benefit. He still will not attain any of the fruits of the holy path. So he must be taught to contemplate his own body in the manner given previously and again create a skeleton, making it brilliantly white like a snow-covered mountain. He should then fix his thoughts and concentrate his mind on his navel, or within his pelvis, and follow the breath as it goes in and out....[79]

His mind then becomes calm and still. He sees his body's skin as a white silk bag. When he has seen this, he no longer sees his bones or knows where the organ of his heart lies. He must then be instructed to arouse his imagination further, turning his own body—his heart and mind, and trunk and limbs—into white jade. When he has seen this, he must again fix his thoughts on his coccyx within his pelvis and prevent his mind from wandering. He will then suddenly see above his body a light roughly the size of a coin, which gradually grows larger until it is the size of the eye of a giant *makara* fish. The light encircles him like a gathering cloud. It is like a white cloud within which there is a white light, like that of a crystal mirror. The brightness keeps increasing until his entire body is radiant. Then a further white light appears, perfectly round like a cartwheel, bright both within and without, brighter than the sun.

When he has seen these things, he must count the breath as before...either singly or doubly, long or short as he wishes. In this manner, dwelling in a secluded place he should fix his thoughts and not allow his mind to scatter. Then he must fix his thoughts and again contemplate his coccyx. As he contemplates it, his mind settles and ceases to stir.

He now again sees his body, and it becomes even brighter than before, [the light above it now] roughly the size of a large coin. Redoubling his efforts, he again sees his body, and the light is even brighter, grown to the size of the mouth of a water pitcher. It is brighter than every bright thing in the world. When he has seen this light, he redoubles his striving and does not allow his mind to slacken. Now he sees the light before his chest, roughly the size of a mirror. When

---

79. I elide a three-sentence-long description of counting and following the breath here, and also a shorter one below.

he has seen this light, he must strive vigorously as if extinguishing a fire on his head, exerting himself without cease. He sees the light become even more intense, brighter than a heavenly jewel. It is very pure, devoid of imperfection. Seven kinds of light, which shine like the seven precious substances, emerge from his chest and enter the light. When these signs have appeared, the practitioner becomes extremely happy and spontaneously joyful. His mind feels incomparably peaceful.[80]

In the carving, these instructions read as if they are intended for anyone "with much lust," as it says in the first line. In the full text of the *Chan Essentials,* however, the target is far more specific: meditators who remain plagued by lust despite having already obtained the "*samādhi* of the contemplation of the Buddha" and its attendant visions, described earlier (*Chan Essentials* 2.19.1–2). And in the ensuing passage, when setting the carving against the full text, we see clearly that the carving has studiously avoided reference to any of the many visions that accompany and confirm each stage of progress.

In the passages immediately following the citation above, the *Chan Essentials* describes further visions that the meditator will encounter: seven lights merging into a single bright light (2.20.8), a spear-like light emerging from the crown of his head (2.20.9), and a cloud of light within which Śākyamuni Buddha appears in all his splendor (2.20.10). Subsequent meditations on the body lead to still further visions (2.20.11–14), culminating in a vision of the seven buddhas of the past. Omitting all of this, the carving resumes again. Passages that in the original describe the preaching of these visionary buddhas—a traditional typology of the impermanence of the body (2.20.15–17)—become in the carving merely a continuation of the earlier instructions on breath meditation. Once again the carving has transformed the *Chan Essentials,* with its unremitting emphasis on visions and visionary confirmation, into a relatively staid set of instructions for basic forms of Buddhist meditation.

Yet, while the carved excerpts avoid connecting meditative attainment to visionary experience, they do not suppress all mention of meditative visions. After giving the instructions for breath meditation, the carving continues:

> As when practicing breath counting, [the meditator] should focus his mind. He must diligently maintain the precepts, upholding them single-mindedly. He must take even minor transgressions very seriously, repenting them with remorse and taking care not to conceal even tiny violations. If he conceals any violation, he will see the many radiant lights as rotten wood. When he sees this, it will be known that he has violated the precepts.
>
> [In such a case,] he must again arouse a sense of shame and remorse, repent and rebuke himself, sweep the sanctuary, clean the floors, and perform many kinds of menial service.... After cultivating merit in this manner, with full

---

80. *Chan Essentials* 2.20.1–4 (*CMY,* T.613:15.256c22–257a23); Bemmann and Hua 2018, 104.

remorse, he should count his breaths as before. He will again see the light, radiant and exquisite, just as before.[81]

In the original, this passage is one of dozens that interpret visions as signs of past-life sin and hence of the need to repent. These passages, in turn, form a counterpoint to the many others that explain visions as signs of meditative progress or attainment. In the cave 59 carving, however, this passage is the only one that mentions these kinds of visionary experiences at all. Its meaning thereby changes rather dramatically. Read on their own, the excerpts most readily imply that meditative visions are generally problematic and associated primarily with those who violate the precepts.[82]

Chan in Sichuan and the Limits of Chan Originality

As a new version of the *Chan Essentials* that dramatically attenuates, if not entirely eliminates, the long-standing idea that meditative attainment is something linked to and confirmed by elaborate visionary experience, the cave 59 carving seems to move in parallel with the early Chan writings that use similar contrasts to distinguish the *chan* of the Bodhidharma lineage from its alternatives. Both envision a world in which meditative visions are at best signs of delusion or sin and where accomplished meditators are never deemed so by virtue of having experienced them.

Given their affinity in this respect, we might wonder if the cave 59 carving, or the text it reproduces, was the product of individuals or groups associated with the early Chan School in some way. A number of groups answering to such a description were indeed active in Sichuan, in areas near the Wofoyuan, throughout the eighth century. Sources speak of a prominent early Chan lineage descending from the fifth patriarch Hongren through Zhishen 智詵 (609–702) and Chuji 處寂 (665–732) that was based in Zizhou 資州 prefecture nearby.[83] Chuji was supposedly the ordination master of Mazu 馬祖 (709–788), whose disciples dominated late-Tang-dynasty Chan.[84] Chuji was also the teacher of Wuxiang 無相, who in 739 was appointed abbot of the famous Jingzhong 淨眾 temple in the Sichuan capital. Zongmi 宗密 (780–841), whose writings provide our most detailed account of the various factions of early Chan, mentions two additional Chan groups based in Sichuan: the so-called

---

81. Bemmann and Hua 2018, 105–106; *Chan Essentials* 2.20.6–7 (*CMY*, T.613:15.257b3–12).

82. To one reading the excerpts alone, the statement in the final line that those who repent will eventually see the light "just as before" might have aroused a vague sense that "good" visions were also possible, but even if so this sense is severely restricted compared to the original *Chan Essentials*. More likely, this passage would have just been difficult to understand, since the earlier passages describing the light seen by those who reach meditative attainment were not included in the carving.

83. *Lengqie shi zi ji*, T.2837:85.1289c11–12 (Yanagida 1971a, 273); *Song gao seng zhuan*, T.2061:50.836b8–29; *Li dai fa bao ji*, T.2075:51.184c3–16 (Yanagida 1971b, 140; Adamek 2007, 334–335).

84. On Mazu's early life, see Jia 2006, 12–13, and Poceski 2007, 22–23.

Baotang 保唐 School of Wuzhu 無住 (714–774), of which the *Records of the Dharma Jewel through the Generations* discussed earlier was a product, and a lineage descended from Xuanshi 宣什 (n.d.), another supposed heir of the fifth patriarch, that was inherited by several groups based in the central Sichuan prefectures immediately northeast of Anyue.[85]

Our knowledge of these groups, their teachings, and the sectarian identity (if any) their members would have claimed is clouded, often hopelessly so, by the polemical agendas of the sources that describe them. Still, it does seems quite likely that in the years leading up to 735, when the cave 59 carvings were made, prominent Buddhist teachers active in Sichuan were identifying with the Bodhidharma lineage and may well have been promoting understandings of meditation similar to what was proposed in the early Chan writings discussed earlier. Be this as it may, there is no reason for seeing the cave 59 carving as having any direct connection to such groups or to the Chan School more broadly. Apart from its apparent devaluing of meditative visions, nothing else in the cave 59 carving is evocative of early Chan literature, where classical Buddhist topics that figure prominently in the carvings, such as bodily impurity, rarely held much interest.

Moreover, the cave 59 version of the *Chan Essentials* is not the only source from this historical period that attests to a broader, nonsectarian suspicion of meditative visions as a matter of general principle. Consider, for example, the following passage from the *Essential Formulas of True Speech* (*Zhen yan yao jue* 真言要決), an anonymous, early eighth-century compendium of short Buddhist essays on a variety of topics:[86]

> When cultivating the Way by sitting in meditation (*zuochan*) alone and applying yourself diligently, you might see the bodies of buddhas, bodhisattvas, arhats, the heavenly venerable lord Lao, the immortals, or other famous worthies of the past. They might speak marvelous teachings to you, expound on the Way, or bestow on you the Dharma. If you take these happenings to be true, this is a big, big mistake.... To enter into the demon's net is much worse than not cultivating the Way at all, so with this in mind, *when doing seated meditation, one must not take any visions at all as confirmation.* Even if you emit a great light, or if the earth shakes,

---

85. *Yuan jue jing da shu shi yi chao,* Z.245:9.534c20–535a5. According to Zongmi these masters were the monks Wei 未 of Guozhou 果州 and Yunyu 蘊玉 of Langzhou 閬州, and the nun Yisheng 一乘 of Xiangru 相如 district, also in Guozhou.

86. The *Zhen yan yao jue* is attested in three Dunhuang manuscripts and one Japanese manuscript from Ishiyamadera 石山寺. Two of the original six scrolls survive. Full of quotations from Buddhist scriptures and the Confucian and Daoist classics, it happily declares that Confucius and Laozi were also sages (*Zhen yan yao jue,* T.2825.85.1231a13). As suggested by Zheng Acai (1989), its emphasis on the equality of the "three teachings" points to a date in the Kaiyuan 開元 reign period (713–741), when Emperor Xuanzong himself composed commentaries to the *Diamond Sutra,* the *Dao de jing,* and the *Classic of Filial Piety.* The only firm external evidence is a Japanese record of its having been copied in the year 751 (*Dai nihon komonjo,* 11:259), which makes a dating to the Kaiyuan era plausible.

> you must not believe it [to be a true sign]. Just focus your mind and keep it still, and then these demonic manifestations will of themselves go away.[87]

In its sweeping suggestion that no visions (*jingjie*) should ever be taken as confirmation (*zheng* 證) when practicing seated meditation, the *Essential Formulas of True Speech* makes an argument very similar to the one put forth more vehemently and polemically in early Chan writings. Yet this text, long available to scholars in the modern Taishō edition of the Chinese Buddhist canon, has never been considered to have any connection to early Chan. Indeed, nothing else in its style, doctrines, or rhetoric suggests that it did.

Thus rather than attribute influence from early Chan, we might do best to accept the version of the *Chan Essentials* carved in cave 59 of the Wofoyuan as evidence that the manner in which early Chan School partisans claimed superiority for their approach to meditation was not, in fact, theirs alone. To reject meditative visions as the form in which confirmatory signs of attainment most readily occur was indeed, in the broader history of Chinese Buddhism, something new. Early Chan School treatises were thus not wrong when they claimed that such an understanding of *chan* was distinctive relative to what most people in China had hitherto seen as authoritative. But it was not only among the self-proclaimed heirs of Bodhidharma that these ideas had currency. This new semiotic ideology of meditative experience was more broadly in the air in the early eighth century.

The Politics of Meditative Attainment

If the Chinese Buddhists who rejected the semiotic potential of concrete meditative visions in the eighth century were arguing against a perspective that had endured without substantial challenge for several centuries, one might wonder why that stance came to the fore at that particular historical moment and why it subsequently endured as one possible (but never the only) expression of Chinese Buddhist orthodoxy. A full exploration of these questions lies well beyond the scope of this study, as it would likely require nothing less than an evaluation of Buddhism's place in China's so-called Tang-Song transition, long hypothesized as an epochal social and cultural transformation comparable in scope to the changes that occurred in Europe at the dawn of the early modern era and in the wake of the Protestant Reformation.[88] But even if we cannot fully answer this question here, we can undertake a brief sketch of some of the social and political conditions that were possibly rele-

---

87. 修道獨處坐禪用心精進，或見佛身、菩薩身、真人羅漢身、天尊老君身、神仙身、及過往有名號賢德身。并談說妙言，稱道授法。即以為真者，此大大邪惑…若入魔網，全不及元不修道。以此而議，坐禪所有境界，並不得取以為證。縱使放光動地，彌不得信之。但當正心不動，魔事即自亡滅。(*Zhen yan yao jue*, T.2825:85.1229c15–1230a)

88. The destructive and socially transformative An Lushan rebellion in 755 is an event often pointed to as the start of the Tang-Song transition. The first generation or two of the early Chan School lies just before this.

vant and the changes taking place within them that might have allowed for or encouraged the rise of this new approach to Buddhist meditation at this particular historical juncture.

The *Scripture on the Ten Wheels* in Cave 59

An initial clue to these developments comes from a second inscription in cave 59 of the Wofoyuan, a passage from Xuanzang's mid-seventh-century translation of the *Scripture on the Ten Wheels* (*Da sheng da ji Dizang shi lun jing* 大乘大集地藏十輪經). Carved at the same time and by the same sponsor as the *Chan Essentials* excerpts, this passage enumerates twenty rules for those who wish to practice meditation, most of them unremarkable—for example, meditators must follow the precepts, not speak vulgar words, not be attached to sleep or music, and so forth. Yet the first rule given seems to be of a slightly different character. Held up as an example of problematic behavior is someone who "desires to cultivate meditation but, lacking the necessary material resources, causes disturbance by traveling about seeking for them."[89]

Whether "disturbance" here means a disturbance for the meditator or, conversely, for those from whom donations are sought is left ambiguous. Regardless, this first rule seems to have been central to the meaning of the passage as a whole. For after all the rules have been listed, the consequences of violating them are summarized, and here again the main difficulty is the problems faced by meditators who lack sufficient donations:

> One who cultivates meditation and performs even one [of these bad deeds] will never achieve *samādhi*, or if he has already achieved it, will immediately regress. If he is unable to achieve *samādhi*, then even though he has amassed heaps of other virtues, because of seeking out and then making use of the donations of the faithful he will give rise to an evil mind and evil mental states. In the presence of kings and ministers he will commit various crimes, and then be scolded, beaten, or mutilated. He will then become sick and suffer for a long time or die unexpectedly and then be reborn successively in the negative states of rebirth, including even in the Avīci hell.[90]

This passage brings together several different ideas. First is the standard notion that transgressions of the precepts impede meditative attainment. This idea is then linked to the similarly common trope that monks and nuns who receive offerings from the laity while in such a state of impurity are

---

89. 雖欲修定，而乏資緣，經求擾亂。(*Da sheng da ji Dizang shi lun jing*, T.411:13.735b16–17). Here and below I give the Chinese text as it appears in the carving (Bemmann and Hua 2018, 93–99). The received version, which I cite for reference, has only a few inconsequential differences.

90. 若修定者隨有一行，終不能成諸三摩地，設使先成，尋還退失。若不能成諸三摩地，雖集所餘諸善法聚，而有是事，追求受用信施因緣，發起惡心心所有法，於諸國王、大臣等所犯諸過罪，或被呵罵，或被捶打，或被斷截支節手足。由是因緣，或成重病長時受苦，或疾命終於三惡趣，隨生一所，乃至或生無間地獄。(*Da sheng da ji Dizang shi lun jing*, T.411:13.735c10–18)

thereby guilty of still further transgressions. At the same time, this passage seems also to claim that all these problems connect back to the first rule from the list of twenty—that meditators who actively seek out donations will, by virtue of this seeking, produce trouble both for themselves, leading to evil states of mind, and for the wider society. This trouble is then specified concretely by the curious claim that such monks will somehow find themselves violating secular laws and being subjected to criminal punishments, not to mention eventually falling into hell.

None of these ideas on their own would necessarily raise any eyebrows. But the conclusion that the *Scripture on the Ten Wheels* then draws from them is arguably somewhat unexpected. For now the Buddha issues a command, and given its position at the conclusion of the text included in the inscription, we may suspect that it is this command in particular that the organizers of the carving of this passage in cave 59 wanted to highlight:

> I permit [i.e., command][91] you to give to monks who meditate in hermitages the best quality lodgings, the best quality bedding, and the best quality food and drink, and to exempt them from all monastic duties. Why? If those who cultivate meditation are lacking in supplies and requisites, they will give rise to various evil states of mind and be unable to achieve *samādhi* and [will experience the other problems enumerated previously] up to falling into the Avīci hell.[92]

In contrast, those who practice meditation while being well supplied will attain *samādhi* and eventually liberation. A final verse then states that meditation is the highest of all monastic vocations and that its practitioners must be honored and supported by gods and kings alike.

Even on its own this is a remarkable passage. That it would have been plucked out of the *Scripture on the Ten Wheels* and carved in a public or semi-public space is even more remarkable. The idea that meditators require material support of the best quality is, for one thing, a striking inversion of the common image of meditators as paragons of asceticism. Notable too is the further claim that, for those who meditate, it is the absence of such donations that provokes evil mental states and transgressions both religious and secular. That meditation is a high-risk, high-reward activity—that it places its practitioners in a state of special sensitivity productive of both great benefit but also great danger—is an ancient idea in Buddhism. (As the *Dhammapada* memorably states it, "Like a blade of sharp grass, the ascetic's life wrongly grasped leads one straight to hell.") Far less common, however, is to

---

91. In the idiom of canonical *vinaya* literature (specifically the *vastu* sections), the Buddha institutes various monastic rules, in response to particular situations, by "permitting" the monks and nuns to do various things. It is this idiom that is here invoked, and the force of this permission is that of a command.

92. 吾聽汝等給阿練若修定芯芻最上房舍、最上臥具、最上飲食，一切僧事皆應放免。所以者何。諸修定者，若乏資緣，即便發起一切惡心心所有法，不能成就諸三摩地，乃至墮於無間地獄。(*Da sheng da ji Dizang shi lun jing*, T.411:13:735c22–26)

blame such problems not on the ascetics themselves but on those who have failed to support them.

In one way, the act of carving this passage in cave 59 can be taken as an assertion, a claim that one part of the Sangha—those who cultivate meditation—is particularly worthy of offerings, because of their pursuit of this practice.[93] Yet, at the same time, this assertion cannot be taken as a straightforward reflection of reality. That someone would publicly make a claim this bold—one that goes so far as to blame the criminality of Buddhist monastics on remiss donors—implies an anxiety over just this point. Someone here felt the need to argue that meditators *should* have a status they evidently did not automatically enjoy. Here too we might see something similar in the stance of early Chan, where the ideology of the Bodhidharma lineage, in attributing to an elite cohort of masters an authority analogous to that derived from the imperial lineage (Jorgensen 1987), arguably reflects an anxiety over precisely that authority, rather than, as the situation has sometimes been imagined, a newly confident Chinese Buddhism willing to throw off the shackles of India and declare some of its own to be fully realized buddhas.

The Authority of Meditation in the Kaiyuan Era

That a diversity of otherwise unaligned Chinese Buddhists whose sense of status and authority derived from their practice or putative mastery of meditation would in the early 700s have found this status under threat, and would have responded in sometimes similar ways, fits with broader patterns and even some specific details concerning the relations between the Buddhist church and the state during the reign of Emperor Xuanzong 玄宗 (r. 712–756).

This long and relatively stable period politically, until its disastrous ending in the An Lushan rebellion, came just on the heels of the era of the woman Emperor Wu (r. 684–705).[94] After engineering the abdication of his father Ruizong 睿宗 (r. 710–712), the new emperor Xuanzong quickly adopted an increasingly restrictive attitude toward the Buddhist establishment.[95] This was part of a calculated turn away from the previous administrations of Emperor Wu and her son and immediate successor, Zhongzong 中宗 (r. 705–710), under which the Buddhist church had enjoyed considerable power, status, and freedom. The extent to which official government policy, visible to us through surviving edicts and official histories, had real impact on a

---

93. To conjoin such a claim with the rejection of an inherent link between meditative attainment and visionary experience (as implied by the selective excerpts from the *Chan Essentials* in the same cave) suggests another vague parallel to early Chan writings, which similarly impute special authority to the mastery of *chan*, but only the putatively true kind in which no visions intrude.

94. Wu Zetian 武則天, often *Empress* Wu in English-language scholarship. She in fact reigned under the title Emperor (*huangdi* 皇帝). Although East Asian historians ancient and modern invariably call her Empress (后), she purposely abandoned this title at the height of her rule.

95. Weinstein 1987, 49–54; Tonami 1986, 444–470, and 1988; Faure 1997, 76–78.

society-wide level is, of course, always open to question. But Xuanzong, whose reign also brought about a newly expansive level of imperial control over the general Chinese populace (Palumbo 2017, 145), does seem to have success-fully engineered, in a relatively short period of time, a significant change in elite Buddhist clerics' own sense of status and position.

In 714, not long after coming to power, Xuanzong issued an edict de-manding that Buddhist monks and nuns perform acts of reverence—that is, bow—to their secular families. In 733, just two years prior to the cave 59 carvings, he ordered that the clergy must bow to the emperor as well (Tonami 1988, 44). The question of clerical ritual obeisance to secular or familial au-thorities was a long-standing and symbolically potent one in Buddhist church–state relations in China. Many previous emperors had attempted to assert their symbolic—and to the extent they were in fact obeyed, actual—authority over the Sangha by requiring such acts of reverence. None, however, had succeeded.[96] And while Xuanzong's policies too were eventually reversed, this occurred only after his death. Whether or not they were regularly fol-lowed in practice, he was the first Chinese emperor to have such rules offi-cially in place for any significant stretch of time. Moreover, in contrast to previous occasions when emperors had issued, or even merely contemplated issuing, similar edicts, there is no record of public clerical opposition to these new policies.[97] From this alone we may conclude that Xuanzong really did manage to instill a new measure of Buddhist clerical subservience to the throne, one that would have been experienced, at the court at least, as a comparatively sudden change in public status.

We need not assign this sudden loss of face a determinative causal power to see it as contributing to the appeal of the kinds of claims simultaneously being made, with increasing fervor, by early Chan partisans. As Wendi Adamek has cogently observed, outside a few favorites, the ordinary Chinese Buddhist cleric during Xuanzong's reign was at risk of "acquiring a worldly status that put him on par with an official but steadily losing the otherworldly

---

96. On the early bowing debates, see, among other studies, Michihata 1968, 163–219.

97. This point is made by Adamek 2000, 77. It has been suggested by some scholars that the 714 edict was quickly repealed in the wake of resistance or protest (Twitchett 1979, 362; Weinstein 1987, 34; Faure 1997, 76). I am unable to find any firm evidence of this. The *Tang hui yao* (47:836) passage cited by Faure mentions only the order, not its cancellation. Weinstein meanwhile cites the *Jiu tang shu* (8.172) and *Fo zu tong ji* (T.2035:49:373b9), but the former does not say that the order was rescinded, and the latter is of questionable reliability. For after the *Fo zu tong ji* first states that "in the fourth month [of 714] was rescinded [the edict] compelling veneration [by the clergy of their parents]" (四月罷致敬), the editor, Zhipan 志磐 (fl. 1260), adds a comment noting that since that time the clergy have not had to bow to their parents. This claim, however, blatantly contradicts the edict of 733 (Kaiyuan 21), where reverence of parents was reiterated, an edict the *Fo zu tong ji* conveniently fails to mention in its entry for that year (T.2035:49:375a1–2). It is possible that Zhipan has inadvertently or intentionally taken the *Jiu tang shu* entry for the fifth month of 714 (Kaiyuan 2; *Jiu tang shu*, 8.173) to the effect that a certain Wei Zhigu 魏知古 had been "removed from the post of Manager of Affairs" (罷知政事), and read it to mean that he "canceled the compelling of reverence" (罷致敬).

status that allowed him to look benevolently down upon the emperor" (Adamek 2000, 78). We can, Adamek suggests, see the increasingly radical "sudden" Chan rhetoric and the exclusivist, one-per-generation lineage claims of Shenhui 神會 (684–758) as having been appealing to contemporaries in part because they promised to recapture a real or imagined special status for some part of the clergy during a time when its charisma was under unprecedented threat.

Interest in, and the apparent appeal of, a reconfiguration of the semiotics of meditative experience and attainment—seen in early Chan literature but also more broadly in the early 700s—is also something for which the climate of Xuanzong's reign may have been a decisive factor. Though this was not their only concern, at least some of Xuanzong's edicts targeted the authority of meditation (*chan*) in particular. In 714, an edict prohibiting officials from privately employing Buddhist or Daoist clerics explains its motivations as follows:

> We have heard that many among the families of the hundred officials maintain relations with Buddhist and Daoist clerics as if they were members of their households, their wives and children interacting with them freely. Some [of these clerics] deceitfully claim the authority of meditative contemplation to make false statements about good and bad fortune. They tread upon the sinister path![98]

Similarly, in the eleventh month of the next year, new regulations for Buddhist and Daoist temples were justified on the grounds of a general lack of discipline among the clergy, but also by the existence of those who, "claiming to have mastered meditative contemplation, falsely prophesize about either disasters or auspicious happenings."[99]

Governmental fear of religious figures claiming prophetic powers is, of course, a perennial theme of Chinese history down to the present day. But worth our notice is the way these edicts in Xuanzong's time link such fears to the authority of meditative contemplation (*changuan* 禪觀) in particular. So too is an edict issued in 724, which, after requiring all Buddhist monastics to memorize two hundred pages of scriptures and pass a triennial exam thereon (or face defrocking), takes the trouble to note that these requirements could *not* be replaced by expertise in seated meditation (*zuochan* 坐禪).[100] These comments bespeak an active effort by Xuanzong's

---

98. 如聞，百官家多以僧尼、道士等為門徒往還，妻子等無所避忌，或詭託禪觀，禍福妄陳，事涉左道。(*Tang hui yao*, 860). See, similarly, *Quan tang wen*, 21.1a; *Song ben ce fu yuan gui*, 159.11b. The title of the edict in the *Quan tang wen*, "Order prohibiting interaction between officials and Buddhist and Daoist clergy" (禁百官與僧道往還制), was added by the much later editors of this collection and is misleading. The edict does not prohibit all contact between officials and the clergy, but merely requires officials who host religious rituals to ensure that all attending clergy are approved by the local government office (Gernet 1995, 284; cf. Weinstein 1987, 51).

99. 稱解禪觀妄說災祥。(*Song ben ce fu yuan gui*, 159.8b9–10)

100. *Tang hui yao*, 49:861 (Weinstein 1987, 111; Michihata 1967, 46–47).

administration to undermine claims to tangible status based on expertise in *chan*, claims that had, evidently, previously been possible at least in theory.

When the government is issuing edicts accusing those who "deceitfully claim the authority of meditative contemplation" of destabilizing the country with their supposedly prophetic powers, it is easy to see why claiming or being seen to claim a kind of meditative attainment founded on visionary experience may have become more precarious than it once had been. Rejecting the long-standing link between meditative attainment and visionary experience, which we have seen occurring in the early eighth century in early Chan writings and elsewhere, may have been at least in part a response to this climate—an argument, in short, that claims to the authority conferred by mastery of *chan* do not require, and are even antithetical to, any claim to a potentially subversive visionary power.

The insistence on lineage characteristic of the early Chan School was perhaps another such response. Although the notion of the Bodhidharma lineage does predate Xuanzong's reign, it still is noteworthy that the major early Chan sources in which the Bodhidharma lineage is glorified in the manner to which we have become accustomed all postdate Xuanzong's ascension in 712.[101] These lineage texts, moreover, sometimes make what looks like a concerted effort to distance the so-called *chan* practiced by the Chan School from anything that might be construed as similar to what Xuanzong's edicts condemn. The *Records of the Masters and Disciples of the Laṅkāvatāra*, written around the year 716, thus presents the following words as those by which the first Chan patriarch, after arriving in China from India, replied to the emperor's request that he teach:

> The master then began to teach the Chan teachings, saying: "In this land [of China]...practitioners have [hitherto] fallen either into the Lesser Vehicle, the Two Vehicles, the ninety-five heterodox ways, *or else into demonic chan, in which*

---

101. The earliest mention of the Chan lineage—that is, a lineage from Bodhidharma descending through the East Mountain masters to a living or recently deceased Chinese teacher—is usually held to be the epitaph of Faru (d. 689), discussed earlier. Scholars sometimes assert that this epitaph was written immediately after Faru's death (Cole 2009, 73). In fact, the epitaph is undated, as even Yanagida noted (1967, 40), though he too assumed it was written close in time to Faru's death. Another possibly very early source that discusses the Bodhidharma lineage, the funerary stele for Shenxiu 神秀 (d. 706) composed by Zhang Yue 張說 (d. 730), is also undated (*Quan tang wen*, 231.1b4–6). Epitaphs for early members of the Chan lineage were often written decades after their deaths. We should not, therefore, assume anything about the dates of these two, and this calls into question the precise history of the ideology of the Chan lineage. The other, more securely datable epitaphs in which modern scholars have discerned some connection to either the Chan lineage or distinctly Chan ideas all date to later than 712 (Ibuki 2008), as do, though only just, the earliest surviving Chan lineage texts (the *Lengqie shi zi ji* and the *Chuan fa bao ji*). Early Chan obviously did not spring into being fully formed in 712, and figures such as Shenxiu clearly were famous during the pre-Xuanzong era. Still, to a degree that modern historians seem not to have acknowledged, there are few if any sources for early Chan proper that are securely dated before Xuanzong's reign. "Early Chan," as we know it, may well be a largely post-712 phenomenon.

*one contemplates and then sees all things, knowing the good and bad fortune of others.
How sad!... [Doing such things, they but] falsely say that they sit in meditation
and practice contemplation.*[102]

There is nothing novel to the basic claim that apart from the "true" meditation taught by the Chan patriarchs there are many wrongheaded forms of it,
based on inferior Buddhist understanding, non-Buddhist teachings, or even
the influence of demons. But given the date of the *Records of the Masters and
Disciples of the Laṅkāvatāra,* its author, the monk Jingjue 淨覺 (683–ca. 750),
was surely aware of Xuanzong's 714 edict. (Jingjue was the brother of a
former empress and hence not likely to have been ignorant of recent events
at court.) In this light, the opening lines of Jingue's account of the Chan
lineage seem designed to assure his readers, sympathetic or hostile, that the
"chan" mastered by those in the Chan lineage is something very different
from what Xuanzong's edicts condemn. Xuanzong's policies were surely not
the only reason for the increasing popularity of the lineage-based authority
claims that characterized the early Chan School. Contemporary developments in Indian Buddhism that were becoming more widely known in China
at this time—such as ideas about secret or esoteric transmission from guru
to disciple associated with Tantra—may also have played a role (Sharf 2017).
What the Chinese political climate may account for, however, is the particular manner in which these new ideas about lineage came to be joined to the
problem of the authority of meditative experience and meditative attainment
and the proper status of the *chan* master.

The political climate of the early 700s may also help to explain why
similar efforts to disassociate meditative attainment from visionary experience turn up both in early Chan writings and in other, apparently unrelated
projects such as the cave 59 carving of the *Chan Essentials* at the Wofoyuan.
Xuanzong's policies toward Buddhism were clearly being felt in Sichuan by
the 730s, when the cave 59 carvings were made.[103] And certainly the associated carving of the *Scripture on the Ten Wheels* passage shows that at least some
members of the local Buddhist community felt that the status associated with
their (or others') claims to special expertise in meditation was under threat.
Those who felt this way were evidently comfortable taking a public stand
against this loss of status. Yet other passages included in the cave 59 carvings

---

102. 於是就開禪訓，三藏云，此土...或墜小乘二乘法，或墮九十五種外道法，或墮鬼神禪，觀見一
切物，知他人家好惡事。苦哉...詐言我坐禪觀行。(*Lengqie shi zi ji,* T.2837:85.1284a1–8; Yanagida
1971a, 93; Faure 1989, 102). The figure here is not Bodhidharma but Guṇabhadra, whom the
Lengqie shi zi ji, uniquely among early Chan sources, presents as the first patriarch.

103. The efforts of the central government to raise the status of Daoism at the expense
of Buddhism in Sichuan are visible in a 724 edict, inscribed on a stele that stands to this day,
ordering the return to local Daoists of a property on Qingcheng Mountain (青城山) that had
previous been a Buddhist monastery (Long and Huang 1997, 23). Sculpture projects carried
out at various Sichuan sites during this time also often reveal an implicit effort to assert the
subservience of Buddhism to Daoism (Mollier 2010).

also suggest that, just as in the opening lines of the *Records of the Masters and Disciples of the Laṅkāvatāra*, it was necessary to pair this protest with a clear acknowledgment of the justice and wisdom of the kinds of criticism of meditation that appear in the edicts and regulations of Xuanzong. The final sections of the cave 59 carving associated with meditation include excerpts from the third scroll of the *Chan Essentials,* where, as in the passage from the *Scripture on the Ten Wheels,* the Buddha issues a series of rules, pertaining in this case to those who improperly claim association with meditation:

> There may be monks, nuns, laymen, or laywomen who, while within the Buddhist fold, ceaselessly covet personal gain. Out of desire for fame they dissemble and perform evil. Not actually practicing seated meditation, heedless in their conduct of body and speech, they only claim to practice meditation out of greed for personal gain.[104]

Such practitioners, the excerpt goes on to say, are guilty of a grave transgression that, if not immediately repented, will lead to long suffering in hell. The Buddha also rebukes monks and nuns who make false claims to actual meditative attainments, those who "have not in fact seen the white bones but claim to have seen them."[105] This transgression is even more serious than merely claiming to be a meditator—no atonement is possible, and guilty parties will be reborn in the deepest hell for an entire eon.

Taken together and read as a single integral statement, the cave 59 carvings on meditation give a nuanced message concerning meditation and its power. Those who meditate are to be honored and materially supported above all other Buddhists. Yet at the same time, those who falsely claim to meditate or falsely claim the power of meditation are guilty of the most heinous of crimes. Indeed, as is then suggested by the final significant excerpt from the *Chan Essentials,* meditative attainment of the traditional, visionary kind is not necessary:

> Their minds free of distraction, [practitioners should] sit upright in absorption, concentrate their minds in a single place, and block off their sense faculties. *Even though they do not obtain any confirmatory visions,* such people, their minds calm, will by the power of their concentrated minds be reborn in Tuṣita heaven, where they will meet Maitreya.[106]

---

104. 若有比丘、比丘尼、優婆塞、優婆夷，於佛法中，為利養故，貪求無厭。為好名聞，而假偽作惡。實不坐禪，身口放逸，行放逸行，貪利養故，自言坐禪。(Bemmann and Hua 2018, 113; *Chan Essentials* 4.32.5; *CMY,* T.613:15.268a19–22)

105. 實不見白骨，自言我見白骨。(Bemmann and Hua 2018, 114; *Chan Essentials* 4.32.7; *CMY,* T.613.15:268b3)

106. 心不散亂，端坐正受，住意一處，閉塞諸根。此人安心，念定力故，雖無境界，捨身他世，生兜率天，值遇彌勒。(Bemmann and Hua 2018, 115–116; *Chan Essentials* 4.32.12; *CMY,* T.613:15.268c15–18). This passage is, interestingly, one of two from the *Chan Essentials* included

In the context of the original scripture, this passage represents a consolation prize for those who do not reach the higher, more elaborate visions and attainments to which the text devotes most of its attention. But in the carving, where such attainments are not described at all, this reads as the conclusion, and what is reiterated here is the attitude toward meditative visions that seems to have motivated the editing process itself. Read together, the passage from the *Scripture on the Ten Wheels* and the excerpts from the *Chan Essentials* uphold meditators as the supreme "fields of merit" for the faithful while deflecting any expectation that the meditators will possess or claim to possess the kind of visionary powers that might arouse government suspicion.

Setting the cave 59 carvings in dialog with early Chan literature allows us to see two very different ways of responding to a climate in which the visionary powers of the *chan* masters of old were no longer a possession that living individuals could safely or easily claim, and where, accordingly, it was necessary or desirable to reevaluate long-standing ideas about the semiotics of meditative attainment. The Wofoyuan carvings were hardly the basis for an enduring solution to this problem, since their rewriting of the *Chan Essentials* did little more than edit away offending material from an earlier source of meditation lore deeply invested in the traditional paradigm. It is not surprising, then, that the new vision of *chan* that spread throughout China and eventually East Asia was not this one, but rather the one inspired, with many future variations, by the literature of the early Chan School. Still, even if the understanding of *chan* reflected in the cave 59 carvings was of limited long-term importance, this example retains great historical value. With its help, we can see something of the shared conditions out of which the early Chan understanding of meditation and its authority emerged.

Toward a New Era

The previous chapters of this book showed that a relatively uniform approach to *chan*, Buddhist meditation, began in China in the early 400s, prevailed for well over two hundred years, and achieved consolidation in a variety of literary genres and topics and across different kinds of media. In this chapter, we turned from this shared and relatively stable terrain to the significant historical and ideological changes in the Chinese understanding of Buddhist meditation that accompanied, and to some degree defined, the emergence of the Chan School in the early eighth century. The argument I have made throughout is that we can only properly discern what was new about the Chan approach to *chan* (and there was indeed something new about it) when we read the early Chan writings on this topic as they were situated and intended to be read—as criticisms of, and an alternative to, the theretofore prevailing

---

in the *Zhong jing yao lan* 眾經要攬, a collection of scriptural citations known from the Dunhuang manuscripts (*Secrets of Buddhist Meditation*, appendix 1, no. 2).

treatment of the relationship between meditation, meditative experience, and meditative attainment in Chinese Buddhism.

In addition to its many other novel arguments concerning the authority of lineage and spiritual descent, early Chan proposed a new semiotic ideology of meditative experience. In it, the visionary experiences that previous generations of Chinese Buddhists had looked to as signs of success, not just for meditators but in any number of domains of religious life, were stripped of their potential for communicative power and asserted to be never more than hallucinations. Early Chan writers claimed that meditative attainment especially was simply not the kind of thing that one could know had occurred on the basis of such crude evidence. To the extent that this claim bypassed specific *methods* of meditation to target, at a higher order, the norms and procedures by which meditative attainment and authority could be confirmed, it was indeed radical. We should acknowledge this radicalness. Even if we agree that it did not lead to a wholesale reorganization of Buddhist monastic life, as earlier and overly romantic views of the Chan School and its place in Chinese Buddhism once had it, we must consider why it proved appealing and important and what else it might have implicated. As we will see in the epilogue, the approach to the semiotics of meditative experience that Chan proposed never succeeded in completely replacing the one that had come before it. But it did make permanently available the *possibility* of adopting an entirely different framework for understanding the kinds of things meditation might be good for and the kinds of experiences or other signs one might uphold as evidence for mastery of it. To this extent, Chan unsettled what had once been unproblematic and in doing so changed the face of Chinese Buddhism.

Epilogue

THIS BOOK HAS told a story about what Buddhist meditation was in early medieval China. Unsurprisingly, in this telling it was not a universal mental science that stood apart from the ritual, religious, or institutional trappings of Buddhism itself. After several decades of post-Orientalist scholarship, the decidedly recent genealogy of that understanding of Buddhist meditation is now well known. But if that view is wrong, what would it mean to get things right? I have tried to answer this question, within a particular cultural and historical setting, with the goal of arriving at an understanding of how Buddhists themselves (however loosely we define that term) thought about Buddhist meditation that is not the mere negation or inverse of a modernist fantasy of it, that is not "a view of others as a back-projection from who we think we are" (Keane 2007, 12).

Our words, of course, threaten to betray us from the start. To call *meditation* what the seated Buddhist adept is doing, or is supposed to be doing, is already to subscribe to a particular understanding of this activity. This is one reason I have framed the topic of this book as *chan* (禪), the word that in East Asia has most often pointed to that thing in the world—the activity of the motionless, cross-legged Buddhist contemplative—that the words "Buddhist meditation" usually point to for us. But linguistic fiddling hardly solves the difficulties. Whether we call it *chan* or meditation, the object in question is a challenge for historical analysis because central to it are the inner experiences of those who pursue it—matters not directly accessible even to contemporaneous observers. Moreover, even at the level of purely external, observable behavior, the practice of meditation was (and is) of such importance in the normative ideals of Buddhism that in most cases we cannot take the written records concerning those who carried it out, and what happened to them when they did, as purely descriptive historical accounts.

This book has taken these methodological challenges not as limitations to be overcome but as indications of how Buddhist meditation could ever have mattered to anyone, and hence its nature as a social, cultural, historical, and experiential object. This has meant demonstrating the existence, tracing the contours, and charting parts of the history not of Buddhist meditation itself,

249

whose presence must be inferred for the most part rather than grasped directly in specific instances, but of that which made it possible for meditation and its fruits to exist within a social world. It is in this *semiotic ideology of meditative experience* that we see the assumptions that medieval Chinese Buddhists held concerning what the experiential signs of meditative attainment are, how they should be read, and what consequences can and should result from that reading, as well as the textual, hermeneutic, and social activities they carried out informed by and in furtherance of those assumptions.

One of the central arguments in this study, then, has been that in early medieval China, between the years 400 and 700, there was a coherent set of real ideals—ideals regularly taken up *as* ideals, for the purpose of understanding, categorizing, and acting upon reality—concerning the practice of Buddhist meditation as an established monastic regime, the significance of meditative experiences largely visionary in form, and meditative attainment as a recognizable social (and emically, metaphysical) fact. By attending to these ideals, as well as the forms and tools through which they were made available for use (a major function of meditation literature), I have endeavored to tell a history of Buddhist meditation that lies between the circumstantial limits of what any specific Chinese Buddhists actually did or experienced, on the one hand, and the *mere* ideology of meditation in the sense of the normative and purely theoretical accounts of it that were canonized and transmitted to future generations, on the other. Taking its specifically *semiotic* ideology as our object of inquiry lets us think about the ways that the social and doctrinal histories of Buddhist meditation were and are necessarily commingled. We can and should, I have suggested, attend simultaneously to meditation as represented in normative scriptures, where an explicit topic of concern is how its success should be recognized, and to meditative experiences as things that impinged on real human lives, endowing those who had or persuasively claimed them with meditative attainment or, going further, the title of master of meditation. These were categories of social being that had real consequences for specific individuals precisely because they transcended their purely local contexts to articulate with a shared, "canonical" system of value and meaning, however broadly conceived.

Alongside this question of what it would mean to take up Buddhist meditation as a social and cultural object has been a more specific argument about what we actually find in the normative literature of Buddhist meditation in early medieval China. It is certainly true that during this time, and throughout premodern Buddhist history, meditation was in practice a decidedly elite endeavor carried out only by a small number of religious virtuosos. But the Buddhist meditation texts seen as most authoritative and held to be canonical by early medieval Chinese Buddhists have shown us that even normatively this activity was not supposed to utterly transcend the textures of Buddhism that ordinary people too encountered. Even when directed at seemingly abstract goals that we might think were of prime concern only to elite monastics, such as the realization of emptiness or non-self, Buddhist meditation during this era was still supposed to produce (and was hence judged in terms of) the same kinds of visionary experience that counted as potential signs of miraculous confirmation in many other domains of Chinese Buddhism and Chinese religion more generally. Meditation was thus fully embedded, *not just in practice but also in theory,* in the same world of cultic and ritual practice that all Chinese Buddhists participated in, because its goals were conceived in relation to that world and its outcomes had consequences relative to it.

Seeing this enmeshment of meditation in a shared ritual, ethical, and experiential world has not required looking outside the transmitted textual "canon" of Chinese Buddhism. This larger question of the relationship between canonical Buddhist literature and the wider worlds in which that literature was produced lies at the heart of ongoing methodological debates in the field of Buddhist Studies in recent decades. While this book is not a comprehensive assessment of this question, it does offer a useful site in which to consider it, since the practice of meditation is a key, arguably even *the* key, canonical Buddhist ideal. If so, one conclusion suggested by the material taken up in this study is that it is far too sweeping, if not a patent error, to say that in reading elite, canonical Buddhist literature "we are almost always sampling topics that were of prime interest only to a minority of Buddhists" or that deriving an understanding of Buddhism from such sources will invariably tend to "reduce the humanity of Buddhist devotees to intellect" (Lewis 2014, 1–2).

It is, to be sure, true that only a small minority of Buddhists wrote and read what we now call "canonical" Buddhist literature. But this does not mean, as certain strains of contemporary scholarship have often suggested or implied, that for this reason its authors were necessarily alienated from the worlds in which they lived, either in the interests and aspirations they were attempting to express in their writings or in what they reveal to us through them. That Buddhist scripture and doctrine were composed by a "small, literate, almost exclusively male and certainly atypical professionalized subgroup" does not in itself mean, as Gregory Schopen has it, that this literature as a rule has no bearing on "what religious people of all segments of a given community actually did and how they lived."[1]

What the meditation texts that were canonical during the fifth through seventh centuries in China suggest is that Buddhist scripture and doctrine, even when written in a technical idiom of limited accessibility, were not intended to be normative in the sense of a simplistic or categorical prescription of orthodoxy. Just as modern academic authors themselves purport to be able to do, those who wrote in this restricted idiom could and did use it to talk about—to *theorize,* we might say—matters of broad concern. Rather than prescribing orthodox belief or action, which we might then wish to contrast with the beliefs and actions actually held and carried out on the ground, Buddhist doctrine could, and often did, "ratify decisions that had

---

1. Schopen 1987, 193 (reprinted in Schopen 1997, 114).

already been made at a different level," to use Hans Belting's characterization of medieval Christian theological writings on the worship of icons (1994, 9). If Buddhist scriptural and canonical literature, taken as a class, has sometimes appeared to contemporary scholars to "reduce the humanity of Buddhist devotees to intellect," this is perhaps a sign not that we have read too much of this literature but that we have not read it closely enough.

In recovering a more penetrating understanding of what Buddhist meditation was in medieval China, I have argued that answering questions concerning what it was and why it was important for those who may never have practiced it, or even wanted to practice it themselves, does not necessarily require finding new *kinds* of sources unblemished by the supposed obfuscation of normative literature. It has required simply not limiting ourselves to those portions of the canon, as medieval Chinese Buddhists defined it, on which our textbook views have hitherto been based. It has also required making sure we know how to properly read this material—in other words, before saying that the norms of Buddhist doctrine were not instantiated on the ground, we must consider what Buddhists themselves thought instantiating those norms would look like. Indeed, if the abstract nature of the "canonical," and hence the flexibility of its application in reference to real things and events in the world, is, as Roy Rappaport suggests (1999), a feature of religion rather than a bug, how could we purport to prejudge when canonical norms are or are not being instantiated?

Seen in this light, our task as historians of Buddhism is not to peer beneath, behind, or around canonical norms or doctrines so as to uncover what really happened "on the ground," but rather to discern the varied ways that what really happened was (and could be) taken as an instance of norms or the embodiment of doctrine, and hence, given value and thereby made into a basis for social life. How *this* happens is a matter of semiotic ideology. And the range of possible ways it could occur—a range that while not completely fixed is also not infinitely flexible in any given time and place—is likely to be less obvious from the written formulation of those norms than we think. It is without question a great deal less obvious than most Orientalist scholarship on Buddhism assumed. It might even turn out (taking an example from this book) that instantiating the norm of "realizing emptiness" meant seeing four snakes emerging from a golden vase.

To be clear, I am certainly not calling for scholars of Buddhism to return en masse to the textual and literary canon or to abandon their many efforts to draw from sources that are "new" relative to the traditional concerns of academic Buddhology and which were produced by a wider range of the social, intellectual, and professional classes of Buddhist societies past and present. My argument is simply that we should stop reflexively framing the local, popular, noncanonical, or on-the-ground forms of Buddhism discoverable through such sources as something invariably different from, let alone actively concealed by, the Buddhism of canonical scripture and doctrine. Dialectically, such an embrace of the hermeneutics of suspicion was probably necessary when it was a novel idea to study anything other than the tracts of high church doctrine or elite practices such as meditation. Yet the value of a methodologically and topically plural field of Buddhist Studies is now well accepted. Given that, to continue to insist that ethnography, material culture, noncanonical literature, or descriptive rather than prescriptive sources will show us a kind of Buddhism that canonical literature never can, or that they reveal the "limits" of the influence of Buddhist doctrine (Schopen 2014b), is arguably highly misleading. For this framing reinforces the patently false notions that we already fully understand Buddhist doctrine and have already fully read and explored the totality of "canonical" Buddhist literature, and to this extent, it has the perverse effect of entrenching the claims to accuracy and completeness of earlier (and often dubious) scholarly analyses of those things.

This is not merely a matter of recognizing that Buddhists may be more comfortable with a divergence between precept and practice than are we. Nor need it involve saying that by thinking of Buddhism as a *repertoire* of potentially contradictory elements rather than a unified and coherent system, we can find a place for its disparate understandings and practices without relegating any to secondary status.[2] My point is different, and simpler, but not, I think, less important—namely, that we should recognize the difference between "textual" Buddhism and *textbook* Buddhism. Much of what has been said to malign the former, as an incomplete or ideologically suspect source of evidence for what Buddhism is, was, or should be, has the latter as its true object of criticism.

Yet as most scholars of Buddhism would probably agree upon reflection, what the vast Buddhist canon actually contains, and how any bit of it has served Buddhists across time and space, is by no means the same thing as the depiction, by earlier generations of modern scholars, of what the claims of Buddhist doctrine are, much less what beliefs and modes of life they thought such claims rightly authorize. Many persistent ideas about the latter—about what someone properly motived by Buddhist norms would rightly do or think, and hence how we might judge, from what they actually do or think, their relationship to those norms—were first formulated by Orientalist scholars who *assumed* as a methodological starting point that the living realities of Buddhism had lost sight of its original doctrines.[3] It can hardly be surprising that the prescriptions of Buddhist doctrine and the

---

2. See for example Campany 2012; McDaniel 2011; Young 2015; and Stone 2016. See also Hymes 2002, in the case of Chinese religion more broadly. The powerful model of culture as a "repertoire"—in effect, a critique of scholars for whom cultures are unified, shared, and coherent—has been developed most systematically by sociologist Ann Swidler (1986; 2001), on whom all of these works have drawn to good effect.

3. For example, such scholarship often proposed that the doctrine of non-self is incompatible with a well-financed Buddhist funeral industry, such that the presence of the latter implies a loss of understanding of the former. As Jacqueline Stone points out, this is a dubious reading of the doctrine of non-self at best (2016, 9–13).

concerns expressed in canonical literature, when understood in such terms, will usually fail to match Buddhism on the ground.

Chan Before Chan has largely been concerned with a broadly shared and relatively stable culture of Buddhist meditation that developed in China between the early fifth and late seventh centuries. Its final chapter depicted the early Chan School of the mid-Tang dynasty as a potent challenge to that culture and the semiotic ideology of meditation that had sustained it. Early Chan writers usually do not make it immediately clear what alternative they are proposing. Many of the later innovations of the Chan School, in rhetorical, literary, and institutional matters, can be seen in part as attempts to resolve this question—to say, in positive terms, what then *does* make a Chan master if it is not confirmation by visionary meditative experience. Without going into that later history any further, we may simply note that in challenging not any particular technique of meditation but, at a higher order, a set of norms about how claims to meditative experience can or cannot (even potentially) serve as evidence for matters of public significance, the Chan School was indeed seeking to overturn a previously settled order, and generations of East Asian Buddhists and modern scholars alike have not been wrong to see it as radical, even Protestant-like in its message, even if this radicalness did not extend to new material forms of Buddhist life, where it was, if anything, conservative (Foulk 1993).

With regard to the question of historical change, it is important to further note that the culture of meditation and meditative experience explored in this book did not ever go away, in either China or East Asia more broadly. The Chan School did in large measure (though perhaps less than its partisans claimed) succeed in appropriating the word *chan* to its new vision. But what I have called *chan* before Chan did not simply disappear. Accordingly, many of the figures and traditions discussed in this study have histories extending far past my brief treatment of them. For example, the semiotics of meditative confirmation in early Tiantai literature explored in Chapter 3 is but the tip of a larger iceberg extending into the Tang, Song, and later dynasties (Stevenson 2007). The same is true of Tang-dynasty Pure Land figures such as Shandao as well. And we have not even touched upon the Tantric literature of the later Tang and beyond, another obvious area where one might look to find similar semiotic ideologies of meditative experience. Suffice it to say that long after the fifth, sixth, and seventh centuries, Chinese Buddhists, even when no longer calling it *chan*, continued (and still continue) to engage in meditative practices of various kinds in which they sought out, obtained, and told others about their extraordinary experiences and visions, often with real consequences.

It is appropriate, then, that we end with a final example that gestures toward that later history. This example—a document from the trove of Dunhuang manuscripts that have provided so much social-historical data for scholars of medieval China—also serves as a suitable capstone to this book by providing, in a way that most of the sources I have used cannot, a well and truly documentary perspective concerning meditation and meditative experience, something rarely if ever available within the annals of premodern Buddhism writ large. This document provides an almost ethnographic, unfiltered glimpse of how specific individuals laid claim to concrete meditative experiences, the context in which those claims were solicited and made, and the way they were then deemed to be consequential, or not.

This short text, which I will call the *Dunhuang Record of Visions,* dates from the early 900s and was preserved by chance when its unused side was recycled, as part of the verso of Pelliot manuscript no. 3556. Cut off at both beginning and end, it now comprises a list of fifty-six names of individuals who are known from surviving census registers to have been nuns who lived in the Dunhuang area in the early 900s, and each name is followed by a set of notes.[4] The original text of the *Dunhuang Record of Visions* appears to have been an inclusive survey of the residents of at least two local nunneries and possibly more.[5] The notes that follow each name record the nun's meditative visions on two separate occasions. The record for the nun Zhenyi (no. 21; fig. 8, third from left) is typical:

> Zhenyi: While meditating in the practice place, saw a woman give her two silver bowls, but then take them back and leave. Further: Saw nothing.[6]

Almost all the notes begin with the words "while meditating in the practice place" followed by either a brief description of a vision or a note indicating that no vision was obtained. Most also include, after a blank space and the word "further" (又), a second report. Details of the paleography show that these second reports were not transcribed onto the manuscript immediately after their respective first reports, but were added later, sequentially and as a group.[7] In other words this manuscript was itself used to collect the relevant informa-

---

4. For a transcription of the *Dunhuang Record of Visions* and a brief analysis of its contents, see Hao 1998, 43–49, and Wei 2011, 608–614.

5. The names of the nuns seem to have been arranged by temple of residence. After the initial thirteen names, there is a sizeable blank space followed by *sheng* (乘). This must denote the Dasheng 大乘 nunnery, whose name was abbreviated this way in local administrative documents (*Dunhuang xue da ci dian,* 628). As Hao Chunwen has verified (see previous note), some of the names listed here in the *Dunhuang Record of Visions* are associated with that nunnery on contemporaneous census registers. The first thirteen names, therefore, are presumably the last entries for a different temple (the large blank space was probably left to allow for more names at a later date).

6. 真意。於道場思惟次。見一女人與二銀碗，卻收將去。又，不見。(Hao 1998, 45). I take *ci* 次 in a post-verbal position, meaning "right when" (*Tang wu dai yu yan ci dian,* 69).

7. It is relatively easy to see that the calligraphy in any given first report differs from that in the associated second report, and all the second reports are similar. Even more telling is that, in some cases, several adjacent second reports are written in a shared, lighter shade of ink. In these instances, the person writing seems to have been momentarily using a slightly more watery ink mixture while moving sequentially between the second reports (this can been seen in fig. 8, lines 7–8 from the right).

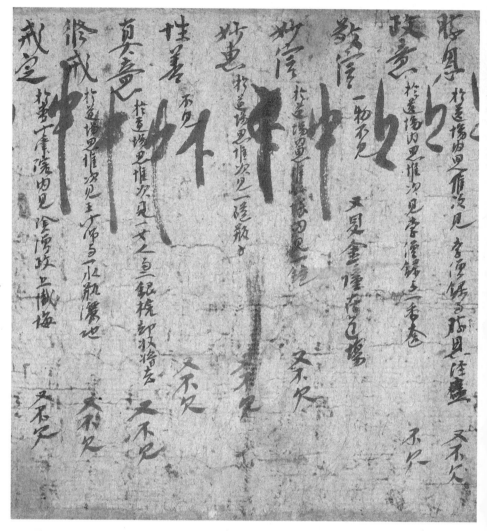

Figure 8. *Dunhuang Record of Visions*, Pelliot no. 3556, verso. This section contains the entries (*right to left*) for Sheng'en 勝恩, Zhengyi 政意, Jingxin 敬信, Miaoxin 妙信, Miaohui 妙惠, Xingshan 性善, Zhenyi 真意, Xiujie 修戒, and Jieding 戒定. Xingshan's entry records "saw nothing" (不見) on the first and second reports and is ranked "inferior" (下). The entries with visions are ranked "middle-grade" (中) or "superior" (上). That of Jingxin is graded superior even though she is only credited with a vision on the second report (this shows the ranking was done after both reports were recorded). For Miaohui, there seems to have been some hesitation about the ranking, with "inferior" perhaps being overwritten. Note also the uniformly light shading of ink in the second reports for Miaohui, Xingshan, Zhenyi, and Xiujie, showing that they were recorded sequentially, not immediately after their respective first reports. Bibliothèque Nationale de France.

tion on two separate occasions. Accordingly, it is an administrative rather than a purely literary document, and it shows us not only the content of the meditative visions claimed by or attributed to these nuns, but something of the manner in which those claims or attributions were collected and then used.

Zhenyi's vision is representative of the lot—simple but pointedly enigmatic. Many are of objects with vague but not definitive Buddhist connotations: a clay water pitcher (Miaohui, no. 19), or a golden censer (Jiexin, no. 28). Some involve animals: Xiangmao (no. 30) "saw a white dog enter the practice place"; Jieyuan (no. 43), a "white bird." In other cases, the vision is of a person who bestows an object or does a simple activity: Yuanjie (no. 13) sees a monk give her a string of pearls; Xingxian (no. 32) sees a monk sprinkling water on the ground; Dingxue (no. 46) sees an old man holding a bowl of yogurt. Local, presumably familiar personages appear in a few cases: Xiujie (no. 22) sees "Dharma master Wang," who gives her a pitcher of water; Zhengyuan (no. 26) sees "the monk Chen" leading a camel; Miaoda (no. 14) sees "controller of monks Fan" (氾僧統), who we know from other sources held this post at Dunhuang in the early 900s.

As interesting as these visions are, the records of the *absence* of a vision are potentially even more significant. Often, as for Zhenyi as cited above, a vision is followed by a note saying that on the second occasion nothing was seen.[8] In other cases, nothing is seen the first time, while the second report describes a vision. No nun is attributed with two visions. Nearly half the nuns—twenty out of fifty-six—experienced nothing, as with Miaobao (no. 4), who "did not see a single thing. Further: did not see anything" (一物不見。又不見). Entries such as this show that the *Dunhuang Record of Visions* is not hagiography. It is not a commemoration of only the extraordinary, normative, or idealized experiences of a privileged few. It is rather an artifact of an inclusive census of claims to meditative experience in which even those with nothing to declare had to go on record to that effect.

The *Dunhuang Record of Visions* also attests to a third and final event. Written alongside each name, in large, quickly executed strokes, are one of three words: "superior" (上), "middle-grade" (中), or "inferior" (下). Someone has ranked or graded each nun and her visions. The principles governing these judgments are unclear. Not unexpectedly, the nuns reporting no visions are all deemed inferior. Yet so too are some nuns who did have visions, namely, Jiexin (no. 2), who saw "two Uighurs" (!), and Zhenxin (no. 37), who saw a "mulberry fruit." What precisely distinguished the middle-grade visions from the superior ones is also unclear. Xiangmao, who saw a white dog, is superior, but Jieyuan, who saw a white bird, is only middle-grade. Both Zuishengzhi (no. 1),[9] who saw a monk with a bowl of fragrant water, and Miaohui (no. 19),

---

8. Absence of a vision is noted variously as "did not see [anything]" (不見), "did not see a single thing" (一物不見), or "did not see anything at all" (甚也不見).

9. 最勝智. Over thirty nuns with three-character monastic names beginning with *Zuisheng* 最勝 are known from ninth- and tenth-century Dunhuang documents (Dohi 2015, 905–907).

who merely saw a water pitcher, are middle-grade; apparently neither vision was as good as the golden pillar seen by the superior Jingxin (no.17).

The *Dunhuang Record of Visions* leaves us with many questions. What kind of meditation led to these visions?[10] Who evaluated the visions? What did the assigned ranks mean, and what further consequences did this classification entail? But even without this information, we have here an unrivaled picture of the social life of Buddhist meditative experience and attainment in the early 900s in Dunhuang. Neither a prescriptive manual nor a hagiography of meditative virtuosity, nor even merely a first-person account of a meditative experience, the *Dunhuang Record of Visions* is a trace of the activities by which those things that happened to these nuns while meditating, and to which it was assumed that they and only they could attest, were solicited, recorded, collected, and then, finally, judged and thereby made to matter in a relatively public way.

We cannot directly connect these happenings to any of the specific materials or contexts studied in this book. And we do not know if any of the early meditation manuals we have examined at length was known to these nuns or to those who judged their experiences. Be this as it may, the *Dunhuang Record of Visions* reflects a semiotic ideology of meditative experience more or less continuous with the one made available by the fifth-, sixth-, and seventh-century sources investigated earlier in this study. In the second and third chapters particularly, we saw that concrete but enigmatic visions were considered significant meditative experiences that the meditator alone had access to and that he or she had to declare to others and discuss with them, since what they revealed about the person who experienced them, if anything, was not obvious and required the interpretative skill of one possessing sufficient knowledge of the signs.

If the *Dunhuang Record of Visions* shows us that this approach to meditative experience persisted long after it was challenged by the early Chan School, it also provides us with a precious example of its instantiation at levels less rarified than those we have glimpsed hitherto. Now, we should indeed refrain from attributing to premodern Buddhists a modernist privileging of personal experience over and against all other forms of authority (Sharf 1995). But, as I have suggested, there is a difference between privileging personal experience in the sense of taking it (or arguing that it should be taken) as a stand-alone epistemic criterion and in the sense of requiring, as a matter of social practice and semiotic ideology, that individuals look within and report to others those things that have happened to them and to which they are deemed necessarily and reliably privy. The *Dunhuang Record of Visions*

---

10. The word used is *siwei* (to meditate), one of the common Chinese translations of *chan* (see *DZDL*, T.1509:25.185b16). It is impossible to say what specific method or technique of meditation was at issue here. That the *Dunhuang Record of Visions* does not use the word *chan* may be insignificant. But it may also reflect a post–Chan School era, in which *chan* was no longer as easily associated with practices in which confirmation by concrete visions was hoped for.

shows us that the nuns at Dunhuang in the early 900s routinely laid claim to personal meditative experiences in the latter sense. They were called upon, in an organized, collective, and ongoing fashion,[11] to give an account of what had happened to them in meditation—to declare what concrete things they and they alone had seen or, conversely, that they had not seen anything. And the giving of these accounts had consequences for them.

Yet even as this is so, we must further recognize that for these nuns, and for those who compiled this record and used it in the ways they did, the work of Buddhist meditation did not lie merely, if at all, in the *generating* of normative experiences. The experiences these nuns reported did not in and of themselves exemplify any Buddhist doctrines or ways of being in the world. Rather, they were patently personal, idiosyncratic, and unambiguously local in character, featuring people (Dharma master Wang), ethnic groups (Uighurs), wildlife (camels), and foodstuffs (yogurt) that even those who claimed them would have known to be particular to the Dunhuang region and thus not likely to populate the visions of those living in other times and places. The dominant model by which scholars of religion have sought to assess the nature of religious experience in recent years—in which such experiences are explained not as direct perceptions but as the "internalized residues of earlier social worlds" (McCutcheon 2012, 8)—seems here, if not to fail, then at least to not be very interesting. According to fifth- and sixth-century Chinese Buddhist meditation texts, and to the *Dunhuang Record of Visions*, which shows us an instantiation of similar ideals long thereafter, significant meditative experiences might well be anything. The culture of Buddhist meditation, accordingly, lay not in the creation of normative experiences but in the *taking* of a nearly infinite variety of truly personal—which is not to say unmediated or unconditioned—experiences as indicative of a limited range of normative statuses.

Thus it is incorrect, or at least incomplete, to say that for Buddhists "there is nothing new to discover in the course of their meditation . . . [because] the objective of meditation is to gain deeper understanding of the truths handed down by the tradition" (Franco 2009, 9), or that Buddhists have traditionally held that meditation does not lead to new knowledge because "yogic perception would not provide any new *information* from what had been given by philosophy" (Tillemans 2013, 299, emphasis in original). These contemporary scholars of Buddhism certainly do right in rejecting the popular notion that Buddhist meditation is a kind of scientific inquiry, an open-ended, nondogmatic investigation of the mind and world. But if in its place we propose a merely inverse perspective—that Buddhist meditation was thought to be only

---

11. Importantly, we know that the *Dunhuang Record of Visions* was not unique. The Haneda collection preserves a single sheet of an unconnected but clearly comparable document (*Tonkō hikyū*, 9.98–99; no. 699). This document differs in some important respects: it includes four visionary reports from each person and no cases of a failure to obtain visions. It also lacks the grading seen on Pelliot no. 3556. I thank Hao Chunwen for bringing this document to my attention.

the inculcation or, at best, the discovery of truths already authorized by a tradition—we overlook something important. For the point is not merely that meditation, in traditional Buddhist understanding and in traditional Buddhist societies, gives access to truths first, and fully, revealed by the Buddha. It is rather that gaining access to those truths is valued not as the acquisition of new propositional knowledge but as the means, and hence the *sign,* of meditative attainment. (Formally, it is the acquiring of wisdom that uproots the defilements, not the other way around.) It is an indication that one has become a certain kind of person who can now act on the world in new ways, because other things about them, such as their fate after death, are now known to be true. The new information that Buddhists *do* claim can and must be discovered through meditation is whether or not the meditator in question has in fact gained understanding of the truths handed down by the tradition and is thus enlightened. And this is so even if the manner in which the meditator's experiences afford the discovery of this knowledge is, as we have seen, constrained—constrained, but not fully determined in advance. This is just what it means to say that there is a semiotic ideology of meditative experience.

Thus, to claim that there was such an ideology, in any particular time and place, is not to say that everything was already figured out or that to meditate was simply to emulate an unambiguous norm of thought or behavior handed down by tradition or given in the inescapable web of language and culture. Like all norms that have social lives—what I have called "real ideals," ideals that were actually taken up *as* ideals—it was something that had to be worked out, between people, by way of objects, experiences, texts and other sources of "canon," and other semiotic forms, in space and across time. It is here that we should situate the history of Buddhist meditation—not merely in the ideal practices that canonical texts describe (or prescribe), nor in the meditation practice (if any) that real people engaged in and the experiences they may have had while doing so, but rather in the various ways that meditation was sustained as a cultural form permitting individuals, their practices, and their experiences to become things that others could recognize and respond to. Indeed, the practices, ideologies, and concrete judgments involved in turning the messy particulars of experience into instances of something more—the turning of visions into prophecies, a moment of blissful calm into *samādhi,* and meditators into arhats, bodhisattvas, buddhas, or Zen masters, among many other things—may well be the better part of the reality of Buddhism, if not of human existence itself.

References

Primary Texts, Collections, and Reference Works

A Chinese English Dictionary. Beijing: Foreign Language Teaching and Research Press, 1997.

Abhidharmakośabhāṣyam. Edited by P. Pradhan. Patna: K. P. Jayaswal Research Center, 1975.

Aṅguttara-nikāya. Edited by R. Morris and E. Hardy. London: Pali Text Society, 1885–1900.

Apidamo da piposha lun 阿毘達磨大毘婆沙論, T.1545, vol. 27.

Apidamo jushe lun 阿毘達磨俱舍論, T.1558, vol. 29.

Apidamo shun zheng li lun 阿毘達磨順正理論, T.1562, vol. 29.

Apitan ba jiandu lun 阿毘曇八犍度論, T.1543, vol. 26.

Aweiyuezhishu jing 阿惟越致遮經, T.266, vol. 9.

Bai hu tong yi 白虎通義. *Si bu cong kan* 四部叢刊 edition.

Baoshan Lingquan si 寶山靈泉寺. Zhengzhou: Henan ren min chu ban she, 1992.

Bei hua jing 悲華經, T.157, vol. 3.

Bian zheng lun 辯正論, T.2110, vol. 52.

Biqiuni zhuan 比丘尼傳, T.2063, vol. 50.

Biqiuni zhuan jiao zhu 比丘尼傳校註. Edited by Wang Rutong 王孺童. Beijing: Zhong hua shu ju, 2006.

Bukkyō daijiten 佛教大辭典. 10 vols. Edited by Mochizuki Shinkō 望月信亨. Tokyo: Sekai seiten kankō kyōkai, 1958–1963.

Chan fa yao jie 禪法要解, T.616, vol. 15.

Chan men zhang 禪門章, Z.907, vol. 55.

Chan mi yao fa jing 禪祕要法經, T.613, vol. 15.

Chan yao jing 禪要經, T.609, vol. 15.

Chang ahan jing 長阿含經, T.1, vol. 1.

Cheng shi lun 成實論, T.1646, vol. 32.

Chu san zang ji ji 出三藏記集, T.2145, vol. 55.

Chu yao jing 出曜經, T.212, vol. 4.

Da banniepan jing 大般涅槃經, T.374, vol. 12.

Da banniepan jing shu 大般涅槃經疏, T.1767, vol. 38.

Da bannihuan jing 大般泥洹經, T.376, vol. 12.

Da bao ji jing 大寶積經, T.310, vol. 11.

Da fang bian fo bao en jing 大方便佛報恩經, T.156, vol. 3.

Da fang deng da ji jing 大方等大集經, T.397, vol. 13.

Da fang deng tuoluoni jing 大方等陀羅尼經, T.1339, vol. 21.

Da sheng bei fentuoli jing 大乘悲分陀利經, T.158, vol. 3.

Da sheng da ji Dizang shi lun jing 大乘大集地藏十輪經, T.411, vol. 13.

Da sheng qi xin lun 大乘起信論, T.1666, vol. 32.

Da sheng qi xin lun shu 大乘起信論義疏, Z.755, vol. 45.

Da sheng qi xin lun yi shu 大乘起信論義疏, T.1843, vol. 44.

Da sheng yi zhang 大乘義章, T.1851, vol. 44.

Da tang nei dian lu 大唐內典錄, T.2149, vol. 55.

Da zhi du lun 大智度論, T.1509, vol. 25.

Dai nihon komonjo: hennen monjo 大日本古文書: 編年文書. 25 vols. Tokyo: Tōkyō teikoku daigaku, 1901–1940.

Damoduoluo chan jing 達摩多羅禪經, T.618, vol. 15.

Dao di jing 道地經, T.607, vol. 15.

Dao xing bore jing 道行般若經, T.224:8.

Dao zang 道藏. 36 vols. Beijing: Wen wu chu ban she, 1988.

Dao zang zi mu yin de 道藏子目引得. Edited by Weng Dujian 翁獨健. Beijing: Hafo Yanjing xue she, 1935.

Dengyō daishi shōrai taishū roku 傳教大師將來台州錄, T.2159, vol. 55.

Dīgha-nikāya. Edited by T. W. Rhys Davids, J. E. Carpenter, and W. Stede. London: Pali Text Society, 1975.

Dunhuang xue da ci dian 敦煌學大辭典. Shanghai: Shanghai ci shu chu ban she, 1998.

Fa hua sanmei chan yi 法華三昧懺儀, T.1941, vol. 46.

Fa hua wen ju ji 法華文句記, T.1719, vol. 34.

Fa hua yi shu 法華義疏, T.1721, vol. 34.

Fa hua zhuan ji 法華傳記, T.2068, vol. 51.

Fa jing jing 法鏡經, T.322, vol. 12.

Fa yuan zhu lin 法苑珠林, T.2122, vol. 53.

Fan fan yu 翻梵語, T.2130, vol. 54.

Fan wang jing pusa jie ben shu 梵網經菩薩戒本疏, T.1813, vol. 40.

Fang deng sanmei xing fa 方等三昧行法, T.1940, vol. 46.

Fo guang da ci dian 佛光大辭典. 8 vols. Gaoxiong Shi: Fo guang chu ban she, 1988.

Fo shuo guan jing 佛說觀經, T.2914, vol. 85.

Fo zu tong ji 佛祖統紀, T.2035, vol. 49.

Fu fa zang yin yuan zhuan 付法藏因緣傳, T.2058, vol. 50.

Gao seng Faxian zhuan 高僧法顯傳, T.2085, vol. 51.

Gao seng zhuan 高僧傳, T.2059, vol. 50.

Gen ben shuo yi qie you bu pi'naiye 根本說一切有部毘奈耶, T.1442, vol. 23.

Gen ben shuo yi qie you bu pi'naiye za shi 根本說一切有部毘奈耶雜事, T.1451, vol. 24.

Gu xiao shuo gou chen 古小說鉤沉. *Lu Xun quan ji* 魯迅全集, vol. 8, 121–657. Beijing: Ren min wen xue chu ban shen, 1973.

Guan fo sanmei hai jing 觀佛三昧海經, T.643, vol. 15.

Guan Mile pusa shang sheng doushuai tian jing 觀彌勒菩薩上生兜率天經, T.452, vol. 14.

Guan nian Emituo fo xiang hai sanmei gongde fa men 觀念阿彌陀佛相海三昧功德法門, T.1959, vol. 47.

Guan Puxian pusa xing fa jing 觀普賢菩薩行法經, T.277, vol. 9.

Guan Wuliangshou fo jing 觀無量壽佛經, T.365, vol. 12.

Guan Wuliangshou fo jing shu 觀無量壽佛經疏, T.1753, vol. 37.

Guan Wuliangshou jing yi shu 觀無量壽佛經義疏, T.1749, vol. 37.

Guan Xukongzang pusa jing 觀虛空藏菩薩經, T.409, vol. 13.

Guan Yaowang Yaoshang er pusa jing 觀藥王藥上二菩薩經, T.1161, vol. 20.

Guang hong ming ji 廣弘明集, T.2103, vol. 52.

Guo qing bai lu 國清百錄, T.1934, vol. 46.

Han wei nan bei chao mu zhi hui bian 漢魏南北朝墓誌彙編. Edited by Zhao Chao 趙超. Tianjin: Tianjin gu ji chu ban she, 2008.

Han yu da ci dian 漢語大詞典. Edited by Luo Zhufeng 罗竹风. Beijing: Zhong hua shu ju, 1986.

Hong ming ji 弘明集, T.2102, vol. 52.

Hou han shu 後漢書. Beijing: Zhong hua shu ju, 1973.

Hua yan jing 華嚴經, T.278, vol. 9.

Jātaka. Edited by V. Fausboll. 6 vols. London: Pali Text Society, 1963.

Ji shen zhou san bao gan tong lu 集神州三寶感通錄, T.2106, vol. 52.

Jie tuo dao lun 解脫道論, T.1648, vol. 32.

Jin gang bore boluomi jing 金剛般若波羅蜜經, T.235, vol. 8.

Jin guang ming jing 金光明經, T.663, vol. 16.

Jin guang ming jing shu 金光明經疏, T.1787, vol. 39.

Jin guang ming jing wen ju 金光明經文句, T.1785, vol. 39.

Jing lü yi xiang 經律異相, T.2121, vol. 53.

Jiu tang shu 舊唐書. Beijing: Zhong hua shu ju, 1975.

Jiumoluoshi fa shi da yi 鳩摩羅什法師大義, T.1856, vol. 45.

Kai yuan shi jiao lu 開元釋教錄, T.2154, vol. 55.

Kōsetsu Bukkyōgo daijiten 広說佛教語大辞典. Edited by Nakamura Hajime 中村元. Tokyo: Tōkyō shoseki, 2001.

Le Grand Ricci. Online edition, *Grand dictionnaire Ricci de la langue chinoise*, Paris: Institut Ricci, 2001. Brill Online Chinese Reference Shelf, 2013. https://chinesereferenceshelf.brillonline.com/grand-ricci.

Lengqie shi zi ji 楞伽師資記, T.2837, vol. 85.

Lengqieaboduoluo bao jing 楞伽阿跋多羅寶經, T.670, vol. 16.

Li dai fa bao ji 曆代法寶記, T.2075, vol. 51.

Li dai san bao ji 歷代三寶紀, T.2034, vol. 49.

Liu du ji jing 六度集經, T.152, vol. 3.

Lü xiang gan tong zhuan 律相感通傳, T.1898, vol. 45.

Lun heng jiao shi 論衡校釋. Edited by Huang Hui 黃暉. 4 vols. Beijing: Zhong hua shu ju, 1990.

Luoyang qielan ji 洛陽伽藍記, T.2092, vol. 51.

Majjhima-nikāya. Edited by V. Trenckner and R. Chalmers. London: Pali Text Society, 1979.

Manorathapūraṇī. Edited by M. Walleser and H. Kopp. London: Pali Text Society, 1924–1957.

Meisōden shō 名僧傳抄, Z.1523, vol. 77.

Milindapañho. Edited by V. Trenckner. London: Pali Text Society, 1962.

Mohe zhi guan 摩訶止觀, T.1911, vol. 46.

Mohesengqi lü 摩訶僧祇律, T.1425, vol. 22.

Nan hai ji gui nei fa zhuan 南海寄歸內法傳, T.2125, vol. 54.

Nan qi shu 南齊書. Beijing: Zhong hua shu ju, 1974.

Nihon genson hasshu issaikyō mokuroku 日本現存八種一切経目録. Tokyo: Kokusai bukkyōgaku daigakuin daigaku gakujutsu furontia jikkō iinkai, 2006.

Paṭisambhidāmagga. Edited by A. C. Taylor. London: Pali Text Society, 1905–1907.

Pini mu jing 毘尼母經, T.1463, vol. 24.

Piposha lun 鞞婆沙論, T.1547, vol. 28.

Pusa jie yi shu 菩薩戒義疏, T.1811, vol. 40.

Qi fo ba pusa suo shuo da tuoluoni shen zhou jing 七佛八菩薩所說大陀羅尼神咒經, T.1332, vol. 21.

Qi xin lun shu 起信論疏, T.1844, vol. 44.

Qianrimoni bao jing 遣日摩尼寶經, T.350, vol. 12.

Qing Guanshiyin pusa xiao fu du hai tuoluoni zhou jing 請觀世音菩薩消伏毒害陀羅尼呪經, T.1043, vol. 20.

Quan tang wen 全唐文. 11 vols. Beijing: Zhong hua shu ju, 1983.

Ren wang bore jing shu 仁王般若經疏, T.1707, vol. 33.

Samantapāsādikā. Edited by J. Takakusu and M. Nagai. London: Pali Text Society, 1924–1947.

Sammohavinodanī. Edited by A. P. Buddhadatta Thero. London: Pali Text Society, 1980.

Saṃyutta-nikāya. Edited by L. Feer. London: Pali Text Society, 1991.

San guo shi 三國志. Beijing: Zhong hua shu ju, 1964.

Sapoduo pini piposha 薩婆多毘尼毘婆沙, T.1440, vol. 23.

Shan jian lü piposha 善見律毘婆沙, T.1462, vol. 24.

She ji bai yuan jing 撰集百緣經, T.200, vol. 4.

Shen seng zhuan 神僧傳, T.2064, vol. 50.

Shi chan boluomi ci di fa men 釋禪波羅蜜次第法門, T.1916, vol. 46.

Shi jing tu qun yi lun 釋淨土群疑論, T.1960, vol. 47.

Shi san jing zhu shu 十三經注疏. Beijing: Zhong hua shu ju, 1980.

Shi shuo xin yu jiao jian 世說新語校箋. Edited by Yang Yong 楊勇. Beijing: Zhong hua shu ju, 2006.

Shi song lü 十誦律, T.1435, vol. 23.

Shi zhu piposha lun 十住毘婆沙論, T.1521, vol. 26.

Shinsan Dai Nihon zoku zōkyō 新纂大日本續藏經. Edited by Nishi Yoshio 西義雄 and Tamaki Kōshirō 玉城康四郎. 90 vols. Tokyo: Kokusho kankōkai, 1975–1989. CD-ROM and DVD. Chinese Buddhist Electronic Text Association (CBETA), 2008–2016.

Si fen biqiuni chao 四分比丘尼鈔, Z.724, vol. 40.

Si fen lü 四分律, T.1428, vol. 22.

Si fen lü shan fan bu que xing shi chao 四分律刪繁補闕行事鈔, T.1804, vol. 40.

Si wei lüe yao fa 思惟略要法, T.734, vol. 15.

Song ben ce fu yuan gui 宋本冊府元龜. 4 vols. Beijing: Zhong hua shu ju, 1989.

Song gao seng zhuan 宋高僧傳, T.2061, vol. 50.

Song shu 宋書. Beijing: Zhong hua shu ju, 1974.

Śrāvakabhūmi. Edited by Śrāvakabhūmi Study Group. 3 vols. Tokyo: Sankibō busshorin, 1998–2018.

Sui Tiantai Zhizhe da shi bie zhuan 隋天台智者大師別傳, T.2050, vol. 50.

Taishō shinshū daizōkyō 大正新修大藏經. Edited by Takakusu Junjirō 高楠順次朗 and Watanabe Kaigyoku 渡邊海旭. 85 vols. Tokyo: Taishō issaikyō kankōkai, 1924–1932. CD-ROM and DVD. Chinese Buddhist Electronic Text Association (CBETA), 2008–2016.

Tang hui yao 唐會要. Beijing: Zhong hua shu ju, 1955.

Tang wu dai yu yan ci dian 唐五代语言词典. Edited by Jiang Liansheng 江蓝生 and Cao Guangshun 曹广顺. Shanghai: Shanghai jiao yu chu ban she, 1997.

Tonkō hikyū: Kyōu Shooku zō 敦煌秘笈: 杏雨書屋蔵. 10 vols. Osaka: Takeda kagaku shinkō zaidan, 2009.

Vinayapiṭaka. Edited by H. Oldenberg. London: Pali Text Society, 1997.

Visuddhimagga. Edited by C. A. F. Rhys Davids. London: Pali Text Society, 1975.

Wang Li gu han yu zi dian 王力古漢語字典. Edited by Wang Li 王力. Beijing: Zhong hua shu ju, 2000.

Wei shu 魏書. Beijing: Zhong hua shu ju, 1974.

Weimojie suo shuo jing 維摩詰所說經, T.475, vol. 14.

Wu fen lü 五分律, T.1421, vol. 22.

Wu men chan jing yao yong fa 五門禪經要用法, T.619, vol. 15.

Xian yu jing 賢愚經, T.202, vol. 4.

Xiang fa jue yi jing 像法決疑經, T.2870, vol. 85.

Xiao zhi guan 小止觀 (*Xiu xi zhi guan zuo chan fa yao* 修習止觀坐禪法要), T.1915, vol. 46.

Xing qi xing jing 興起行經, T.197, vol. 4.

Xinjiang shi ku: Tulufan Bozikelike shi ku 新疆石窟: 吐魯番伯孜克里克石窟. Urumchi: Xinjiang ren min chu ban she, 1990.

Xiu chan yao jue 修禪要訣, Z.1222, vol. 63.

Xiu xing dao di jing 修行道地經, T.606, vol. 15.

Xu gao seng zhuan 續高僧傳, T.2060, vol. 50.

Xunzi ji jie 荀子集解. Edited by Wang Xianqian 王先謙. Beijing: Zhong hua shu ju, 1988.

Yi qie jing yin yi 一切經音義, T.2128, vol. 54.

Yongjing Bingling si 永靖炳灵寺. Beijing: Wen wu chu ban she, 1989.

Yuan jue jing da shu shi yi chao 圓覺經大疏釋義鈔, Z.245, vol. 9.

Za ahan jing 雜阿含經, T.101, vol. 2.

Zang wai fo jiao wen xian 藏外佛教文獻. Edited by Fang Guangchang 方廣錩. 16 vols. Beijing: Zong jiao wen hua chu ban she, 1995–.

Zeng yi ahan jing 增一阿含經, T.125, vol. 2.

Zhao lun 肇論, T.1858, vol. 45.

Zhen yan yao jue 真言要訣, T.2825, vol. 85.

Zheng fa hua jing 正法華經, T.263, vol. 9.

Zheng fa nian chu jing 正法念處經, T.721, vol. 17.

Zhi chan bing mi yao fa 治禪病祕要法, T.620, vol. 15.

Zhong ahan jing 中阿含經, T.26, vol. 1.

Zhong ben qi jing 中本起經, T.196, vol. 4.

Zhong jing mu lu 眾經目錄 (of Fajing 法經), T.2146, vol. 55.

Zhuangzi ji shi 莊子集釋. Edited by Wang Xiaoyu 王孝魚. 3 vols. Beijing: Zhong hua shu ju, 2004.

Zuo chan sanmei jing 坐禪三昧經, T.614, vol. 15.

Secondary Sources

Abe Takako 阿部貴子. 2006. "Nyūshutsu sokunen no daijōteki tenkai: *Daijikkō* o chūshin to shite" 入出息念の大乗的展開: 『大集経』を中心として. *Chizan gakuhō* 智山学報 55:113–132.

———. 2014. "*Zenhiyōhōkyō* ni okeru hakkotsukan ni tsuite" 『禅秘要法経』における白骨観について. *Bukkyō bunka ronshū* 仏教文化論集 11:332–363.

Adam, Martin T. 2003. "Meditation and the Concept of Insight in Kamalaśīla's *Bhāvanākramas*." PhD diss., McGill University.

Adamek, Wendi. 2000. "Robes Purple and Gold: Transmission of the Robe in the 'Lidai fabao ji' (Record of the Dharma-Jewel through the Ages)." *History of Religions* 40 (1):58–81.

———. 2007. *The Mystique of Transmission*. New York: Columbia University Press.

———. 2009. "A Niche of Their Own: The Power of Convention in Two Inscriptions for Medieval Chinese Buddhist Nuns." *History of Religions* 49 (1):1–26.

———. 2015. "Addressing the Mind: Developments in the Culture of Confession in Sui-Tang China." *Journal of Chinese Buddhist Studies* 28:117–152.

Agostini, Giulio. 2002. "Indian Views of the Buddhist Laity: Precepts and Upāsaka Status." PhD diss., University of California, Berkeley.

Akamatsu Akihiko. 2015. "Early Advaita Vedānta and Mahāyāna Buddhism." *Acta Asiatica* 108:63–74.

Allan, Sarah. 1984. "Drought, Human Sacrifice and the Mandate of Heaven in a Lost Text from the *Shang shu*." *Bulletin of the School of Oriental and African Studies* 47 (3):523–539.

Anālayo. 2003. "Nimitta." In *Encycylopaedia of Buddhism: Volume 7*, edited by W. G. Weeraratne, 177–179. Sri Lanka: Department of Buddhist Affairs.

———. 2009. "Vimuttimagga." In *Encycylopaedia of Buddhism: Volume 8*, edited by W. G. Weeraratne, 622–632. Sri Lanka: Department of Buddhist Affairs.

———. 2011. *A Comparative Study of the Majjhima-nikāya*. Taipei: Dharma Drum Publishing Corporation.

———. 2015. "The Buddha's Fire Miracles." *Journal of the Oxford Centre for Buddhist Studies* 11:9–42.

———. 2016. "The Gradual Path of Training in the Dīrghāgama, From Sense-restraint to Imperturbability." *The Indian International Journal of Buddhist Studies* 17:1–24.

Andersen, Poul. 1979. *The Method of Holding the Three Ones: A Taoist Manual of Meditation of the Fourth Century A.D.* London: Curzon.

————. 1994. "Talking to the Gods: Visionary Divination in Early Taoism." *Taoist Resources* 5 (1):1–24.

Andō Toshio 安藤俊雄. 1957. "Tendai shoki no zenhō" 天台初期の禅法. *Ōtani gakuhō* 大谷学報 36 (4):15–28.

————. 1962. "Rozan Eon no zen shisō" 盧山慧遠の禅思想. In *Eon kenkyū* 慧遠研究, edited by Kimura Eiichi 木村英一, 249–286. Tokyo: Sōbunsha.

————. 1968. *Tendai gaku* 天台学. Kyoto: Heirakuji shoten.

Andrews, Allan A. 1993. "Lay and Monastic Forms of Pure Land Devotionalism: Typology and History." *Numen* 40 (1):16–37.

Andrews, Fred H. 1948. *Wall Paintings from Ancient Shrines in Central Asia*. London: Oxford University Press.

Aoki Takashi 青木隆. 1989. "*Shidai zenmon* ni okeru ichi, ni no mondai" 『次第禅門』における一、二の問題. *Indogaku Bukkyōgaku kenkyū* 38 (1):221–224.

App, Urs. 2012. *The Cult of Emptiness: The Western Discovery of Buddhist Thought and the Invention of Oriental Philosophy*. Rorschach: University Media.

Asada Masahiro 浅田正博. 1978. "*Shidai zenmon* ni okeru zen hōben shisō no denshō to hatten" 『次第禅門』における前方便思想の伝承と展開. *Bukkyōgaku kenkyū* 仏教学研究 34:23–57.

Attwood, Michael Jayarava. 2008. "Did King Ajātasattu Confess to the Buddha and Did the Buddha Forgive Him?" *Journal of Buddhist Ethics* 15:279–307.

Austin, J. L. 1962. *How to Do Things with Words*. Oxford: Clarendon Press.

Balkwill, Stephanie. 2015. "Empresses, Bhikṣuṇīs, and Women of Pure Faith." PhD diss., McMaster University.

Bapat, P. V., and A. Hirakawa. 1970. *Shan-Chien-P'i-P'o-Sha*. Poona: Bhandarkar Oriental Research Institute.

Barbieri-Low, Anthony J., and Robin D. S. Yates. 2015. *Law, State, and Society in Early Imperial China*. Leiden: Brill.

Barnes, Nancy J. 1993. "The *Triskandha*." In *Studies on Buddhism in Honour of A. K Warder*, edited by N. K. Wagle and F. Watanabe, 1–20. Toronto: Center for South Asian Studies.

————. 1999. "Rituals, Religious Communities, and Buddhist Sūtras in India and China." In *Buddhism across Boundaries*, 485–515. Taipei: Foguang Cultural Enterprise.

Barrett, T. H. 1990. "'Kill the Patriarchs!'" *Buddhist Forum* 1:87–97.

————. 1991. "The Date of the Leng-chia shih-tzu chih." *Journal of the Royal Asiatic Society* 1 (series 3):255–259.

Bautze-Picron, Claudine. 1998. "Lumière et obscurité: L'Éveil de Shâkyamuni et la victoire sur Mâra." *Annali dell'Istituto Universitario Orientale, Naples* 58 (1–2):1–49.

————. 2009. *The Indian Night: Sleep and Dreams in Indian Culture*. New Delhi: Rupa and Co.

Becker, Carl B. 1984. "Religious Visions: Experiential Grounds for the Pure Land Tradition." *Eastern Buddhist*, n.s. 17 (1):138–153.

Belting, Hans. 1994. *Likeness and Presence: A History of the Image before the Era of Art*. Chicago: University of Chicago Press.

Bemmann, Martin, and Sun Hua, eds. 2018. *Buddhist Stone Sutras in China: Sichuan Province 4.* Wiesbaden: Harrassowitz.

Bendall, Cecil. 1902. *Çikshāsamuccaya.* St. Petersbourg: Bibliotheca Buddhica 1.

Benn, James A. 2007. *Burning for the Buddha: Self-immolation in Chinese Buddhism.* Honolulu: University of Hawai'i Press.

Berkowitz, Alan J. 2000. *Patterns of Disengagement: The Practice and Portrayal of Reclusion in Early Medieval China.* Stanford, CA: Stanford University Press.

Bernon, Olivier de. 2000. "Le manual des maîtres de kammaṭṭhāna: étude et presentation de rituals de meditation dans la tradition du bouddhisme khmer." PhD diss., Institut National des Langues et Civilisations Orientales.

Beyer, Stephan. 1977. "Notes on the Vision Quest in Early Mahayana." In *Prajnaparamita and Related Systems: Studies in Honor of Edward Conze,* edited by Lewis Lancaster, 329–340. Berkeley, CA: Group in Buddhist Studies.

Bielefeldt, Carl. 1988. *Dōgen's Manuals of Zen Meditation.* Berkeley: University of California Press.

Blum, Jason N. 2014. "The Science of Consciousness and Mystical Experience: An Argument for Radical Empiricism." *Journal of the American Academy of Religion* 82 (1):150–173.

Bodhi, Bhikkhu. 2012. *The Numerical Discourses of the Buddha.* Boston: Wisdom.

Bokenkamp, Stephen R. 1983. "Sources of the Ling-pao Scriptures." In *Tantric and Taoist Studies in Honor of R. A. Stein,* edited by Michel Strickmann, 434–486. Bruxelles: Institut Belge des Hautes Études Chinoises.

———. 2005. "Sackcloth and Ashes: Self and Family in the Tutan Zhai." In *Scriptures, Schools, and Forms of Practice in Taoism,* edited by Poul Andersen and Florian C. Reiter, 33–48. Wiesbaden: Harrassowitz.

———. 2007. *Ancestors and Anxiety: Daoism and the Birth of Rebirth in China.* Berkeley: University of California Press.

———. 2013. "Zao qi Lingbao jing zhong de ding xing chan hui wen" 早期靈寶經中的定型懺悔文. In *Chen lun, chan hui yu jiu du* 沉淪懺悔與救度, edited by Li Fengmao 李豐楙 and Liao Zhaoheng 廖肇亨, 119–138. Taipei: Zhong yang yan jiu yuan Zhongguo wen zhe yan jiu suo.

Boucher, Daniel. 2006. "Dharmarakṣa and the Transmission of Buddhism to China." *Asia Major,* 3rd ser., 19 (1–2):13–37.

Brashier, K. E. 2011. *Ancestral Memory in Early China.* Cambridge, MA: Harvard University Press.

Braun, Erik. 2002. "Confession and the *Paṭimokkha* in the Pāli Vinaya." *Sagar* 9:95–117.

———. 2013. *The Birth of Insight: Meditation, Modern Buddhism, and the Burmese Monk Ledi Sayadaw.* Chicago: University of Chicago Press.

Bretfeld, Sven. 2003. "Visuelle Reprasentation im sogenannten 'Yoga-Lehrbuch' au Qïzïl." In *Indien und Zentralasien Sprach – und Kulturkontakt,* edited by Sven Bretfeld and Jens Wilkens, 167–205. Wiesbaden: Harrassowtiz.

———. 2015. "Purifying the Pure: The Visuddhimagga, Forest-Dwellers and the Dynamics of Individual and Collective Prestige in Theravāda Buddhism." In

Discourses of Purity in Transcultural Perspective (300–1600), edited by Nikolas Jaspert and Stefan Köck Matthias Bley, 320–347. Leiden: Brill.

Bronkhorst, Johannes. 1986. *The Two Traditions of Meditation in Ancient India*. Stuttgart: Franz Steiner Verlag.

———. 1995. "The Buddha and the Jainas Reconsidered." *Asiatische Studien* 49 (2):333–350.

———. 1998. "Did the Buddha Believe in Karma and Rebirth?" *Journal of the International Association of Buddhist Studies* 21 (1):1–20.

Brose, Ben. 2008. "Crossing Thousands of Li of Waves: The Return of China's Lost Tiantai Texts." *Journal of the International Association of Buddhist Studies* 29 (1):21–62.

Bryder, Peter. 1985. *The Chinese Transformation of Manichaeism: A Study of Chinese Manichaean Terminology*. Löberöd: Bokförlaget Plus Ultra.

Bucknell, Roderick S. 1984. "The Buddhist Path to Liberation: An Analysis of the Listing of Stages." *Journal of the International Association of Buddhist Studies* 7 (2):7–40.

Bucknell, Roderick S., and Chris Kang. 1997. *The Meditative Way: Readings in the Theory and Practice of Buddhist Meditation*. Richmond: Curzon.

Buswell, Robert E., Jr. 1989. *The Formation of Ch'an Ideology in China and Korea*. Princeton, NJ: Princeton University Press.

Buswell, Robert E., Jr., and Robert M. Gimello, eds. 1992. *Paths to Liberation: The Mārga and Its Transformations in Buddhist Thought*. Honolulu: University of Hawai'i Press.

Cabezón, José Ignacio. 2017. *Sexuality in Classical South Asian Buddhism*. Somerville, MA: Wisdom.

Caciola, Nancy. 2003. *Discerning Spirits: Divine and Demonic Possession in the Middle Ages*. Ithaca, NY: Cornell University Press.

Caillat, Collet. 1960. "Deux études de moyen-indien." *Journal Asiatique* 248:41–64.

———. 1965. *Les expiations dans le rituel ancien des religieux Jaina*. Paris: Boccard.

Campany, Robert Ford. 1991. "Notes on the Devotional Use and Symbolic Functions of *Sutra* Texts as Depicted in Early Chinese Buddhist Miracle Tales and Hagiographies." *Journal of the International Association of Buddhist Studies* 14 (1):28–69.

———. 1996. *Strange Writing: Anomaly Accounts in Early Medieval China*. Albany: State University of New York Press.

———. 2007. "Two Religious Thinkers of the Early Eastern Jin: Gan Bao and Ge Hong in Multiple Contexts." *Asia Major*, 3rd ser., 18 (1):175–224.

———. 2009. *Making Transcendents: Ascetics and Social Memory in Early Medieval China*. Honolulu: University of Hawai'i Press.

———. 2012. *Signs from the Unseen Realm: Buddhist Miracle Tales from Early Medieval China*. Honolulu: University of Hawai'i Press.

———. 2015. "Abstinence Halls (*zhaitang* 齋堂) in Lay Households in Early Medieval China." *Studies in Chinese Religions* 1:1–21.

Cassaniti, Julia. 2015. *Living Buddhism: Mind, Self, and Emotion in a Thai Community*. Ithaca, NY: Cornell University Press.

————. 2018. *Remembering the Present: Mindfulness in Buddhist Asia*. Ithaca, NY: Cornell University Press.

Cassaniti, Julia L., and Tanya Marie Luhrmann. 2014. "The Cultural Kindling of Spiritual Experiences." *Current Anthropology* 55 (supp. 10):333–343.

Chan, Yiu Wing. 2013. "An English Translation of the *Dharmatrāta-Dhyāna-Sūtra* with Annotation and a Critical Introduction." PhD diss., University of Hong Kong.

Chappell, David. 1983. "The Teachings of the Fourth Ch'an Patriarch Tao-hsin (580–651)." In *Early Ch'an in China and Tibet,* edited by Whalen Lai and Lewis R. Lancaster, 89–130. Berkeley: University of California Press.

————. 1986. "From Dispute to Dual Cultivation: Pure Land Responses to Ch'an Critics." In *Traditions of Meditation in Chinese Buddhism,* edited by Peter N. Gregory, 163–198. Honolulu: University of Hawai'i Press.

————. 2005. "The *Precious Scroll of the Liang Emperor.*" In *Going Forth: Visions of Buddhist Vinaya,* edited by William M. Bodiford, 40–67. Honolulu: University of Hawai'i Press.

Chavannes, Edouard. 1910. *Cinq cents contes et apologues*. Paris: E. Leroux.

Chen, Frederick Shih-Chung. 2013. "In Search of the Identity of the Eight Trigram Deities on the Northern Liang Votive Stupas in Dunhuang and Turfan." *Asia Major*, 3rd ser., 26 (1):55–78.

Chen, Jinhua. 1999. *Making and Remaking History: A Study of Tiantai Sectarian Historiography*. Tokyo: International College for Advanced Buddhist Studies.

————. 2014a. "From Central Asia to Southern China: The Formation of Identity and Network in the Meditative Traditions of Fifth-Sixth Century Southern China (420–589)." *Fudan Journal of Humanities and Social Sciences* 7 (2):171–202.

————. 2014b. "Meditation Traditions in Fifth Century Northern China." In *Across Asia: Networks of Material, Intellectual, and Cultural Exchange*, edited by Tansen Sen, 111–139. Singapore: Institute of Southeast Asian Studies.

Chen Shu-fen 陳淑芬. 2000. "A Study of Sanskrit Loanwords in Chinese." *Qinghua xuebao* 清華學報 30 (3):375–426.

Chen Zhiyuan 陳志遠. 2015. "Qihuan si ju shi zhi zheng zai kao" 祇洹寺踞食之爭再考. *Zhongguo zhong gu shi yan jiu* 中國中古史研究 5:38–54.

Chi Limei 池麗梅. 2008. *Tōdai Tendai Bukkyō fukkō undō kenkyū josetsu* 唐代天台仏教復興運動研究序說. Tokyo: Daizō shuppan.

Chittick, Andrew. 2020. *The Jiankang Empire in Chinese and World History*. Oxford: Oxford University Press.

Clarke, Shayne. 1999. "Pārājika: The Myth of Permanent and Irrevocable Expulsion from the Buddhist Order." MA thesis, University of Canterbury.

————. 2009. "Monks Who Have Sex: *Pārājika* Penance in Indian Buddhist Monasticism." *Journal of Indian Philosophy* 37:1–43.

Cole, Alan. 1996. "Upside Down / Right Side Up: A Revisionist History of Buddhist Funerals in China." *History of Religions* 35 (4):307–338.

————. 2009. *Fathering Your Father: The Zen of Fabrication in Tang Buddhism*. Berkeley: University of California Press.

Collins, Steven. 1982. *Selfless Persons*. Cambridge: Cambridge University Press.

———. 1998. *Nirvana and Other Buddhist Felicities*. Cambridge: Cambridge University Press.

Cone, Margaret. 2001. *A Dictionary of Pāli. Part I, a–kh*. Oxford: Pali Text Society.

Conze, Edward. 1973. *The Perfection of Wisdom in Eight Thousand Lines and Its Verse Summary*. Bolinas, CA: Book People.

———. 1975. *Buddhist Meditation*. New York: Harper and Row.

Cook, Joanna. 2010. *Meditation in Modern Buddhism: Renunciation and Change in Thai Monastic Life*. Cambridge: Cambridge University Press.

Cousins, L. S. 1973. "Buddhist Jhāna: Its Nature and Attainment According to Pali Sources." *Religion* 3:115–131.

———. 2009. "Scholar Monks and Meditator Monks Revisited." In *Destroying Māra Forever: Buddhist Ethics Essays in Honor of Damien Keown*, edited by John Powers and Charles S. Prebish, 31–46. Ithaca, NY: Snow Lion.

Cowell, Edward B. 1895. *The Jātaka*. 6 vols. Cambridge: Cambridge University Press.

Crosby, Kate. 1999. "History versus Modern Myth: The Abhayagirivihāra, the *Vimuttimagga* and *Yogāvacara* Meditation." *Journal of Indian Philosophy* 27:503–550.

———. 2000. "Tantric Theravāda: A Bibliographic Essay on the Writings of François Bizot and Others on the Yogāvacara Tradition." *Contemporary Buddhism* 1 (2):141–193.

———. 2013. *Traditional Theravada Meditation and Its Modern-Era Suppression*. Hong Kong: Buddha-Dharma Centre of Hong Kong.

Crosby, Kate, and Andrew Skilton. 2008. *The Bodhicaryāvatāra*. Oxford University Press.

Cutler, Sally Mellick. 1997. "Still Suffering After All These Eons: The Continuing Effects of the Buddha's Bad Karma." In *Indian Insights: Buddhism, Brahmanism and Bhakti*, edited by Peter Connolly and Sue Hamilton, 63–82. London: Luzac Oriental.

Dantinne, Jean. 1983. *La splendeur de l'inébranlable (Akṣobhyavyūha)*. Louvain: Université Catholique de Louvain, Institut orientaliste.

———. 1991. *Les qualités de l'ascete (dhutaguṇa)*. Brussels: Thanh-Long.

Davis, Erik W. 2016. *Deathpower: Buddhism's Ritual Imagination in Cambodia*. New York: Columbia University Press.

Day, Matthew. 2010. "Magic Feathers, Wittgensteinian Boxes and the Politics of Deeming." *Religion* 40:293–295.

DeFrancis, John, ed. 2003. *ABC Chinese-English Comprehensive Dictionary*. Honolulu: University of Hawai'i Press.

Deleanu, Florin. 1993. "Śrāvakayāna Yoga Practices and Mahāyāna Buddhism." Special issue, *Bulletin of the Graduate Division of Literature Waseda University* 20:3–12.

———. 2006. *The Chapter on the Mundane Path (Laukikamārga) in the Śrāvakabhūmi*. Tokyo: International Institute for Buddhist Studies.

———. 2012. "Far from the Maddening Strife for Hollow Pleasures: Meditation and Liberation in the Śrāvakabhūmi." *Journal of the International College for Postgraduate Buddhist Studies* 16:1–38.

Demiéville, Paul. 1954. "La Yogācārabhūmi de Saṅgharakṣa." *Bulletin de l'École Française d'Extrême-Orient* 44 (2):339–436.

———. 1973. "Le miroir spirituel." In *Choix d'études bouddhiques (1929–1970)*, 135–156. Leiden: Brill.

Desjarlais, Robert R. 1997. *Shelter Blues: Sanity and Selfhood Among the Homeless.* Philadelphia: University of Pennsylvania Press.

Dhammajoti, Bhikkhu KL. 2009a. *Sarvāstivāda Abhidharma.* Hong Kong: Centre for Buddhist Studies, University of Hong Kong.

———. 2009b. "The Aśubhā Meditation in the Sarvāstivāda." *Journal of the Centre for Buddhist Studies (Sri Lanka)* 7:248–295.

Dohi Yoshikazu 土肥義和. 2015. *Hasseiki makki–jūisseiki shoki Tonkō shizoku jinmei shūsei* 八世紀末期~十一世紀初期燉煌氏族人名集成. Tokyo: Kyūko shoin.

Donner, Neal. 1977. "The Mahāyānization of the Chinese Dhyāna Tradition." *Eastern Buddhist*, n.s., 10 (2):49–65.

Drège, Jean Pierre. 1981. "Clefs des songes de Touen-houang." In *Nouvelles contributions aux études de Touen-houang*, edited by M. Soymié, 205–249. Gèneve: Droz.

———. 1991. *Les bibliothèques en Chine au temps des manuscrits.* Paris: École Française d'Extrême-Orient.

Drège, Jean Pierre, and Dimitri Drettas. 2003. "Oniromancie." In *Divination et société dans la chine médiévale*, edited by Marc Kalinowski, 369–401. Paris: Bibliothèque Nationale de France.

Dreyfus, Georges. 2011. "Self and Subjectivity: A Middle Way Approach." In *Self, No Self? Perspectives from Analytical, Phenomenological, and Indian Traditions*, edited by Evan Thompson, Mark Siderits, and Dan Zahavi, 114–156. Oxford: Oxford University Press.

Du Jiwen 杜繼文 and Wei Daoru 魏道儒. 1993. *Zhongguo chan zong tong shi* 中国禅宗通史. Jiangsu: Jiangsu gu ji chu ban she.

Dumoulin, Heinrich. 1994. *A History of Zen Buddhism.* New York: Macmillan.

Dundas, Paul. 2011. "Textual Authority in Ritual Procedures: The Śvetāmbara Jain Controversy concerning Īryāpathikīpratikramaṇa." *Journal of Indian Philosophy* 39:327–350.

Durrant, Stephen W., Wai-yee Li, and David Schaberg. 2016. *Zuozhuan.* Seattle: University of Washington Press.

Edgerton, Franklin. 1927. "The Hour of Death: Its Importance for Man's Future Fate in Hindu and Western Religions." *Annals of the Bhandarker Institute* 8:219–249.

———. 1953. *Buddhist Hybrid Sanskrit Grammar and Dictionary.* New Haven, CT: Yale University Press.

Egge, James R. 2002. *Religious Giving and the Invention of Karma in Theravāda Buddhism.* Richmond: Curzon.

Ehara, N. R. M., Soma Thera, and Kheminda Thera. 1961. *The Path of Freedom (Vimuttimagga).* Colombo: Dr. D. Roland D. Weerasuria.

Eifring, Halvor. 2016. "What Is Meditation?" In *Asian Traditions of Meditation*, edited by Halvor Eifring, 1–26. Honolulu: University of Hawai'i Press.

Eliade, Mircea. 1969. *Yoga: Immortality and Freedom.* Translated by Willard R. Trask. Princeton, NJ: Princeton University Press.

Eltschinger, Vincent. 2012. "Debate, Salvation and Apologetics: On the Institution-alization of Dialectics in the Buddhist Monastic Environment." In *Devadattīyam, Johannes Bronkhorst Felicitation Volume*, edited by Francois Voegeli et al., 429–489. Bern: Peter Lang.

Endō Junichirō 遠藤純一郎. 1996. "*Shakumakaenron* Shiragi seiritsusetsu ni kansuru kōsatsu" 『釋摩訶衍論』新羅成立説に関する考察. *Chizan gakuhō* 智山学報 45:85–102.

Enomoto Fumio. 1989. "On the Annihilation of *karman* in Early Buddhism." *Transactions of the International Conference of Orientalists in Japan* 34:43–55.

———. 1994. "A Note on Kashmir as Referred to in Chinese Literature: Ji-bin." In *A Study of the Nilamata. Aspects of Hinduism in Ancient Kashmir*, edited by Ekari Yasuke, 357–365. Kyoto: Institute for Research in the Humanities, Kyoto University.

———. 2002. "The Extinction of Karman and Prāyaścitta." In *Buddhist and Indian Studies in Honor of Professor Sodo Mori*, 235–246. Hamamatsu: Kokusai Bukkyoto Kyokai.

Esler, Dylan. 2012. "Note d'oniromancie Tibétaine: réflexions sur le chapitre 4 du *Bsam-gtan mig-sgron* de Gnubs-chen sangs-rgyas ye-shes'." *Acta Orientalia Belgica* 25:317–328.

Espesset, Grégoire. 2002. "Criminalized Abnormality, Moral Etiology, and Redemptive Suffering in the Secondary Strata of the *Taiping jing*." *Asia Major*, 3rd ser., 15 (2):1–50.

Fang Guangchang 方廣錩, ed. 1995a. "Tianzhu guo Putidamo chan shi lun" 天竺國菩提達摩禪師論. In *Zang wai fo jiao wen xian* 藏外佛教文獻, vol. 1, 32–44. Beijing: Zong jiao wen hua chu ban she.

———, ed. 1995b. "Zui miao sheng ding jing" 最妙勝定經. In *Zang wai fo jiao wen xian* 藏外佛教文獻, vol. 1, 338–348. Beijing: Zong jiao wen hua chu ban she.

Faure, Bernard. 1986a. *Le traité de Bodhidharma*. Paris: Éditions le mail.

———. 1986b. "The Concept of One-Practice Samādhi in Early Ch'an." In *Traditions of Meditation in Chinese Buddhism*, edited by Peter N. Gregory, 99–128. Honolulu: University of Hawai'i Press.

———. 1989. *Le bouddhisme Ch'an en mal d'histoire*. Paris: École Française d'Extrême-Orient.

———. 1996. *Visions of Power: Imagining Medieval Japanese Buddhism*. Princeton, NJ: Princeton University Press.

———. 1997. *The Will to Orthodoxy: A Critical Genealogy of Northern Chan Buddhism*. Stanford, CA: Stanford University Press.

———. 2017. "Can (and Should) Neuroscience Naturalize Buddhism?" *International Journal of Buddhist Thought and Culture* 27 (1):139–159.

Felbur, Rafal. 2017. "Essays of Sengzhao." In *Three Short Treatises by Vasubandhu, Sengzhao, and Zongmi*, 49–138. Moraga, CA: Bukkyo Dendo Kyokai America.

———. 2019. "Kumarajiva: 'Great Man' and Cultural Event." In *A Companion to World Literature: Volume 1, Third Millennium BCE to 600 CE*, edited by Ken Seigneurie. Hoboken, NJ: John Wiley & Sons.

Felski, Rita. 2015. *The Limits of Critique*. Chicago: University of Chicago Press.

Feugère, Laure. 1989. "A Meditation Cave in Kizil." In *South Asian Archaeology 1985*, edited by Karen Frifelt and Per Sørensen, 380–386. London: Curzon Press.

Fitzgerald, Timothy. 2000. "Experience." In *Guide to the Study of Religion*, edited by Willi Braun and Russell T. McCutcheon, 125–139. New York: Cassell.

Flanagan, Owen J. 2011. *The Bodhisattva's Brain: Buddhism Naturalized.* Cambridge, MA: MIT Press.

Fong, Benjamin Y. 2014. "On Critics and What's Real: Russell McCutcheon on Religious Experience." *Journal of the American Academy of Religion* 82 (4):1127–1148.

Forte, Antonino. 1979. "Chōsai." *Hōbōgirin* 5:392–407.

———. 1995. *The Hostage An Shigao and His Offspring.* Kyoto: Istituto Italiano di Cultura Scuola di Studi sull'Asia Orientale.

Foulk, T. Griffith. 1987. "The 'Ch'an School' and Its Place in the Buddhist Monastic Tradition." PhD diss., University of Michigan.

———. 1992. "The Ch'an *Tsung* in Medieval China: School, Lineage, or What?" *Pacific World* 8:18–31.

———. 1993. "Myth, Ritual, and Monastic Practice in Sung Ch'an Buddhism." In *Religion and Society in T'ang and Sung China*, edited by Peter N. Gregory and Patricia B. Ebrey, 147–209. Honolulu: University of Hawai'i Press.

———. 2007. "The Spread of Chan (Zen) Buddhism." In *The Spread of Buddhism*, edited by Ann Heirman and Stephan Peter Bumbacher, 433–456. Leiden: Brill.

Franco, Eli. 2009. "Meditation and Metaphysics: On Their Mutual Relationship in South Asian Buddhism." In *Yogic Perception, Meditation and Altered States of Consciousness*, edited by Eli Franco, 93–132. Vienna: Verlag der Österreichischen Akademie der Wissenschaften.

Frank, Georgia. 2000. *The Memory of the Eyes: Pilgrims to Living Saints in Christian Late Antiquity.* Berkeley: University of California Press.

Frauwallner, Erich. 1995. *Studies in Abhidharma Literature and the Origins of Buddhist Philosophical Systems.* Albany: State University of New York Press.

Freiberger, Oliver. 2006. "Early Buddhism, Asceticism, and the Politics of the Middle Way." In *Asceticism and Its Critics*, edited by Oliver Freiberger, 235–258. Oxford: Oxford University Press.

Fujihira Kanden 藤平寛田. 1986. "Tendai shikan ni okeru gomonzen" 天台止観における五門禅. *Tendai gakuhō* 天台学報 28:183–186.

Fujino Iwatomo 藤野岩友. 1976. "Tonshu kō" 頓首考. In *Chūgoku no bungaku to reizoku* 中国の文学と礼俗, 339–363. Tokyo: Kadokawa shoten.

Fujita Kōtatsu 藤田宏達. 1970. *Genshi jōdo shisō no kenkyū* 原始浄土思想の研究. Tokyo: Iwanami shoten.

Fukui Kōjun 福井康順. 1965. *Dōkyō no kisoteki kenkyū* 道教の基礎的研究. Tokyo: Shoseki Bunbutsu Ryūtsūkai.

Fukushima Kōsai 福島光哉. 1965a. "Chigi no shoki zengaku ni kan suru ichi kōsatsu" 智顗の初期禅学に関する一考察. *Indogaku Bukkyōgaku kenkyū* 13(1): 251–254.

———. 1965b. "Shidai zen mon no naihōben" 次第禅門の内方便. *Ōtani gakuhō* 大谷学報 44 (3):31–45.

———. 1974. "Tendai shikan to gōsō" 天台止観と業相. *Bukkyōgaku seminā* 佛教学セミナー 20:272–284.

Funayama Tōru 船山徹. 1995. "Rikuchō jidai ni okeru bosatsukai no juyō katei: Ryūsō, Nansei ki o chūshin ni" 六朝時代における菩薩戒の受容過程: 劉宋・南斉期を中心に. *Tōhō gakuhō* 東方学報 67:1–135.

———. 1998. "*Mokuren mon kairitsuchū gohyaku keijūji* no genkei to hensen" 『目連問戒律中五百軽重事』の原型と変遷. *Tōhō gakuhō* 東方学報 70:203–290.

———. 2004. "The Acceptance of Buddhist Precepts by the Chinese in the Fifth Century." *Journal of Asian History* 38 (2):97–120.

———. 2006. "Masquerading as Translation: Examples of Chinese Lectures by Indian Scholar-Monks in the Six Dynasties Period." *Asia Major*, 3rd ser., 19 (1–2):39–55.

———. 2007a. " 'Nyozegamon' ka 'nyozegamon ichiji' ka — Rikuchō Zui-Tō no 'nyozegamon' kaishakushi e no shin shikaku" 「如是我聞」か「如是我聞一時」か — 六朝隋唐の「如是我聞」解釋史への新視角. *Fagu foxue xuebao* 法鼓佛學學報 1:241–275.

———. 2007b. "Rikuchō butten no honyaku to henshū ni miru chūgokuka no mondai" 六朝仏典の翻訳と編輯に見る中国化の問題. *Tōhō gakuhō* 東方学報 80:1–18.

———. 2013. *Butten wa dō kan'yaku sareta no ka: sūtora ga kyōten ni naru toki* 仏典はどう漢訳されたのか: スートラが経典になるとき. Tokyo: Iwanami shoten.

———. 2015. "Buddhism during the Liang Dynasty: Some of Its Characteristics as a Form of Scholarship." *Acta Asiatica* 109:71–100.

Furuta Shōkin 古田紹欽. 1980. "Bodaidaruma izen no zen" 菩提達磨以前の禅. In *Furuta Shōkin chosaku shū* 古田紹欽著作集, 14 vols., 2:3–31. Tokyo: Kōdansha.

Ge Zhaoguang 葛兆光. 2001. *Zhongguo si xiang shi* 中國思想史. 3 vols. Nanjing: Fudan da xue chu ban she.

Geaney, Jane. 2002. *On the Epistemology of the Senses in Early Chinese Thought*. Honolulu: University of Hawai'i Press.

Georgieva, Valentina. 1996. "Representations of Buddhist Nuns in Chinese Edifying Miracle Tales During the Six Dynasties and the Tang." *Journal of Chinese Religions* 24:47–76.

Gernet, Jacques. 1995. *Buddhism in Chinese Society*. New York: Columbia University Press.

Geslani, Marko. 2018. *Rites of the God-King: Śānti and Ritual Change in Early Hinduism*. Oxford: Oxford University Press.

Gethin, Rupert. 1994. "*Bhavaṅga* and Rebirth according to the Abhidhamma." *Buddhist Forum* 3:11–35.

———. 1997. "Cosmology and Meditation: From the Aggañña Sutta to the Mahāyāna." *History of Religions* 36:183–219.

———. 1998. *The Foundations of Buddhism*. Oxford: Oxford University Press.

———. 2004. "On the Practice of Buddhist Meditation According to the Pali Nikāyas and Exegetical Sources." *Buddhismus in Geschichte und Gegenwart* 9:17–37.

———. 2006. "Mythology as Meditation: From the Mahāsudassana Sutta to the Sukhāvativyūha Sūtra." *Journal of the Pāli Text Society* 28:63–112.

Gifford, Julie. 2011. *Buddhist Practice and Visual Culture: The Visual Rhetoric of Borobudur*. London: Routledge.

Gimello, Robert M. 1976. "Chih-yen (602-668) and the Foundations of Hua-yen Buddhism." PhD diss., Columbia University.

———. 1983. "Mysticism in Its Contexts." In *Mysticism and Religious Traditions*, edited by Steven T. Katz, 61–88. Oxford: Oxford University Press.

Girard, Frédéric. 1990. *Un moine de la secte Kegon à l'époque de Kamakura: Myōe (1173–1232) et le "Journal de ses rêves."* Paris: École Française d'Extrême-Orient

Gjertson, Donald E. 1981. "The Early Chinese Buddhist Miracle Tale: A Preliminary Survey." *Journal of the American Oriental Society* 101:287–301.

Gnoli, Raniero. 1977. *The Gilgit Manuscript of the Saṅghabhedavastu.* Roma: Istituto italiano per il Medio ed Estremo Oriente.

Goldman, Robert P. 2005. *Rāmāyaṇa. Book One, Boyhood.* New York: New York University Press.

Gombrich, Richard F. 1988. *Theravāda Buddhism.* London: Routledge and Kegan Paul.

———. 2009. *What the Buddha Thought.* London: Equinox Publishing.

Gombrich, Richard F., and Gananath Obeyesekere. 1988. *Buddhism Transformed: Religious Change in Sri Lanka.* Princeton, NJ: Princeton University Press.

Gómez, Luis O. 1983. "Indian Materials on the Doctrine of Sudden Enlightenment." In *Early Ch'an in China and Tibet*, edited by Whalen Lai and Lewis R. Lancaster, 393–434. Berkeley: University of California Press.

Gong Jun 龔隽. 2006. *Chan shi gou chen* 禅史钩沉. Beijing: San lian shu dian.

Goossaert, Vincent. 2004. "The Quanzhen 全真 Clergy, 1700–1950." In *Religion and Chinese Society: Volume II, Taoism and Local Religion in Modern China*, edited by John Lagerwey, 699–772. Paris: École Française d'Extrême-Orient.

Greene, Eric M. 2006. "Of Bones and Buddhas: Contemplation of the Corpse and Its Connection to Meditations on Purity as Evidenced by 5th Century Chinese Meditation Manuals." MA thesis, University of California, Berkeley.

———. 2013. "Death in a Cave: Meditation, Deathbed Ritual, and Skeletal Imagery at Tape Shotor." *Artibus Asiae* 73 (2):265–294.

———. 2016a. "Seeing *Avijñapti-rūpa:* Buddhist Doctrine and Meditative Experience in India and China." In *Buddhist Meditative Traditions: Comparison and Dialog (Fo jiao chan xiu chuan tong: bi jiao yu dui hua* 佛教禪修傳統: 比較與對話), edited by Kuo-pin Chuang 莊國彬, 107–170. Taipei: Dharma Drum Publishing Corporation.

———. 2016b. "Visions and Visualizations: In Fifth-century Chinese Buddhism and Nineteenth-century Experimental Psychology." *History of Religions* 55 (3):289–328.

———. 2017a. "Atonement of *pārājika* Transgressions in Fifth-century Chinese Buddhism." In *Rules of Engagement: Vinaya Texts and Contexts*, edited by Cuilan Liu, Susan Andrews, and Jinhua Chen, 363–402. Hamburg: Hamburg University Press.

———. 2017b. "Doctrinal Dispute in the Earliest Phase of Chinese Buddhism: Anti-Mahāyāna Polemics in the Scripture on the Fifty Contemplations." *Journal of the International Association of Buddhist Studies* 40:63–109.

———. 2018. "The *Scripture on the Secret Essentials of Meditation:* The Authority of Meditation in the Kaiyuan Era." In *Buddhist Stone Sutras in China: Sichuan Province 4*, edited by Martin Bemmann and Sun Hua, 75–92. Wiesbaden: Harrassowitz.

———. 2020. "The Dust Contemplation: A Study and Translation of a Newly Discovered Chinese Yogācāra Meditation Treatise from the Haneda Dunhuang Manuscripts of the Kyo-U Library." *The Eastern Buddhist* 49 (2):1–50.

———. 2021. *The Secrets of Buddhist Meditation: Visionary Meditation Texts from Early Medieval China.* Honolulu: University of Hawai'i Press.

Griffiths, Paul J. 1983. "Buddhist Jhana: A Form Critical Study." *Religion* 13:55–68.

Guenther, Herbert. 1957. *Philosophy and Psychology in the Abhidharma.* Lucknow: Buddha Vihara.

Gunaratana, Henepola. 1985. *The Path of Serenity and Insight: An Explanation of the Buddhist Jhānas.* Delhi: Motilal Banarsidass.

Gyatso, Janet. 1999. "Healing Burns with Fire: The Facilitations of Experience in Tibetan Buddhism." *Journal of the American Academy of Religion* 67 (1):113–147.

———. 2002. "The Ins and Outs of Self-Transformation: Personal and Social Sides of Visionary Practice in Tibetan Buddhism." In *Self and Self-Transformation in the History of Religions,* edited by David Shulman and Guy G. Stroumsa, 183–194. Oxford: Oxford University Press.

Hallisey, Charles. 1995. "Roads Taken and Not Taken in the Study of Theravāda Buddhism." In *Curators of the Buddha,* edited by Donald S. Lopez Jr. Chicago: University of Chicago Press.

Han, Christina. 2011. "Territory of the Sage: Neo-Confucian Discourse of Wuyi Nine Bends *Jingjie*." PhD diss., University of Toronto.

———. 2014. "Envisioning the Territory of the Sages: The Neo-Confucian Discourse of *Jingjie*." *Journal of Chinese Philosophy and Culture* 22:86–108.

Hanks, William F. 1996. *Language and Communicative Practices.* Boulder: Westview Press.

———. 2010. *Converting Words: Maya in the Age of the Cross.* Berkeley: University of California Press.

Hansen, Valerie. 1998. "The Path of Buddhism into China: The View from Turfan." *Asia Major,* 3rd ser., 11 (2):37–66.

Hao Chunwen 郝春文. 1998. *Tang hou qi wu dai song chu Dunhuang seng ni de she hui sheng huo* 唐后期五代宋初敦煌僧尼的社会生活. Beijing: Zhongguo she hui ke xue chu ban she.

Harrison, Paul. 1978. "Buddhānusmṛti in the *Pratyutpanna-buddha-saṃmukhāvasthita-samādhi-sūtra*." *Journal of Indian Philosophy* 6 (1):35–57.

———. 1990. *The Sāmadhi of Direct Encounter with the Buddhas of the Present.* Tokyo: International Institute for Buddhist Studies.

———. 2003. "Mediums and Messages: Reflections on the Production of Mahāyāna Sutras." *Eastern Buddhist* 35 (1–2):115–152.

Harrison, Paul, and Jens-Uwe Hartmann. 2001. "Ajātaśatrukaukṛtyavinodanāsūtra." In *Buddhist Manuscripts: Volume 1,* edited by Jens Braarvig, vol. 1 of Manuscripts in the Schøyen Collection, 167–216. Oslo: Hermes Publishing.

Harvey, Peter. 2018. "The Four Jhānas and Their Qualities in the Pali Tradition." *Buddhist Studies Review* 35 (1–2):3–27.

Haskett, Christian. 2010. "Revealing Wrongs: A History of Confession in Indian Buddhism." PhD diss., University of Wisconsin.

Hatchell, Chris. 2013. "Buddhist Visual Worlds 2: Practices of Visualization and Vision." *Religion Compass* 7 (9):349–360.

Hayashiya Tomojirō 林屋友次郎. 1941. *Kyōroku kenkyū* 經錄研究. Tokyo: Iwanami shoten.

Heiler, Freidrich. 1922. *Die Buddhistische Versenkung*. Munich: Verlag von Ernst Reinhardt.

Heim, Maria. 2018. *Voice of the Buddha: Buddhaghosa on the Immeasurable Words*. Oxford: Oxford University Press.

Heirman, Ann. 2001. "Chinese Nuns and their Ordination in Fifth Century China." *Journal of the International Association of Buddhist Studies* 24 (2):275–304.

Hinüber, Oscar von. 1996. *A Handbook of Pāli Literature*. Berlin: Walter de Gruyter.

Hirakawa Akira 平川彰. 1960. *Ritsuzō no kenkyū* 律蔵の研究. Tokyo: Sankibō busshorin.

———. 1964. *Genshi Bukkyō no kenkyū* 原始仏教の研究. Tokyo: Shunjūsha.

———. 1990. "Sange to kushama: daijō kyōten to ritsuzō no taihi" 懺悔とクシャマ：大乗経典と律蔵の対比. In *Jōdo shisō to Daijōkai* 浄土思想と大乗戒, 431–453. Tokyo: Shunjūsha.

———. 1993–1994. *Nihyaku-gojukkai no kenkyū* 二百五十戒の研究. 4 vols. Tokyo: Shunjūsha.

———. 1997. *Bukkyō Kan-Bon daijiten* 佛教漢梵大辞典. Tokyo: Reiyūkai, Hatsubaimoto Innātorippusha.

Hiraoka Satoshi 平岡聡. 1991. "The Idea of Confession in the *Divyāvadāna*." *Indogaku Bukkyōgaku kenkyū* 40 (1):512–507.

———. 2002. *Setsuwa no kōkogaku* 説話の考古学. Kyōto: Daizō shuppan.

———. 2007. "*Shutsuyōkyō* no seiritsu ni kansuru mondai" 『出曜経』の成立に関する問題. *Indogaku Bukkyōgaku kenkyū* 55 (2):848–842.

Hitch, Doug. 2009. "The Special Status of Turfan." *Sino-Platonic Papers* 186.

Hong, De. 2014. "The Development of Buddhist Repentance in Early Medieval China." PhD diss., University of the West.

Horner, I. B. 1938–1971. *The Book of the Discipline (Vinaya-piṭaka)*. 6 vols. London: H. Milford.

———. 1963. *Milinda's Questions*. 2 vols. London: Luzac.

Howard, Angela F., and Giuseppe Vignato. 2015. *Archaeological and Visual Sources of Meditation in the Ancient Monasteries of Kuča*. Leiden: Brill.

Hsieh Shu-wei 謝世維. 2010. "Shou guo yu chan hui: zhong gu shi qi zui gan wen hua zhi shen tan" 首過與懺悔: 中古時期罪感文化之探討. *Qinghua xuebao* 清華學報 40 (4):735–764.

Hu Shih. 1937. "The Indianization of China: A Case Study in Cultural Borrowing." In *Independence, Convergence, and Borrowing*, 219–247. Cambridge, MA: Harvard University Press.

Huang Qingping 黃青萍. 2008. "Dunhuang bei zong wen ben de jia zhi ji qi chan fa: Chan ji de li lai xing yu wen ben xing" 敦煌北宗文本的價值及其禪法—禪籍的歷史性與文本性. PhD diss., Guo li Taiwan shi fan da xue 國立臺灣師範大學.

Hubbard, Jamie. 2001. *Absolute Delusion, Perfect Buddhahood: The Rise and Fall of a Chinese Heresy*. Honolulu: University of Hawai'i Press.

Hulsewé, A. F. P. 1955. *Remnants of Han Law*. Leiden: Brill.

———. 1985. *Remnants of Ch'in Law*. Leiden: Brill.

Hureau, Sylvie. 2006. "Preaching and Translating on *poṣadha* Days: Kumārajīva's Role in Adapting an Indian Ceremony to China." *Journal of the International College for Postgraduate Buddhist Studies* 10:86–118.

———. 2010. "Buddhist Rituals." In *Early Chinese Religion, Part Two: The Period of Division (220–589)*, edited by John Lagerwey and Lü Pengzhi, 1207–1244. Leiden: Brill.

Hurvitz, Leon. 1956. *Treatise on Buddhism and Taoism*. Kyoto: Jimbunkagaku Kenkyusho.

———. 1977. "The Abhidharma on the 'Four Aids to Penetration.' " In *Buddhist Thought and Asian Civilization*, edited by Leslie Kawamura, 59–104. Emeryville, CA: Dharma Publishing.

Huxley, Andrew. 1996. "The *Vinaya*: Legal System or Performance-Enhancing Drug?" *The Buddhist Forum* 4:141–163.

Hymes, Robert P. 2002. *Way and Byway: Taoism, Local Religion, and Models of Divinity in Sung and Modern China*. Berkeley: University of California Press.

Ibuki Atsushi 伊吹敦. 1998. "Shoki zenshū bunken ni miru zenkan jissen" 初期禅宗文献に見る禅観実践. *Zen bunka kenkyūjo kiyō* 禅文化研究所紀要 24:19–46.

———. 2008. "Boshimei ni miru shoki no zenshū (jō)" 墓誌銘に見る初期の禅宗(上). *Tōyōgaku kenkyū* 東洋学研究 45:75–89.

Ikeda Eijun 池田英淳. 1937. "Kumarajū yakushutsu no zenkyōten to rozan Eon" 鳩摩羅什譯出の禅經典と廬山慧遠. *Taishō daigaku gakuhō* 大正大学学報 26:101–118.

Ikeda Rosan 池田魯参. 1982. *Kokusei hyakuroku no kenkyū* 國清百録の研究. Tokyo: Daizō shuppan.

Inagaki, Hisao. 1999–2001. "Shan-tao's *Exposition of the Method of Contemplation on Amida Buddha*." Pts. 1–3. *Pacific World* 1:77–89; 2:207–228; 3:277–288.

Ingram, Daniel M. 2008. *Mastering the Core Teachings of the Buddha*. London: Aeon Books.

Inokuchi Taijun 井ノ口泰淳. 1966. "Saiiki shutsudo no bonbun yugaron shū" 西域出土の梵文瑜伽論集. *Ryūkoku daigaku ronshū* 龍谷大学論集 381:2–15 (L).

Inosaki Jikidō 猪崎直道. 1998a. "*Saimyōshōjō kyō* kō" 『最妙勝定経』考. *Komazawa daigaku bukkyō gakubu ronshū* 駒沢大学仏教学部論集 29:312–328.

———. 1998b. "*Zenmonkyō* kō" 『禅門経』考. *Komazawa daigaku daigakuin bukkyōgaku kenkyūkai nenpō* 駒沢大学大学院仏教学研究会年報 31:33–52.

Ishii Kōsei 石井公成. 1988. "*Shakumakaenron* no seiritsu jijō" 『釋摩訶衍論』の成立事情. In *Chūgoku no Bukkyō to bunka: Kamata Shigeo hakushi kanreki kinen ronshū* 中国仏教と文化: 鎌田茂雄博士還暦記念論集, 345–364. Tokyo: Daizō shuppan.

Itō Kokan 伊藤古鑑. 1931. "Zenshū no kyōgaku hattatsu ni tsuite (ichi)" 禅宗の教学発達に就いて(一). *Zengaku kenkyū* 禅学研究 16: 1–26.

Jaini, Padmanabh S. 1992. "*Ākāravattārasutta*: An 'Apocryhpal' Sutta from Thailand." *Indo-Iranian Journal* 35 (2–3):193–223.

Jan Yün-hua 冉雲華. 1983. "Dunhuang wen xian yu Sengchou de chan fa" 敦煌文獻與僧稠的禪法. *Huagang fo xue xue bao* 華岡佛學報 6:73–103.

———. 1990. *Zhongguo chanxue yanjiu lunji* 中國禪學研究論集. Taibei: Dongchu chu ban she.

Jensen, Christopher. 2018. "Dreaming Betwixt and Between: Oneiric Narratives in

Huijiao and Daoxuan's 'Biographies of Eminent Monks.' " PhD diss., McMaster University.

Ji Yun 纪赟. 2009. *Huijiao* Gao seng zhuan *yan jiu* 慧皎《高僧传》研究. Shanghai: Shanghai gu ji chu ban she.

Johnston, Sarah Iles. 2001. "Charming Children: The Use of the Child in Ancient Divination." *Arethusa* (34):97–117.

Jones, Charles B. 2004. "Buddha One: A One-Day Buddha-Recitation Retreat in Contemporary Taiwan." In *Approaching the Land of Bliss: Religious Praxis in the Cult of Amitābha,* edited by Richard K. Payne and Kenneth K. Tanaka, 264–280. Honolulu: University of Hawai'i Press.

Jordt, Ingrid. 2007. *Burma's Mass Lay Meditation Movement.* Athens: Ohio University Press.

Jorgensen, John. 1987. "The 'Imperial' Lineage of Ch'an Buddhism: The Role of Confucian Ritual and Ancestor Worship in Ch'an's Search for Legitimacy in the mid-T'ang Dynasty." *Papers on Far Eastern History* 35:89–133.

Jülch, Thomas. 2014. *Bodhisattva der Apologetik: die Mission des buddhistischen Tang-Mönchs Falin.* Munich: Utz.

Kaltenmark, Max. 1974. "Miroirs Magiques." In *Mélanges de Sinologie offerts à Monsieur Paul Demiéville,* 151–166. Paris: Collège de France.

Kamata Shigeo 鎌田茂雄. 1982. *Chūgoku Bukkyō shi* 中国仏教史. 6 vols. Tokyo: Tōkyō Daigaku shuppankai.

Kāṇe, Pāṇḍuraṅga Vāmana. 1930–1962. *History of Dharmaśāstra.* 5 vols. Poona: Bhandarkar Oriental Research Institute.

Kanno Hiroshi 菅野博史. 2010. "Tōshin, nanbokuchō no Bukkyō no shisō to jissen" 東晋・南北朝の仏教の思想と実践. In *Nanbokuchō Bukkyō no tōden to juyō* 南北朝仏教の東伝と受容, edited by Okimoto Katsumi 沖本克己, 118–169. Tokyo: Shohan.

Kanno Ryūshō 菅野龍清. 2002. "Kumarajū yaku zenkyōrui ni tsuite" 鳩摩羅什訳禅経類について. In *Bukkyōgaku Bukkyō shi ronshū: Sasaki Koken hakushi koki kinen ronshū* 仏教学仏教史論集: 佐々木孝憲博士古稀記念論集, 77–90. Tokyo: Sankibō busshorin.

Kapstein, Matthew. 2004. "Rethinking Religious Experience: Seeing the Light in the History of Religions." In *The Presence of Light: Divine Radiance and Religious Experience,* edited by Mathew Kapstein. Chicago: University of Chicago Press.

Karashima, Seishi. 2010. *A Glossary of Lokakṣema's Translation of the Aṣṭasāhasrikā Prajñāpāramitā.* Tokyo: International Research Institute for Advanced Buddhology, Soka University.

———. 2016. "Meanings of *bian* 變, *bianxiang* 變相, and *bianwen* 變文." *Annual Report of the International Research Institute for Advanced Buddhology* 19:257–278.

Karnes, Michelle. 2011. *Imagination, Meditation, and Cognition in the Middle Ages.* Chicago: University of Chicago Press.

Kashiwagi Hiroo 柏木弘雄. 1981. *Daijō kishinron no kenkyū* 大乗起信論の研究. Tokyo: Shunjūsha.

Kasuga Reichi 春日礼智. 1936. "Jōdokyō shiryō toshite no *Meisōden shijishō, Meisōden yōbunshō,* narabi ni *Miroku Nyorai kannōshō* daishi shoin no *Meisōden* ni tsuite" 浄土教史料としての名僧傳指示抄名僧傳要文抄並びに弥勒如來感應抄第四所引の名僧傳に就いて. *Shūgaku kenkyū* 宗學研究 12:53–118.

Katz, Paul R. 2009. *Divine Justice: Religion and the Development of Chinese Legal Culture.* London: Routledge.

Katz, Steven T. 1978. "Language, Epistemology, and Mysticism." In *Mysticism and Philosophical Analysis,* edited by Steven T. Katz, 22–74. Oxford: Oxford University Press.

———. 1983. "The 'Conservative' Character of Mystical Experience." In *Mysticism and Religious Traditions,* edited by Steven T. Katz, 3–60. Oxford: Oxford University Press.

Keane, Webb. 2003. "Semiotics and the Social Analysis of Material Things." *Language and Communication* 23:409–425.

———. 2005. "Signs Are Not the Garb of Meaning." In *Materiality,* edited by Daniel Miller, 182–206. Durham, NC: Duke University Press.

———. 2007. *Christian Moderns.* Berkeley: University of California Press.

———. 2008. "The Evidence of the Senses and the Materiality of Religion." *Journal of the Royal Anthropological Institute* 14:110–127.

———. 2018. "Semiotic Ideology." *Signs and Society* 6 (1):64–87.

Kellner, Birgit. 2019. "Buddhist Philosophy and the Neuroscientific Study of Meditation: Critical Reflections." *American Philosophical Association Newsletters: Asian and Asian-American Philosophers and Philosophies* 19 (1):36–40.

Ketelaar, James E. 1991. "Strategic Occidentalism: Meiji Buddhists at the World's Parliament of Religions." *Buddhist-Christian Studies* 11:37–56.

Kieffer-pülz, Petra. 2018. "Sex-change in Buddhist Legal Literature with a Focus on the Theravāda Tradition." *Annual Report of the International Research Institute for Advanced Buddhology* 21:27–62.

Kieschnick, John. 1997. *The Eminent Monk: Buddhist Ideals in Medieval Chinese Hagiography.* Honolulu: University of Hawai'i Press.

Kimura Eiichi 木村英一, ed. 1960. *Eon kenkyū: yibun hen* 慧遠研究: 遺文篇. Tokyo: Sōbunsha.

King, Sallie B. 1988. "Two Epistemological Models for the Interpretation of Mysticism." *Journal of the American Academy of Religion* 56 (2):257–279.

King, Winston Lee. 1980. *Theravāda Meditation.* University Park: Pennsylvania State University Press.

Kinnard, Jacob N. 1999. *Imaging Wisdom: Seeing and Knowing in the Art of Indian Buddhism.* Richmond: Curzon.

Kleeman, Terry F. 2016. *Celestial Masters: History and Ritual in Early Daoist Communities.* Cambridge, MA: Harvard University Asia Center.

Knoblock, John. 1988. *Xunzi: A Translation and Study of the Complete Works.* 3 vols. Stanford, CA: Stanford University Press.

Knoblock, John, and Jeffrey K. Riegel. 2000. *The Annals of Lü Buwei.* Stanford, CA: Stanford University Press.

Kobayashi Masayoshi 小林正美. 1993. *Rikuchō Bukkyō shisō no kenkyū* 六朝佛教思想の研究. Tokyo: Sōbunsha

Kongō Daigaku Bukkyō Bunka Kenkyūjo 剛大學佛教文化研究所. 2017. *Tonkō shahon Daijōkishinronsho no kenkyū* 敦煌寫本『大乘起信論疏』の研究. Tokyo: Kokusho kankōkai.

Kroll, Paul W. 2015. *A Student's Dictionary of Classical and Medieval Chinese*. Leiden: Brill.

Kuo, Li-ying 郭麗英. 1994. *Confession et contrition dans le bouddhisme chinois du Ve au Xe siècle*. Paris: École Française d'Extrême-Orient.

———. 2015. "Liu shi ji shang ban ye Dunhuang xie ben *Da fang deng tuoluoni jing* xin tan" 六世紀上半葉敦煌寫本《大方等陀羅尼經》新探. *Dunhuang Tulufan yan jiu* 敦煌吐魯番研究 15:257–278.

Kuramoto Shōtoku 倉本尚德. 2016. *Hokuchō Bukkyō zōzōmei kenkyū* 北朝仏教造像銘研究. Kyoto: Hōzōkan.

La Vallée Poussin, Louis de. 1927. *La morale bouddhique*. Paris: Nouvelle Librairie Nationale.

———. 1937. "Mūsila and Nārada: le chemin du nirvāṇa." *Mélanges chinois et bouddhiques* 5:189–222.

———. 1988. *Abhidharmakośabhāṣyam*. Translated by Leo M. Pruden. 4 vols. Berkeley, CA: Asian Humanities Press.

Lagerwey, John. 2004. "Deux écrits taoïstes anciens." *Cahiers d'Extrême-Asie* 14:139–171.

———. 2009. "Le rituel taoïste du IIe au VIe siècle." In *Religion et société en Chine ancienne et médiévale*, edited by John Lagerwey, 565–600. Paris: Éditions du Cerf.

Lai Wenying 賴文英. 2002. "Liu, qi shi ji Gaochang fo jiao de jing tu chan guan" 六七世紀高昌佛教的淨土禪觀. *Yuan guang fo xue xue bao* 圓光佛學學報 7:113–134.

Lai, Whalen. 1983. "T'an-ch'ien and the Early Ch'an Tradition: Translation and Analysis of the Essay 'Wang-shih-fei-lun.'" In *Early Ch'an in China and Tibet*, edited by Whalen Lai and Lewis R. Lancaster, 65–88. Berkeley: University of California Press.

———. 2003. "The Century of the Holy Man in Chinese History (316–439): The Death of Hsuan-Kao." *Pacific World*, 3rd ser., 5:143–162.

Lai, Whalen, and Lewis R. Lancaster, eds. 1983. *Early Ch'an in China and Tibet*. Berkeley: University of California Press.

Langer, Rita. 2007. *Buddhist Rituals of Death and Rebirth: Contemporary Sri Lankan Practice and Its Origins*. London: Routledge.

Ledderose, Lothar, and Sun Hua, eds. 2014. *Buddhist Stone Sutras in China: Sichuan Province: Volume 1*. Wiesbaden: Harrassowitz.

Lee, Sangyop. 2020. "The Invention of the 'Eminent Monk': Understanding the Biographical Craft of the *Gaoseng zhuan* through the *Mingseng zhuan*." *T'oung Pao* 106 (1):1–85.

Lee, Soyna S. 2009. "The Buddha's Words at Cave Temples." *Ars Orientalis* 36:36–76.

Lévi, Jean. 1986. "Vers de céréales et dieux du corps dans le taoïsme." In *Corps des dieux: le temps de la réflexion*, vol. 7, edited by Charles Malamoud, 99–119. Paris: Gallimard.

Lewis, Todd. 2014. *Buddhists: Understanding Buddhism through the Lives of Practitioners*. Chichester: Wiley Blackwell.

Li Fuhua 李富华 and He Mei 何梅. 2003. *Han wen fo jiao da zang jing yan jiu* 汉文佛教大藏经研究. Beijing: Zong jiao wen hua chu ban she.

Li Xiaorong 李小榮. 2005. *Hong ming ji Guang hong ming ji shu lun gao* 《弘明集》《廣弘明集》述論稿. Chengdu: Ba shu shu she.

Lin, Fu-shih. 1995. "Religious Taoism and Dreams: An Analysis of the Dream-Data Collected in the Yün-Chi Ch'i-Ch'ien." *Cahiers d'Extrême-Asie* 8:95–112.

Lin, Li-ko'uang. 1949. *L'Aide-mémoire de la vraie loi*. Paris: Adrien-Maisonneuve.

Lin, Wei-cheng. 2015. "Sign." In *Key Terms in Material Religion*, edited by S. Brent Plate, 201–206. London: Bloomsbury.

Link, Arthur. 1976. "Evidence for Doctrinal Continuity of Han Buddhism from the Second through the Fourth Centuries." In *Papers in Honor of Professor Woodbridge Binham*, edited by James B. Parsons, 55–126. San Francisco: Chinese Materials Center.

Liu Shufen 劉淑芬. 2008. *Zhong gu de fo jiao yu she hui* 中古的佛教與社會. Shanghai: Shanghai gu ji chu ban she.

Liu Wenying 刘文英. 1989. *Meng de mi xin yu meng de tan suo* 夢的迷信与夢的探索. Beijing: Zhongguo she hui ke xue chu ban she.

Liu Yi 劉屹. 2010. *Jing dian yu li shi: Dunhuang dao jing yan jiu lun ji* 經典與歷史: 敦煌道經研究論集. Beijing: Ren min chu ban she.

LLoyd, Geoffrey. 1999. "Divination: Traditions and Controversies, Chinese and Greek." *Extrême-Orient, Extrême-Occident* 21:155–166.

Loewe, Michael. 2010. "Social Distinctions, Groups and Privileges." In *China's Early Empires: A Re-appraisal*, edited by Michael Nylan and Michael Loewe, 296–307. Cambridge: Cambridge University Press.

Long Xianzhao 龍顯昭 and Huang Haide 黃海德. 1997. *Ba shu dao jiao bei wen ji cheng* 巴蜀道教碑文集成. Chengdu: Sichuan da xue chu ban she.

Lopez, Donald S., Jr. 2005. "Introduction." In *Critical Terms for the Study of Buddhism*, edited by Donald S. Lopez Jr. Chicago: University of Chicago Press.

———. 2008. *Buddhism and Science*. Chicago: University of Chicago Press.

Lowe, Bryan. 2017. *Ritualized Writing: Buddhist Practice and Scriptural Cultures in Early Japan*. Honolulu: University of Hawai'i Press.

Lü Pengzhi 呂鵬志. 2008. *Tang qian dao jiao yi shi shi gang* 唐前道教儀式史綱. Beijing: Zhong hua shu ju.

Lu, Yang. 2004. "Narrative and Historicity in the Buddhist Biographies of Early Medieval China: The Case of Kumārajīva." *Asia Major*, 3rd ser., 17 (2):1–43.

Luhrmann, Tanya. 2012. *When God Talks Back: Understanding the American Evangelical Relationship with God*. New York: Alfred A. Knopf.

———. 2016. "Comment on *The Anti-Witch*." In *Somatosphere Presents: A Book Forum on The Anti-Witch by Jeanne Favret Saada*, edited by Eugene Raikhel, 6–7. http://somatosphere.net/2016/05/book-forum-jeanne-favret-saadas-the-anti-witch.

Luhrmann, Tanya, and Rachel Morgain. 2012. "Prayer as Inner Sense Cultivation: An Attentional Learning Theory of Spiritual Experience." *Ethos* 40 (4):359–389.

Lutz, Antoine, John D. Dunne, and Richard J. Davidson. 2007. "Meditation and the Neuroscience of Consciousness." In *The Cambridge Handbook of Consciousness*, edited by Morris Moscovitch, Philip David Zelazo, and Evan Thompson, 497–549. Cambridge: Cambridge University Press.

Magnin, Paul. 2002. "L'orthodoxie en question: une étude du *Soutra de la concentration la plus profonde et souveraine*." In *Bouddhisme et lettrés dans la Chine médiévale*, edited by Catherine Despeux, 229–300. Paris: Éditions Peeters.

Mai, Cuong T. 2009. "Visualization Apocrypha and the Making of Buddhist Deity Cults in Early Medieval China." PhD diss., Indiana University.

Mair, Victor. 1986. "Records of Transformation-tableaux (*pien-hsiang*)." *T'oung Pao* 72 (1):3–43.

Makita Tairyō 牧田諦亮 and Ochiai Toshinori 落合俊典, eds. 1994–2000. *Nanatsudera koitsu kyōten kenkyū sōsho* 七寺古逸經典研究叢書. 6 vols. Tokyo: Daitō shuppansha.

Mather, Richard B. 1971. "The Fine Art of Conversation: The Yen-yu P'ien of the Shi-shuo hsin-yu." *Journal of the American Oriental Society* 91 (2):222–275.

Mathews, R. H. 1996. *Mathews' Chinese-English Dictionary*. Cambridge, MA: Harvard University Press.

Matsumoto Bunzaburo 松本文三郎. 1911. *Daruma* 達磨. Tokyo: Morie honten.

Matsunami Seiren 松濤誠廉. 1967. *Bukkyō ni okeru shin to gyō* 佛教における信と行. Kyoto: Heirakuji.

Mayer, Alexander L. 2006. "Dreams." In *Encyclopedia of Buddhism*, edited by Robert E. Buswell Jr., 1:238–239. New York: Macmillan Reference USA.

McCutcheon, Russell T. 2012. "Introduction." In *Religious Experience: A Reader*, edited by Craig Martin, Russell T. McCutcheon, and Leslie Dorrough Smith, 1–18. Bristol, CT: Equinox.

McDaniel, Justin. 2011. *The Lovelorn Ghost and the Magical Monk: Practicing Buddhism in Modern Thailand*. New York: Columbia University Press.

McGuire, Beverley Foulks. 2014. *Living Karma: The Religious Practices of Ouyi Zhixu*. New York: Columbia University Press.

McMahan, David. 2002. *Empty Vision: Metaphor and Imagery in Mahāyāna Buddhism*. London: Routledge.

———. 2017. "How Meditation Works." In *Meditation, Buddhism, and Science*, edited by David L. McMahan and Erik Braun, 21–46. Oxford: Oxford University Press.

McMahan, David L., and Erik Braun. 2017. *Meditation, Buddhism, and Science*. Oxford: Oxford University Press.

Mcnair, Amy. 2013. "Patronage of Buddhist Buildings and Sovereignty in Medieval China." In *Stifter und Mäzene und ihre Rolle in der Religion*, edited by Barbara Schuler, 19–42. Wiesbaden: Harrassowitz.

McRae, John R. 1986. *The Northern School and the Formation of Early Ch'an Buddhism*. Honolulu: University of Hawai'i Press.

Mei Lin 梅林. 2005. "Tanwupi yu Tanwupi ming shi bian" 曇摩毗與曇摩蜱名實辨. *Dunhuang yan jiu* 敦煌研究 91:80–86.

Mertz, Elizabeth. 2007. "Semiotic Anthropology." *Annual Review of Anthropology* 36:337–353.

Michihata Ryōshū 道端良秀. 1967. *Tōdai Bukkyōshi no kenkyū* 唐代仏教史の研究. Tokyo: Hōzōkan

———. 1968. *Bukkyō to Jukyō rinri* 仏教と儒教倫理. Kyōto: Heirakuji shoten.

Mittal, Kusum. 1957. *Dogmatische Begriffsreihen im Älteren Buddhismus*. Berlin: Akademi-Verlag.

Miyaji Akira 宮治昭. 1992. *Nehan to Miroku no zuzōgaku: Indo kara chūō Ajia e* 涅槃と弥勒の図像学: インドから中央アジアへ. Tokyo: Yoshikawa kobunkan.

———. 1995a. "Turufan, Toyoku sekkutsu no zenkankutsu hekiga ni tsuite: Jōdozu,

Jōdo kansōzu, fujō kansō zu" トゥルファン・トヨク・石窟の禅観窟壁画について: 浄土図浄土観想図不浄観想図." Pt. 1. *Bukkyō geijutsu* 仏教芸術 221:15–41.

———. 1995b. "Turufan, Toyoku sekkutsu no zenkankutsu hekiga ni tsuite." Pt. 2. *Bukkyō geijutsu* 仏教芸術 223:15–36.

———. 1996. "Turufan, Toyoku sekkutsu no zenkankutsu hekiga ni tsuite." Pt. 3. *Bukkyō geijutsu* 仏教芸術 226:38–83.

Mizuno Kōgen 水野弘元. 1957. "Zenshū seiritsu yizen no shina zentei shisōshi josetsu" 禅宗成立以前のシナの禅定思想史序説. *Komazawa daigaku kenkyū kiyō* 駒沢大学研究紀要 15:15–54.

———. 1974. "Gō ni kansuru jakkan no kōsatsu" 業に関する若干の考察. *Bukkyōgaku seminā* 佛教学セミナー 20:1–25.

Mochizuki Shinkō 望月信亨. 1946. *Bukkyō kyōten seiritsu shiron* 佛教經典成立史論. Kyoto: Hōzōkan.

Mohr, Michel. 2006. "Imagining Indian Zen: Tōrei's Commentary on the *Ta-mo-to-lo ch'an ching* and the Rediscovery of Early Meditation Techniques during the Tokugawa Era." In *Zen Classics*, edited by Steven Heine and Dale S. Wright, 215–246. Oxford: Oxford University Press.

Mollier, Christine. 2008. *Buddhism and Taoism Face to Face*. Honolulu: University of Hawai'i Press.

———. 2010. "Iconizing the Daoist-Buddhist Relationship: Cliff Sculptures in Sichuan during the Reign of Emperor Tang Xuanzong." *Daoism: Religion, History and Society* 2:95–133.

Monier-Williams, Monier. 1986. *A Sanskrit-English Dictionary*. Delhi: Motilal Banarsidass.

Moretti, Costantino. 2016. *Genèse d'un apocryphe bouddhique: le Sūtra de la Pure Délivrance*. Paris: Collége de France.

Morgan, David. 2016. "Divination, Material Culture, and Chance." *Material Religion: The Journal of Objects, Art and Belief* 12 (4):502–504.

———. 2018. *Images at Work*. Oxford: Oxford University Press.

Mori Shōji 森章司. 1998. "Genshi bukkyō kyōten ni okeru 'kṣama' (sange) ni tsuite" 原始仏教経典における 'kṣama(懺悔)' について. *Tōyōgaku ronsō* 東洋学論叢 23:66–103.

———. 1999. "Genshi bukkyō kyōten ni okeru sange: 'pratikaroti'" 原始仏教経典における懺悔: 'pratikaroti.' *Chūyō gakujutsu kenkyū kiyō* 中央学術研究所紀要 27:2–31.

Moro Shigeki 師茂樹. 2012. "Senzatsukyō no seiritsu to juyō: naze uranai ga hitsuyō to sareta no ka" 占察経の成立と受容: なぜ占いが必要とされたのか. *Nihon bukkyō gakkai nempō* 日本仏教学会年報 77:135–157.

Morrison, Elizabeth. 2010. *The Power of Patriarchs: Qisong and Lineage in Chinese Buddhism*. Leiden: Brill.

Müller, Gotelind. 1992. "Zum Begriff des Traumes und seiner Funktion im chinesischen buddhistischen Kanon." *Zeitschrift der Deutschen Morgenländischen Gesellschaft* 142 (2):343–377.

Murakami Yoshimi 村上嘉実. 1961. "Kosōden no shin'i ni tsuite" 高僧伝の神異について. *Tōhō shūkyō* 東方宗教 17:1–17.

Muranaka Yūshō 村中祐生. 1986. *Tendai kanmon no kichō* 天台観門の基調. Tokyo: Sankibō busshorin.

———. 2004. "Shikan ni okeru gōsōhatsu to shūhō niin" 止観における業相発と習報二因." In *Onozuka kichō hakase koki kinen ronbunshū: Kūkai no shisō to bunka (ge)* 小野塚幾澄博士古稀記念論文集：空海の思想と文化＜下＞, 51–70. Tokyo: Nonburu sha.

Mutō Akinori 武藤明範. 2004. "*Ryō kosōden* ni mirareru zenkan jisshū no dōkō" 『梁高僧伝』にみられる 禅観実修の動向. *Sōtōshū kenkyūin kenkyū kiyō* 曹洞宗研究員研究紀要 34:17–76.

———. 2005a. "*Tōkōsōden* ni mirareu zenkan jisshū no dōkō (1)" 『唐高僧伝』にみられる 禅観実修の動向 (1). *Bunkenkai kiyō* 文研会紀要 16:47–69.

———. 2005b. "*Tōkōsōden* ni mirareu zenkan jisshū no dōkō (2)." *Sōtōshū kenkyūin kenkyū kiyō* 曹洞宗研究員研究紀要 35:33–61.

———. 2006. "*Tōkōsōden* ni mirareu zenkan jisshū no dōkō (3)." *Sōtōshū kenkyūin kenkyū kiyō* 曹洞宗研究員研究紀要 36:89–120.

———. 2007. "*Tōkōsōden* ni mirareu zenkan jisshū no dōkō (4)." *Bunkenkai kiyō* 文研会紀要 18:19–50.

———. 2009. "*Tōkōsōden* myōritsuhen, gohōhen ni mirareu zenkan jissen no dōkō" 『唐高僧伝』明律篇・護法篇にみられる禅観実修の動向. *Tōkai bukkyō* 東海仏教 54:17–35

Myōjin Hiroshi 明神洋. 1993a. "Kumarajū to nenbutsukan" 鳩摩羅什と念仏観. *Indogaku Bukkyōgaku kenkyū* 42 (1):246–248.

———. 1993b. "Zenkan kyōten ni okeru nenbutsukan: so no imi to kigen ni tsuite" 禅観経典における念仏観：その意味と起源について. *Bukkyōgaku* 仏教学 35:59–79.

Nakajima Ryūzō 中島隆蔵. 1991. "Chūgoku chūsei ni okeru zange shisō no tenkai" 中国中世における懺悔思想の展開. In *Ju-Butsu-Dō sankyō shisō ronkō: Makio Ryōkai hakushi kiju kinen* 儒-仏-道三教思想論攷: 牧尾良海博士喜寿記念, 493–506. Tokyo: Sankibō busshorin.

———. 1997. *Shutsusanzōkishū jōkan yakuchū* 出三蔵記集序巻訳注. Tokyo: Heirakuji shoten.

Ñāṇamoli, Bhikkhu. 1987. *The Dispeller of Delusion (Sammohavinodanī)*. London: Pali Text Society.

———. 1991. *The Path of Purification: Visuddhimagga*. 5th ed. Kandy, Sri Lanka: Buddhist Publication Society.

Ñāṇamoli, Bhikkhu, and Bhikkhu Bodhi. 1995. *The Middle Length Discourses of the Buddha*. Somerville, MA: Wisdom.

Narayanan, Vasudha. 2000. "Diglossic Hinduism: Liberation and Lentils." *Journal of the American Academy of Religion* 68 (4):761–779.

Nattier, Jan. 2003. *A Few Good Men: The Bodhisattva Path According to the Inquiry of Ugra (Ugraparipṛcchā)*. Honolulu: University of Hawai'i Press.

———. 2004. "Beyond Translation and Transliteration: A New Look at Chinese Buddhist Terms." Paper presented at the meeting of the American Oriental Society, Western Branch.

———. 2008. *A Guide to the Earliest Chinese Buddhist Translations*. Tokyo: International Research Institute for Advanced Buddhology, Soka University.

———. 2010. "Re-evaluating Zhu Fonian's *Shizhu duanjie jing* (T309): Translation or

Forgery?" *Annual Report of the International Research Institute for Advanced Buddhology* 13:231–258.

———. 2014. "Now You Hear it, Now You Don't: The Phrase 'Thus Have I Heard' in Early Chinese Buddhist Translations." In *Buddhism across Asia: Networks of Material, Intellectual and Cultural Exchange*, edited by Tansen Sen, 39–64. Singapore: Institute of Southeast Asian Studies.

Ning Qiang. 2007. "Visualization Practice and the Function of the Western Paradise Images in Turfan and Dunhuang in the Sixth to Seventh Centuries." *Journal of Inner Asian Art and Archaeology* 2:133–142.

Nishimoto Teruma 西本照眞. 1998. *Sangaikyō no kenkyū* 三階教の研究. Tokyo: Shunjūsha.

Nitta Masaaki 新田雅章. 1981. *Tendai jissōron no kenkyū* 天台実相論の研究. Kyoto: Heirakuji shoten.

Niu Hong 牛宏. 2007. "Dunhuang zang wen, han wen chan zong wen xian dui du" 敦煌藏文、汉文禅宗文献对读—P.t.116(191–242) 与 P.ch.2799, S.ch.5533, P.ch.3922. *Dunhuang xue ji kan* 敦煌學輯刊 4:188–205.

Nobel, Johannes. 1937. *Suvarṇabhāsottamasūtra*. Leipzig: Otto Harrassowitz.

Nolot, Édith. 1987. "Saṃghāvaśeṣa-, saṃghātiśeṣa-, saṃghādisesa." *Bulletin d'études indiennes* 5:251–272.

———. 1996. "Studies in Vinaya Technical Terms 1–3." *Journal of the Pali Text Society* 22:75–150.

Nukariya Kaiten 忽滑谷快天. 1925. *Zengaku shisōshi* 禪學思想史. Tokyo: Genkōsha.

O'Flaherty, Wendy Doniger. 1984. *Dreams, Illusions, and Other Realities*. Chicago: University of Chicago Press.

Obeyesekere, Gananath. 2012. *The Awakened Ones: The Phenomenology of Visionary Experience*. New York: Columbia University Press.

Ochiai Toshinori 落合俊典. 2004. *Kongōji issaikyō no kisoteki kenkyū to shinshutsu butten no kenkyū* 金剛寺一切経の基礎的研究と新出仏典の研究. Tokyo: Research Report.

Ōchō Enichi 横超慧日. 1958–1979. *Chūgoku bukkyō no kenkyū* 中国仏教の研究. 3 vols. Kyoto: Hōzōkan.

Ōchō Enichi 横超慧日 and Suwa Gijun 諏訪義純. 1982. *Rajū* 羅什. Tokyo: Daizō shuppan.

Odani Nobuchiyo 小谷信千代. 1996. "Zenkyō ni okeru yugagyōsha: daijō ni kakehashi suru mono" 禅経における瑜伽行者―大乗に架橋する者. *Bukkyōgaku zeminā* 仏教学ゼミナー 63:22–34.

Ōfuchi Ninji 大淵忍爾. 1974. "On *Ku Ling-pao-ching*." *Acta Asiatica* 27:33–56.

———. 1991. *Shoki no Dōkyō* 初期の道教. Tokyo: Sōbunsha.

Okimoto Katsumi 沖本克己. 1988. "Shoki zenshūshi no ichi shiten" 初期禅宗史の一視点. In *Chūgoku no Bukkyō to bunka: Kamata Shigeo hakushi kanreki kinen ronshū* 中国仏教と文化: 鎌田茂雄博士還暦記念論集, 187–204. Tokyo: Daizō shuppan.

Olivelle, Patrick. 1995. "Deconstructing the Body in Indian Asceticism." In *Asceticism*, edited by Vincent L. Wimbush and Richard Valantasis, 188–210. Oxford: Oxford University Press.

Olson, Carl. 2015. *Indian Asceticism: Power, Violence, and Play*. Oxford: Oxford University Press.

Ōmatsu Hisanori 大松久規. 2013. "*Shaku zenharamitsu shidai hōmon* 'ken zen'aku konjō' ni tsuite"『釈禅波羅蜜次第法門』「験善悪根性」について. *Indogaku Bukkyōgaku kenkyū* 62 (1):39–42.

———. 2016. "*Zoku kōsōden* shūzen hen ni mirareru zenkan"『続高僧伝』習禅篇に見られる禅観. *Indogaku Bukkyōgaku kenkyū* 65 (1):198–203.

Ōminami Ryūshō 大南竜昇. 1975. "Sanmai kyōten ni okeru kenbutsu to kanbutsu" 三昧経典における見仏と観仏. *Indogaku Bukkyōgaku kenkyū* 23 (2):235–238.

Ong, Robert K. 1985. *The Interpretation of Dreams in Ancient China.* Bochum: Studienverlag.

Ōno Hideto 大野栄人. 1994. *Tendai shikan seiritsushi no kenkyū* 天台止観成立史の研究. Kyoto: Hōzōkan.

———. 2012. *Tendai shidai zenmon no kenkyū: dai ikkan* 天台次第禅門の研究: 第 1 巻. Tokyo: Sankibō busshorin.

Orofino, Giacomella. 1994. "Divination with Mirrors." In *Proceedings of the 6th Seminar of the International Association of Tibetan Studies,* vol. 2, edited by Per Kvaerne, 612–628. Oslo: The Institute for Comparative Research in Human Culture.

Orsi, Robert A. 2016. *History and Presence.* Cambridge, MA: Harvard University Press.

Ōtake Susumu 大竹晋. 2017. *Daijō kishinron seiritsu mondai no kenkyū: "Daijō kishinron" wa Kanbun Bukkyō bunken kara no pacchiwāku* 大乗起信論成立問題の研究:『大乗起信論』は漢文仏教文献からのパッチワーク. Tokyo: Kokusho kankōkai.

Ōtani Tetsuo 大谷哲夫. 1970. "Gishin dai ni okeru shūzensha no keitai: toku ni shūzensha no shin'i to shinsenka ni tusite" 魏晋代における習禅者の形態: 特に習禅者の神異と神遷家について. *Indogaku Bukkyōgaku kenkyū* 19 (1):267–268.

———. 1972. "Gishin dai ni okeru shūzensha no keitai, ni: toku ni shūzensha no shin'i to shinsenka ni tusite" 魏晋代における習禅者の形態–2–特に習禅者の神異と神遷家について. *Indogaku Bukkyōgaku kenkyū* 20 (2):152–153.

Ōtsuka Nobuo 大塚伸夫. 2013. *Indo shoki mikkyō seiritsu katei no kenkyū* インド初期密教成立過程の研究. Tokyo: Shunjūsha.

Palumbo, Antonello. 2003. "Dharmarakṣa and Kaṇṭhaka: White Horse Monasteries in Early Medieval China." In *Buddhist Asia,* edited by Giovanni Veradi and Silvio Vita, 167–216. Kyoto: Italian School of East Asian Studies.

———. 2013. *An Early Chinese Commentary on the Ekottarika-āgama.* Taipei: Dharma Drum Publishing.

———. 2017. "Exemption not Granted: The Confrontation between Buddhism and the Chinese State in Late Antiquity and the 'First Great Divergence' between China and Western Eurasia." *Medieval Worlds* 6:118–155.

Parmentier, Richard J. 1994. *Signs in Society: Studies in Semiotic Anthropology.* Bloomington: Indiana University Press.

———. 2016. *Signs and Society: Further Studies in Semiotic Anthropology.* Bloomington: Indiana University Press.

Pas, Julian F. 1995. *Visions of Sukhāvatī: Shan-tao's Commentary on the Kuan Wu-liang shou-fo ching.* Albany: State University of New York Press.

Payne, Richard K. 1996. "The Five Contemplative Gates of Vasubandhu's *Rebirth Treatise* as a Ritualized Visualization Practice." In *The Pure Land Tradition: History and Development,* edited by James Foard et al., 233–266. Berkeley, CA: Berkeley Buddhist Studies Series.

Peirce, Charles Sanders. 1931–1966. *Collected Papers of Charles Sanders Peirce.* Edited by Charles Hartshorne, Paul Weiss, and Arthur W. Burks. 8 vols. Cambridge, MA: Belknap Press.

Pelliot, Paul. 1920. "Meou-tseu ou les doutes levés." *T'oung Pao* 19:255–433.

Penkower, Linda. 2000. "In the Beginning... Guanding 灌頂 (561–632) and the Creation of Early Tiantai." *Journal of the International Association of Buddhist Studies* 23 (2):245–296.

Pettazzoni, Raffaele. 1932. *La confession des péchés.* Paris: Librairie Ernest Leroux.

Pettit, J. E. E. 2013. "Learning from Maoshan: Temple Construction in Early Medieval China." PhD diss., Indiana University.

Ping Qiyong 馮其庸 and Deng Ansheng 鄧安生, eds. 2006. *Tong jia zi hui shi* 通假字彙釋. Beijing: Beijing da xue chu ban she.

Poceski, Mario. 2007. *Ordinary Mind as the Way: The Hongzhou School and the Growth of Chan Buddhism.* Oxford: Oxford University Press.

———. 2015. "Conceptions and Attitudes towards Contemplative Practice within the Early Traditions of Chan Buddhism." *Journal of Chinese Buddhist Studies* 28:67–116.

Prebish, Charles S. 1975. *Buddhist Monastic Discipline: The Sanskrit Prātimokṣa sūtras of the Mahāsāṃghikas and Mūlasarvāstivādins.* University Park: Pennsylvania State University Press.

Proudfoot, Wayne. 1985. *Religious Experience.* Berkeley: University of California Press.

Python, Pierre. 1973. *Vinaya-viniścaya-upāli-paripṛcchā.* Paris: Adrien-Maisonneuve.

Quinter, David. 2010. "Visualizing the *Mañjuśrī Parinirvāṇa Sutra* as a Contemplation Sutra." *Asia Major*, 3rd ser., 23 (2):97–128.

Rambelli, Fabio. 2013. *A Buddhist Theory of Semiotics.* London: Bloomsbury.

Rappaport, Roy A. 1999. *Ritual and Religion in the Making of Humanity.* Cambridge: Cambridge University Press.

Ren Jiyu 任繼愈. 1985. *Zhongguo fo jiao shi* 中國佛教史. 3 vols. Beijing: Zhongguo she hui ke xue chu ban she.

Ri, Ki-yong. 1982. *Aux origines du "Tch'an houei": aspects bouddhiques de la pratique pénitentielle.* Seoul: Korean Institute for Buddhist Studies.

Rickett, W. Allyn. 1971. "Voluntary Surrender and Confession in Chinese Law." *Journal of Asian Studies* 30 (4):797–814.

Robinet, Isabelle. 1993. *Taoist Meditation.* Translated by Julian F. Pas and Norman J. Girardot. Albany: State University of New York Press.

Rotman, Andy. 2008. *Divine Stories: Divyāvadāna.* Boston: Wisdom.

———. 2009. *Thus Have I Seen: Visualizing Faith in Early Indian Buddhism.* Oxford: Oxford University Press.

Rozenberg, Guillaume. 2010. *Renunciation and Power: The Quest for Sainthood in Contemporary Burma.* New Haven, CT: Yale University Southeast Asia Studies.

Ruegg, David Seyfort. 1967. "On a Yoga Treatise in Sanskrit from Qizil." *Journal of the American Oriental Society* 87 (2):157–165.

Sakaino Kōyō 境野黄洋. 1935. *Shina Bukkyō seishi* 支那佛教精史. Tokyo: Sakaino Kōyō hakushi ikō kankōkai.

Sakamoto Kōbaku 坂本広博. 1981. "Ryō kosōden ni mirareru zenkan: shūzen hen shin'i hen nitusite" 梁高僧伝に見られる禅観: 習禅篇、神異篇について. *Tendai gakuhō* 天台学報 23:93–97.

———. 1982. "Ryō kosōden ni mirareru zenkan: bōshin hen, myōritsu hen o chūshin to shite" 梁高僧伝に見られる禅観: 亡身篇、明律篇を中心として. *Tendai gakuhō* 天台学報 24:122–126.

Sakurabe Hajime. 1980. "On the *Wu-T'ing-Hsin-Kuan*." In *Indianisme et bouddhisme: mélanges offerts à Mgr Étienne Lamotte*, 307–312. Louvian: Publications de l'Institut Orientaliste de Louvain.

Samuel, Geoffrey. 2014. "Between Buddhism and Science, Between Mind and Body." *Religions* 5:560–79.

Sasaki Kentoku 佐々木憲徳. 1978. *Zenkan hattenshiron* 禅観発展史論. Tokyo: Pitaka.

Satō Mitsuo 佐藤密雄. 1963. *Genshi bukkyō kyōdan no kenkyū* 原始仏教教団の研究. Tokyo: Sankibō busshorin.

Satō Seijun 佐藤成順. 1988 "Chūgoku bukkyō ni okeru rinjū ni matsuwaru gyōgi" 中国仏教における臨終にまつわる行儀. In *Jōdoshū tenseki kenkyū: Tōdō Kyōshun hakushi koki kinen* 浄土宗典籍研究: 藤堂恭俊博士古稀記念, 177–209. Kyoto: Dōhōsha.

Satō Taishun 佐藤泰舜. 1931. *Kokukyaku issai kyō: kyōshūbu* 國譯一切經: 經集部. Vol. 4. Tokyo: Daitō shuppansha.

Satō Tatsugen 佐藤達玄. 1986. *Chūgoku Bukkyō ni okeru kairitsu no kenkyū* 中国仏教における戒律の研究. Tokyo: Mokujisha.

Satō Tetsuei 佐藤哲英. 1961. *Tendai daishi no kenkyū* 天台大師の研究. Kyoto: Hyakkaen.

Schafer, Edward H. 1951. "Ritual Exposure in Ancient China." *Harvard Journal of Asiatic Studies* 14 (1–2):130–184.

Schieffelin, Bambi B., Kathryn Ann Woolard, and Paul V. Kroskrity. 1998. *Language Ideologies*. Oxford: Oxford University Press.

Schipper, Kristofer. 1985. "Vernacular and Classical Ritual in Taoism." *Journal of Asian Studies* 45 (1):21–57.

———. 1995. "The Inner World of the *Lao-Tzu Chung-Ching*." In *Time and Space in Chinese Culture*, edited by Chun-chieh Huang and Erik Zürcher, 114–131. Leiden: Brill.

Schipper, Kristofer, and Franciscus Verellen, eds. 2004. *The Taoist Canon: A Historical Companion to the Daozang*. Chicago: University of Chicago Press.

Schlingloff, Dieter. 1964. *Ein Buddhistisches Yogalehrbuch*. Berlin: Akademie-Verlag.

Schlütter, Morten. 2005. "Vinaya Monasteries, Public Abbacies, and State Control of Buddhism under the Song (960–1279)." In *Going Forth: Visions of Buddhist Vinaya*, edited by William M. Bodiford, 136–160. Honolulu: University of Hawai'i Press.

Schopen, Gregory. 1987. "Burial *Ad Sanctos* and the Physical Presence of the Buddha in Early Indian Buddhism." *Religion* 17:193–225.

———. 1997. *Bones, Stones, and Buddhist Monks*. Honolulu: University of Hawai'i Press.

———. 1998. "Marking Time in Buddhist Monasteries: On Calendars, Clocks, and Some Liturgical Practices." In *Sūryacandrāya: Essays in Honour of Akira Yuyama on the Occasion of His 65th Birthday*, edited by Paul Harrison and Gregory Schopen, 157–180. Swisttal-Odendorf: Indica et Tibetica Verlag.

———. 2004. *Buddhist Monks and Business Matters*. Honolulu: University of Hawai'i Press.

———. 2014a. *Buddhist Nuns, Monks, and Other Worldly Matters*. Honolulu: University of Hawai'i Press.

———. 2014b. "Liberation Is Only for Those Already Free: Reflections on Debts to Slavery and Enslavement to Debt in an Early Indian Buddhist Monasticism." *Journal of the American Academy of Religion* 82 (3):606–635.

Schuster, Nancy. 1984. "Yoga-Master Dharmamitra and Clerical Misogyny in Fifth Century Buddhism." *Tibet Journal* 9 (4):33–46.

Scott, Joan Wallach. 1991. "The Evidence of Experience." *Critical Inquiry* 17: 773–797.

Sekiguchi Shindai 関口真大. 1961. *Tendai shōshikan no kenkyū: shogaku zazen shikan yōmon* 天台小止観の研究: 初学座禅止観要文. Tokyo: Tendaigaku kenkyūjo.

———. 1969. *Tendai shikan no kenkyū* 天台止觀の研究. Tokyo: Iwanami Shoten.

Senda Takuma 千田たくま. 2004. "Gikyō *Zenmonkyō* no kenkyū" 偽経『禅門経』の研究. *Zengaku kenkyū* 禅学研究 83:71–90.

Sengoku Keisho 仙石景章. 1980. "*Shidai zenmon* ni yinyōserareru zenkyō nitsuite"『次第禅門』に引用せられる禪經について. *Indogaku Bukkyōgaku kenkyū* 29:134–135.

———. 1985. "Zenshū to zenkyō" 禅宗と禅経. *Shūgaku kenyū* 宗学研究 27:188–193.

Sharf, Robert H. 1993. "The Zen of Japanese Nationalism." *History of Religions* 33 (1):1–43.

———. 1995. "Buddhist Modernism and the Rhetoric of Meditative Experience." *Numen* 42 (3):228–283.

———. 1998. "Experience." In *Critical Terms in Religious Studies*, edited by Mark C. Taylor, 94–116. Chicago: University of Chicago Press.

———. 2001. "Visualization and Mandala in Shingon Buddhism." In *Living Images: Japanese Buddhist Icons in Context*, edited by Elizabeth Horton Sharf and Robert H. Sharf, 151–198. Stanford, CA: Stanford University Press.

———. 2002. "On Pure Land Buddhism and Ch'an / Pure Land Syncretism in Medieval China." *T'oung Pao* 88:282–331.

———. 2013. "Art in the Dark: The Ritual Context of Buddhist Caves in Western China." In *Art of Merit: Studies in Buddhist Art and its Conservation*, edited by Kuenga Wangmo, David Park, and Sharon Cather, 38–65. London: Courtauld Institute of Art.

———. 2014a. "Is Nirvāṇa the Same as Insentience? Chinese Struggles with an Indian Buddhist Ideal." In *India in the Chinese Imagination: Myth, Religion, and Thought*, edited by John Kieschnick and Meir Shahar, 131–160. Philadelphia: University of Pennsylvania Press.

———. 2014b. "Mindfulness and Mindlessness in Early Chan." *Philosophy East and West* 64 (4):933–964.

———. 2015. "Is Mindfulness Buddhist? (and Why It Matters)." *Transcultural Psychiatry* 52 (4):470–484.

———. 2017. "Buddhist Veda and the Rise of Chan." In *Chinese and Tibetan Esoteric Buddhism*, edited by Yael Bentor and Meir Shahar, 85–120. Leiden: Brill.

Shaw, Sarah. 2006. *Buddhist Meditation: An Anthology of Texts from the Pāli Canon*. London: Routledge.

———. 2016. "Meditation Objects in Pāli Buddhist Texts." In *Asian Traditions of Meditation*, edited by Halvor Eifring, 122–144. Honolulu: University of Hawai'i Press.

Shengkai 圣凯. 2004. *Zhongguo fo jiao chan fa yan jiu* 中国佛教忏法研究. Beijing: Zong jiao wen hua chu ban she.

Shi Darui 釋大睿. 2000. *Tiantai chan fa zhi yan jiu* 天台懺法之研究. Taipei: Fa gu wen hua.

Shi Huimin 釋惠敏. 1994. *Shōmonji ni okeru shoen no kenkyū* 『声聞地』における所縁の研究. Tokyo: Sankibō busshorin.

———. 2001. "Jiumuluoshi suo chuan shu xi guan chan fa zhi po xi" 鳩摩罗什所传数息观禅法之剖析. In *Jiumuluoshi he Zhongguo minzu wenhua* 鳩摩罗什和中国民族文化, 31–49. Urumqi: Xinjiang meishu sheying chubanshe.

Shi Yichun 釋依淳. 1989. *Ben sheng jing de qi yuan ji qi kai zhan* 本生經的起源及其開展. Kao-hsiung: Fo guang chu ban she.

Shibata Taisen 柴田泰山. 2006. *Zendō kyōgaku no kenkyū* 善導教学の研究. Tokyo: Sankibō busshorin.

Shih, Robert. 1968. *Biographies des moines éminents de Houei-Kiao*. Louvain: Institut orientaliste.

Shinohara, Koichi. 1988. "Two Sources of Chinese Buddhist Biographies." In *Monks and Magicians: Religious Biographies in Asia*, edited by Phyllis Granoff and Koichi Shinohara, 119–228. Oakville: Mosaic Press.

———. 1992. "Guanding's Biography of Zhiyi." In *Speaking of Monks: Religious Biography in India and China*, 97–232. Oakville: Mosaic Press.

———. 2007a. "The Moment of Death in Daoxuan's Vinaya Commentary." In *The Buddhist Dead*, edited by Brian J. Cuevas and Jacqueline I. Stone, 105–134. Honolulu: University of Hawai'i Press.

———. 2007b. "Writing the Moment of Death: Chinese Biographies of Eminent Monks." In *Heroes and Saints: The Moment of Death in Cross-cultural Perspectives*, edited by Phyllis Granoff and Koichi Shinohara, 47–72. Newcastle: Cambridge Scholars Publishing.

———. 2010. "Removal of Sins in Esoteric Buddhist Rituals: A Study of the *Dafengdeng Dhāraṇī* Scripture." In *Sin and Sinners: Perspectives from Asian Religions*, edited by Phyllis Granoff and Koichi Shinohara, 243–275. Leiden: Brill.

———. 2014. *Spells, Images, and Maṇḍalas*. New York: Columbia University Press.

———. 2018. "Fotudeng's Spell Practice and the Dhāraṇī Recitation Ritual." In *Texts and Transformations: Essays in Honor of the 75th Birthday of Victor H. Mair*, edited by Haun Saussy, 271–288. Amherst, NY: Cambria Press.

Shioiri Ryōdō 塩入良道. 1959. "Senpō no seiritsu to chigi no tachiba" 懺法の成立と智顗の立場. *Indogaku Bukkyōgaku kenkyū* 7 (2):45–55.

———. 2007. *Chūgoku bukkyō ni okeru senpō no seiritsu* 中国仏教における懺法の成立. Tokyo: Taishō daigaku tendaigaku kenkyūshitsu.

Shizutani Masao 静谷正雄. 1974. *Shoki daijō bukkyō no seiritsu katei* 初期大乗仏教の成立過程. Kyoto: Hyakkaen.

Shukla, K., ed. 1973. *Śrāvakabhūmi*. Patna: K. P. Jayaswal Research Institute.

Shushan, Gregory. 2014. "Extraordinary Experiences and Religious Beliefs: Deconstructing Some Contemporary Philosophical Axioms." *Method and Theory in the Study of Religion* 26:384–416.

Silk, Jonathan A. 1997. "Further Remarks on the *yogācāra bhikṣu*." In *Dharmadūta: mélanges offerts au vénerable Thich Huyên-Vi à l'occasion de son soixante-dixième anniversaire*, edited by Bhikku Pasadika and Bhikkhu Tampalawela Dhammaratana, 233–250. Paris: Éditions You Feng.

———. 2000. "The *Yogācāra Bhikṣu*." In *Wisdom, Compassion, and the Search for Understanding: The Buddhist Studies Legacy of Gadjin M. Nagao*, edited by Jonathan A. Silk, 265–314. Honolulu: University of Hawai'i Press.

———. 2007. "Good and Evil in Indian Buddhism: The Five Sins of Immediate Retribution." *Journal of Indian Philosophy* 35 (3):253–286.

———. 2019. "Chinese Sūtras in Tibetan Translation: A Preliminary Survey." *Annual Report of the International Research Institute for Advanced Buddhology* 22: 227–246.

Silverstein, Michael. 1979. "Language Structure and Linguistic Ideology." In *The Elements: A Parasession on Linguistic Units and Levels*, edited by William F. Hanks, Paul R. Clyne, and Carol F. Hofbauer, 193–247. Chicago: Chicago Linguistic Society.

Singer, Milton B. 1984. *Man's Glassy Essence: Explorations in Semiotic Anthropology*. Bloomington: Indiana University Press.

Skilton, Andrew, and Phibul Choompolpaisal. 2015. "The Ancient Theravāda Meditation System, Borān Kammaṭṭhāna." *Buddhist Studies Review* 32 (2):207–229.

Smart, Ninian. 1958. *Reasons and Faiths*. London: Routledge and Paul.

Somiyé, Michel. 1959. "Les songes et leur interprétation en Chine." In *Les songes et leur interprétation*, 274–305. Paris: Le Seuil.

Soothill, William Edward, and Lewis Hodous. 1937. *A Dictionary of Chinese Buddhist Terms*. London: K. Paul, Trench, Trubner and Co.

Sørensen, Henrick H. 2012. "The History and Practice of Early Chan." In *Readings of the Platform Sutra*, edited by Morten Schlütter and Stephen F. Teiser, 53–76. New York: Columbia University Press.

Stein, Rolf A. 1967. "Remarques sur les movements du taoïsme politico-religieux au IIe siècle ap. J.-C." *T'oung Pao* 50:1–78.

Stevenson, Daniel B. 1986. "The Four Kinds of Sāmadhi in Early T'ien T'ai Buddhism." In *Traditions of Meditation in Chinese Buddhism*, edited by Peter N. Gregory, 45–97. Honolulu: University of Hawai'i Press.

———. 1987. "The T'ien-t'ai Four Forms of Sāmadhi and Late North-South Dynasties, Sui and Early T'ang Buddhist Devotionalism." PhD diss., Columbia University.

———. 1993. "The Problematic of the *Mo-ho chih-kuan* and T'ien-t'ai History." In Neal Donner and Daniel B. Stevenson, *The Great Calming and Contemplation: A Study and Annotated Translation of the First Chapter of Chih-I's Mo-Ho Chih-Kuan*, 62–96. Honolulu: University of Hawai'i Press.

———. 1995a. "Death-Bed Testimonials of the Pure Land Faithful." In *Buddhism in Practice*, edited by Donald S. Lopez Jr., 592–602. Princeton, NJ: Princeton University Press.

———. 1995b. "Pure Land Buddhist Worship and Meditation in China." In *Buddhism in Practice*, edited by Donald S. Lopez Jr., 359–379. Princeton, NJ: Princeton University Press.

———. 1999. "Zhiyi on the Concept of Ritual Repentance." In *Sources of Chinese Tradition: Volume 1*, 467–471. New York: Columbia University Press.

———. 2007. "Where Meditative Theory Meets Practice: Requirements for Entering the 'Halls of Contemplation/Penance' (觀/懺堂) in Tiantai Monasteries of the Song." Special issue (Essays from the International Tendai Conference), *Tendai gakuhō* 天台学報, 71–142.

Stone, Jacqueline I. 2016. *Right Thoughts at the Last Moment: Buddhism and Deathbed Practices in Early Medieval Japan*. Honolulu: University of Hawai'i Press.

Storch, Tanya. 2014. *The History of Chinese Buddhist Bibliography*. Amherst, NY: Cambria Press.

———. 2016. "Fei Changfang's *Record of the Three Treasures throughout the Successive Dynasties* (*Lidai sanbao ji* 歷代三寶紀) and Its Role in the Formation of the Chinese Buddhist Canon." In *Spreading Buddha's Word in East Asia: The Formation and Transformation of the Chinese Buddhist Canon*, edited by Jiang Wu and Lucille Chia, 109–142.

Strawson, Galen. 2017. "Consciousness Never Left." In *The Return of Consciousness*, edited by K. Almqvist and A. Haag, 89-103. Stockholm: Axel and Margaret Axson Johnson Foundation.

Strickmann, Michel. 1988. "Dreamwork of Psycho-Sinologists: Doctors, Taoists, Monks." In *Psycho-Sinology: The Universe of Dreams in Chinese Culture*, edited by C. T. Brown, 25–46. Washington, DC: Woodrow Wilson International Center for Scholars.

———. 1996. *Mantras et mandarins: le bouddhisme tantrique en Chine*. Paris: Gallimard.

———. 2002. *Chinese Magical Medicine*. Stanford, CA: Stanford University Press.

Struve, Lynn A. 2012. "Deqing's Dreams: Signs in a Reinterpretation of His Autobiography." *Journal of Chinese Religions* 40:1–44.

Stuart, Daniel M. 2015. *A Less Traveled Path: Saddharmasmṛtyupasthānasūtra, Chapter 2*. Beijing: China Tibetology Publishing House; Vienna: Austrian Academy of Sciences Press.

———. 2017a. "Unmanifest Perceptions." In *Śrāvakabhūmi and Buddhist Manuscripts*, edited by Jundo Nagashima and Seongcheol Kim, 109–171. Tokyo: Nombre Inc.

———. 2017b. "Insight Transformed: Coming to Terms with Mindfulness in South Asian and Global Frames." *Religions of South Asia* 11 (2–3):158–181.

Su Bai 宿白. 1997. "Dong han wei jin nan bei chao fo si bu ju chu tan" 東漢魏晉南北朝佛寺佈局初探. In *Qing zhu Deng Guangming jiao shou jiu shi hua dan lun wen ji* 慶祝鄧廣銘教授九十華誕論文集, 31–49. Shijiazhuang: Hebei jiao yu chu ban she.

Su Shuhua 蘇樹華. 2006. *Xin yi Shi chan bo luo mi* 新譯釋禪波羅蜜. Taibei: San min shu ju.

Sun Yinggang 孫英剛. 2014. *Shen wen shi dai: chen wei, shu shu yu zhong gu zheng zhi yan jiu* 神文時代: 讖緯、術數与中古政治研究. Shanghai: Shanghai gu ji chu ban she.

Swanson, Paul L. 2017. *Clear Serenity, Quiet Insight: T'ien-t'ai Chih-i's Mo-ho chih-kuan*. Honolulu: University of Hawai'i Press.

Swidler, Ann. 1986. "Culture in Action: Symbols and Strategies." *American Sociological Review* 51:273–86.

———. 2001. *Talk of Love: How Culture Matters.* Chicago: University of Chicago Press.

Taber, John A. 2009. "Yoga and Our Epistemic Predicament." In *Yogic Perceptions, Meditation, and Altered States of Consciousness,* edited by Eli Franco and Dagmar Eigner, 71–92. Vienna: Verlag der Österreichischen Akademie der Wissenschaften.

Tada Kōshō 多田孝正. 1976. "Shidai zenmon shochū no hokkoku shozenji no tsūmyōkan" 次第禅門所出の北国諸禅師の通明観. *Shūkyō kenkyū* 宗教研究 50 (1):1–21.

———. 1981. "Sange ni kansuru chūgokuteki kōsatsu" 懺悔に關する中國的考察. *Bukkyōgaku* 佛教學 11:41–63.

Takahashi Shin'ya 高橋審也. 1993. "Kanmuryōjukyō no seiritsuchi ni tsuite" 観無量寿経の成立地について. In *Shūkyōteki shinri to gendai: Undō Gidō sensei kiju kinen ronbunshū* 宗教的真理と現代: 雲藤義道先生喜寿記念論文集, 279–292. Tokyo: Kyōiku Shinchōsha.

Takemura Makio 竹村牧男. 1985. "*Daijokishinron* no shikan ni tsuite" 『大乗起信論』の止観について. *Indogaku Bukkyōgaku kenkyū* 33 (2):494–499.

Tambiah, Stanley Jeyaraja. 1984. *The Buddhist Saints of the Forest and the Cult of Amulets.* Cambridge: Cambridge University Press.

Tan Shibao 谭世保. 1991. *Han Tang fo shi tan zhen* 汉唐佛史探真. Guangzhou: Zhongshan da xue chu ban she.

Tanabe, George. 1992. *Myōe the Dreamkeeper.* Cambridge, MA: Harvard University Press.

Tanaka, Kenneth. 1990. *The Dawn of Chinese Pure Land Buddhist Doctrine: Ching-ying Hui-yuan's Commentary on the Visualization Sutra.* Albany: State University of New York Press.

Tanaka Ryōshō 田中良昭. 1983. *Tonkō zenshū bunken no kenkyū* 敦煌禪宗文献の研究. Tokyo: Daitō shuppansha.

———. 2009. *Tonkō zenshū bunken no kenkyū dai ni* 敦煌禪宗文献の研究第二. Tokyo: Daitō shuppansha.

Tanaka Ryōshō 田中良昭 and Cheng Zheng 程正. 2014. *Tonkō zenshū bunken bunrui mokuroku* 敦煌禪宗文獻分類目錄. Tokyo: Daitō shuppansha.

Tang, Li. 2004. *A Study of the History of Nestorian Christianity in China and Its Literature in Chinese.* New York: Peter Lang.

Tang Yongtong 湯用彤. (1938) 2001. *Han wei liang jin nan bei chao fo jiao shi* 漢魏兩晉南北朝佛教史. 2 vols. Taibei: Foguang shu ju.

Taves, Ann. 1999. *Fits, Trances, and Visions: Experiencing Religion and Explaining Experience from Wesley to James.* Princeton, NJ: Princeton University Press.

———. 2009. *Religious Experience Reconsidered.* Princeton, NJ: Princeton University Press.

Teiser, Stephen F. 1994. *The Scripture on the Ten Kings and the Making of Purgatory in Medieval Chinese Buddhism.* Honolulu: University of Hawaiʻi Press.

Tillemans, Tom J. F. 2013. "Yogic Perception, Meditation, and Enlightenment: The Epistemological Issues in a Key Debate." In *A Companion to Buddhist Philosophy,* edited by Steven Emmanuel, 290–306. Oxford: John Wiley and Sons.

Tōdō Kyōshun 藤堂恭俊. 1960a. "Kumarajū yakushutsu to iwareru zenkyōten no setsuji suru nenbutsukan" 鳩摩羅什訳出と言われる禅経典の説示する念仏観. In *Fukui hakushi shōju kinen tōyō shisō ronshu* 福井博士頌壽記念東洋思想論集, 398–411. Tokyo: Fukui Hakushi shōju kinen ronbunshū kankōkai.

———. 1960b. "*Zazensanmai kyō* ni setsuji suru nenbutsukan no seiritsu haikei" 『坐禅三昧経』に説示する念仏観の成立背景. *Indogaku Bukkyōgaku kenkyū* 8 (2):70–73.

Tokuno, Kyoko. 1990. "The Evaluation of Indigenous Scriptures in Chinese Buddhist Bibliographic Catalogs." In *Chinese Buddhist Apocrypha*, edited by Robert E. Buswell Jr., 31–74. Honolulu: University of Hawai'i Press.

Tonami Mamoru 礪波護. 1986. *Tōdai seiji shakaishi kenkyū* 唐代政治社會史研究. Kyoto: Dōhōsha.

———. 1988. "Policy towards the Buddhist Church in the Reign of T'ang Hsüan-tsung 玄宗." *Acta Asiatica* 55:27–47.

Tsai, Kathryn Ann. 1994. *Lives of the Nuns: Biographies of Chinese Buddhist Nuns from the Fourth to Sixth Centuries*. Honolulu: University of Hawai'i Press.

Tsuchiya Masaaki 土屋昌明. 1994. "Gokan ni okeru shika to shuka ni tsuite" 後漢における思過と首過について. In *Dōkyō bunka e no tenbō* 道教文化への展望, edited by Dōkyō bunka kenkyūkai, 271–293. Tokyo: Hirakawa shuppansha.

———. 2002. "Confession of Sins and Awareness of Self in the *Taiping jing*." In *Daoist Identity*, edited by Livia Kohn and Harold D. Roth, 39–57. Honolulu: University of Hawai'i Press.

Tsukamoto Zenryū 塚本善隆. 1955. *Jōron kenkyū* 肇論研究. Kyoto: Hōzōkan

———. 1957. "The Śramaṇa Superintendent T'an-Yao 曇曜 and His Time." *Monumenta Serica* 16 (1–2):363–396.

———. 1968. *Chūgoku Bukkyō tsūshi* 中国仏教通史. Tokyo: Suzuki gakujutsu zaidan.

———. 1974. *Gisho Shakurōshi no kenkyū* 魏書釈老志の研究. Tokyo: Daitō shuppansha.

———. 1975. *Chūgoku chūsei Bukkyōshi ronkō* 中国中世仏教史論考. Tokyo: Daitō shuppansha.

Tsukinowa Kenryū 月輪賢隆. 1971. *Butten no hihanteki kenkyū* 仏典の批判的研究. Kyoto: Hyakkaen.

Tucci, Giuseppe. 1958. *Minor Buddhist Texts, Part 2: First Bhāvanākrama of Kamalaśīla*. Roma: Istituto Italiano per il Medio ed Estremo Oriente.

———. 1971. *Minor Buddist Texts, Part 3: Third Bhāvanākrama*. Roma: Istituto Italiano per il Medio ed Estremo Oriente.

Twitchett, Denis. 1979. "Hsüan-Tsung (reign 712–56)." In *The Cambridge History of China: Volume 3, Sui and T'ang China, 589–906, Part I*, edited by Denis Twitchett and John K. Fairbank, 333–463. Cambridge: Cambridge University Press.

Ueyama Daishun 上山大俊. 1976. "Chibeto yaku tongo shinshū yōketsu no kenkyū" チベット訳『頓悟真宗要決』の研究. *Zen bunka kenkyūjo kiyō* 禅文学研究所紀要 8:33–103.

Vaidya, P. L. 1958. *Avadānaśatakam*. Darbhanga.

Vajirañāṇa, Parawahera. 1962. *Buddhist Meditation in Theory and Practice*. Colombo: Gunasena.

Van Schaik, Sam. 2015. *Tibetan Zen*. Boston: Snow Lion.

Van Zoeren, Steven Jay. 1991. *Poetry and Personality: Reading, Exegesis, and Hermeneutics in Traditional China.* Stanford, CA: Stanford University Press.

Vande Walle, W. 1979. "Lay Buddhism among the Chinese Aristocracy during the Period of the Southern Dynasties: Hsiao Tzu-liang (460–494) and His Entourage." *Oreintalia Lovaniensia Periodica* 10:275–279.

Varsano, Paula M. 1999. "Looking for the Recluse and Not Finding Him In: The Rhetoric of Silence in Early Chinese Poetry." *Asia Major*, 3rd ser., 12 (2):39–70.

Verellen, Franciscus. 2019. *Imperiled Destinies: The Daoist Quest for Deliverance in Medieval China.* Cambridge, MA: Harvard University Asia Center.

Vetter, Tilmann, and Stefano Zacchetti. 2004. "On *Jingfa* 經法 in Early Chinese Buddhist Translations." *Annual Report of the International Research Institute for Advanced Buddhology* 7:159–166.

Waldschmidt, E. 1930. "Wundertätige Mönche in der ostturkistanischen Hinayana Kunst." *Ostasiatische Zeitschrift,* n.s., 1:3–9.

Wallace, B. Alan. 2009. *Mind in the Balance: Meditation in Science, Buddhism, and Christianity.* New York: Columbia University Press.

Walshe, Maurice, trans. 1995. *The Long Discourses of the Buddha.* Boston: Wisdom.

Wang, Huei-hsin. 2001. "Zhiyi's Intepretation of the Concept '*Dhyāna*' in his *Shi Chan Boluomi Tsidi* [sic] *Famen.*" PhD diss., University of Arizona.

Wang Juan 汪娟. 1998. *Dunhuang li chan wen yan jiu* 敦煌禮懺文研究. Taibei: Fa gu wen hua shi ye gu fen you xian gong si.

———. 2008. *Tang Song gu yi fo jiao chan yi yan jiu* 唐宋古逸佛教懺儀研究. Taibei: Wen jin chu ban she.

Wang, Yi-tung. 1984. *A Record of Buddhist Monasteries in Lo-yang.* Princeton, NJ: Princeton University Press.

Watson, James L. 1982. "Of Flesh and Bones: The Management of Death Pollution in Cantonese Society." In *Death and the Regeneration of Life*, edited by Maurice Bloch and Jonathan Parry, 155–186. Cambridge: Cambridge University Press.

Wayman, Alex. 1974. "The Mirror as a Pan-Buddhist Metaphor-Simile." *History of Religions* 13 (4):251–269.

Wei Yingchun 魏迎春. 2011. "Wan tang wu dai Dunhuang seng ni shi jing yu kao ke zhi du yan jiu" 晚唐五代敦煌僧尼試經與考課制度研究. In *Fo jiao wen xian yu wen xue* 佛教文獻與文學, edited by Zheng Acai 鄭阿財, 597–617. Gaoxiong: Fo guang wen hua shi ye.

Weinstein, Stanley. 1987. *Buddhism under the T'ang.* Cambridge: Cambridge University Press.

White, David Gordon. 2009. *Sinister Yogis.* Chicago: University of Chicago Press.

Willemen, Charles, Bart Dessein, and Collett Cox. 1998. *Sarvāstivāda Buddhist Scholasticism.* Leiden: Brill.

Williams, Bruce. 2002. "Mea Maxima Vikalpa: Repentance, Meditation and the Dynamics of Liberation in Medieval Chinese Buddhism, 500–650 CE." PhD diss., University of California, Berkeley.

Williams, Crispin. 2011. "Early References to Collective Punishment in an Excavated Chinese Text: Analysis and Discussion of an Imprecation from the Wenxian

Covenant Texts." *Bulletin of the School of Oriental and African Studies* 74 (3):437–462.

Wilson, Jeff. 2014. *Mindful America: The Mutual Transformation of Buddhist Meditation and American Culture*. Oxford: Oxford University Press.

Wright, Arthur F. 1948. "Fo-t'u-teng." *Harvard Journal of Asiatic Studies* 11 (3–4):321–371.

———. 1954. "Biography and Hagiography: Hui-chiao's *Lives of Eminent Monks*." In *Silver Jubilee Volume of the Zinbun-Kagaku-Kenkyusho, Kyoto University*, 383–432. Kyoto: Kyōto daigaku jinbun kagaku kenkyūjo.

———. 1957. "Sengrui Alias Hui-rui." *Sino-Indian Studies* 5 (3–4):272–294.

Wu, Jiang, and Lucille Chia, eds. 2016. *Spreading Buddha's Word in East Asia: The Formation and Transformation of the Chinese Buddhist Canon*. New York: Columbia University Press.

Wu, Pei-yi. 1979. "Self-Examination and the Confession of Sins in Traditional China." *Harvard Journal of Asiatic Studies* 39 (1):5–38.

Wynne, Alexander. 2007. *The Origin of Buddhist Meditation*. New York: Routledge.

Xu Fuchang 徐富昌. 1993. *Shuihudi qin jian yan jiu* 睡虎地秦簡研究. Taibei: Wen shi zhe chu ban she.

Xu Wenming 徐文明. 2004. *Zhong tu qian qi chan xue si xiang shi* 中土前期禪學思想史. Beijing: Beijing shi fan da xue.

Xuan Fang 宣方. 2001. *Han wei jin chanxue yanjiu* 漢魏晉禪學研究. Dashu: Fo guang wen hua jiao ji jin hui.

Yabuki Keiki 矢吹慶輝. 1927. *Sangaikyō no kenkyū* 三階教の研究. Tokyo: Iwanami.

Yagi Sendai 八木宣諦. 1986. "Sōden shiryō to shite no himei" 僧伝資料としての碑銘. *Taishō daigaku sōgō bukkyō kenkyūjo nenpō* 大正大学綜合佛教研究所年報 8:1–18.

Yamabe Nobuyoshi 山部能宜. 1997. "An Shigao as a Precursor of the Yogācāra Tradition: A Preliminary Study." In *Bukkyō shisō bunkashi ronsō: Watanabe Takao Kyōju kanreki kinen ronshū* 仏教思想文化史論叢: 渡邊隆生教授還暦記念論集, 153–194. Kyoto: Nagata bunshōdō.

———. 1999a. "An Examination of the Mural Paintings of Toyok Cave 20 in Conjunction with the Origin of the *Amitayus Visualization Sutra*." *Orientations* 4:38–44.

———. 1999b. "The Sūtra on the Ocean-like Samādhi of the Visualization of the Buddha." PhD diss., Yale University.

———. 2002. "Practice of Visualization and the *Visualization Sutra:* An Examination of Mural Paintings at Toyok, Turfan." *Pacific World*, 3rd ser., 4:123–152.

———. 2004. "An Examination of the Mural Paintings of Visualizing Monks in Toyok Cave 42." In *Turfan Revisited*, edited by Desmond Durkin-Meisterernst, 401–407. Berlin: Dietrich Reimer Verlag.

———. 2005. "Visionary Repentance and Visionary Ordination in the Brahma Net Sutra." In *Going Forth: Visions of Buddhist Vinaya*, edited by William M. Bodiford, 17–39. Honolulu: University of Hawai'i Press.

———. 2009. "The Paths of Śrāvakas and Bodhisattvas in Meditative Practice." *Acta Asiatica* 96:47–75.

———. 2010. "Zai tan shi ku yong tu" 再探石窟用途. In *Tulufan xue yan jiu* 吐魯番學研究,

edited by Tulufan xue yan jiu yuan 吐鲁番学研究院, 784–806. Shanghai: Shanghai gu ji chu ban she.

———. 2014. "Toyok Cave 20: Paintings and Inscriptions." In *Epigraphic Evidence in the Pre-modern Buddhist World*, edited by Kurt Tropper, 217–262. Vienna: Arbeitskreis für Tibetische und Buddhistische Studien, Universität Wien.

———. 2014b. "Yogācāra Influence on the Northern School of Chan Buddhism." In *Fo jiao chan xiu chuan tong: qi yuan yu fa zhan* 佛教禪修傳統: 起源與發展, edited by Zhuang Guobin [Chuang Kuo-pin] 莊國彬, 249–314. Taipei: Xin wen feng 新文豐.

———. 2016. "Āraya shiki setsu no jissenteki haikei ni tsuite" アーラヤ識説の實踐的背景について. *Tōyō no shisō to shūkyō* 東洋の思想と宗教 33:1–30.

Yamabe, Nobuyoshi, and Fumihiko Sueki. 2009. *The Sutra on the Concentration of Sitting Meditation*. Berkeley, CA: Numata Center for Buddhist Translation and Research.

Yamada Akihiro 山田明広. 2004. "Dōkyō sai ni okeru jigyakuteki kōi no kōnō oyobi suitai" 道教斎における自虐的行為の効能および衰退につして. In *Chūgoku shisō ni okeru shintai shizen shinkō* 中国思想における身体自然信仰, 383–398. Tokyo: Tōhō shoten.

Yamada, Isshi. 1968. *Karuṇāpuṇḍarīka*. London: School of Oriental and African Studies.

Yamada Toshiaki 山田利明. 1995. "The Evolution of Taoist Ritual: K'ou Ch'ien-chih and Lu Hsiu-ching." *Acta Asiatica* 68.

———. 1999. *Rikuchō dōkyō girei no kenkyū* 六朝道教儀禮の研究. Tokyo: Tōhō shoten.

Yamaguchi Susumu 山口益. 1968. "Sange ni tsuite" 懺悔について. *Bukkyōgaku seminā* 佛教学セミナー 9:1–14.

Yamauchi Shun'yu 山内舜雄. 1986. *Zen to tendai shikan* 禅と天台止観. Tokyo: Daizō shuppansha.

Yampolsky, Phillip B. 1967. *The Platform Sutra of the Sixth Patriarch*. New York: Columbia University Press.

Yanagida Seizan 柳田聖山. 1967. *Shoki zenshū shisho no kenkyū* 初期禅宗史書の研究. Kyoto: Hōzōkan.

———. 1969. *Daruma no goroku* 達摩の語録. Tokyo: Chikuma shobō.

———. 1970. "Daruma zen to so no haikei" ダルマ禅とその背景. In *Hokugi Bukkyō no kenkyū* 北魏佛教の研究, edited by Ōchō Enichi 横超慧日, 115–177. Kyoto: Heirakuji shoten.

———. 1971a. *Shoki no zenshi I* 初期の禅史 I. Tokyo: Chikuma shobō.

———. 1971b. *Shoki no zenshi II* 初期の禅史 II. Tokyo: Chikuma shobō.

———. 1983. "The Li-tai fao-pao chi and the Cha'n Doctrine of Sudden Awakening." In *Early Ch'an in China and Tibet*, edited by Lewis R. Lancaster and Whalen Lai, 13–50. Berkeley, CA: Asian Humanities Press.

———. 1999a. "Zekkanron no honbun kenkyū" 絶觀論の本文研究. In *Zen bukkyō no kenkyū: Yanagida Seizan shū dai ichi kan* 禅仏教の研究: 柳田聖山集第一巻, 77–133. Tokyo: Hōzōkan.

———. 1999b. "Zenmon kyō ni tsuite" 禅門経について. In *Zen bukkyō no kenkyū: Yanagida Seizan shū dai ichi kan* 禅仏教の研究: 柳田聖山集第一巻, 301–314. Tokyo: Hozōkan.

Yang Liangsheng 楊聯陞. 1961. "Dao jiao zhi zi bo yu fo jiao zhi zi pu" 道教之自博與佛教之自撰. In *Bukkyō shigaku ronshū: Tsukamoto Hakushi shōju kinen* 佛教史學論集: 塚本博士頌壽記念, 962–969. Kyoto: Tsukamoto hakushi shōju kinenkai.

Yang Mingfen 杨明芬. 2007. *Tang dai xi fang jing tu li chan fa yan jiu* 唐代西方净土礼忏法研究. Beijing: Min zu chu ban she.

Yang Zengwen 杨曾文. 1996. *Shen hui he shang chan yu lu* 神會和尚禪語錄. Beijing: Zhong hua shu ju.

Yi, Joy Lidu. 2018. *Yungang: Art, History, Archeology, Liturgy.* London: Routledge.

Yokota Zenkyō 横田善教. 1999. "*Kanmuryōjukyō* ni okeru 'kan' no go" 『観無量寿経』における「観」の語. In *Jōdokyō no sōgōteki kenkyū* 浄土教の総合的研究, 157–176. Kyoto: Bukkyō daigaku sōgō kenkyūjo.

Yoshikawa Tadao 吉川忠夫. 1987. "Seishitsu kō" 静室考. *Tōhō gakuhō* 東方学報 59:125–162.

———. 1998. *Chūgokujin no shūkyō ishiki* 中国人の宗教意識. Kyoto: Sōbunsha.

Yoshikawa Tadao 吉川忠夫 and Funayama Tōru 船山徹, trans. 2009–2010, *Kōsōden* 高僧伝. 4 vols. Tokyo: Iwanami shoten.

Young, Serinity. 1999. *Dreaming in the Lotus: Buddhist Dream Narrative, Imagery and Practice.* Boston: Wisdom.

Young, Stuart H. 2015. *Conceiving the Indian Buddhist Patriarchs in China.* Honolulu: University of Hawai'i Press.

Zacchetti, Stefano. 2003. "The Rediscovery of Three Early Buddhist Scriptures on Meditation." *Annual Report of the International Research Institute for Advanced Buddhology* 6:251–300.

———. 2008. "The Nature of the *Da anban shouyi jing* 大安般守意經 T602 Reconsidered." *Journal of the International Association of Buddhist Studies* 31 (1–2):421–484.

———. 2010. "Defining An Shigao's 安世高 Translation Corpus: The State of the Art in Relevant Research." In *Xi yu li shi yu yan yan jiu ji kan dai san ji* 西域歷史語言研究集刊第三輯, edited by Shen Weirong 沈衞榮, 249–270. Beijing: Ke xue chu ban she.

———. 2016. "Notions and Visions of the Canon in Early Chinese Buddhism." In *Spreading Buddha's Word in East Asia: The Formation and Transformation of the Chinese Buddhist Canon,* edited by Jiang Wu and Lucille Chia, 81–108.

Zhang, Zhenjun. 2014. *Buddhism and Tales of the Supernatural in Early Medieval China: A Study of Liu Yiqing's (403–444) Youming lu.* Leiden: Brill.

Zhao Junping 趙君平 and Zhao Wencheng 趙文成. 2006. *Heluo Muke Shiling* 河洛墓刻拾零. Beijing: Beijing tu shu guan chu ban she.

Zheng Acai 鄭阿財. 1989. "Dunhuang xie ben *Zhen yan yao jue* yan jiu" 敦煌寫本《真言要決》研究. *Fa shang xue bao* 法商學報 23:211–229.

Zheng Zhiming 鄭志明. 1986. *Zhongguo she hui yu zong jiao* 中國社會與宗教. Taibei: Taiwan xue sheng shu ju.

Zhou Yuru 周玉茹. 2014. "Liu chao Jiangnan biqiuni chan xiu kao lun" 六朝江南比丘尼禅修考论. *Ren wen za zhi* 人文杂志 12:14–20.

Zhu Qingzhi 朱慶之. 1990. "Ye ma yi zheng" 野馬義證. *Gu han yu yan jiu* 古漢語研究 7:17–18.

Ziegler, Harumi Hirano. 2015. *The Collection for the Propagation and Clarification of Buddhism: Volume 1.* Moraga, CA: Bukkyo Dendo Kyokai America.

———. 2017. *The Collection for the Propagation and Clarification of Buddhism: Volume 2.* Moraga, CA: Bukkyo Dendo Kyokai America.

Zürcher, E. 1972. *The Buddhist Conquest of China.* Leiden: Brill.

———. 1980. "Buddhist Influence on Early Taoism: A Survey of Scriptural Evidence." *T'oung Pao* 66 (1–3):84–147.

———. 1999. "Buddhism across Boundaries: The Foreign Input." In *Buddhism across Boundaries: Chinese Buddhism and the Western Regions*, 1–60. Sanchung: Foguang Cultural Enterprise.

———. 2006. "Buddhist *Chanhui* and Christian Confession in Seventeenth Century China." In *Forgive Us Our Sins: Confession in Late Ming and Early Qing China*, edited by Nicolas Standaert and Ad Dudink, 103–127. Nettetal: Steyler Verlag.

Index

Page numbers in **boldface** refer to figures or tables.

About the Author

Eric M. Greene teaches in the Department of Religious Studies at Yale University. His research focuses on the early history of Buddhism in China and the dynamics of the transmission and translation of Indian Buddhist practices and literature to China between the second and ninth centuries. His articles have appeared in *T'oung Pao, Journal of Chinese Religions, Artibus Asiae, Journal of the International Association of Buddhist Studies, Asia Major, History of Religions,* and *Journal of the American Oriental Society,* among other places. He is presently working on a project concerning the earliest Chinese translations of Indian Buddhist literature and the Chinese Buddhist literature of the second and third centuries.

**Kuroda Institute
Studies in East Asian Buddhism**

Studies in Ch'an and Hua-yen
Robert M. Gimello and Peter N. Gregory, editors

Dōgen Studies
William R. LaFleur, editor

The Northern School and the Formation of Early Ch'an Buddhism
John R. McRae

Traditions of Meditation in Chinese Buddhism
Peter N. Gregory, editor

Sudden and Gradual: Approaches to Enlightenment in Chinese Thought
Peter N. Gregory, editor

Buddhist Hermeneutics
Donald S. Lopez, Jr., editor

Paths to Liberation: The Mārgā and Its Transformations in Buddhist Thought
Robert E. Buswell, Jr., and Robert M. Gimello, editors

Sōtō Zen in Medieval Japan
William M. Bodiford

The Scripture on the Ten Kings *and the Making of Purgatory
in Medieval Chinese Buddhism*
Stephen F. Teiser

The Eminent Monk: Buddhist Ideals in Medieval Chinese Hagiography
John Kieschnick

Re-Visioning "Kamakura" Buddhism
Richard K. Payne, editor

Original Enlightenment and the Transformation of Medieval Japanese Buddhism
Jacqueline I. Stone

Buddhism in the Sung
Peter N. Gregory and Daniel A. Getz, Jr., editors

*Coming to Terms with Chinese Buddhism:
A Reading of* The Treasure Store Treatise
Robert H. Sharf